PROJECT MANAGEMENT
FIFTH EDITION

Project Management

Fifth edition

Dennis Lock

Gower

First Edition published 1968
Second Edition 1977
Third Edition 1984
Fourth Edition 1988
Reprinted 1993 (twice)

Published by
Gower Publishing
Gower House
Croft Road
Aldershot
Hants GU11 3HR
England

Gower Publishing
Distributed in the United States by
Ashgate Publishing Company
Old Post Road
Brookfield
Vermont 05036
USA

CIP catalogue records for this book are available
from the British Library

ISBN 0–566–07339–0 Hardback
ISBN 0–566–07340–4 Paperback

Typeset in 10pt Palatino by Photoprint, Torquay, S. Devon
Printed and bound in Great Britain by
Biddles Ltd, Guildford and King's Lynn

Contents

List of illustrations

Preface to fifth edition

This edition started from an intensely self-critical review, strengthened by advice and support from colleagues, and put into effect by setting aside a whole year in which to concentrate on the project. The occasion which triggered this fresh approach was *Project Management*'s twenty-first anniversary, when it seemed fitting to aim for an improved edition that could look forward with confidence to the twenty-first century. The result is this completely rewritten and enlarged fifth edition.

The sequence of topics throughout the book remains the same, but there are many substantial additions and changes. These are far too numerous to describe here in detail, but I can list some of the main features.

There are three new chapters. Chapter 2 (project organization) is a revised version of material that was previously part of the introductory chapter. Chapter 5 (commercial management) is an important addition, included to reinforce this book's approach to project management as a complete subject, rather than treating it simply as a collection of separate techniques. Techniques are, however, not forgotten and the new Chapter 9 describes some of the more advanced possibilities open to the experienced planner or project manager.

In recent years, precedence networks have become more

popular, and some computer software (although not the programs recommended in this book) can only process precedence logic. This trend has been recognized by revisions and corrections in Chapter 6, and by the inclusion of a precedence example in Chapter 9.

Another improvement is the attachment of further reading lists to some chapters. This has been done for topics which are particularly specialized, where some readers may wish to pursue their study in greater depth.

Project Management has always aimed to be a readable book with a practical approach, and it has depended for this partly on the number and quality of its illustrations. Several new illustrations have been introduced in this edition, but many others have been replaced and all the rest were scrutinized with special care to make sure that every figure is up to date and as clear and informative as possible.

Some of the changes made for this edition result from suggestions made by The Open University, to whom I am particularly grateful for their support and helpful criticism. I am also indebted to K&H Project Systems, Lucas Management Services and Welcom Software Technology International for general advice and for their practical help in illustrating Chapters 8 and 9.

Dennis Lock
1992

1

The nature and purpose of project management

Project management has evolved in order to plan, coordinate and control the complex and diverse activities of modern industrial and commercial projects. Clearly, man-made projects are not new; monuments surviving from the earliest civilizations testify to the incredible achievements of our forebears and still evoke our wonder and admiration. Modern projects, for all their technological sophistication, are not necessarily greater in scale than some of those early mammoth works. But economic pressures of the industrialized world, competition between rival contractors, and greater regard for the value and well-being (and hence the employment costs) of the people who constitute the project work-force have all led to the development of new techniques for managing projects.

All projects share one common characteristic – the projection of ideas and activities into new endeavours. The ever-present element of risk and uncertainty means that the steps and tasks leading to completion can never be described with absolute accuracy in advance. For some complex projects the achievement of a successful outcome may even be in question. The function of project management is to foresee or predict as many of the dangers and problems as possible and to plan, organize and control activities so that the project is completed success-

1

fully in spite of the risks. This process starts before any resources are committed and must continue until all work is finished. The aim is for the final result to satisfy the project sponsor or purchaser, within the promised timescale and without using more money and other resources than those which were originally set aside or budgeted for.

Much of the development in project management methods has taken place in the second half of the twentieth century, spurred by impatient project purchasers (who want their projects finished quickly so that their investments can be put to profitable use as soon as possible). Competition between nations for supremacy in weapons and defence systems has played a major part in the development of sophisticated management techniques, and the process has been accelerated further by the widespread availability of powerful, reliable and relatively cheap computers. Project management is more effective when it makes appropriate use of these sophisticated techniques and, in this sense, is a *specialized* branch of management.

Planning and control must, of course, be exercised over all the activities and resources involved in a project. The project manager therefore needs to be able to understand, at least in outline, how the various participants operate, and to appreciate their particular problems (or recognize their failings). This demands sufficient and fairly wide experience. Thus, in this practical sense, project management is akin to *general* management.

It is important, therefore, to understand that there is far more to the practice of effective project management than the application of a few sophisticated computer programs. It embodies a whole framework of logical and progressive decision-making, the use of common sense and perception, proper organization, effective commercial and financial management, painstaking attention to documentation and routine clerical tasks, and a clear grasp of proven and long-established principles of management and leadership.

Projects

The principal identifying characteristic of a project is its novelty. It is a step into the unknown, fraught with risk and uncertainty.

No two projects are ever exactly alike, and even a repeated project will differ in one or more commercial, administrative, or physical aspect from its predecessor.

It is convenient to classify projects under four main headings:

1 Civil engineering, construction, petrochemical, mining and quarrying projects

Projects in this category are those which spring most readily to mind whenever industrial projects are mentioned. They have in common the fact that the fulfilment phase must be conducted on a site which is exposed to the elements, remote from the contractor's head office.

These projects incur special risks and problems of organization and communication. They often require massive capital investment and they require rigorous management of progress, finance and quality. The amount of finance and other resources in such projects may be too great for one contractor to invest, in which case the organization and communications are further complicated by the participation of several contractors, working in some kind of joint venture.

2 Manufacturing projects

Manufacturing projects aim at the production of a piece of equipment or machinery, ship, aircraft, land vehicle, or some other item of specially designed hardware. The finished product may be purpose built for a single customer, or the project could be generated and funded from within a company for the design and development of a new product for manufacture and sale in quantity.

Manufacturing projects are usually conducted in a factory or other home-based environment, where the company should be able to exercise on-the-spot management and provide an optimum environment. Of course, these conditions do not always apply; for example one notable exception is the expensive development of a product by a consortium of companies (possible overlapping international borders), with consequent problems of risk, communication, coordination and control.

Manufacturing projects may involve work away from the home base, for example in installation, commissioning and start-up, initial customer training and subsequent service and maintenance.

3   Management projects

This class of projects proves the point that every company, whatever its size, can expect to need project management expertise at least once in its lifetime. These are the projects that arise when companies relocate their headquarters, develop and introduce a new computer system, prepare for a trade exhibition, produce a feasibility or other study report, mount a stage show, or generally engage in any operation that involves the management and coordination of activities to produce an end result that is not identifiable principally as an item of hardware or construction.

4   Research projects

Projects for pure research can consume vast sums of money, last for many years, and end up with results that please, surprise or disappoint and produce nothing of value. These projects carry the highest risk because they aim to extend the boundaries of current scientific knowledge. Unlike all other types of project, their end objectives are usually difficult or impossible to define. Research projects may, therefore, not be amenable to strict project management.

However, some form of control must be attempted. Budgets must be set, in line with available funding. Expenditure can be controlled to some extent by conducting regular management reviews and reassessments, and by authorizing and releasing funds in periodic, controlled and carefully considered steps.

It should also be noted that although the research itself may be outside the scope of project control methods, the provision of necessary buildings or equipment may well constitute capital investment projects on which proper project management can and must be exercised.

Project objectives

The objectives of any project can be grouped under three headings:

1 Performance and quality

The end result of the project must be fit for the purpose for which it was intended. The specification must be satisfied.

If a copper refinery is designed and built to process 200 000 tonnes of cathode copper per annum, then it must be able to do so, and to produce copper at the rated purity. The plant must function reliably, efficiently and safely. In these enlightened times there will be serious trouble for all concerned if operation of the plant causes environmental pollution.

Development projects for consumer goods must produce articles that satisfy the market requirements. The design concept, engineering and quality have to result in a reliable product. At one time responsibility for quality was seen primarily as that of the quality control department, relying on inspection and testing to discover faults and arrange for their rectification. In more recent years the concept of total quality management has come to the fore, with responsibility for quality shared by all the staff and work-force from top management downwards. Most of this book is about achieving the time and cost objectives. For the quality, performance and reliability objective competence in engineering and design is obviously essential. But this must be complemented by adequate quality procedures, for which BS 5750 or ISC 9000 are accepted as the controlling standards and the starting point from which to implement a quality management system.

2 Budget

The project must be completed without exceeding the authorized expenditure.

For most commercial or industrial projects failure to achieve this objective will lead to reduced profits and lower return on capital investment or actual losses. Many projects are undertaken where there is no direct commercial profit motive (for instance, some management projects, research projects and projects carried out by national or local government authorities) but proper attention to cost budgets and financial management is always essential. In extreme cases a project may have to be abandoned if funds run out, in which case the work and funds already invested are forfeit and must be written off.

3   Time to completion

Actual progress must match planned progress, so that all significant stages of the project take place no later than their specified dates, leading to final completion on or before the planned date.

This timescale objective is extremely important. Quite apart from the effect on the project purchaser or sponsor, late running will disrupt resource plans for following projects. Especially important is the likely effect on costs. If the planned timescale is exceeded, the original cost estimates and budgets are almost certain to be exceeded too. A particular danger occurs time and again when project starts are delayed (waiting for information, funds, other resources, approval or authorization), placing the project managers in a difficult or impossible situation from the outset.

A project costs money during every day of its existence, working or non-working, weekday or weekend, from day one of the programme right through until the last payment has been made. These costs arise through a variety of reasons.

There are the obvious 'variable' or 'direct' costs of materials and all the man-hours expended in design and production or construction activities. These are time-related in several ways. The most often quoted cause is cost inflation, so that a job done later than planned may cost more in money terms owing to intervening price rises for materials and wage or salary increase awards. There are other, less easily quantifiable, causes where the argument equates late working with inefficient working, and therefore with wasted or lost time that has to be paid for.

The 'fixed' or 'overhead' costs of management, administration, accommodation, services and general facilities must also be borne. These costs are directly time-related: they are incurred day by day, every day, regardless of any work actually achieved.

Another important time-related cost is that of financing. In many cases the contractor is only able to recover the costs of work-in-progress against invoices to the customer which are independently certified to verify the amount of work done. Work in progress does not only include work carried out in a factory or at a construction site, but also encompasses all the unbilled costs of engineering and design. If the work is late, invoices cannot be issued, and the contractor must finance the project himself in the meantime. Where the contractor has an overdraft at the bank or relies on other loan financing, there is interest to be paid on the loan. If the contractor finances work in progress from his own funds, there is the notional loss of interest or dividends that the same funds could have earned had the contractor invested them elsewhere (such as in a deposit account at a bank or in bonds).

Delays on a major project can easily cause additional costs amounting to thousands of pounds per day. There can also be the ignominy of cost penalties in contracts which provide the project customer with the sanction of penalty payment for each day or each week by which the contractor fails to meet the delivery obligation. In the very worst case, the contractor could suffer severe cash flow problems – even bankruptcy – through the inability to issue valid invoices.

If, however, work is carefully monitored, and managed so that it proceeds against a sensible, achievable plan, much of the cost control battle will already have been won. TIME IS MONEY.

The performance/cost/time triangle

It may be necessary to identify one of the three objectives (performance, cost or time) as being of particular importance, depending on the needs of the project client or customer. The allocation or resources and management attention can then be biased accordingly.

This has been illustrated as a triangle of objectives in Figure 1.1. This concept was featured in a television programme 'Have Project – Will Manage', screened in the UK in Autumn 1989 on BBC television, and was the subject of a paper 'Project Management Framework' by Martin Barnes in the *International Project Management Yearbook 1985*, published in association with

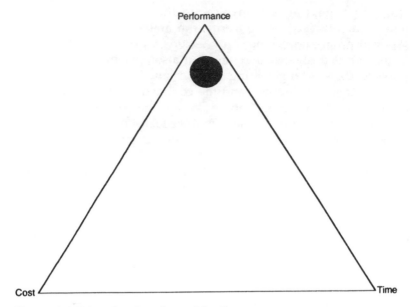

Figure 1.1 Triangle of project objectives
This diagram illustrates that the three principal project objectives of
performance, cost and time are interrelated. In some cases conflicting
priorities may lead to the client giving particular weight to one of these
objectives when the project is defined and planned. The performance
objective is indicated as paramount in this example. (*Diagram after
Martin Barnes, Deloitte, Haskins & Sells*)

the *International Journal of Project Management,* by Butterworth
Scientific.

INTERNET and the Association of Project Managers

The profession of project management is represented by the
International Association of Project Management (INTERNET).
Its corporate member in the UK is The Association of Project
Managers, and further information is available from their
secretariat at: The Association of Project Managers, 85 Oxford
Road, High Wycombe, Buckinghamshire HP11 2DX. Member-
ship of the Association, which arranges seminars and meetings

and publishes the magazine *Project* and the *International Journal of Project Management*, is a good way for project managers to meet other project managers and to maintain current awareness of modern techniques, practices and available computer systems.

2
Project management organization

It should be obvious that, if all the project objectives are to be achieved, the people, communications, jobs and resources must be properly organized. But the form which this organization should take may not be so obvious. This chapter concentrates on the management structure in which people and participating organizations are going to work.

A good organization will ensure that clear lines of authority exist, and that every member of the project knows what he or she must do to make the project a success. This is part of the management communication framework, essential for motivating all the staff employed. A well motivated group can be a joy to work with. A badly informed group, with vague responsibilities and ambiguous levels of status and authority, is likely to be poorly motivated, slow to achieve results, costly to run and frustrating to work with.

The complement of good management communications is the provision of adequate feedback paths through and across the organization. These allow progress to be monitored, difficulties to be reported back to executive management and expert specialist advice on technical or commercial problems to be sought by any participant.

The subject of project management organization can be

introduced conveniently by means of a simple example, based on a small light engineering company.

Project management organization in a manufacturing company

Suppose that a light engineering company employs about 200 people and is selling some sort of specialized equipment or components. Manufacture might take place in batches, or in a continuous flow, or as a mixture of both. The whole production operation would probably be conducted under the supervision of a production manager who would rely upon a small production control department to schedule all the work.

In normal conditions the backlog of work awaiting issue to the shops might run, at most, into a few weeks (less if a successful just-in-time system were in operation). Loading of production departments and their machines must be arranged to ensure a reasonably smooth flow of work without bottlenecks and without too much idle time, but planning methods would be straightforward and within the capability of a competent production control department. If exceptional work peaks or bottlenecks did occur, these could be overcome by rearranging the existing schedules or by the short-term employment of subcontractors.

Estimators, job planners and production engineers will analyse manufacturing drawings and specifications. The time required for every manufacturing operation can therefore be assessed with reasonable accuracy, based on past experience of similar or identical operations. No need will be found for any specialized planning or scheduling technique other than the application of well-proven production control methods, such as daily loading charts (using either simple wallboards or a suitable computer system).

Job costing can be carried out in arrears by recording man-hours and materials used. The time cycle from start to finish of each operation will be fairly short, and the total cost of each unit produced should become evident fairly soon using normal accounting procedures.

However, this small company is ambitious and the sales department is going all out to secure more orders. Not only will these orders increase in quantity, but some customers may ask for non-standard items which do not form part of the customary catalogued production range. Many of these special items may be trivial variations on the normal production theme, but other requested changes could prove to be more radical or complex, presenting something of a challenge to the company's design and production departments.

In the course of time the customers will themselves be expanding. Some of their orders will grow bigger not only in volume, but also in the time needed to fulfil them. Although these orders might consume large quantities of labour and materials, it is also possible that the actual number of finished products could be very small. Some will have become so specialized that no possible market can be found for them outside the needs of each specific purchaser. This state of affairs is sometimes summed up as being a transition from high-volume/low-cost to high-cost/low-volume production.

To give an example, suppose that this particular company was originally engaged in the manufacture of street lamps and other associated 'street' items. Later, the company's expertise and activities could have been extended to include the design and manufacture of automatic traffic signals (that is, traffic lights), each system sold comprising a control box, vehicle sensing elements and the signal lamps themselves.

As traffic demands becomes heavier, traffic systems have to be planned on a larger scale and the firm must increase its design, engineering and manufacturing concepts accordingly. Instead of considering just one crossroads or T-junction individually, whole road systems will have to be taken into account and subjected to analysis in order to arrive at solutions in which the sequencing and operation of signals is coordinated over specified areas to ensure optimum traffic flow. When an order is finally placed for a town traffic system, the contractor could therefore be involved in much more than the supply and installation of a single set of traffic lights. He might find himself caught up in the provision of automatic diversion signs, remote-controlled television cameras, car parking instrumentation, several sets of traffic lights, other highly sophisticated paraphernalia, much of which is linked to and controlled by one or more computers.

The company is no longer concerned with the sale of equipment or 'hardware' alone. It now has to support its sales with a high proportion of customer consultation, systems engineering and other services or 'software'. Instead of being able to satisfy each customer order by supplying direct from a finished stocks warehouse, it has to design, manufacture, install and commission complex systems to highly specialized customer requirements. Whereas delivery times were once achieved in days or a few weeks, these complex projects might take many months, if not years, to complete.

When the stage has been reached where simple jobs have given way to complex projects, the old methods of production planning and control will no longer be effective by themselves. Any attempt at work scheduling and control must take into account all the activities necessary to bring the project to a successful conclusion, including the many software tasks. Cost control (an essential factor in achieving profitability) itself becomes more complex, so that the cost office and accounts department are only contributors to the mechanism; they must be helped by experts who can define the detail of the total work content and report on achievement and cost implications as time proceeds. Possibly some of the items purchased outside the firm must be considered as special, and they too will have to be brought into the control function – they might even rank as projects in their own right.

A clearer picture of some of the problems encountered in project handling can be derived from a study of the organization structure of the company's supervision and management. A small engineering company might be organized along the lines shown in Figure 2.1. Line organizations of this type are set up to control work within departmental boundaries. Thus the chief engineer in this case will be responsible for design and development and very little else, leaving the works manager to concentrate on the production aspects of the business. Each manager looks only at those reporting to him in the line, concentrating on his own department or division, with no direct responsibilities outside those boundaries. Of course, no company could ever exist on such a rigid basis. Functional interplay

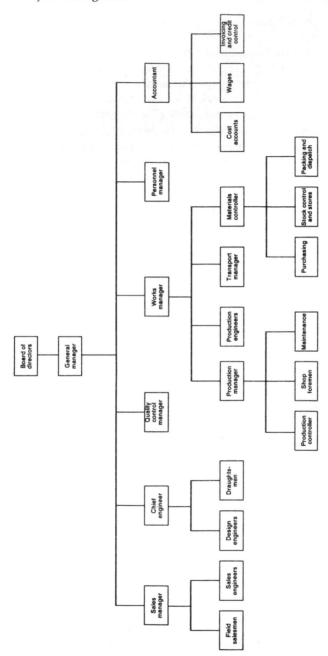

Figure 2.1 Example of a manufacturing company organization chart
This type of organization defines line responsibilities but makes no special provision for the coordination of project activities.

must take place between managers. Nevertheless, any such functional relationships which do exist are seen as secondary to the main line structure. They are not defined or brought under any form of control.

One might reasonably ask whether general managers should not play a significant part in coordinating all the various functions. The answer, of course, is that they do. Their prime task, however, is to implement policies and carry out general administration, rather than to become involved with the day-to-day running of projects or with technical detail. In the organization structure depicted in Figure 2.1 there is, in fact, no obvious person who can logically be charged with the direct responsibility for following a major project through all its stages. The positions of line responsibility are clearly shown, but the coordination between them, necessary for effective project control, is missing.

All engineering projects, in common with most other customer-funded projects, are cyclical in nature. This is illustrated in Figure 2.2, which shows some of the key stages for a manufacturing project. Each project is conceived when the customer and sales department first make contact, and is brought to life when an order is placed or a contract signed. Thereafter many other stages must be passed through in turn, until the project finally arrives back at the customer as a completed work package. Clockwise rotation around the cycle only reveals the main stream. Within this flow many small tributaries, cross-currents and even whirlpools are generated before the project is finished.

As instructions are issued from one department to another, information must be fed back along the communication channels to signal the results obtained as each instruction is carried out. These feedback data are used to correct any errors arising from engineering design or during the execution of production work, and for the essential task of controlling the general progress of the project.

Much project information will not flow along the defined lines of authority, but will cross them in complex and changing patterns. In fact, when a manufacturing project is compared with routine production, the emphasis has shifted from looking principally at the line relationships to consideration of the

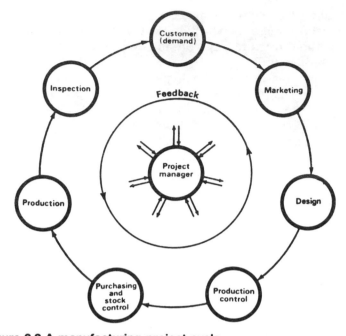

Figure 2.2 A manufacturing project cycle
A diagrammatic representation of the key stages in the progress of a typical manufacturing project.

functional connections. This has to be reflected in the formal organization structure if the project is to be coordinated and managed satisfactorily. Someone must be made responsible for managing the project as an entity, rather than having this responsibility spread vaguely over a number of managers contained within the departmental line structure. What is needed is a kind of project champion, who can ensure that all the activities are planned, coordinated and directed towards the clear aim of achieving the project objectives. Thus, at the hub of the project cycle, a new figure has emerged – the project manager.

Figure 2.3 shows how a project manager might relate functionally in a manufacturing company which is undertaking a special, complex project alongside its more routine manufacturing activities. This arrangement is often used, allowing the general line organization of the company and its management roles to continue normally while providing for special manage-

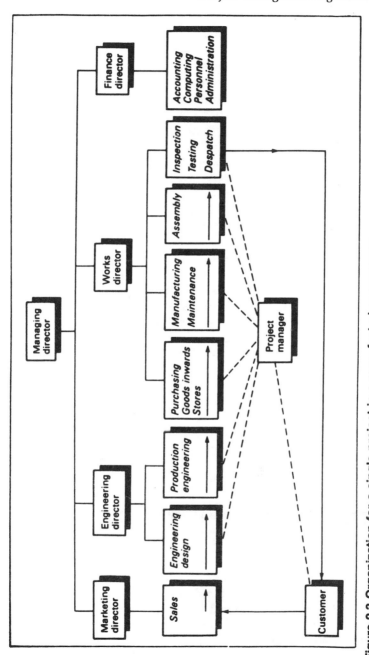

Figure 2.3 Organization for a single project in a manufacturing company
In this example the company is carrying out general batch production of engineering products, and also has one more complex project going through all phases of design and production. A project manager has been appointed, in a functional role, to coordinate and progress the project work through the company's normal organization structure.

ment attention to the 'intruding' project. In this case the role of the project manager is functional, with no direct line authority over other managers. But, when conflict or unresolved problems arise the project manager *must* be able to call on the support of the company's senior managers to exert *their* authority over the relevant line managers.

Figure 2.4 is an organization chart for a manufacturing company which handles more than one project at a time. Each project manager has claim to some of the common company resources but, as in the single project case, the direct day-to-day management and supervision of the project work-force remains firmly within the responsibility of the line managers. The project managers have no direct line authority of their own. This is an example of a matrix organization.

It is, of course, possible to arrange things differently. A complete work group or team can be created for a specific project, organized as a self-contained entity within the main company, and with the project manager placed at its head with direct line authority over all the team members. This arrangement may be impracticable in a manufacturing company owing to the nature of the facilities and heavy machinery required, all of which form part of the company's more permanent manufacturing resources, the use of which must be shared by other projects and routine manufacturing work.

Differences between the team and matrix approaches to project organization are discussed later in this chapter, where the argument is extended beyond this introductory case of manufacturing projects to include general engineering and construction projects.

The project manager in manufacturing projects

It can happen that, when a company is examined to discover the existence of a project manager, the first results are fruitless because no one with that job title can be found. The project manager's identity is often hidden behind some other organizational role. This is especially true for specialized, in-house projects where, for example, a person with the title 'facilities

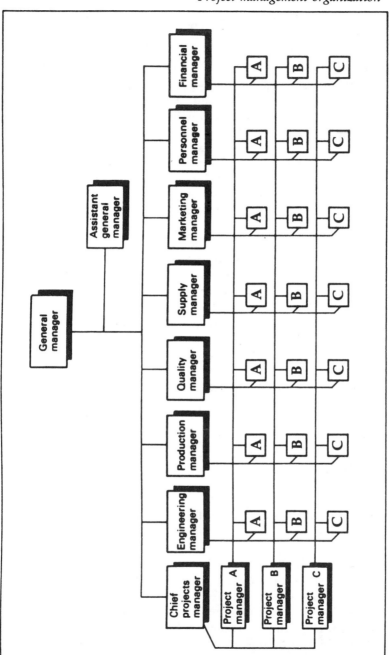

Figure 2.4 Organization for handling several simultaneous projects in a manufacturing company
Several projects (Projects A, B and C are shown here) are being handled by a manufacturing company. All projects must share the common resources of the company's usual engineering, production and administrative departments. Each project manager exercises a functional, coordinating role for his own project, but has to rely on cooperation from departmental line managers to get work through against competition from all other work priorities.

manager' might act as project manager during a major reorgan-
ization of accommodation or a 'senior engineer' might be
responsible for managing a costly project for developing a new
product.

Even where project management is accredited with the importance of a full-time appointment, the situation can be made
less clear by the variety of titles used to describe the job. Contract manager, scheduling and estimating manager, project coordination engineer, programme engineer, project coordinator
are but a few of the titles which have been used. Previous
editions of this book have recommended the adoption of
'project manager' as a standard title (which has long been the
usual practice in the construction industry). The trend in recent
years has been encouraging, and project management is now
widely recognized as a profession that deserves reasonable
status and rewards, with its own professional associations (The
Association of Project Managers and INTERNET) and with far
less confusion over the job title.

In any company which is caught up in industrial expansion or
in the so-called technological explosion, the project manager
will represent only one of the several specialized roles introduced. He might be numbered, for example, among the senior
industrial engineers, organization and methods practitioners,
systems analysts or other operational research individuals. The
project manager might have started his career in one of these
activities, or could have been a commercial manager, sales
engineer or a senior design and development engineer. Not
infrequently the job of project manager is associated with that of
the contracts manager. This is a logical link because both will be
expected to coordinate commercial and technical aspects of a
company's work and both will occupy a position in the
organization that emphasizes functional rather than line
responsibilities.

One of the more common routes to project management lies
through the engineering design department. Frequently the
engineer in command of a particular project is charged with a
degree of overall responsibility for seeing work right through to
completion. When this situation develops, the engineer per-
forms a double roll, exercising direct line authority and
supervision in controlling and guiding the engineering and

design staff while acting in a functional role when attempting to influence the other departments engaged on the project.

The project management function in a small company may be conducted entirely on a part-time basis by one of the existing department heads, or by some other individual as in the case of the engineer just described. Other companies may be forced to recognize the need for a full-time project manager, the incumbent being held responsible for either one individual project or for several projects which are being handled simultaneously. Very large companies even have whole departments devoted to project management, where specialist teams operate as a central service.

Seniority of the project manager in manufacturing projects

The questions 'How senior is the project manager?' and 'To whom should the project manager report?' now arise. A consideration of the general organization, possibly helped by reference to Figures 2.3 and 2.4, may suggest a solution.

The person appointed will be expected to provide the company's general management with relevant facts whenever it becomes necessary for them to exert their senior authority or take other executive action to maintain the project on its specified financial, technical and delivery course. The project manager should therefore have reasonable access to general management.

Much of the project manager's time will be spent in coordination – steering and integrating the activities of some departments and relying on others for information or supporting services. This demands cooperation with and from the managers of most departments in the company, whether these departments are directly engaged in project fulfilment (such as engineering and production) or are service departments (such as accounts and personnel). Ideally, therefore, the project manager should not be handicapped by being placed in an organizationally inferior position to any departmental manager in particular or to departmental managers in general.

Thus the appointment level for the project manager in a manufacturing company appears to be indicated on a management plane which is at least equivalent to that occupied by the company's departmental managers. This view is reinforced when it is realized that the person appointed will probably be called upon to supervise subcontractors and (once the marketing people have finished taking the order) to represent the company to the customer. The project manager is, in fact, a significant part of the corporate image which the company projects to the outside world.

Project management organization in capital projects

It is now time to widen the argument beyond projects conducted wholly within a manufacturing company by considering some organization aspects of large capital projects. The examples used are based on projects which include an element of site construction, but many of the arguments put forward will also be valid for more complex manufacturing projects, especially where these involve large organizations or more than one participating organization.

Project teams versus functional group organizations

Consider a company which is about to embark upon a project for the first time. A competent project manager is available, but this firm has never had to handle a complex capital project before and now has to set up the most suitable organization. If the project manager were asked to advise, he would immediately be faced with the question that often causes controversy:

- Should the company take all the key people destined to work on the project and place them under the direct management of the project manager, so that he is asked to manage a purpose-built project team?

Or, alternatively

- Would it be better to have the project manager to act in a purely functional capacity? He would still be responsible for the whole project, but with no direct authority over the work-force, having instead to coordinate the work provided from specialist groups and other departments, each of which is supervised by and reports directly to its own separate line manager within the company or wider organization.

Team organization

Figure 2.5 illustrates a project team organization structure which could be set up to carry out all the work necessary to devise the processes and reagent flows, specify and purchase the plant and equipment, design the buildings and other facilities for a chemical processing plant. This is a team which has been specially assembled for the purpose. The project manager is in direct command, with complete authority for directing the participants so that the project meets all the objectives.

When the project has been finished, the team and its project manager have no further purpose. As various aspects of the project are finished, so the team will gradually be reduced in size until it is finally disbanded when the project is finished.

Functional or matrix organization

Figure 2.6 shows a different organization structure which would also be able to accommodate the chemical plant project. In this case, however, there is no special project team. Instead, permanently established groups of people are organized according to their special skills or disciplines. Every project handled by the firm within this functional, or matrix, organization has its own project manager, but all these project managers draw upon the same specialist groups for their manpower and other resources. Their influence is functional, and the people in the specialist groups remain administratively responsible to their own departmental line managers.

For the manufacturing project counterpart to this chemical plant example see Figure 2.4, which also shows several projects being managed functionally in a matrix organization.

Which type of organization is best?

Project teams have the advantage that they can each be directed to a single purpose: the successful completion of one project. A team can be completely autonomous. It is provided with and relies on its own resources. There is no clash of priorities

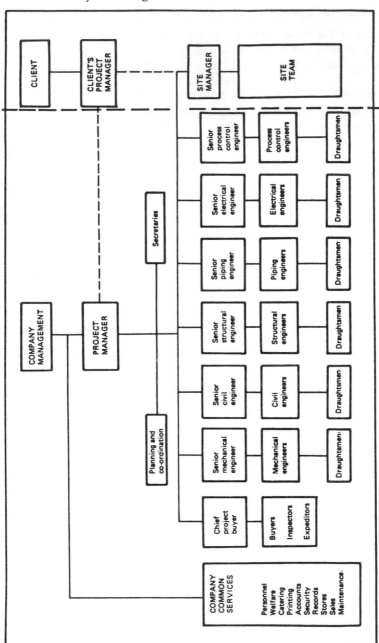

Figure 2.5 Project team organization

Here is one way in which a company can organize resources for the design, procurement, construction and commissioning of a chemical process plant. This is a project team. All the members report through their respective lines of command to the project manager. Not only does the project manager have complete responsibility for all aspects of the project; he also has the clear authority of direct command.

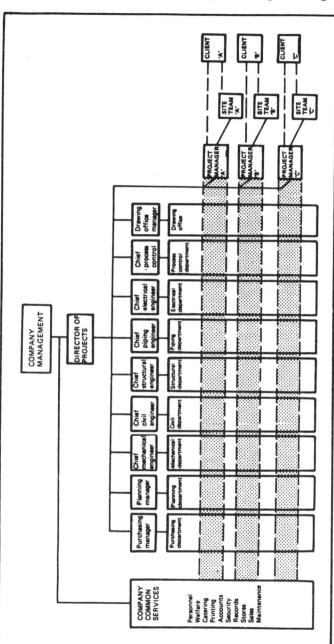

Figure 2.6 Matrix organization

This chart shows a company organized functionally for the execution of capital projects. If the chemical process plant project of Figure 2.5 were to be handled by this company, it would not be accorded a particular team but would instead be distributed over the specialist groups. The assigned project manager would be responsible for directing and coordinating the work, but would have no line authority over any member of any group. It is clear that the lines of command are complex, and individuals working in any one of the groups find themselves responsible to their own chief, but with added responsibility to the project manager regarding some elements of their work. Such complexity can lead to conflict, but there are compensating features. These are discussed in the text and summarized in Figure 2.7.

resulting from a clamour of different projects in competition for common (shared) resources.

Much is rightly said and written about the importance of motivating people who work on projects. An important aspect of motivation is the generation of a team spirit, in which all members of the team strive to meet common goals. It is obviously easier to establish a team spirit when a project team actually exists, as opposed to the case where the people are dispersed over a matrix organization which has to deal with many projects.

If the work is being conducted for a government defence contract, or for any other project that requires a secret or confidential environment, the establishment of a project team greatly helps the organizers to contain all the work and its information within closed, secure boundaries.

Unless the project is very large, however, the individual specialist subgroups set up to perform all the varied activities within the project will prove too small to allow sufficient flexibility of labour and other resources. Where, for example, a common manufacturing facility of 100 people is coping with several projects, the absence of a few workers through sickness may result in some rescheduling but would be unlikely to cause disaster. If, on the other hand, a project team had been set up to include its own independent production group, perhaps only needing six people, the infection of three of these with flu could pose a more serious problem.

Inflexibility associated with small groups is seen more keenly in some of the experienced administrative and specialist discipline work functions, where it is often more difficult, if not impossible, to rectify matters at short notice using temporary employees. In the manufacturing case it is quite possible that only one or two people will be responsible for all project purchasing, or for project production control – indeed it is not unknown for one person to be made responsible for both of these activities on a small project team. When this situation is allowed to develop, the fate of the project may depend on the capabilities and health of just one individual, who becomes virtually indispensable.

Returning to the example of the chemical plant project, suppose that the company responsible employs ten civil engineers. If the company operates a matrix organization, these engineers would work together in a department under their own chief engineer, with work allocated to the various projects as necessary (see Figure 2.6). In the project team case (see Figure 2.5) a small project might only need one civil engineer, whose unplanned absence for any reason could prove disastrous.

There is a danger that specialist engineers located in small project teams are deprived of the benefits of working in a department with colleagues of their own specialist discipline, namely the ability to discuss technical problems with their peers and having access to the valuable fund of general historic technical and professional data plus current awareness that such departments accumulate.

If a project is of sufficient size to justify its own exclusive team, not all the problems of project coordination will be overcome. Very often it may be found impossible to house all the participants under one roof, or even in the same locality. Much of the project manager's time could be spent in sorting out special problems, such as technical difficulties or labour relations and other line management matters, rather than being concentrated on managing the project itself. Although the project team organization may be logical, and ideal for the project, a general lack of coordination between the functions is still possible.

One problem with a project team organization is the question of what happens when the project comes to an end. When each project is finished and its team disbanded, the team members can suffer serious or even traumatic withdrawal symptoms. Organizational change usually brings problems, with dissatisfactions, rivalries and career worries created among those whose roles must change.

Another possible danger is that something may go wrong with the project after its supposed completion, with expert attention required from the team's engineers to satisfy the customer and put matters right. If the team no longer exists, and the engineers who designed the project have been dispersed, events could take an embarrassing, even ugly, turn.

On the other hand, the matrix option allows the establishment of specialist functional groups which have 'eternal life', independent of the duration of individual projects. This continuity of work promotes the gradual build-up of expertise and experience. Specialist skills are concentrated. Pooling of skills provides for flexibility in deploying resources. Each member of every specialist group enjoys a reasonably stable basis for employment (provided the order book is full). There is a clear promotion path within the discipline up to at least chief engineer level, and each person in the group is able to compete against his colleagues for more senior positions within the group as vacancies arise in the long term. Performance assessment of each individual, and any recommendation for improved salary or other benefits, is carried out by a chief engineer or other manager of the same engineering discipline within the stable group, and this is more likely to result in a fair assessment and employee satisfaction. These possibilities are not readily available to the specialist engineer working alone in a multi-disciplined project team.

The matrix organization has its own characteristic disadvantages. Not least of these is the split responsibility which each group member faces between his line manager and the project manager (see Figure 2.6).

The arguments will no doubt continue as to which is the better of the two organizations. Some of the pros and cons are summarized in Figure 2.7. As a general rule (but it is dangerous to generalize in this subject) large projects of long duration will probably require the formation of project teams. Functional organizations are indicated for companies which handle a number of small projects in which neither the amount of resources nor the timescale needed for each project is great.

The hybrid option

Sometimes companies adopt the solution of a hybrid organization, operating a matrix organization in general, but with teams set up for certain projects when the need arises.

An example of such an organization is shown in Figure 2.8. It is arranged principally as a matrix, with specialist groups under their respective highly qualified and experienced chief engineers. The project management group contains project managers and project engineers who draw on the resources of the specialist groups for the skilled engineering and expert advice needed for most projects.

CHARACTERISTIC	ORGANISATION INDICATED	
	TEAM	MATRIX
Maximum authority for the project manager	✔	
Freedom from duplicated or ambiguous lines of command	✔	
Maximum motivation of staff to meet difficult time and cost targets	✔	
High security: where information has to be confined to those working on the project — by enclosing project work in secure areas	✔	
— by restricting the total number of staff who need to know about the work	✔	
Most flexible deployment of total company resources		✔
Most effective availability, company-wide, of experts with rare specialist skills		✔
Large project, employing many people for a long time	✔	
Several projects, each needing a few people for a short time		✔
Career motivation of individuals — by creating senior job positions (and opportunities for promotion) for specialists (eg electrical engineers)		✔
Career motivation of individuals — by long-term continuity of management structure, allowing managers time to assess individuals' performance, give guidance and ensure fair long-term rewards		✔
Provision of advice or service to construction personnel on site, and after-sales advice and service to customers after completion of project design work (which may prove very difficult to arrange if a team has been disbanded)		✔
Establishment of information banks, in which accumulated experience can be kept for retrieval on later projects		✔

Figure 2.7 Project team versus matrix organization

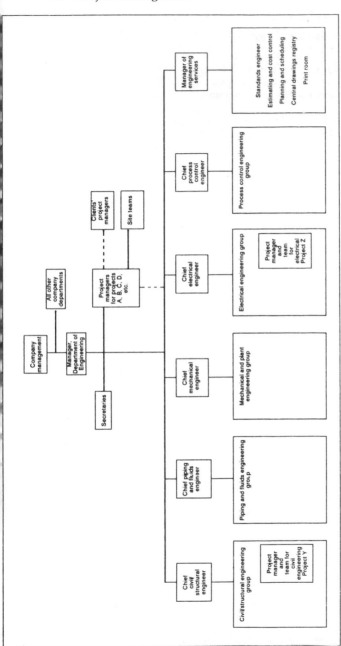

Figure 2.8 A hybrid organization
This organization is similar to an actual project engineering organization in a mining company which operated in the winning of non-ferrous metals and other minerals worldwide. Although at first sight this is a matrix, the company would set up a project team whenever the occasion demanded, thus running a hybrid organization mixing the team and matrix concepts. In this example, a large earthmoving project has been set up as a team project in the civil/structural group, and the electrical group is handling the replacement of a mine generator as a group team project. In these team cases, the team leader within the group acts as project manager and has access to the client. In all other projects, project managers are drawn from the project managers' group.

If, however, a project should arise which is predominantly within one of the specialist skills, the company might decide to appoint a project manager from within the relevant specialist group, managing a team contained within the group. For example, a project to install a new electrical generator in an existing plant might be regarded as a project that could be handled entirely by a team within the electrical department. Similarly, a land reclamation project might be assigned solely to the civil engineering group, who would set up their own internal team to deal with it under a civil engineer as project manager.

A variation of the hybrid organization occurs when a company operates generally as a project matrix organization but sets up a separate, autonomous team whenever the size and scope of a project justifies the arrangement.

Organizations with more than one project manager

In all probability the overall organization of any sizeable project will be found to contain more than one project manager.

Whenever a company sells a project to a customer, that customer will probably wish to monitor progress in order to assure himself that there is every chance of the work being completed in accordance with the contract. For simple manufacturing contracts this role might be performed by the customer's purchasing department, using its expediting and inspecting personnel. But, except in this very simple case, the customer may wish to appoint his own project manager to oversee the contract. That was the situation in the example given at Figure 2.5. The customer will certainly need his own project manager where the project involves him in planning to accommodate, install and start up plant supplied under the project.

The project contractor may in turn be a major purchaser (that is customer) having to buy in expensive equipment or other items or services to be built into the project before it can be delivered to the end user. For large projects some of these subcontracts may amount to significant projects in their own right, each needing planning and management similar to that used by the main contractor. These subcontractors may need project managers to manage these subprojects. Indeed, the project contractor may even insist that such project managers are appointed, and may wish to inspect and approve the project management procedures used, possibly as a precondition of the subcontracts.

There is often more than one project contractor. Here is another reason for finding more than one project manager. In such multi-contractor projects it is most probable that one contractor would be nominated by the project customer as the main or the managing contractor, with overall responsibility to the customer for managing or coordinating all the other contractors and subcontractors and completing the project.

Sometimes the customer will seek the services of an independent professional project manager, to act for him in return for a management fee. This role is often undertaken by companies, by professional partnerships or by professional people (such as consulting engineers or architects).

For very large projects several companies may agree to share the technical problems, expense (and risk) by forming a consortium or joint venture company, which adds yet another complication to the organization and at least one more project manager.

Whenever the complexity of a project is increased for any of these reasons, apart from the obvious need to define responsibilities carefully and tie up the contractual ends, it is vital that the lines of communication between all the parties are established and declared in a clear and efficient manner. It is not unusual to find projects where participants are separated by international borders and thousands of miles. The sheer volume of information, whether in the form of drawings, other technical documents, commercial correspondence, telexed queries and even hotel and travel arrangements can be mind-boggling for a large project. In order to avoid over-complicating what can already be an intricate organization, it makes much practical sense to nominate one individual in each of the organizations (including the customer) through whom all project information must be passed (in and out). Ideally, each organization will have its own project manager and they are the obvious nominees (even **where, at some of the busier locations, the bulk of material** actually requires a small army of clerks and other assistants to send/receive, sort, edit, distribute and file all the documents).

Figure 2.9 illustrates some of the possible lines of communication in a complex project organization.

The project manager himself

Before becoming too deeply involved with this subject, it is necessary to consider changing attitudes towards women in industry. In the UK, introduction of the Equal Pay Act (1970) and the 1975 Sex Discrimination Act is now history, and more women should be taking on the role of project managers. It is a fact, however, that industrial project management remains a male-dominated occupation (for example, in the UK women account for less than one per cent of total membership of The Association of Project Managers). Let us hope that this will not always be the case. For the sake of simplicity, masculine pronouns and job titles are used in many cases throughout this book, but these are not intended to apply only to men. When therefore, as in the title to this section, 'the project manager himself' is written, this should be taken to include 'the project manageress herself'.

What is the ideal personality specification for a project manager? If the objectives of project management could be condensed into responsibility for ensuring work completion within time and cost restrictions, then these goals could be achieved by a variety of approaches. One project manager might operate successfully by inducing fear and trepidation in his fellow men, so that his every word is seen as a command to be instantly obeyed. Another might achieve the same results through gentle but firm persuasion. The essential element here is the ability to motivate people, by whatever means: the seasoned expert will be able to vary his management style according to the response of the individual being managed.

The average project participant will appreciate being led by a project manager who displays competence, makes clear decisions, gives clear instructions, delegates well, listens to and

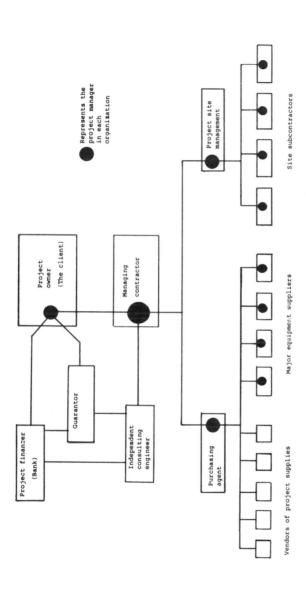

Figure 2.9 Project with more than one project manager

Most projects have at least two project managers – one within the client's organization and the other employed by the managing contractor. This illustration shows that a large project can have people in several parts of the organization who must practise project management skills. Every manufacturer of a major piece of equipment has his own subproject that needs managing, and every site subcontractor of any significance will need to schedule and progress his own work. Many of the techniques described in this book apply to these 'satellite' project managers as well as to the principals.

accepts sound advice, is enthusiastic and confident, and thus generally commands respect by his example and qualities of leadership.

Other essential characteristics of the project manager can be grouped under the heading of perceptiveness. The project manager must be able to select the salient facts for a set of data or a particular arrangement of circumstances. He must then be able to use these facts to best effect by taking action or reporting important exceptions to executive management, while filtering out the unimportant and irrelevant material.

Most project managers will become accustomed to being presented with information that is incomplete, unduly optimistic, inaccurate, deliberately misleading or completely wrong. Without going into all the possible reasons for such inaccuracies, it is possible to lay down that a project manager must never be in any way a gullible individual. He will learn to check much of the information which he receives, particularly by knowing what questions to ask in order to probe its validity. As he gains experience of a particular organization he should be capable of assessing the reliability of individuals or departments, so that he can apply 'confidence factors' to the data which they submit and the stories that they tell.

All project managers of any merit will know the frustration caused not simply by receiving inaccurate information, but also through receiving no information at all. Data deficiencies can take the form of delayed instructions or approvals from the customer, late information from subcontractors and vendors, and tardy release of design and other information within the project manager's own company. On international projects, in particular, it may be very difficult to obtain reliable and regular reports of cost and progress from distant locations. The ability to gather and assess relevant data is, therefore, another essential property for project management. It is no good expecting to obtain the complete picture and manage a project simply by sitting fixed behind a desk for the duration of the project. The project manager must take (and be seen to take) an active interest. He should show himself regularly in those departments of the company on which he is dependent (a process which has been called 'management by walkabout'). It may be necessary for him to visit vendors, subcontractors, the customer and a remote construction site at suitable intervals in order to gather facts, resolve local disputes, generate enthusiasm, or simply to witness progress at first hand.

The project manager in the age of technology could be described as a specialist. His background may be in one of the specialist engineering or other professional disciplines and he will certainly need to be trained in one or more of the current special project management techniques if he is to operate effectively. Nevertheless the term 'specialist' can be misleading, since much of the project manager's time will be taken up with coordinating the activities of project participants from a wide variety of administrative, professional, technical and craft backgrounds. This work, far from requiring specialization, demands a sufficient general understanding of the work carried out by those participants for the project manager to be able to discuss the work sensibly, understand all the commercial and technical data received and appreciate (or question) any reported problems.

The project manager should have a general understanding of administrative procedures as they will be applied throughout the project organization. If a person is asked to handle a flow of project data between different departments, he should be able to use his understanding of the administration and its pro- cedures to recommend or arrange for the information to be presented in the form most likely to be effective in the hands of the various recipients. In the jargon of computer technology, the project manager may be asked to solve interface problems, the solutions to which need some understanding of how the peripheral units operate.

There is little doubt that the evolution process will continue for project planning and control techniques. The project manager must be prepared to keep abreast of this development, undergoing training or retraining whenever necessary, and passing this training on to other members of the firm where appropriate. He must be able to choose and use appropriate techniques, either directly or adapted to suit the project's particular purposes, whenever they are needed. On the other hand, the temptation to impose unsuitable methods on an organization for the sole reason that they represent the height of current fashion must be resisted.

Support, cooperation and training for the project manager

No matter how experienced, competent, enthusiastic and intelligent the person chosen for the job of project manager, he cannot expect to operate effectively alone, without adequate support and cooperation. This obviously includes the willing cooperation of all staff engaged on the project, whether they report to him in the line organization or not. But it also includes support from higher management in the organization, who must at least ensure the provision of essential finance, accommodation, facilities, equipment, manpower and other resources when they are needed and the availability of suitable clerical or other supporting staff. Just as those working on the project need to be properly motivated, so does the project manager himself, and supportive higher management who show constructive and helpful interest in the project can go a long way to achieve this. They can also help in the longer term by providing opportunities for training as new techniques or management systems are developed.

A person who is responsible for the allocation and progressing of work will inevitably be called upon to decide priorities or criticize progress achieved. The project manager, especially in a functional organization, must often arrange for the issue of such work instructions in the full knowledge that he has no direct authority over any one of the departments involved. Each departmental manager alone is responsible for the performance and day-to-day internal management and work allocation of his own department. It has even been known for a departmental manager to tell a project manager to keep out of his department. In such circumstances the project manager's influence can only be exerted as reflected authority from higher management, without whose full backing the project manager must be ineffective.

The main show of authority which the project manager can wield stems from his own personality and ability to persuade or motivate others. In these enlightened times discipline no longer implies the imposition of rigid authoritarian regimes or management by fear through the constant threat of dismissal or other punitive action. Mutual cooperation and established job satisfaction are the more likely elements of an effective approach, especially in the long term. There will, however, be occasions when firm discipline has to be exercised; when, in the last resort, the full backing and support of higher management must be available as a reserve force on which the project manager can call in any hour of need.

Sometimes it would be apt to include project managers in that group of individuals described as 'human dynamos'. There will be times when apathy or inertia of some project participants has to be overcome by an electrifying injection of enthusiasm. The output of any dynamo, however, may be dissipated wastefully if it is switched into an inefficient or wrongly connected circuit. The astute project manager will learn to recognize any wasteful shortcomings in the organization of his project forces. When this happens, and a change in the organization is indicated, the project manager should be able to rely on his superiors to make any administrative changes which he can show to be appropriate and necessary. Higher management, after installing the project manager, must back him up and work with him to create an ideal environment in which to operate.

In order to maintain his company's competitive edge, the project manager should keep abreast of new developments in project control and management techniques and thinking. Senior management must recognize that such training is a continuous process and not simply a question of sending a person away for a two-day course on network analysis. There has been an increasing and welcome tendency for various training authorities to arrange project management seminars where, in addition to the formal training given, delegates from different companies are able to meet and discuss mutual problems and solutions, and exchange views and experiences generally. The effectiveness of these individuals and of the profession as a whole must benefit from this type of exchange.

Just as important as the project manager's own training is the creation of an enlightened and informed attitude to modern project management techniques and organizational procedures among the participants within the contractor's project organization. There is a serious danger that those who are suddenly presented with unfamiliar techniques and procedures on a project, without any explanation of the underlying methods or reasons for their introduction, will decide not to cooperate and fail to provide the feedback and other responses essential for those procedures to be effective. Ideally, when the objectives of a particular project are outlined the project manager should assure himself that participating managers, engineers and line supervisors have at least been given an elementary grounding in the appreciation of network analysis, scheduling, principles of cost and progress control, and the interpretation of associated computer reports, all with specific relevance to the procedures to be used on the particular project. Training or instructions should be given in the use of the various forms and other documents to be used on the project and (where appropriate) in the active use of relevant computer systems. If participating staff understand the procedures and the reasons for them, their essential cooperation is far more likely to be forthcoming and effective.

3

Defining the project

Project definition is a process which starts when the customer or investor first conceives the idea of a project. It does not end until the last piece of information has been filed to describe the project in its finished 'as built' condition. Figure 3.1 shows some of the elements in the overall process. This chapter deals with the part of project definition that should take place before a project is authorized; the part most relevant to setting the project on its proper course and which plays a vital role in helping to establish any initial contractual commitments. Subsequent aspects of project definition are discussed later in this book, particularly in Chapters 14 and 16.

Introduction

Enquiries and subsequent orders for commercial projects generally enter contracting companies through their sales engineering or marketing organization, and it is usually from this source that other departments learn of each new enquiry or firm order. Even when enquiries bypass the sales organization, sensible company rules should operate to ensure referral to the marketing director or sales manager, so that every enquiry is

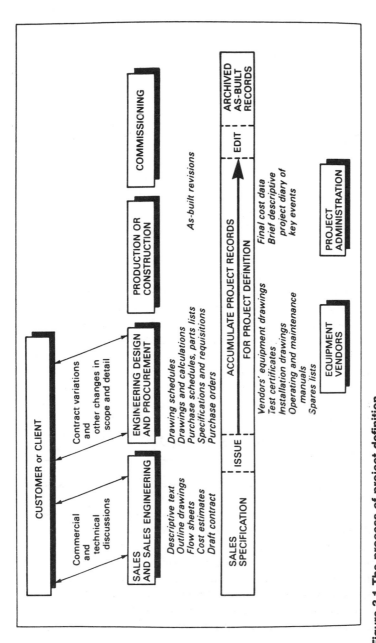

Figure 3.1 The process of project definition
The sales specification is only the first stage in defining a project. The process is not complete until as-built records have been made and safely archived for future retrieval. This diagram shows some of the important elements.

'entered into the system'. This will ensure that every enquiry received can be subjected to a formal screening process for assessing its potential project scope, risk and value. The work involved in preparing a tender can easily constitute a small project in itself, needing significant preliminary engineering design work plus sales and office effort that must be properly authorized and budgeted. The potential customer will almost certainly set a date by which all tenders for the project must be submitted, so that time available for preparation is usually limited. Everything must be planned, coordinated and controlled if a tender of adequate quality is to be delivered on time. Some companies record their screening decision and appropriate follow-up action on a form such as that shown in Figure 3.2.

Before any company can even start the enquiry screening process, and certainly before tender preparation can be authorized, the customer's requirements must be clearly established and understood. The project must be defined as well as possible right at the start. The contracting company must know for what it is bidding and what its commitments would be in the event of winning the contract.

Adequate project definition is equally important for the customer, who must be clear on what he expects to get for his money. Project definition is also just as important for a company considering an in-house project, in which case that company (as the investor in the project) can be regarded as the customer.

Projects which cannot be defined

Most of the procedures and project cases described in this book are written from the contractor's point of view and assume that the customer's project objectives and the contractor's commitments have been well defined in advance, enabling all stages of the project and its expenditure to be managed effectively against clear benchmarks. Of course there are times when a proposed project is so complex, or is fraught with so much uncertainty and risk, that its progress and outcome cannot be foretold at the beginning. In other words, it may simply be impossible for the customer or investor to define the project.

Project title:		Enquiry number	Rev. or case

Client's name and address:

Client's reference:

Enquiry date:

Telephone:

Name and title of contact:

Telex:

Outline description of proposed project:

Screening committee authorization:

Comments

We will bid. Inform client: ☐

We will not bid. Inform client: ☐

Clarify with customer and rescreen: ☐

Signed:

Action	For action by	Authorized budgets			Date wanted
		Labour	Travel	Other expenses	
Define the task					
Review task definition with the client					
Develop project design solutions					
Evaluate client's operating costs					
Review proposed solutions with client					
Estimate our project costs					
Write proposal and prepare artwork					
Printing and binding					
Time allowed for proposal delivery					
Presentation of proposal					
Total budgets					
Name of engineer in charge:					

Figure 3.2 Screening and action plan form for new project proposals

The investor faced with a very uncertain prognosis for an industrial project may wish to start by commissioning a feasibility study from a consultant or professionally orientated contracting company in order to obtain more facts and expert advice. This approach is frequently used to examine and appraise the technical, logistical, environmental, commercial and financial aspects of all kinds of projects requiring major investment. Banks and other institutions asked to finance or otherwise sponsor ill-defined projects may require a satisfactory feasibility study report before committing funds. Government departments often demand or commission reports for projects which have national or international implications. A feasibility study for a large capital project can be quite an undertaking in itself, perhaps taking years to prepare and costing millions of pounds, but a good feasibility study report can do much to point a project in the right direction and define its risks and achievable objectives.

Another approach to starting an ill-defined project is to limit the risk by authorizing work step by step. It may be possible to divide the project into a number of stages for this purpose. Such stages might be set according to:

- the occurrence of significant events in the project that can easily be recognized when they occur or are achieved; or
- the imposition of a time limit for each stage; or
- a budgetary limit for each stage; or
- a combination of any two or all of these.

Funding or authorization of expenditure on each new stage of the project would depend on a critical review of the results achieved to date and a fresh look at the future prospects. This approach has the advantage of limiting the committed risk and, whereas it is still not possible to define the whole project in advance, it should be possible to look the short way ahead necessary to define each limited step. Each step so defined may then be amenable to the project management procedures that cannot be used for the whole project. Pure research projects are good examples of this approach, where the initial setting up and provision of facilities can be treated as a definable project, and subsequent expenditure, the results obtained and future funding can be reviewed regularly at suitable intervals.

In the step-by-step approach it always has to be borne in mind that it may become necessary to abandon the project and write off the expenditure incurred.

A contractor asked to embark upon a project in which his

expected role is not adequately defined can of course accept the order, provided that the payment arrangements guarantee reimbursement of all his costs plus reasonable fees or profits. The contractor should ensure that the customer or investor bears the risk in these cases. Such arrangements can still be inconvenient or potentially difficult for contractors, since it may be difficult for them to arrange and commit resources for a project whose duration is unknown and which could be stopped without much notice.

It is common in construction projects to isolate any small parts of a project which cannot adequately be defined and which are outside the contractor's control, and list these separately in the quotation. An example would be a project to refurbish a building where part of the structure is hidden from view and in uncertain condition. The proposal might assume the structure to be sound, but include a separate provisional estimate of costs that will be charged to the customer should additional work prove to be necessary when the cladding is removed and the structure revealed as the project proceeds.

There are procedures which allow for probabilities or alternative options to be built into initial project planning, so that the project starts with built-in uncertainty. This book, however, deals generally with the more usual deterministic approach, in which firm objectives can be agreed at the beginning with the project customer or investor. Naturally, customer-requested modifications will occur during the course of most projects, and these may change the original objectives. But the main thrust of really effective project management is a positive and determined attitude towards attaining the objectives set, with action taken wherever necessary to keep the project on its planned course.

Defining a project for financial appraisal

There may, of course, be overriding legal, ethical or operational reasons for going ahead with a project where the financial considerations are secondary (for example, a programme of structural works which have been declared necessary in order that a company shall comply with statutory health and safety regulations). In most cases, however, when a commercial project requiring significant expenditure is contemplated the proper approach is for the customer or investor to use one or more of the accepted processes for project financial appraisal. These help to forecast the likely net savings or profits that the investment will yield, put these into perspective against the company's corporate objectives, and assess any risk that the expected benefits might not accrue.

All of this demands proper and extended project definition, the full scope of which would include the evaluation and assessment of some or all of the following parameters:

- An outline description of the project, with its required performance characteristics quantified in unambiguous terms.
- The total amount of expenditure expected to carry out the project and bring its resulting product or structure into use.
- The expected date when the product or structure can be put effectively to its intended use.
- Forecast of any subsequent operating and maintenance costs for the new product or structure.
- The operating and maintenance costs of any existing plant or structure that would be superseded by the new project.
- Any scrap or resale value expected from disposal of the superseded plant or structure.
- The economic working life expected from the new plant or structure.
- Forecast scrap or resale value expected at the end of the working life of the new plant or structure.
- A forecast of the costs of financing likely over the appraisal period (bank interest rates, inflationary trends, international exchange rate trends, and so on, as appropriate).
- Fiscal considerations (taxes or financial incentives expected under national or local government legislation).
- A schedule which sets out all known items of expenditure (cash outflows) against the calendar.
- A schedule which sets out all expected savings or other contributions to profits (cash inflows) against the same calendar.
- A net cash flow schedule (which is the difference between

the inflow and outflow schedules, again tabulated against the same calendar).

For short-term commercial projects the financial appraisal may take the form of a simple payback calculation. This sets out expenditure against time (it could be tabulated or drawn as a graph) and also plots all the financial benefits (savings or profits) on the same chart. Supposing that graphs were drawn, the point where the two graphs intersect is the break-even point, where the project can be said to have 'paid for itself'. The time taken to reach this point is called the payback period.

Any financial sum listed as a saving or cost item in future years will have its significance distorted through the passage of time (for instance, £100 spent today is more expensive than spending £100 in a year's time, owing to lost interest that the money might have earned for the investor on deposit in the meantime). Such distortions can have a considerable effect on the forecast cash flows of a project lasting more than two or three years if factors are not introduced to correct them, and it is best to use a discounting technique for the financial appraisal of long-term projects (see Chapter 5).

Project managers do not, of course, have to be expert in all or any of the techniques of project financial appraisal. It may, however, help to increase their determination to meet the defined objectives if they realize that these were key factors in an earlier appraisal decision; factors (time, money, performance) on which the investor and the contractor are both dependent if the completed project is to be a mutual success.

The customer's project specification

Initial enquiries from customers can take many different forms. Perhaps a set of plans or drawings will be provided, or a written description of the project objectives. A combination of these two, rough sketches, or even a verbal request are other possibilities. Ensuing communications between the customer and contractor, both written and verbal, may result in subsequent qualifications, changes or additions to the original request. All of these factors, taken together and documented, constitute the 'customer specification', to which all aspects of any tender must relate.

Project scope

Should the quotation be successful and a firm order result, the contractor will have to ensure that the customer's specification is satisfied in every respect. His commitments will not be confined to the technical details but will encompass the fulfilment of all specified commercial conditions. The terms of the order may lay down specific rules governing methods for invoicing and certification of work done for payment. Inspection and quality standards may be spelled out in the contract and one would certainly expect to find a well-defined statement of delivery requirements. There may even be a warning that a condition of the resulting contract will provide for penalties to be paid by the contractor should he default on the agreed delivery dates.

Any failure by the contractor to meet his contractual obligations could obviously be very damaging for his reputation. Bad news travels fast throughout an industry, and the contractor's competitors will, to put it mildly, not attempt to slow the process. The contractor may suffer financial loss if the programme cannot be met or if he has otherwise miscalculated the size of the task which he undertook. It is therefore extremely important for the contractor to determine in advance exactly what the customer expects for the money.

The customer's specification should therefore set out all the requirements in unambiguous terms, so that they are understood and similarly interpreted by customer and contractor alike. Much of this chapter deals with the technical requirements of a specification but, equally important, is the way in which responsibility for the work is to be shared between the contractor, the customer, and others. In more precise terms, the scope of work required from the contractor, the size of his contribution to the project, must be made clear.

At its simplest, the scope of work required might be limited to making and delivering a piece of hardware in accordance with drawings supplied by the customer. At the other extreme, the scope of a major construction or process plant project could be defined so that the contractor handles the project entirely, and is responsible for all work until the purchaser is able to accept delivery or handover of a fully completed and proven project (known as a turnkey operation).

Whether the scope of work lies at one of these extremes or the other, there is always a range of ancillary items that have to be considered. Will the contractor be responsible for any training of the customer's staff and, if so, how much (if any) training is to be included in the project contract and price? What about commissioning, or support during the first few weeks or months of the project's working life? What sort of warranty or guarantee is going to be expected? Are any training, operating or maintenance instructions to be provided? If so, in what language?

Answers to all of these questions must be provided, as part of project definition, before cost estimates, tenders and binding contracts can be considered. Checklists are a useful way of ensuring that nothing important is forgotten.

Use of checklists

Contractors who have amassed a great deal of experience in their particular field of project operation will learn the type of questions that must be asked of the customer in order to fill in most of the information gaps and arrive at a specification that is sufficiently complete.

The simplest level of checklist use is seen when a sales engineer takes a customer's order for equipment that is standard, but which can be ordered with a range of options. The sales engineer will use a pad of preprinted forms, ticking off the options that the customer requires. People selling replacement windows with double glazing use such pads. So do some automobile salesmen. The forms are convenient and help to ensure that no important details are omitted when the order is taken and passed back to the factory for action.

Companies about to tender for construction or mining projects can make good use of checklists. One checklist may be concerned with ensuring that plant performance or building accommodation needs are properly specified. Local climatic and geological data at the intended project site may have to be defined. If the project site is in a foreign country, the contractor may not know about potential hazards such as high winds or earth tremors, and it may also be necessary to check on any special statutory regulations which operate in the region. Other data might cover national working practices and the influence of local trade unions, the availability of suitable local labour, facilities to be provided for the contractor's expatriot staff and so on. Many, many questions will have to be asked and answered. Checklists are ideal in these circumstances. The example in Figure 3.3 illustrates some of the items that might feature in a complete list.

The manufacturer of special purpose machining systems may have a host of questions to ask about details of the products which the machines must eventually produce, and how the customer wants any loading and unloading points, locating lugs, jigs, fixtures and so on arranged. The standard network diagram which appears later in this book as Figure 11.4 was used by a company as a sequenced checklist for such cases.

The contractor's project specification

When serious consideration of the customer's specification encourages any contractor to prepare a tender, he must obviously put forward technical and commercial proposals for carrying out the work. These proposals will also form a basis for the contractor's own provisional design specification. It is usually necessary to translate the requirements defined by the customer's specification into a form compatible with the contractor's own normal practice, quality standards, technical methods and capabilities. The design specification will provide this link.

It is well known that the desired end results of a project can often be achieved by a variety of technical or logistical concepts. There could be considerable differences between proposals submitted by companies competing for the same order. Once an order has been won, however, the successful contractor knows the general solution which has been chosen. The defeated alternative options will usually be relegated to history. But there will still remain a considerable range of possibilities for the

Project site and other local conditions

Availability of utilities
— Electrical power
— Potable water
— Other water
— Sewerage
— Other
Existing roads.
Access restrictions (e.g. low road bridges, weight limits)
Nearest rail point. Any width, length or height loading restrictions?
Nearest suitable seaport
Nearest commercial airport
Local airstrip
Seismic conditions
Climatic conditions
— Temperature range
— Rainfall or other precipitation
— Humidity
— Wind force and direction
— Sunshine
— Dust
— Barometric pressure
Site plans and survey
Soil investigation and foundation requirements
Local workshop and manufacturing facilities
Local transport and insurance arrangements
Local sources of bulk materials
Local plant hire
Local manpower resources available
— Professional
— Skilled
— Unskilled
Site accommodation arrangements for:
— Offices
— Secure stores
Site living accommodation arrangements for:
— Expatriot managers and engineers
— Artisans
— Short stay visitors
Site catering and messing arrangements
Are married quarters to be provided? If yes, see separate checklist
Site safety and security
First aid, medical and hospital facilities
Hotel or other accommodation available for VIPs
Local banking arrangements
Information communications available or possible at site:
— General mail and airmail service
— Special mail, Datapost or courier service
— Telephone over public network
— Telephone by direct line or satellite
— Telex
— Facsimile
— Other

Figure 3.3 Part of a project definition checklist
The first two pages from a checklist which might be used by an international company to assist with project definition in the pre-project or very early stages of a project. Every company with sufficient project experience can compile such lists.

Contractual and commercial

How firm are proposals?
What are the client's relative priorities for:
— Time?
— Money?
— Quality?
What are the client's delivery requirements?
What are the client's cost objectives? Do we know what budgets he has set?
Scope of work envisaged:
— Basic design only?
— Full detailed design?
— Procurement responsibility — ourselves, client or other?
— Construction responsibility — ourselves, client or managing contractor?
— Commissioning, customer training, manuals, etc. (specify)
How accurate are existing estimates:
— Ball park?
— Comparative?
Have below-the-line estimate items been checked against the checklist in the estimating manual?
How is the project to be financed?
What do independent reports indicate about the client's:
— Present financial status?
— Recent invoice payment performance?
Is project financing to be guaranteed by a bank or other suitable organization?
Are any restraints or special approval requirements expected to be imposed by the client for
    financing purchases?
Is the contract expected to contain any form of penalty clause?
Is the project to be quoted firm price?
How are the payments to be arranged:
— Initial deposit?
— Stage payments?
— Payment on handover?
— Retention?
How are payments to be approved and authorized?
What insurances will we be asked to arrange or should we arrange?
What guarantees of performance are we to offer?

Project organization

Is the overall project organization known?
Is there an organization chart?
Obtain the following information as relevant for each company or organization involved:
— Name of organization
— Name of project manager or other person in charge
— Names, job titles and responsibilities of other key personnel
— Name of addressee for all correspondence, if not the project manager
— Mail address and post code
— Street address for goods and all non-postal deliveries
— Telephone number
— Telex number
— Facsimile number

Initial design and technical information

Flowsheets
Layouts
Is further information required from the client?
Process parameters
Design parameters
Design standards, drawing sheets to be used, drawing numbering, etc.
Special local engineering standards or statutory design regulations
Any similar previous projects from which useful design information can be retrieved and re-used?
continued on next sheet

Figure 3.3 *concluded*

detailed design and make-up of the project within the defined boundaries of the accepted proposal and its resulting contract.

Taking just a tiny element of a technical project as an example, suppose that a plant is being designed in which there is a requirement to position a lever from time to time by automatic remote control. Any one or combination of a number of drive mechanisms might be chosen. Possibilities include hydraulic, mechanical, pneumatic, or electromagnetic devices. Each of these could be subdivided into a further series of techniques. If, for example, an electromagnetic system were chosen this might be a solenoid, a stepping motor or a servo motor. There are still further possible variations within each of these methods. The device chosen might have to be flameproof or magnetically shielded, or special in some other respect. Every time the lever has been moved to a new position, several ways can be imagined for measuring and checking the result. Electro-optical, electrical, electronic or mechanical methods could be considered. Very probably the data obtained from this positional measurement would be used in some sort of control or feedback system to correct errors. There would, in fact, exist a very large number of permutations between all the possible ways of providing drive, measurement and positional control. The arrangement eventually chosen might depend not so much on the optimum solution (if such exists) as on the contractor's usual design practice or simply on the personal preference of the engineer responsible.

With the possibility of all these different methods for such a simple operation, the variety of choice could approach infinite proportions when the permutations are considered for all the design decisions for a major project. It is clear that coupled with all these different possibilities will be a correspondingly wide range of different costs, since some methods by their very nature must cost more than others. When a price or budget is quoted for a project, this will obviously depend not only on economic factors (such as the location of the firm and its cost/profit structure) but also on the system and detailed design intentions.

Ways of estimating project costs are considered in Chapter 4. It can already be seen, however, that owing to their cost implications, the main technical proposals must be established before serious attempts at estimating can start. Once these design guidelines have been decided, they must be recorded in a provisional design specification. If this were not done, there would be a danger that a project could be costed, priced and sold against one set of design solutions but actually executed using a different, more costly, approach. This danger is very real. It occurs in practice when the period between submitting a quotation and actually receiving the order exceeds a few months, allowing the original intentions to be forgotten. It also happens when the engineers carrying out the project work decide not to agree with the original proposals (sometimes called the 'not invented here' syndrome). Projects in this author's experience have strayed so far from their original design concept for such reasons that their total costs reached more than double their budgets.

Similar arguments apply concerning the need to associate the production methods actually used in manufacturing projects with those assumed in the cost estimates and subsequent budgets. It can happen that certain rather bright individuals come up with suggestions during the proposal stage for cutting corners and saving expected costs – all aimed at securing a lower and more competitive tender price. Provided that these ideas are recorded with the estimates, all will be well and the cost savings can be achieved when the project goes ahead. Now imagine what could happen if, for instance, a project proposal were to be submitted by one branch of the organization, but that when an order eventually materialized responsibility for carrying out the work was switched to a production facility at some other location in the organization, with no record of the production methods originally envisaged. The cost consequences could prove to be nothing short of disastrous. Unfortunately, it is not necessary to transfer work between locations for mistakes of this kind to arise. Even the resignation of one production engineer from a manufacturing company could produce such consequences if his intentions had not been adequately recorded. The golden rule, once again, is to define and document the project in all essential respects before the estimates are made and translated into budgets and price.

Construction projects offer another example of work which has to be defined by specification. The need to apply for planning permission from the local authority means that plans must be drawn up in any case before work can begin. There are, however, many detailed aspects of a building which can greatly affect its costs, including for instance the style of interior decoration and the quality of the fittings and installed equipment. Disputes can be minimized, if not prevented altogether, when a contractor produces his own detailed project specification and asks the customer to accept it before the contract is signed. Any changes subsequently requested by the customer can then be charged as additions to the original order.

Specifications for product development projects

Development programmes aimed at the introduction of additions or changes to a company's product range are perhaps more prone than most to overspending on cost budgets and timescale. One possible cause of this phenomenon is that chronic engineer's disease which might be termed 'creeping improvement sickness'. Many will recognize the type of situation illustrated in the following example.

A company producing electronic and audio equipment for domestic users has carried out a market survey. From the results of this study the company plans to introduce a new 'fun' model stereo tape cassette player. The aim is for a device with attractive styling, dual mains or battery operation, reasonable performance, but at a low price and calculated to appeal to the tastes of teenage customers against the competition of foreign imports.

The launching of the new product design can be visualized, starting with a meeting in the chief engineer's office in the company's development laboratories. In addition to the chief engineer the meeting would probably include representatives from other interested departments, such as sales and production. The other member needed to establish the necessary quorum is, of course, the design engineer assigned to carry out the actual development work.

Discussion would undoubtedly be aimed at setting the engineer off on the right track to create the unit envisaged by the company's directors on the basis of the market survey. Thus the engineer (George) will be provided with a set of objectives. Let us assume, however, that, as often happens, these objectives are fairly broadly based and not written into a formal product specification. George can be imagined emerging from the meeting with mental notes from the verbal briefing given to him during all the discussions, plus possibly his own rough notes and sketches. He will undoubtedly have been given some idea of target production costs, styling, performance, the preferred selling price and an approximate date for stocks to be available for distribution and release to the market. By any standards this design job can be regarded as a small project, requiring budgeting and some degree of programme control but not dependent for its success on state-of-the-art project management techniques.

We can safely assume that George will be fairly bubbling over with enthusiasm. Most competent engineers become keen when suddenly given responsibility for a new project on which their creative abilities can be unleashed. After a few weeks of activity behind the closed doors of his laboratory, George can be expected to emerge with the first experimental model of the new cassette player. This working model must then be subjected to the critical attention of various experts, among whom may be marketing staff, an industrial designer and production engineers or other suitable representatives of the department that will eventually have to manufacture the product.

Following successful evaluation of the prototype, and incorporation of recommendations from the experts, the next stage in the project will be the preparation of production drawings, bills of materials and specifications from which a small pilot production batch can be manufactured. One might reasonably expect, from experience, that this preproduction phase of the project would take considerably longer than the original design of the laboratory model. The production department may decide to go ahead with some limited tooling, and the production engineers and others will want to set up trial manufacturing procedures, check on tolerances, test-programme any automatic operations and think generally about methods for assembly and testing.

A period of waiting must therefore be endured by George, during which, apart from having to check drawings or answer occasional queries he is free to reflect upon his design. This leads him to having second thoughts. He has discovered that he could have specified a different amplifier, giving improved performance while slightly reducing the cost of bought-out components. George decides to implement the change which, incidentally, requires a redesign of the printed circuit boards at a stage when they have been drawn and ordered in production prototype quantities. George puts the redesign in hand and cancels the order for prototype boards.

Modified drawings and parts lists are issued to the production and purchasing departments. The production cost estimators find that the cost saving expected from changing to the new amplifier will amount to less than one per cent of the total estimated production cost per unit. So far, the change has caused a three-week hold-up in the programme and has caused preparatory work in several departments to be scrapped and restarted.

George, in the meantime, has received a visit from a representative of the company which he chose to supply the loudspeakers. The representative is delighted with the potential business but, taking a technical brochure from his brief case, wishes George to know that he can offer, at modest cost, new loudspeakers that would suit the size and shape of the cabinet, extend the bass response by a whole octave, and be better able to withstand the increased power of the new amplifier. The slightly increased size of the replacement loudspeakers will result in further drawing modifications and the scrapping of some work already carried out on the pilot batch. George considers this a small price to pay for the significant increase in performance and decides to make the change.

At length, and in spite of the delays and additional expense, the prototype batch is completed and passed back to the laboratory for evaluation. George is dismayed to find that every single one of the prototype batch exhibits two faults which were not apparent on the first laboratory-built experimental model. There is a significant amount of rumble from the tape cassette drive motor, now shown up as a result of the improvement in base response. For the same reason, mains hum is audible.

Three possible choices are now open to George. He could revert to the original design, using the original amplifier and loudspeakers. George, however, has high ideals and the idea of degrading the performance does not appeal to him. The second option would be to introduce a simple filter circuit to cut the bass response to attenuate the rumble and hum; this again would degrade the performance. George therefore decides to do the only proper thing. He modifies the mains power unit to remove the mains hum and specifies a higher quality tape drive motor which produces less rumble. These changes again cause delay and result in increased development and unit manufacturing costs. The eventual result, however, is outstandingly good. The performance of the modified prototype finally measures up to George's most critical requirements. George is well pleased with the results of his labours and congratulates himself on a job well done.

The management might not be so well pleased. The new model has been produced several months later than the original target date, and the manufacturing cost per unit has become so high that it will not be possible to sell the unit economically at the intended price. In any case, the gap in the market where the demand originally lay has since been filled by a competitor's product, which would not have happened if the unit had been produced at the right time. George has, in fact, designed a very good unit but not the product which he was asked to design. He has allowed his own ideas to intrude and he has lost sight of the original objectives. He has allowed the 'best' to become the enemy of the 'good'.

This simple example serves to show some of the pitfalls which can happen in an uncontrolled product development project without an adequate project specification. One can see that, in addition to the delayed completion, the development costs must have exceeded original estimates. The oft-repeated phrase 'time is money' is as true in project management as anywhere, and it is usually fairly safe to assume that if a planned timescale has been exceeded the budget will also have been overspent.

It might be as well to take a second look at this imaginary project and see how the course of events would have run under a regime which employed some of the essential elements of project control.

The first noticeable difference would be the provision of a project specification. The main part of this specification would be a technical product specification, written to ensure that all the design objectives were clearly defined from the start. Such product specifications should include an account of the expected performance (with quantified data), quality and reliability standards, styling guidelines, any size and weight limits and so on.

Commercial objectives for the product development project must also be specified, and these would probably include the maximum permissible unit production costs and an indication of the required selling price. Because such manufacturing cost and price data must always be related to the quantities produced, and for the purposes of project appraisal, a sales forecast covering at least three years ahead should be made. In order to assess the probable rate of return on capital investment (as part of project appraisal) the management must start with a fair idea of what this investment will be. Budgets for development expenditure, production tooling and other costs should therefore be compiled and agreed at the beginning and recorded in the commercial part of the specification.

Finally, there is the question of timescale. The target date for market release must be decided carefully in advance to ensure that it is an objective which can be achieved. Quite often the date chosen will aim to launch the product in time for its announcement at an important trade exhibition.

A more effective check could have been kept on progress in our example if a simple programme schedule (such as a bar chart) had been included as part of the project specification. Provided that this identified all the important project events ('milestones'), regular management checks would have indicated the danger of late running soon enough for corrective action to be taken.

Now suppose that George has reached the stage in the project where previously he was allowed to introduce his first design change (the amplifier). Under conditions of effective control he would not have been allowed to introduce any change after the issue of production drawings without prior discussion with other departments likely to be affected. It is usual for changes of this nature to be brought up for approval before a representative 'change committee'. The committee will assess all the possible effects of any proposed change on stocks and work-in-progress, reliability, costs, timescale and so on before giving their consent or other instructions. In our example we can be sure that at least some of the adverse effects of George's proposed change would have been foreseen by a change committee. Apart from any technical reasons, this change would have been nipped in the bud because of the threat it posed to the timescale.

Detailed procedures for controlling modifications are given in Chapter 14. It is enough at this stage to note that the other modifications which were introduced in the cassette player project would also have met with an early demise under a sound administration. George would have been kept along the right lines by the provision of a formal product specification and development programme, by the sensible control of modifications and, of course, by the day-to-day supervision of his superiors.

Developing and documenting the project specification

Given the importance of specifying project requirements as accurately as possible, it is appropriate to end this chapter with some thoughts on the preparation of a specification document.

Although the customer may be clear from the very first about his needs, it is usual for dialogue to take place between the customer and one or more potential contractors before a contract is signed. During this process each contractor can be expected to make various proposals for executing the profit that effectively add to or amend the customer's initial enquiry document. In some companies this pre-project phase is aptly known as solution engineering, since the contractor's sales engineers work to produce and recommend an engineering solution which they consider would best suit the customer (and win the order).

Solution engineering may last a few days, several months, or even years. It can be an expensive undertaking (especially when the resulting tender fails to win the contract). Although it is a nice tidy theory to imagine the contractor's sales engineers putting their pens to paper and writing the definitive project specification at the end of the solution engineering phase, the practice is likely to be quite different. An original descriptive text, written fairly early in the proceedings, will undergo additions and amendments as the solution develops, and there will probably be a pile of drawings, artists' impressions, flowsheets, schedules (or other documents appropriate to the type of project) which themselves have undergone amendments and substitutions.

A fundamental and obvious requirement when the contract is signed is to be able to identify positively which of these versions record the actual contract commitment. Remember that the *latest* issue of any document may not be the *correct* issue.

Consider, therefore, the composition of a project specification. The following arrangement provides the basis for unambiguous definition of project requirements at any stage by reference to the specification serial number and its correct revision number. The total specification will comprise:

1   *Binder or folder*   The specification for a large project is going to be around for some time and receive considerable handling. It deserves the protection of an adequate binder or folder. This should carry the project number and title, prominently displayed for easy identification. The binder should be loose-leaf, to allow for the addition or substitution of amended pages.

2   *Descriptive text*   The narrative describing the project should be written clearly and concisely. The text should be preceded by a contents list, and be divided logically into sections, with all pages numbered. Every amendment must be given an identifying serial number or letter, and the overall amendment (or revision) number for the entire specification must be raised each time the text is changed. Amended paragraphs or additional pages must be highlighted, for example by placing the relevant amendment number alongside the change (possibly within an inverted triangle in the manner often used for engineering drawings).

3   *Supporting documents*   Most project specifications need a number of supporting engineering and other documents that may be too bulky for binding in the folder. All these documents must be listed and treated as part of the specification (see the next item).

4   *Control schedule of specification documents*   This vital part of the specification should be bound in the folder along with

the main text (either in the front or at the back). This schedule must list every document which forms part of the complete specification or which is otherwise relevant to adequate project definition (for example, a standard engineering specification). Minimum data required for each document are its serial and correct revision numbers. Preferably the title of each document should also be given. Should any of the associated documents itself be complex, it should have its own inbuilt control schedule. It usually helps if a control schedule is given the same serial and amendment numbers as the main document which it is controlling. There is more information of general relevance to the clerical control of amended multi-page documents at the end of the purchase specification section in Chapter 13. The procedure should provide that the amendment state of any issue of the entire project specification (with all its associated documents) can be identified simply by the amendment number of the relevant control schedule.

4

Cost estimates

An accurate estimate of project costs provides an essential part of the proper basis for management decisions and control. The most obvious reason for producing cost estimates is to assist in pricing decisions, but that is by no means the whole story. Cost estimates are usually needed for all commercial projects, including in-house projects and those sold without fixed prices. Timescale planning, pre-allocation of project resources, the establishment of budgets for funding, manpower and cost control, and the measurement of achievement against expected performance all demand the provision of sound estimates.

Essential cost definitions and principles

It is generally understood in accounting circles that the word 'cost' should never be used alone, without a qualifying adjective. It must always be made clear exactly what kind of costs are meant. There are many ways in which costs can be described but, within the space of this chapter, it is necessary to outline some of the terms with which the the cost estimators and project manager should be acquainted. There is no need to explain obvious, self-explanatory terms (such as labour costs, material costs and so on) and the following list has been limited to a few essentials that may not be familiar to all readers. Items are listed in alphabetical order.

Below-the-line costs

This term is used as a collective name for the various allowances that are added once a total basic cost estimate has been made. They can include allowances for cost escalation, exchange rate fluctuation and other contingency allowances.

Cost variance

A cost variance is any deviation measured between estimated, planned or budgeted costs and the corresponding cost actually measured. Variances are particularly important in cost reports, because they satisfy the rule of reporting or managing by exception. The term variance is also used in standard costing to describe the errors (small, it is hoped) that result from using calculated averages, errors that are revealed when payroll and purchase ledger accounts are reconciled periodically with project costing.

Direct costs

Costs which can be attributed directly to a job or piece of project equipment are termed direct costs. Thus if a person spends two hours in the manufacture of a component which is specifically identifiable as being required for a particular project, then the cost of that person's time is a direct cost, and it can be recorded as such and charged to the project.

Factory cost

Applicable to manufacturing projects, the factory cost is the total cost of a job or project before the addition of mark-up for profit. It comprises all direct and indirect costs for labour, materials and expenses. A very simple example which shows the relationship of factory cost in the pricing structure is given in Figure 4.1. Although design costs are often treated as indirect in manufacturing, they are direct in this example because this is a project to design and make a one-off special component, so that the engineering costs can be directly related and charged to the job.

Fixed costs

Costs are said to be fixed when they remain unchanged and must continue to be incurred even though the workload might fluctuate between zero and the maximum capacity. These costs include such things as management and administrative salaries, rent, business rates or property tax, heating, insurance and so on. Fixed costs are usually equatable with indirect (overhead) costs.

Indirect costs (overhead costs or overheads)

The provision of factory and office accommodation, general management and administration, heating, lighting, maintenance and so on are all costs that must generally be incurred in running a business. They cannot, however, be applied directly to one job or project and are therefore termed indirect costs. They can include labour, materials and expenses. These indirect costs are often referred to as overhead costs, or simply the overheads.

Note that the provision of site facilities for a construction project, although these could include accommodation and services that would be classed as indirect back at the main or home office, can be classed as direct costs. This is because they are provided specifically for the project in question, and can therefore be identified solely with that project and charged directly to it.

There are considerable differences between companies in the interpretation of direct and indirect costs. Some firms charge the cost of plan printing, for example, to projects and recover the costs by billing them to the client or customer. Other firms would regard such costs as indirect, and charge them to overheads. Sometimes the classification of costs as direct or indirect even varies from project to project, depending on what each customer has contracted to pay for as a direct charge.

Cost estimators and project managers must be clear on what constitutes direct and indirect costs in their particular company and must also pay attention to any special provisions contained in the proposal or contract for each project.

Indirect costs, although they are predominantly fixed costs, can sometimes include an element of variable costs. Maintaining a permanent headquarters would be a fixed indirect cost, since it must be incurred irrespective of normal workload fluctuations. Providing temporary office staff in administrative departments would be a variable cost, since the amount spent must depend on the workload and management can decide to increase or reduce the number of temporary staff (and hence their cost) at will. Classification of overheads into fixed and variable costs is not relevant to much of the argument in this book, but is important in manufacturing and process industries as a control in relating prices, profitability and the volume of production. In all work, however, including industrial projects, management will wish to keep the overhead expenses as low as possible, because high overheads can kill a company's chances of being competitive in the market-place. It is in the variable overhead costs where the easiest and quickest savings can be made (short of relocating the company's headquarters or dismissing some of the permanent administrative and management staff).

Labour burden
The labour burden is an amount, usually expressed as a percentage, that is added to the basic hourly or weekly rate for employees to compensate for holidays, the statistical probability of illness or other absence, and *per capita* amounts payable by the employer as employee benefits or by law (in the UK, for example these include the employer's part of the National Insurance contribution).

Materials burden
Materials purchased for a project, which are themselves treated as a direct cost, are typically marked up by contractors in order to recover their administrative and handling costs. These mark-ups generally range from 15 per cent (or less), for very large items shipped directly to site, to up to 25 per cent on small low-cost items that have high handling costs relative to their value. A common all-round rate used for the materials burden is 15 per cent.

Overhead costs – see Indirect costs

Overhead recovery
Most project costing systems work on the basis of charging

direct labour costs (including the labour burden) as time recorded on the job multiplied by the standard hourly cost applicable to the grade. An amount can then be added proportional to this labour cost (usually as a rate per cent) to recover a part of the company's indirect, overhead costs. The example in Figure 4.1, although very simple, illustrates this principle.

The same overhead rate (75 per cent in Figure 4.1) would be applied over all similar projects carried out by the company. In some industries the overhead rate can rise to 100 per cent, 200 per cent or even higher (as, for example, in companies with a very high level of research and development to fund). In labour intensive industries, with little research and development and no high grade premises, the overhead rate might be 50 per cent or even less. It is not possible to state norms for the purposes of this book, since the circumstances of companies vary considerably from one to another (even where they are carrying out similar work). Obviously the company which manages to keep its indirect costs (and overhead rate) to a minimum has a competitive cost and pricing advantage.

This method of recovering overheads as a 'levy' on direct labour costs is called absorption costing. Setting the rate is an accounting task demanding perception and skill. Getting the answer right depends on accurate workload forecasts and effective overhead cost estimating and control. If the planned workload does not materialize, less direct labour can be charged out, resulting in a corresponding reduction in the planned overhead recovery. When this happens, the condition is called overhead under-recovery.

Overhead over-recovery will occur if workload and direct labour billings exceed expectations, so that the per cent rate set proves to be too high. Although this can increase profitability in the short term, it may not be desirable because it can imply that the company's pricing is not sufficiently competitive in the market, with damaging consequences for future order prospects.

Clients for large capital projects may be very critical of proposed overhead rates chargeable to their projects. They often ask for detailed explanations of what proposed overhead costs are intended to include. In fact, the overhead rate for a large

Item	£	£	£
Direct materials			
Brass sheet		50.00	
Brass rod		25.00	
Other		20.00	
Total direct material cost			95.00
Direct labour (at standard rates)			
Design			
10 hours engineer	at 25.00	250.00	
15 hours draughtsman	at 15.00	225.00	
1 hour checker	at 17.00	17.00	
Manufacture			
20 hours sheet metal	at 13.00	260.00	
3 hours turner	at 13.00	39.00	
1 hour assembly	at 13.00	13.00	
1 hour inspection	at 16.00	16.00	
Total direct labour cost			820.00
Prime cost			915.00
Overheads at 75% of direct labour			615.00
Factory cost			1530.00
Mark up at 50%			765.00
Selling price			2295.00

Figure 4.1 Cost and price structure for a simple manufacturing project.

project may even have to be negotiated before an order can be won.

Prime cost
The sum of all direct costs needed to fulfil a particular job or

project (direct labour plus direct materials plus direct expenses) is sometimes called the prime cost.

Standard costs

When carrying out estimating, budgeting, accounting and cost reporting for any job or project, it would be tedious and impracticable to attempt using all the different rates of pay earned by individuals. Two engineers with similar capabilities and identical job titles might, for example, be earning quite different salaries. Such differences can obviously occur for quite valid reasons at any level in the management or work-force. The cost estimator cannot possibly name the individuals who will be engaged on jobs that may not be started for months, even years after the estimates are made. Even if names could be pencilled in, there would be no guarantee that those same people would actually do the work.

The well-proven solution to this problem is to adopt standard costing. For labour costs, the first step is to classify people according to some convenient rules (usually based on a combination of the work that they do and their general level in the salary structure). Here, for example, are the categories which one company found suitable for its home office staff in capital projects involving, engineering, purchasing and construction management:

Grade	Those included	Notes
1	Company directors, divisional managers and professional staff of consultant rank	
2	Project managers and departmental managers	Includes chief engineers from all engineering disciplines
3	Project engineers and senior engineers	Irrespective of engineering discipline
4	Engineers and junior engineers	Irrespective of engineering discipline

Grade	Those included	Notes
5	Drawing office group leaders and checkers	
6	Draughtsmen and tracers	
7	Administrative staff	Includes buyers, commercial officers, secretaries, clerical and all staff working in administrative services other than managers regardless of seniority or salary.

It is best if the number of different categories can be kept to a minimum (not more than ten if possible). The accountants work out an average salary cost for those in each standard grade. All estimates and actual jobs are then costed using these grades and standard rates. Because the standards are calculated within the confines of the accounts department, the method also has the advantage of preserving the confidentiality of individuals' earnings: cost estimators and project administration staff need only be given the current standard rates. However, the standard rates themselves should be treated as confidential (they may be of use to a competitor, for example).

Standard cost rates can also be devised for commonly stocked materials and purchased components used in manufacturing companies. Standard costing extends to other production quantities and measurements, but these are not relevant here in the context of project management.

All standard cost rates need to be reviewed by the accountants from time to time, for example when a general wage and salary award takes place or when there is a significant and permanent change in material costs.

See also Cost variance.

Variable costs
Variable costs are those costs which are incurred at a rate

depending on the level of work activity. They are typically confined to the direct costs, but may have a small indirect content.

Estimating accuracy

Estimating must obviously start from some form of project specification. It is clear that the better the project can be defined at the outset, the less chance there should be of making estimating errors. However, the possibility of error can never be reduced to zero, and no sensible person could ever declare the initial cost estimates for a total project to be entirely free from error and completely accurate. Estimating always involves an element of personal judgement. A project, because it is a new venture, must always contain some surprises. If the final project costs did happen to equal the initial estimates, that would obviously be a matter for some congratulation and celebration but it would also be a matter of chance. In many cases it may not even be possible to declare with confidence what the total costs are at the end of a project, owing to the complexities of cost collection, cost apportionment and accounting methods.

Steps can, of course, be taken to remove some possible sources of estimating errors and to ensure that effective systems are in place for subsequent cost measurement. Some of these methods are discussed in this chapter and elsewhere in this book. The cost estimator should be aware of the problems, but must not allow these to deflect him from the primary task, which must always be to use all the data and time available in producing the most accurate estimate possible, in other words a calculated judgement of what the project *should* cost if all goes according to expectations. Estimates made with a high degree of confidence will greatly assist those responsible for any competitive pricing decision, and accurate estimates improve the effectiveness of cost budgets and resource schedules.

Some companies in the construction, petrochemical, civil engineering and other industries find it convenient to classify project cost estimates according to the degree of confidence that the estimators can express in their accuracy. These classifications obviously depend on the quality of information available to the estimators and the time allowed for preparing the estimates. Here is one useful set of estimate categories.

1   *Ball park estimates* are those made before a project starts, when only very hazy information exists and when practically all details of the work need to be formulated. Ball park estimates are also made in emergencies, when all the detailed information is available for a more accurate estimate but when there is insufficient time in which to consider it (for example, when a production manager is presented with a set of detailed manufacturing drawings, he weighs the pile thoughtfully in his hand and, after only a short pause, declares 'There's twenty thousand pounds' worth of work here'). Ball park estimates are widely used in many industries. They are particularly valuable for carrying out preliminary checks on possible resource requirements, for screening enquiries for tenders and for other early planning decisions. Ball park estimates are not likely to provide sufficient accuracy for other purposes; they should never, for example, be used as a basis for fixed price tendering. A well-reasoned ball park estimate might achieve an accuracy of ± 25 per cent, given a generous amount of luck and good judgement.

2   *Comparative estimates,* as their name implies, are made by comparing work to be done on the new project with work done on similar projects in the past. They can be attempted before detailed design work takes place, when there are no accurate materials lists or work schedules. They depend on a good outline project definition, which must enable the estimator to identify all the major elements and assess their degree of size and complexity. The other main requirement is access to cost and technical archives of past projects which contain comparable (they need not be identical) elements. Apart from commercial risks outside the estimator's control (for example foreign exchange rate fluctuations), accuracy will depend very much on the degree of confidence that can be placed in the proposed design solutions, on the working methods eventually chosen and on the closeness with which the new project elements can be matched with those of previous projects. It may not be possible to achieve better

than ± 15 per cent accuracy. Comparative estimates are commonly used as the basis for tenders in manufacturing and other engineering projects, provided that the target profit margin is large compared with the probable estimating error. When the time available for tendering is very short contractors for construction projects may also be obliged to rely on comparative estimates, but they should then build in as many allowances for contingencies as competitive pricing will permit.

3 *Feasibility estimates* can only be derived after a significant amount of preliminary project design has been carried out. In construction projects, for example, the building specification, site data, provisional layouts and drawings for services are all necessary. Quotations must be obtained from potential suppliers of major project equipment or subcontracts, and material take-offs or other schedules should be available to assist with estimating the costs of materials. The accuracy 'confidence factor' for feasibility estimates should be better than ± 10 per cent. This class of estimate is often used for construction tenders.

4 *Definitive estimates* cannot be made until most design work has been finished, all the major purchase orders have been placed at known prices, and actual work on the project construction or assembly is well advanced. Definitive estimates can be produced from scratch, but the best practice is to update the original comparative or feasibility estimates on a regular or continuous basis as part of the cost reporting and control procedure. Estimating accuracy will obviously improve with time as known actual costs replace their corresponding estimates in the total project cost estimate. Estimates can be labelled 'definitive' when the point in time is reached where their declared accuracy is ± 5 per cent or better. Unless the accounting and cost control systems are flawed the figures for actual project costs and the definitive project estimate will converge when the project ends.

Whenever a cost estimate is made, whether it is for a major construction project or for an engineering or a manufacturing project, it is important that the figures given are qualified by a declaration of their expected accuracy. If a classification system such as that outlined above is adopted, then it is a relatively simple matter to label each project estimate as ballpark, comparative, feasibility, definitive or whatever. Provided that the company operates a consistent, well established and well understood procedure, all those concerned in using the estimates for pricing decisions, for the preparation of budgets, for planning, or for any other purpose will know what degree of confidence to place in the estimates and modify their decisions accordingly.

It is difficult to lay down hard and fast rules on what should be a reasonable target for accuracy in estimates intended for pricing and control. For pricing purposes much depends on the size of the intended profit margin, since a large margin will tend to cushion small estimating errors. Margins vary greatly, depending on market conditions and, particularly, on accepted practice in the relevant industry. Reliable estimates are a valuable asset to managers faced with the difficult task of trying to price a project in the teeth of keen competition, where there is no room to allow for the luxury of a safety factor in the shape of a high mark-up, or for the inclusion of contingency allowances.

The vulnerability of planned profits to erosion from costs which exceed estimates is not always appreciated. A simple example will illustrate this point. Consider a project which was sold for a fixed price of £1 m against a total cost estimate of £900 000. The budgeted gross profit was therefore £100 000, or 10 per cent of the selling price. Now suppose that project actually cost £950 000. The difference between the actual cost and that estimated (that is the estimating error) was only about 5.6 per cent. But the effect on the gross profit was drastic; it has been slashed from the expected £100 000 to £50 000, an error not of 5.6 per cent but of 50 per cent. That is how the outcome would be viewed by the company's management and shareholders.

Planned profits are always at risk and may be subject to many variables. Some of these can be predicted but others often come as unpleasant surprises. The aim must be to reduce the number of unknown variables as far as possible, and then to provide a sensible allowance to cover those which remain.

Because profits are so vulnerable they deserve the protection of good estimates. Managing a project which has been underestimated can be a soul-destroying experience, with everything running late and all remaining cost predictions aimed at assessing the amount of the impending loss. Not many project managers would wish to suffer such an experience again: if they were in any way responsible they may not be given the chance.

Labelling project cost estimates

It is quite likely that several different estimates will be made for the costs of a project before the actual work is authorized. These might arise as the result of alternative engineering solutions for meeting one project specification, or it could be that the specification itself undergoes several changes as discussion takes place between the contractor and his potential customer.

In such cases there is a danger of getting the different estimates mixed up, so that the cost estimate which is eventually used for setting budgets and preparing a tender is the wrong version; an estimate that relates to a specification issue or an engineering solution which is different from that which has been agreed.

It is therefore necessary to give each estimate a unique and positive identifying number. This might be based on the enquiry serial number or the specification number, but those numbers can only be main identifiers, which simply link the estimate with the particular enquiry or project. Wherever there is a possibility that two or more different estimates might exist for the same project (which is usual), a case number should be given to each different set of conditions. The relevant estimate in each case can then be identified by always quoting its case number in addition to the main identifier.

Work breakdown

Consider a project aimed at developing a mining complex or other plant for on-the-spot extraction and processing of mineral resources in an area that was previously uninhabited and which is many miles from the nearest rail-head, port or airport. The project for building the plant might cost well over £100 m, but that would represent only one aspect of the total work. It might be necessary to build roads, possibly a railway, an airstrip, housing, schools, churches, hospital, shops and indeed a whole township (all of which would constitute the project infrastructure).

Now imagine trying to estimate the cost of such a major project and attempting to establish budgets and plans against which to manage the work. Most projects, even if they are not on this grand scale, are too complex to be estimated, planned and controlled effectively unless they are first divided into smaller portions of more manageable size. If the project is very big, it may have to be split into smaller projects or subprojects. Each project or subproject must then itself be further divided into smaller work packages and tasks. Such work breakdowns must be handled in a systematic fashion, so that there is a logical, hierarchical structure to the breakdown (in the fashion of a family tree).

The concept of a sequential work breakdown for the large mining project example is shown in Figure 4.2. The figure shows the large work packages identified at the start of the breakdown. In practice the process of work breakdown would continue, leading to more and smaller packages until, right at the bottom, the individual tasks and purchases are reached. See also Figures 4.3 and 4.4, which illustrate a work breakdown for a fairly small manufacturing project.

In addition to regarding the work breakdown as a family tree, it is also possible to visualize it as a jigsaw puzzle, with every piece put in its right place and with no piece missing. This concept is useful on two counts:

1   A method must be found that clearly and simply identifies each piece of the puzzle and its place in relation to all the other pieces.
2   It is important that when the work breakdown is produced every piece of the puzzle is included, with no piece missing to spoil the total picture.

The first of these objectives should be achieved by giving each piece an identification number which, through the use of a carefully devised, logical system, acts as a locator or address

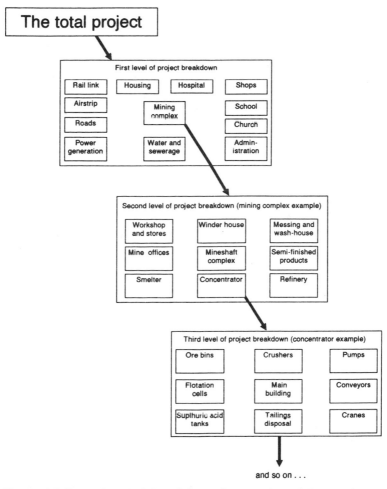

Figure 4.2 Part of a work breakdown for a major mining project
The chart shown here is based on actual experience, but with some
items removed for clarity. It shows how, starting from the total project,
the work breakdown is undertaken in logical steps of steadily increasing
detail. The complete breakdown would continue right down to the level
of all the individual tasks and items of equipment.

(discussed in the following section of this chapter). The second
objective is more difficult, but the risks of omission can be
reduced if checklists are used.

Cost coding

Although this section is headed cost coding, those responsible for designing a coding system must always bear in mind it should not be treated in isolation from other management and engineering information systems in the company. Many benefits can be won if the same system can be applied over all a company's projects, and across other areas of the company's activities in addition to cost estimating, accounting and budgetary control. Some of these benefits are listed later in this section.

A code is a shorthand method for conveying essential data about an item. For project management purposes an item might be anything from the whole project to a small part of it, physical or abstract. It could be a component, a drawing, a job, a manufacturing operation, a piece of construction work, an engineering design activity – anything, in fact, which is necessary for the project. The only thing that all these items have in common is that they are almost always associated with cost; each item (either by itself or grouped with others) has costs that must be estimated, budgeted, spent, measured, reported, assessed and (where appropriate) recovered.

There are many reasons for allocating codes to items, rather than simply describing them in words. For example, codes can be designed to be precise and unambiguous. They also have the advantage, essential in computer systems, of facilitating analysis, editing and sorting for reporting and control.

The functions of a code include the first or both of the following:

1 A code must act as a unique name that *identifies* the item to which it refers.
2 The identifying code, either by itself or by the addition of subcodes, can be arranged so that it categorizes, qualifies or in some other way *describes* the item to which it relates.

The best coding systems are those which manage to combine both these functions as simply as possible in numbers that can be used throughout a company's management information systems.

Listed below is the kind of information that can be contained within the cost code for any item. The systems used as examples are taken from light and heavy engineering and from mining, but the general principles are interchangeable between these and all other types of project.

1 *Project identifier* Figure 4.3 shows a work breakdown, or family tree, for a project to design and build equipment for a radio link. The project number is 110–000, a number which identifies the project for all accounting and engineering purposes. Such project numbers are typically allocated from registers and may be called contract numbers or works order numbers instead. It is possible to choose such numbers in a way that signifies relevant information about each project, in addition to acting as a simple identifier (examples occur in Figures 4.5 and 4.6).

2 *Item identifier* Each number, provided it is unique, is an unambiguous way of naming any item. In practice, however, it is always wise to bracket a concise verbal description with the number whenever the item is referred to, as a simple precaution against clerical errors. Thus it is better to refer to an item as 'Transformer 110–221' in correspondence and on other documents rather than just 'Item number 110–221'.

3 *Relationship within the project* Further examination of Figure 4.3 shows that the code numbers have been designed to correspond with the work breakdown or family tree. Staying with the example of Transformer 110–221, the fact that this component has a cost and part number starting 110–22 identifies the transformer as being used on Modulator 110–220 which in turn is used on Project 110–000 (these numbers will be found on the left-hand side of the family tree in Figure 4.3). This numbering process is continued throughout the work breakdown, so that even individual components can be given codes that relate to the hierarchy. This is illustrated in Figure 4.4, where the code number for the bobbin used on Transformer 110–221 is analysed.

4 *Operation identifier* The task for winding and assembling the purpose-built transformer 110–221 might be given a related cost code, such as 110–221C, where the C suffix denotes the coilwinding operation. A two-digit suffix is more often used

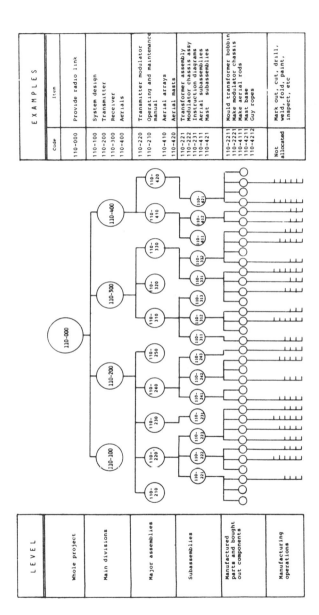

The table in the figure:

E X A M P L E S	
Code	Item
110-000	Provide radio link
110-100	System design
110-200	Transmitter
110-300	Receiver
110-400	Aerials
110-220	Transmitter modulator
110-230	Operating and maintenance manual
110-410	Aerial arrays
110-420	Aerial masts
110-221	Transformer assembly
110-222	Modulator chassis assy
110-233	Instruction diagrams
110-411	Aerial subassemblies
110-421	Mast subassemblies
110-2211	Mould transformer bobbin
110-2221	Make modulator chassis
110-4111	Make aerial rods
110-4211	Mast base
110-4212	Guy ropes
Not allocated	Mark out, cut, drill, weld, fold, paint, inspect, etc

L E V E L
Whole project
Main divisions
Major assemblies
Subassemblies
Manufactured parts and bought out components
Manufacturing operations

Figure 4.3 Work breakdown and cost coding structure for a manufacturing project
The code numbers are allocated within hierarchical groups. Thus, for example, the transformer 110–221 is identifiable from its number as belonging to the transmitter modulator 110–220 and, in turn, to the transmitter 110–200. The first three digits identify all items as belonging to this project, 110–000 (see also Figure 4.4). A logical breakdown such as this is necessary for detailed estimating and for cost accounting. It is folly not to use the same system for part numbers and drawing numbers.

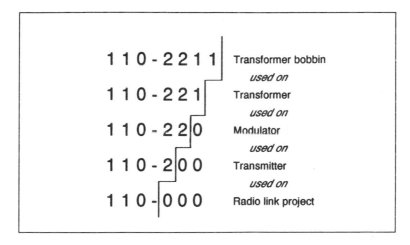

Figure 4.4 Coding system example for a manufacturing project
A transformer bobbin used on the manufacturing project whose
numbering system was demonstrated in Figure 4.3 has been chosen
at random for this example. The analysis shows how the bobbin's
part number acts as a code that places this component on the
correct branch of the family tree. The greatest benefit is obtained
from such generic numbering systems when the part numbers,
drawing numbers and cost codes share a common system.

instead of a single letter, allowing greater scope for detailed
breakdown into individual operations.

5 *Identifiers for department, discipline or trade and labour grade*   A
one- or two-digit subcode is often incorporated to show
which department is responsible for a particular task or cost
item. More digits can be added to denote the trade or
engineering discipline involved. Consider, for instance, the
activity of designing Transformer 110–221. The cost code
might be 110–221–153 with the three-digit subcode 153 in this
case showing that the engineering department (1) is responsible for the task, the engineering discipline is electrical
(coded (5), and the last digit (3) indicates the grade of person
(for example senior engineer, engineer or designer) normally
expected to carry out the task of designing this transformer.
This final digit might also denote a standard cost rate per
hour for the grade of person concerned.

6 *Family identifier*   Many items to be considered for coding can

be classified into families. Such families extend across all projects and can apply to major capital projects or to the smallest engineering and manufacturing projects. The convenience of grouping items into families containing other items having common or similar characteristics is important for manufacturing and other comparative purposes. Family grouping and identification can be built into item codes by including suitable subcode digits. A family might comprise, for example, all pumps specified by a mining or petrochemical company. Another example might be that the digits 01 appearing in a particular place in the item code would always indicate the mainframe assembly in a piece of manufactured equipment. Another type of family is encountered when considering machined objects that share manufacturing similarities by virtue of their shapes and the machining operations to be performed; an application of family coding which is vital to the manufacture of components in group technology cells.

Figure 4.5 shows a coding system, including family identifiers, which is used by a company which carries out manufacturing projects. Figure 4.6 is another system, applicable to an engineering organization carrying out large mining projects.

Some benefits of a logical coding system

Although the primary purpose of a coding system may be to identify parts or to allocate costs, there are many benefits available to the company which is able to maintain a logical coding system in which all the codes and subcodes have common significance throughout the company's management information systems. These benefits increase with time and the accrual of records, provided that the system is used consistently without unauthorized adaptations or additions. The benefits depend on being able to retrieve and process the data effectively, which invariably requires the use of a computer system, preferably with a relational database.

If a coding system is designed logically, taking account of hierarchical structure and families, and is managed effectively, some or all of the following benefits can be expected:

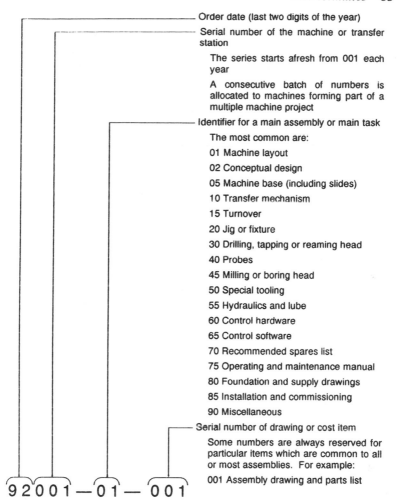

Order date (last two digits of the year)

Serial number of the machine or transfer station

The series starts afresh from 001 each year

A consecutive batch of numbers is allocated to machines forming part of a multiple machine project

Identifier for a main assembly or main task

The most common are:

01 Machine layout

02 Conceptual design

05 Machine base (including slides)

10 Transfer mechanism

15 Turnover

20 Jig or fixture

30 Drilling, tapping or reaming head

40 Probes

45 Milling or boring head

50 Special tooling

55 Hydraulics and lube

60 Control hardware

65 Control software

70 Recommended spares list

75 Operating and maintenance manual

80 Foundation and supply drawings

85 Installation and commissioning

90 Miscellaneous

Serial number of drawing or cost item

Some numbers are always reserved for particular items which are common to all or most assemblies. For example:

001 Assembly drawing and parts list

9 2 0 0 1 — 0 1 — 0 0 1

Figure 4.5 Numbering system used by a heavy engineering company
This company designs and manufactures heavy special-purpose machine tools and machining systems.

- Easy search and retrieval of items from records of past projects which correspond to or are similar to items expected in new projects, essential as a basis for making comparative cost estimates.

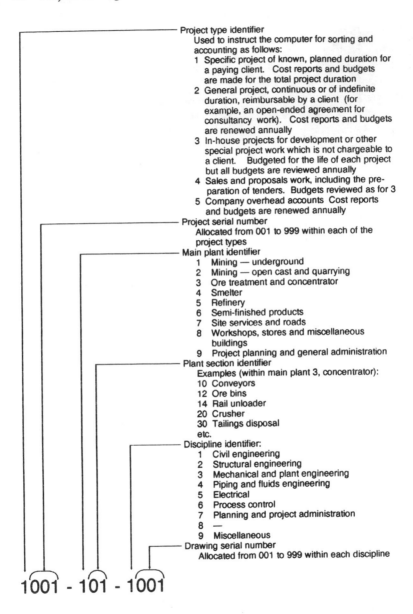

Project type identifier
Used to instruct the computer for sorting and
accounting as follows:
1 Specific project of known, planned duration for
a paying client. Cost reports and budgets
are made for the total project duration
2 General project, continuous or of indefinite
duration, reimbursable by a client (for
example, an open-ended agreement for
consultancy work). Cost reports and budgets
are renewed annually
3 In-house projects for development or other
special project work which is not chargeable to
a client. Budgeted for the life of each project
but all budgets are reviewed annually
4 Sales and proposals work, including the preparation of tenders. Budgets reviewed as for 3
5 Company overhead accounts Cost reports
and budgets are renewed annually

Project serial number
Allocated from 001 to 999 within each of the
project types

Main plant identifier
1 Mining — underground
2 Mining — open cast and quarrying
3 Ore treatment and concentrator
4 Smelter
5 Refinery
6 Semi-finished products
7 Site services and roads
8 Workshops, stores and miscellaneous
buildings
9 Project planning and general administration

Plant section identifier
Examples (within main plant 3, concentrator):
10 Conveyors
12 Ore bins
14 Rail unloader
20 Crusher
30 Tailings disposal
etc.

Discipline identifier:
1 Civil engineering
2 Structural engineering
3 Mechanical and plant engineering
4 Piping and fluids engineering
5 Electrical
6 Process control
7 Planning and project administration
8 —
9 Miscellaneous

Drawing serial number
Allocated from 001 to 999 within each discipline

1001 - 101 - 1001

**Figure 4.6 Numbering system used by a mining engineering
company**

- Easy search and retrieval of design information (especially flowsheets, calculations and drawings) for processes, assemblies or components used on past projects which are relevant to a current project. This 'retained engineering' can result in a considerable saving of engineering design work, time and costs if all or part of the previous design can be re-used or adapted. Not only does such design retrieval avoid the unnecessary costs of designing everything afresh, but it also allows the new project to incorporate designs that have already been proven or debugged, so the scope for errors is reduced. With computer-aided design, or in any other system where the drawings are stored digitally, the scope and possibilities for such retrieval becomes even more practicable and attractive.

- Rapid identification of purchase requisitions and specifications from previous projects for equipment which corresponds to new requirements. This is another example of retained engineering, which can speed the preparation of new purchase specifications (especially when the main texts of the former specifications can be retrieved from files in a word processor).

- Grouping of components into families according to their basic shapes and sizes, relevant to the manufacturing processes needed, in order to maximize production engineering efficiency (as in the case of group technology cells).

- If it is possible to use a common system, cost estimates, budgets, recorded costs, drawing schedules, many other documents and tasks on the project plan can all be related in a database for project administration, management reports and control.

- The ability to carry out statistical analysis on cost and other records from past projects for a variety of reasons, including monitoring performance trends. The following examples from the author's experience had great practical use in a heavy engineering company, and illustrate only two of the many possibilities for exploiting properly coded records:

  1 The averaging of recorded costs for commonly recurring work packages in a range of categories from many past projects allowed the preparation of project estimating

tables (expressed in man-hours and updated materials costs). These tables proved very useful for scheduling new projects and for making global checks on detailed estimates for proposals.

2   Analysis in detail of past shipping records enabled a table to be compiled showing average and probable maximum shipping weights for categorized items used on different types of heavy engineering projects. With the help of a shipping company the table was developed for presentation to the materials control manager as a 'ready-reckoner', which, with occasional updating, was used effectively for estimating future project shipping weights and costs to all relevant countries.

Notes on choosing a coding system

Once a coding system has been established it is difficult and unwise to make any fundamental change. The choice of a system therefore has to be undertaken with a great deal of care. Suppose that a company has been operating for many years with a comprehensive coding method, applied right across all its systems for drawing and other document numbering, cost estimating, cost accounting and part numbering. If this company makes a change to the numbering system, so that numbers which previously had one meaning now denote something entirely different, some of the following problems may arise:

1   Drawings filed under two different systems.
2   Similar inconvenience caused to long-standing customers who maintain their own drawing files for projects.
3   No easy way of identifying similar previous jobs for the purpose of comparative cost estimating.
4   Difficulty in retrieving earlier designs.
5   Staff have to learn and live with two systems instead of one.
6   Problems for storekeepers, with two different systems for part numbers. Parts common to earlier projects may have to be renumbered for newer projects, so that there is a possibility of having identical common parts stored in two places with different part numbers.
7   Mayhem created in any attempt to use a relational database that relies on code numbering.

This is the place to insert another word of warning. It is possible to be too ambitious and try to make numbers include too much information. The result can be numbers that are 14, 15 or even more digits long. The designer of such a system may feel very proud, and computer systems are well able to accept and process such numbers, but please remember the human element – the 'people interface'. People are going to have to work with these numbers, entering them in written or electronic records. Simple codes use less clerical time and result in fewer errors.

Many companies have realized the importance of getting their coding systems right to the extent that they have called in expert independent consultants for advice. One firm of consultants which has built up a considerable reputation in this field is: Brisch Birn & Partners Ltd, 81 Station Road, Marlow, Buckinghamshire SL7 1NS.

What happens when the customer says 'Use my system!'

Not infrequently, an irritating problem arises when customers insist that their own numbering system is used, rather than that normally operated by the project contractor. This happens particularly when a customer is to be presented with a complete set of drawings or prints as part of the contract and wants to be able to file these along with all the other drawings in his system. This, unfortunately, is a case where 'the customer is always right'. This problem of having to use customers' numbering systems is usually restricted to drawings but in some projects it can apply to equipment numbers or part numbers. It also occurs, and is a great nuisance, in the cost coding of work packages or purchased plant for major projects, where the customer and contractor must work together to request, authorize and arrange the release of funds (either from the customer's own resources or from another financing organization). In such cases the customer may insist that all estimates, budgets and subsequent cost reports for the project are broken down against his own capital appropriation or other cost codes.

There are three options that can be considered when the customer asks the contractor to use a 'foreign' coding system:

1   ignore the customer's wishes and continue to use the in-house system for the project;
2   call the project a 'special case', abandon the in-house system, ask the customer for a set of his procedures and use them for the project;
3   compromise and use both systems simultaneously.

To adopt Option 1 may be impossible under the terms of contract and, in any case, would be a short cut to achieving bad customer relations. Option 2 cannot be recommended because:

- the information management benefits of the in-house system would be lost for all data for the project; and
- it will soon be discovered that every other project is a 'special case', leading to a multiplicity of non-related systems throughout the contractor's organization and archives.

Option 3, the compromise course, offers the only proper solution. Every drawing and other affected item must be numbered twice, once for each system. Everything must be diligently cross-referenced between the two systems. This is tedious, time-consuming and means that staff have to learn more than one system. It may be an arguable cause for trying to obtain extra reimbursement from the customer. Fortunately the use of a computer for cross-referencing, sorting and retrieving data makes the use of duplicate systems less of a problem.

Compiling the task list

The first stage in the cost estimating process is to compile a complete list of every known item that is going to attract expenditure. This may prove difficult. But any item inadvertently left out of the cost estimates must obviously result in an underestimate for the project as a whole. This can jeopardize planning and scheduling and (if not realized in time) lead to serious problems and red faces when the time comes to hand the project over to the customer. And, of course, if the project has been sold for a fixed price, the additional work must be paid for not out of the budgeted project funds, but from the contractor's expected profits.

Preparation of a work breakdown (as a family tree or 'goes into chart'), complete with cost codes, is a logical way of considering the total project and should reduce the risk of errors of omission. But at the outset of a project it is most likely that the work breakdown has to be compiled in fairly broad terms, because much of the detail will remain unknown until the project has advanced well into the engineering design phase (well after the contract has been signed and everything has become a firm commitment).

One very useful way of helping to prevent forgotten tasks is to use checklists. Every company with sufficient experience can develop these (see Figure 3.2 for instance). A full checklist would include all possible factors – technical, commercial, statutory, environmental, social and so on – that might eventually have a bearing on the work and its costs. Checklists can prove to be long and detailed documents: typically they list as many possibilities as the compiler can think up, so that they must inevitably include some irrelevancies, and can seem tedious. It is, however, in this very wealth of detail that the importance and strength of checklists lies.

The task list must include not only all the obvious items of project hardware, but also every associated software job. 'Software' is a term which is fairly familiar in the project sense, thanks to the advent of the computer. It should be realized, however, that projects quite remote from computer work can create a software demand. Schedules for production inspection and testing, and instruction and maintenance manuals may have to be specially written. These, together with any other documentation specified in the proposal or contract, should be regarded as tasks which must be included in the estimated costs.

Activities often forgotten during the estimating phase of manufacturing projects, only to be remembered too late for inclusion in the project budgets (and price), include incidental production processes such as paint spraying, inspection and testing. In some firms these may be covered by the general overhead rate, but in many others they will not and must be listed among the direct cost estimates. Protective plating, silk screen printing, engraving and so on are frequently omitted from estimates. A more serious victim of neglect sometimes encountered is the work entailed in final commissioning, handover and customer acceptance of the completed project.

Some contracts demand that the contractor provides training facilities for some of the customer's operatives or technicians. Training sessions can involve the contractor's senior engineers in much hard work, both in the actual training and in preparing the training material beforehand. Incidental expenses may also arise for accommodation and meals, depending on where the training is to be carried out.

Whether the proposal is for a manufacturing project or for a large capital construction project, the business of filling as many gaps as possible in the task list is really part of project definition. Indeed, the project specification may have to be revised and reissued more than once as the task list is developed.

Level of detail in project cost estimating

Some difficulty may be experienced in deciding how much detail to show in the task list. What is a 'task' for this purpose?

Consider the problem of making cost estimates for a manufacturing project proposal. These estimates must be prepared before any detailed design has taken place, and therefore without any production drawings. It would obviously not be possible to list all the operations needed for each separate piece part. It will not even be known at this early stage what or how many parts are going to be needed for the project. It is obvious, therefore, that initial cost estimates, even though they lead to commitments, can only be carried out on a much broader scale than run-of-the-mill production estimates.

Ideally, each task should be selected so that it is small enough to be visualized as a complete entity for estimating purposes. On the other hand, the task must be large enough to represent a measurable part of the whole project. The design and manufacture of each subassembly from a main piece of equipment might rank as a task, while the final assembly of all these subassemblies into one whole main assembly could be regarded as another. Writing, editing and printing an instruction manual is another item that should rank as a discrete task. Separately identifiable major purchases should also be listed, where these are not already included in other tasks. Every one of these examples illustrates an identifiable and specific part of the project, chosen not only to make the job of estimating easier but also (as will be seen later) to provide measurable units of progress and achievement.

Estimating forms

Completion of a task list has established a basis on which project estimates can be made. When the estimates are collected, a large amount of data will be assembled. These should preferably be presented in some sort of tabular arrangement to allow easy reference, detailed analysis and extension into total amounts – for both departments and groups of jobs or tasks.

A certain amount of procedural discipline has to be imposed on the estimating function throughout the organization, and from one project to another. By accruing estimates according to standard procedures, itemized where possible by cost codes, comparisons can readily be made between estimates and historical records of relevant actual costs. Thus a company's estimating skills and accuracy should improve as experience is built up.

Some contracts, especially those for some government departments, may become liable to cost investigation or auditing at one or more stages. These investigations can be exhaustive and taken into considerable detail. Starting off on the right foot by paying careful attention to detail in presenting the estimates and setting them out in orderly fashion can help to establish the good relations between customer and contractor that will be found essential in arriving at a fair price.

Observance of company policy on cost rates and costing methods, as well as the need to determine working budgets, imposes an obligation on the project manager to ensure that the estimates are set down in a standard and logical manner. Calculations performed in odd corners of notebooks, on scraps of paper, and on the backs (or fronts) of envelopes are prone to error and premature loss. They will be unlikely to fulfil any of the conditions already mentioned. In other words, estimating forms are needed.

Project estimating forms can be arranged to fit in with the kind of work breakdown structures that were shown in Figures 4.3, 4.5 and 4.6. One sheet can be allocated to each main project work package or group of tasks, while every row on the forms would be occupied by one task. Each column entry carries data for an activity. Adding the costs along each row yields the estimated cost of the relevant task (which is, incidentally, very convenient for pricing spare parts). Totalling relevant columns gives the commitment expected for each department, and the results can be used for resource scheduling and departmental budgeting.

Some attempts to design estimating forms fail because they are overambitious. There is no need to provide a column for every contingency. Instead, one or more columns can be left with the headings blank, so that these can be filled in as required for any special purposes.

For any project of significant size the use of a computer for collating and aggregating estimates may be desirable, in which case the estimating forms will have to be designed with the computer input format in mind. If the company's procedures have been developed with care and forethought, the estimating data can in fact be fed into a comprehensive management information system that will, as work progresses, be used to compare expenditure and progress against these original estimates.

A project estimating form for manufacturing and general purposes

An example of a general purpose estimating form is given in Figure 4.7. This design is based on a form used by more than one division of a company for projects ranging from military electronic equipment to prefabricated hospital operating theatres. All these projects, although very different in design and content, shared the typical manufacturing project characteristic of requiring special engineering design, followed by project purchasing, leading to manufacture and completion in single or very small batch quantities.

COST ESTIMATE

													Estimate number or case:			

Project number or sales reference:

Estimate number or case:

Estimate date:

Estimate for:

Compiled by:

Sheet ___ of ___ sheets

1	2	3	4	5	6	7	8	9	10	11	12	13	14	15
Code	Item	Qty	Labour times and resulting costs by department or grade						Total direct labour cost	Overhead %	Standard or net cost	Burden %	Longest delivery (weeks)	Total cost 10+11+12+13
			Hours	Cost	Hours	Cost	Hours	Cost	Hours	Cost	Hours	Cost	Hours	Cost			Materials			

Figure 4.7 A general purpose cost estimating form

This general purpose form allows six different grades of labour to be shown and assumes that all hours will be costed at the appropriate standard cost rates. Although it is likely that many companies (and their cost estimates) may need more than six different standard cost grades, it is less likely that more than six grades will be needed for the job or work package listed on one estimating form. The cost estimator will therefore be able to allocate the labour columns (numbered 4 to 9 on this example) to the range of grades necessary for the work being estimated on each particular sheet. The standard grade code and rate used should be entered in the space at the head of each column to show the rates that were current at the time of estimating.

Generally speaking, while wage rates and standard costs change from year to year, the time required to carry out any particular job by a given method will not. Man-time is therefore regarded as a fundamental basis for all estimates, while conversion to money can only be regarded as a derivative, secondary process, dependent on other variable factors. Comparative estimates for labour, therefore, should always be based on man-hours or other time units and never on the relative costs.

It is not necessary to complicate a general purpose estimating form by adding extra columns for such things as special tooling. Such items can easily be accommodated by considering them as separate tasks in their own right. Each can be entered on a row, and the costs added up along the row in the same way as any other task.

The inclusion on the general purpose form of a column headed 'longest lead time' in the materials section is not connected directly with cost estimating. However, those who enter the material costs on the form usually have access to such delivery information and it is better and more efficient to gather all these data from them as early as possible and at the same time. By including longest lead time estimates on the forms, their usefulness is immediately extended, enabling them to be used as a valuable source of information for timescale planning.

Additional columns could be provided on the estimating form to allow mark-ups and selling prices to be shown. These were omitted from the general purpose example in Figure 4.7 deliberately, to stress the fact that relationships between cost estimates and selling prices are sometimes too complex to allow calculation on a simple form. More will be said about project pricing in Chapter 5.

Estimating forms for large construction projects

There are many kinds of forms in use for the purpose of tabulating and summing the cost estimates for large projects in the fields of mining, petrochemicals, construction and civil engineering.

In manufacturing projects the prime costs are likely to comprise mainly labour and materials (often in roughly equal proportions) with a relatively small subcontract element. In large construction contracts the balance is usually shifted: most of the direct labour content is likely to be found in the engineering and project management functions, with much of the actual work of construction and the erection of plant entrusted to a number of subcontractors. It is therefore usual to find a considerable proportion of capital costs expended on subcontracts. Material costs are likely to be divided between bulk supplies (steel, pipework, the constituents of concrete, and so on) plus a considerable investment in specially ordered items of expensive equipment (the provision of some of these constituting significant projects in themselves).

Although construction companies may employ their own direct labour force, much of the work is typically let out to subcontractors. Most of the costs incurred in major construction projects can often be grouped conveniently under a few main headings, for example:

1 engineering and project management (subdivided between home office and site office);
2 purchases (subdivided between bulk construction materials and purchases of major items and equipment for installation);
3 subcontracts and plant hire.

Estimates for home office engineering and project management times can be compiled on general purpose tabulation sheets similar to the example shown in Figure 4.7.

Estimates for many of the bulk materials are often made on very detailed schedules or material 'take-offs' which are designed for each of the particular engineering disciplines involved (for example piping take-offs compiled by fluids engineers and steel take-offs worked out by the civil and structural engineers).

The form shown in Figure 4.8 can be used for listing the cost estimates for major items of equipment required for a project. Provision is made on the form for including freight and duty costs, which are or course especially relevant when the site is distant or overseas from the source of supply. Totals or convenient subtotals from materials take-offs should be transferred to this form in order that the complete materials costs can be summarized and totalled.

Figure 4.9 is another example of a form for listing and estimating capital costs. This version, used by an international mining company for preliminary cost estimates, attempts to include as much detail as possible on one sheet. Each row on this form is allocated to a part of the work breakdown, excluding engineering and management man-hours but including construction subcontract costs, bulk materials costs, equipment costs and freight costs.

A general purpose project cost and price summary form

The form in Figure 4.10 can be used in many cases to summarize project cost estimates and assist in pricing. The form has been designed for flexibility, for use over a wide range of different projects and companies. Although spaces for various rates, allowances and mark-ups are provided, the way in which these are used can be chosen to fit in with a particular company's management and accounting requirements. The form allows the actual figures and formula used in the cost/pricing relationship to be recorded but it does not dictate or suggest the pricing mechanism, which must be considered by management according to the merits of each case.

Manufacturing estimates

Estimates with production drawings

Suppose that an estimate is to be prepared for the routine fabrication of boxes from sheet metal. A set of manufacturing

EQUIPMENT/MATERIAL COST ESTIMATE

Form No 2

Estimate for:

Project number or sales reference:

Estimate number:

Estimate date:

Compiled by:

Sheet of sheets

Specification No (if known)	Equipment or materials	Proposed supplier	Currency	Conversion rate	Unit cost (F.O.B.)	Qty	Total Cost (F.O.B.)	Freight costs	Duties and taxes	Delivered cost

Sheet totals

Reproduced from *ProjectPlanner* by Dennis Lock, Gower, Aldershot, 1990.

Figure 4.8 Form for equipment and material cost estimates

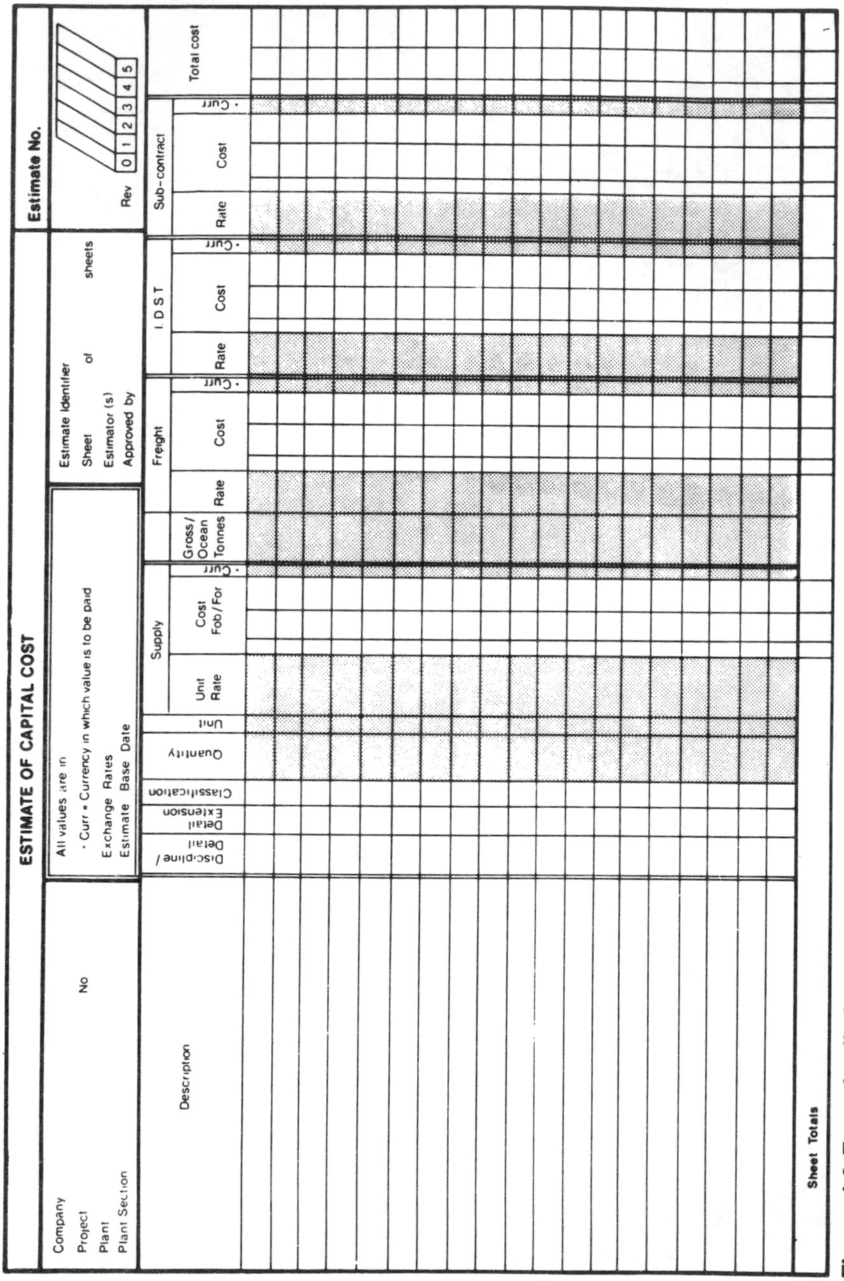

ESTIMATE OF CAPITAL COST

Estimate No.

Company
Project No
Plant
Plant Section

All values are in
• Curr = Currency in which value is to be paid
Exchange Rates
Estimate Base Date

Estimate Identifier
Sheet of sheets
Estimator (s)
Approved by

Rev 0 1 2 3 4 5

Description	Discipline / Detail	Detail Extension	Classification	Quantity	Unit	Supply: Unit Rate	Supply: Cost Fob / For	Supply: • Curr	Freight: Gross / Ocean Tonnes	Freight: Rate	Freight: Cost	Freight: • Curr	I.D.S.T: Rate	I.D.S.T: Cost	I.D.S.T: • Curr	Sub-contract: Rate	Sub-contract: Cost	Sub-contract: • Curr	Total cost
Sheet Totals																			

Figure 4.9 Form for listing cost estimates for capital items

Form No 3

PROJECT COST AND PRICE SUMMARY

Project title: Estimate or sales ref:

Client/customer: Date:

Item		
	LABOUR	
1		
2		
3		
4		
5		
6		>
	EQUIPMENT, MATERIALS AND BOUGHT-OUT SERVICES	
7		
8		
9		
10		
11		>
	OTHER EXPENSES (professional fees, licensing, etc)	
12		
13		
14		>
15	PRIME COST	>
	OVERHEAD COSTS AND HANDLING CHARGES	
	Item numbers charged Charge rate %	
16		
17		
18		>
19	BASIC ESTIMATED PROJECT COST	>
	ALLOWANCES	
20	Escalation allowance at %	
21	Contingencies allowance %	
22		>
23	TOTAL ESTIMATED COST	>
	MARK-UP	
	On items Rate used %	
24		>
25		>
26	INDICATED SELLING PRICE	>

Notes, PC items, etc:

Reproduced from *ProjectPlanner* by Dennis Lock, Gower, Aldershot, 1990.

Figure 4.10 General purpose estimating and pricing form

drawings is needed first. Other important factors likely to influence the answer would be the total quantity of boxes required and the rate at which they were to be produced. Further necessary information would include the type of production facilities which could be deployed and the amount of money to be spent on tooling.

All these facts would allow the job to be considered as a series of production elements or operations. Every single step necessary to convert the raw material into a finished box could be listed in great detail, and in chronological order, on a schedule or 'process sheet'.

An estimate of the labour time required for every individual operation, whether for cutting, folding, punching, welding, riveting or whatever could be made by reference to data accumulated from past experience. In fact, tables of standard times for all routine operations would probably be available. The depth of detail in some sets of standard time tables is very comprehensive. Times for jigging or machine set-up might also be well documented.

In very large-scale mass production estimating and work measurement can reach a pitch where even the times for operator limb movements are considered, these being measured in man-seconds or even finer units of time. Each operation can be broken down into such small elements and the total estimated time for the operation is 'synthesized' by adding the times for all these tiny constituents. Estimating at this level of detail is not shown in Figure 4.3. If it were to be included on the diagram, a separate space would have to be provided below the 'operations' level, labelled 'synthetics'. Routine production times can often be predicted with such accuracy that the answers are given in man-minutes. In the case of this metal box, for example, it is possible to finish up with a very good estimate, obtained by adding all the estimated operation times and factoring the result to allow for a known proportion of non-productive time (for tea breaks, clocking on and off and so on).

If each box had to contain some sort of apparatus or instrumentation the assembly time could also be forecast from standard times with a fair degree of accuracy. The number of screws or rivets to be used; the size, length and number of wires and pipes and the types of connections could all be counted up from the drawings. Once again the estimates could be based on tables derived from the known characteristics and production performance of the organization and its operators.

It is possible to forecast materials expenditure with ease and reasonable certainty for production work. Raw material usage can be assessed by examining the drawings and by then making allowances for cutting wastages, breakages and losses. Other materials and components are listed by the designers on parts lists or bills of material, and it is only necessary to pass these over to the purchasing department or cost office to have the standard costs filled in.

It is now time to admit that this brief account of traditional production estimating has little or nothing to do with the subject of project management. But it has been included to serve as a contrast against which the particular difficulties facing project cost estimators can be discussed. Notice that several common key factors can be identified in the use of routine methods. Work is always broken down into small elements before estimates are applied. The estimates themselves can usually be described as 'standard' or 'known' quantities, and any need for guesswork is either eliminated or reduced to a minimum. Reliance is placed not on personal opinions of how long each job should take, but on the results of long experience and scientific work measurement.

Estimates without detailed production drawings

Suppose now that an estimate is to be prepared for a box filled with instrumentation but that, unlike the example in the previous section of this chapter, no production drawings have been prepared. Only one box of a particular type is to be made, because it will be required for a special project. The only description on which cost estimates can be based is an engineer's written design specification that includes no detail at all of dimensions, materials or the contents of the box other than to state the functional performance expected of the completed product. If the estimator is very lucky, there may be a rough outline sketch of the box.

Standard estimating tables are not likely to be of any help at all in this kind of situation. Build-up of time and cost standards depends upon the establishment of production continuity, which demands in turn that a certain minimum volume of production must take place. Such standards cannot be applied to 'one-off' production, where the unknown variables take over to dominate the picture. In any case, there are no drawings from which to break the work down into operations, so the standards – even if these were valid – could not be applied.

A stage in the project preparation and planning process has now been reached where many professional estimators, production engineers and work study devotees find themselves foundering well out of their normal depth. Their trusted books of standard times, with which they have worked for many years, and much of their professional training will become virtually useless when they are faced with the problem of estimating for work where no drawings exist. These people have learned to regard drawings as their customary means of expression and communication. Without such aids they are rendered helpless. They feel deprived and are quite unwilling to commit themselves to forecasts which may require justification later.

Project cost estimating is not made any easier by the short space of time usually available. All too often a tender has to be prepared within a few days if it is to meet the deadline set by the prospective customer. Failure to meet the closing date could mean that the proposal is automatically disqualified, with the order irrevocably lost to a competitor. Within the short time available, of course, an estimate might be required not just for one box like the one in the example. There could be hundreds of boxes, all different, and all to be manufactured singly. Even if drawings could be found there would be insufficient time to analyse them for detailed cost estimating.

The job of cost estimating can itself be expensive. It is easy to spend a great deal of time and money in the process, especially where there is no pressure to produce the estimates quickly. Low probability of obtaining a project order may not justify such expenditure on estimating and tender preparation.

Project estimating, as has already been seen, is carried out on a much broader scale than run-of-the-mill production work. In the absence of detailed information, larger work packages must be visualized. The only people capable of taking this broader view are likely to be the more senior members of the organization. Departmental managers often become involved, if not in making the estimates at least in approving them. For project manufacturing estimates it is quite likely therefore that the production manager's input will be needed.

There is no simple solution to all these problems, but it is possible to outline an approach which is more likely to yield acceptable results. Fortunately the lack of drawings and the need for making estimates in a short space of time are conditions that both demand a similar handling technique.

With the small example of a small metal box filled with instrumentation, the estimating method might proceed along the following lines. First, a description of the proposed box is needed, with some idea of its contents. The design engineers must provide this information since they are the only people at this stage who can possibly have any real idea what the final, detailed article will be like.

Once a description of the box has been set down it is usually possible to scan the archives to find a previous piece of work which bears some resemblance to the new job. Classification and coding of work and cost records can be a great help when it comes to making such a search. Once again it is only the engineers who can be asked to draw useful comparisons at this early stage. It might well be found that no direct parallel exists but that one previous similar job was carried out which was somewhat simpler than the present object of concern. 'How much simpler?' is the question which must now be asked. The engineer may say that about 10 per cent more components will be needed this time, giving a basis on which the production department can make a comparative estimate.

When the records of actual expenditure on the previous box have been looked up, the production foreman or production manager can reasonably be expected to make an estimate for the new work, given the information that about 10 per cent more components will have to be accommodated and assembled. If the old box took one man-week to fabricate, this may be considered a good enough estimate for the new one. Only a couple more holes are going to be needed to fix the extra components. Wiring and piping must take longer, however, since the 10 per cent increase in the number of components must result in a corresponding increase in the number of connections to be made. A previously recorded assembly time of two man-weeks might therefore be extended to give an estimate of two and a half man-weeks for the more complex box.

These comparative estimates should never, of course, be considered or expressed in terms of man-minutes. Using such fine units of time exposes the estimator to the same trap as the scientist who carries out an experiment using measurement accuracies to three significant figures, and then has the temerity to express the final result using four significant figures. The last two figures of the scientist's result can never be justified. Neither can any talk of man-minutes in production estimates without drawings.

Once the idea has been accepted that production time estimates have to be seen in broad terms, on a scale that equates with packages in the work breakdown, they can be collected and collated in exactly the same way as estimates for design engineering and other non-manufacturing project activities. The estimating system can therefore be standardized, with all cost predictions collected according to the same set of rules and using a common estimating form.

Collecting estimates for labour times

Ideally, project estimates should always be sought from those departments best qualified to provide them. In project work there is a shift of emphasis compared with routine production estimating, where detailed estimates could safely be entrusted to an individual or a group specializing only in estimating or production engineering. Project estimates must usually be obtained from the senior departmental individuals who are going to be responsible for managing the actual project duties later. It would be reasonable, for example, to expect the chief engineer to provide all the design engineering estimates, the chief draughtsman to give those for drawing preparation, and so on. The production manager, the installation or service manager, other managers and supervisors might also become involved.

Decentralizing the estimating function in this way reflects the change in scale when progressing from production estimating to project work. It is not done simply to gain a more accurate estimate of project costs, although that should always be the chief aim. When a large project is being planned the labour time estimates can have a profound influence on the manning and manpower budgets of the affected departments for years to come. Any departmental budget, whatever the type of work involved, can only be really effective if the departmental manager has played a major part in agreeing budget targets – which are to become the manager's future commitments. In the case of any project of significant size this means that departmental managers must either produce or at least agree the estimates for work in their own departments.

If the estimating function is to be decentralized it follows that the set of project estimating forms must be circulated among all the participating departments. This can be done in several ways, with varying degrees of effectiveness.

The first proposition is that one master set of forms could be assembled, attached to a circulation list and sent to the department which is first on the list. That department would be expected to enter its estimates and pass the set of forms on to the next-listed department until, all the estimates having been completed, the bundle should arrive back on the project manager's or proposals manager's desk. Everyone knows how long a library copy of a magazine takes to complete its circulation and of the risks that it faces on its journey – it may never be returned to the library. For the same reasons this method can be dismissed as impracticable for collecting estimates.

A second possibility is to run off a set of pre-headed estimating forms for each department and send them all out simultaneously. This has the advantage of cutting out the serial delays of the first proposition but it still relies on the whole-hearted cooperation of all the departmental heads. Late returns can be expected, while it is known from bitter experience that some sets may even be lost altogether.

It is an indisputable fact that estimating is often regarded as an unpleasant task, a chore to be avoided at all costs if other priorities can be found as an excuse. Therefore no one can expect to rely solely upon written requests for estimating forms to be properly filled in. A more direct approach is needed.

Another way in which to collect the estimates would be to ask for them during the network planning session (described in detail in Chapter 6) and complete a set of estimating sheets on the spot. This occasion provides the opportunity, since all key project members should be on hand. This approach might be considered for very small projects but, for larger projects, there are at least three snags:

1   Network estimates are always made principally for activity durations (that is total elapsed time) rather than for their work content in man-hours. Some form of work content estimates are made at network meetings, in addition to the activity duration estimates, if the network is intended for subsequent resource scheduling.
2   Network planning meetings can involve much effort and take considerable time – perhaps several hours. Protracted meetings do not produce the best results and it is best to avoid asking too much of the members. The law of diminishing returns can apply when any meeting exceeds about two hours. Members will start to fidget, want to get back to their departments to sort out more pressing problems or go home.
3   Material costs are not usually considered at network plan-ning meetings (although they may be relevant if some sophisticated PERT/COST set-up is to be used). A separate estimate collection exercise for material would therefore be needed in most cases.

Short of applying legal compulsion or threat of physical violence, personal canvassing by the project manager, the proposals manager or a suitable delegate is the method most likely to produce quick and dependable results. The process starts by preparing a complete set of estimating sheets for the project, with every known task listed and cost coded. The sheets should be arranged in logical subsets according to the work breakdown structure. The 'canvasser' can then embark on a tour of all the departments involved, installing himself purposefully at each manager's desk in turn. The aim is to remain firmly rooted in each department until all the desired data have been extracted. The person performing this task may become unpopular in the process, but it is not part of any project manager's job to become well liked.

Canvassing affords the project manager or proposals manager an opportunity to assess the estimating capabilities of all the individuals concerned. Any estimate which appears unrealistic or outrageous can be questioned on the spot, and many other details can be sorted out with the least possible fuss and delay. One type of question which must frequently be asked of the estimator takes the form: 'Here is a job said to require four man-weeks; can four men do it in one week, or must the job be spread over four weeks of elapsed time with only one man able to work on it?' The answers to such questions are of obvious importance in scheduling time and resources, of which more will be said in later chapters.

Production staff often need help in their project estimating task. The person collecting the estimates can often supply this help during his tour by translating the design specification into terms that the production people can understand (but care must be taken not to read anything into the specification which is not there). Similarities with past projects can be suggested and any artists' impressions or other sketches which may be available can be amplified by verbal description. Any real doubts which arise over the specification must, however, be referred back to the engineer in charge, since the project manager (or proposals manager) is acting as a coordinator in this case and is not expected to interfere with the design.

Personal estimating characteristics

As a very sound general rule it can be taken that estimates for any work will more frequently be understated than overstated. Many people seem to be blessed with an unquenchable spirit of optimism when asked to predict completion times for any specific task. 'I can polish off that little job in three days', it is often claimed, but three weeks later the only things produced are excuses. Without such optimism the world might be a much duller place in which to live and work, but the project manager's lot would be much easier.

An interesting feature of optimistic estimators is the way in which they allow their cloud-cuckoo land dreams to persist, even after seeing several jobs completed in double the time that they originally forecast. They continue to churn out estimates which are every bit as hopeful as the last and appear quite unable to learn from previous experience. Engineers are perhaps the chief offenders in this respect, with draughtsmen running them a very close second. Fortunately the 'ill wind' proverb holds good, with the wind in this situation blowing to the good of the project manager. The source of consolation in analysing such estimates lies in the fact that they are at least consistent in their trend. In fact, a shrewd project manager will come to learn by experience just how pronounced the trend is in his own particular company. Better still, he will be able to apportion error factors to particular individuals. A typical multiplication factor is 1.5: in other words it is often necessary to add about 50 per cent to the original estimates.

Here, then, is a picture of a project manager or proposals manager obtaining a set of estimates for a project, sitting down with a list of all the estimators who have been involved, complete with the correction factor appropriate to each individual, and then factoring the original estimates accordingly. Far fetched? This method has been proved in practice.

Why should we not try to educate the estimators? After all, prevention is better than cure. But the results of such a re-education programme might be unpredictable, with the effects varying from person to person, upsetting the previous equilibrium. In any case, all of the estimators could be expected to slip back into their old ways eventually and, during the process, their estimating bias could lie anywhere on the scale between extreme optimism and pessimism. Arguing wastes time if nothing is achieved. Accept the situation as it exists and be grateful that it is at least predictable.

Occasionally another kind of individual is encountered who, unlike the optimist of more customary experience, can be relied upon to give regular overestimates for every task. This characteristic is not particularly common and, when it is seen, it might pay to investigate the underlying cause. Possibly the estimator lacks experience or is incompetent. These explanations are unlikely, since the typical symptom of estimating incompetence is random behaviour and not a consistent error trend. The picture becomes clearer, if more unsavoury, when it is remembered that project estimates play a large part in determining total departmental budgets. Higher project estimates mean (if they are accepted) bigger budgets for costs and manpower – expanding departments. This in turn adds to the status of the departmental heads. In these cases, therefore, 'E' stands not only for 'estimator' but also for 'empire builder'. Correction factors are possible, but action is more effective when it is aimed not at the estimates but at their originators.

The inconsistent estimator is the universal bane of the project manager's existence. Here we find a person who is seemingly incapable of estimating any job at all, giving answers that range over the whole spectrum from ridiculous pessimism to ludicrous optimism. The only characteristic reliably displayed is in fact inconsistency. Incompetence or inexperience suggest them-selves as the most likely cause. Complacency could be another. Older people looking forward to retirement rather than pro-motion and staff who were overlooked during the last round of promotions can display these symptoms. Unfortunately this category can manifest itself at departmental head level, just the people in fact most frequently asked to provide estimates. Only time can solve this one.

Finally, it has to be allowed that there is a possibility, however remote, of finding a manager capable of providing estimates for his department which are consistently accurate. The con-tingency is so remote that it can almost be discounted. When this rare phenomenon does occur it is apt to produce a very unsettling effect on the project manager who has, through long experience, learned always to question every report received and never to take an estimate at its face value.

Estimates for material and equipment costs

Materials always need two types of estimate. For each task or work package these are:

1 the total expected cost, including all delivery and other charges;
2 the total lead time (which is the time expected to elapse between starting the purchase order process and receiving the final item needed to complete the task).

Material costs often account for more than half the total cost of a project. Failure to obtain materials on time is a frequent cause of programme slippage and late project completion.

It may also be necessary to make estimates of other factors for operational purposes; for example the volume or weight of materials (information needed for storage and handling).

If detailed design has yet to be carried out, no parts lists, bills of materials or other schedules will exist from which to start the estimating process. Therefore the next best thing must be done by asking the engineers to prepare provisional lists of materials for each task. This may be impossible to carry out in detail, but the problem is not as difficult as it would first seem. In most work the engineers have a very good idea of the major, most expensive items that will have to be purchased. There may be special components, instruments, control gear, bearings, heavy weldments, castings, all depending of course on the type of project. Items such as these can account for a significant proportion of the costs and are frequently those which take the longest time to obtain. In construction projects outline assumptions can be made for the types and quantities of bulk materials needed.

Foreknowledge of these main items of expense reduces the unknown area of estimating and therefore improves the forecasting accuracy. If all the important items can be listed and priced, the remaining miscellaneous purchases can be estimated by intelligent guesswork. Records of past projects can be consulted to help assess the probable magnitude of the unknown element. If, for example, the known main components are going to account for 50 per cent of the total material costs, an error of 10 per cent in estimating the cost of the other materials would amount only to 5 per cent of the total. It is most important, however, to prepare the list of known items very carefully, ensuring that the job is done conscientiously and without serious omissions.

The purchasing department should always be involved, and estimates for prices and delivery times must be obtained through their efforts whenever possible. If the purchasing organization is not allowed to partake in preparing the detailed estimates, a real danger exists that when the time eventually comes to order the goods these will be obtained from the wrong suppliers at the wrong prices. It is far better if the big items of expense can be priced by quotations from the suppliers. The buyer can file all such quotations away in readiness for the time when the project becomes live. If the purchasing department are to be held down to a project materials budget, then it is only reasonable that they should play the major role in producing the material estimates.

Materials estimating responsibility, therefore, lies in two areas. The engineers or design representatives must specify what materials are going to be used, and the purchasing department will be expected to find out how much they will cost and how long they will take to obtain.

Any estimate for materials is not complete unless all the costs of packing, transport, insurance, port duties, taxes and handling have been taken into account (see, for example, the reference to INCOTERMS in Chapter 12). The intending purchaser must be clear on what the price includes, and allowances must be made to take care of any services that are needed but not included in the quoted price. Another cautionary word concerns the period of validity for quotations: it may well be that project cost estimates are made many months – even years – before a contract is awarded. Some quotations for supplies are valid for only 90 days or even less, so that there could be a problem with the cost budget when the time arrives for orders to be placed.

Below-the-line costs

Contingency allowances

A common source of estimating errors is the failure to appreciate that additional costs are bound to arise as the result of design errors, production mistakes, material or component failures and the like. The degree to which these contingencies are going to add to the project costs will depend on many factors, including the type of project, the general efficiency standard of the firm, the soundness (or otherwise) of the engineering concepts and so on. Performance on previous projects is a reliable pointer which can be used to decide just how much to allow on each new project to cover unforeseen circumstances. For a straightforward project, not entailing an inordinate degree of risk, an allowance set at 5 per cent of the above-the-line costs might be adequate. The scope for adding such a contingency allowance will obviously be restricted if there is high price-competition from the market. If the perceived risk suggests the need for a very high contingency allowance, perhaps the company should reconsider whether or not to tender at all.

Cost escalation

Every year wages and salaries increase, raw materials and bought-out components tend to cost more, transport becomes more expensive and plant and buildings absorb more money. All of these increases correspond to the familiar decrease in the real value of money which is termed 'inflation'. This decay is inevitable, and the rate is usually fairly predictable in the short term. A project which is estimated to cost £500 000 (say) in 1992 might cost £550 000 or more if its start were to be delayed for two years.

Suppose that a project was initiated to build a new sea wall along 20 km of coastline at the rate of 2 km per year (a ten-year building programme). The building costs would gradually increase with the passage of time and the resulting cost inflation. The effect is compound, so that an annual inflation rate of about 7.5 per cent would result in the last 2 km of wall costing double the amount needed for the first 2 km.

A cost escalation allowance should be made for any project whose duration is expected to exceed one year. A contract tender is often prepared many months in advance of the actual starting date, and this too can lead to escalation problems. A company will safeguard itself against this risk to some extent by placing a time limit on the validity of any rates or prices quoted in the tender, but delays in signing the contract or in deciding the final technical details can easily add many months to the timescale of a fairly big contract.

The conditions of contract may allow the contractor to claim a price increase in the event of specified cost escalation events that are beyond his control (for example, a national industry wage award), but that is a different case from including escalation in quoted rates and prices as a below-the-line allowance.

The rate chosen by the estimator for below-the-line cost escalation allowances may have to be negotiated with the customer, for example in defence or other contracts to be carried out for a national government.

Provisional sums

It often happens, particularly in construction contracts, that the contractor foresees the possibility of additional work that might arise if particular difficulties are encountered when work actually starts. For example, a client may specify that materials are to be salvaged from a building during demolition work, to be re-used in the new construction. The contractor may wish to reserve his position by including a provisional sum, to be added to the project price in the event that the salvaged materials prove unsuitable for re-use. It is not unusual for a project quotation to include more than one provisional sum, covering several quite different eventualities.

Foreign currencies

Most large projects involve transactions in currencies other than their own national currency. This can give rise to uncertainty and risk when the exchange rates vary. Some mitigation of this effect can be achieved if the contract includes safeguards, or if all quotations can be obtained in the home currency. Otherwise, it is a matter of skill, judgement and foresight.

Common practice in project cost estimating is to nominate one currency as the control currency for the project, and then to convert all estimated costs into that currency using carefully chosen exchange rates. Although contractors would normally choose their home currency, projects may have to be quoted in foreign currencies if the terms of tendering so demand, and if the potential client insists.

Whether or not the contractor wishes to disclose the exchange rates used in reaching his final cost estimates, the rates used for all conversions must be shown clearly on the estimating forms.

Reviewing the estimates

When all the detailed estimates have been entered on estimating forms it should, theoretically, be possible to add them all up and pronounce a forecast of the whole project cost. When this stage has been reached, however, it is never a bad plan to stand well back for a while and view the picture from a wider angle. In particular, try converting the figures for labour times into man-years.

Suppose that the engineering design work needed for a project appears to need 10 000 man-hours (or perhaps 250 man-weeks, according to the estimating units used). Taking 2 000 man-hours or 50 man-weeks as being roughly equivalent to a man-year, rapid division of the estimate immediately shows that five man-years must be spent in order to complete the project design. Now assume that all the design is scheduled to be finished in the first six months of the programme. This could be viewed (simplistically) as a requirement of ten engineers for six months.

The project manager starting this project may receive a rude awakening on referring to records of past projects. These might well show that projects of similar size and complexity took not ten engineers for six months, but expenditure equivalent to ten engineers for a whole year. An apparent error of five man-years exists somewhere. This is, in any language, a king-sized problem. Part of its cause could be the failure of estimators to allow for that part of engineering design which is sometimes called 'after-issue', which means making corrections, incorporating unfunded modifications, answering engineering queries from the work-force or the customer, writing reports and putting records to bed.

It goes without saying that cost estimates for a project are extremely important. Any serious error could prove disastrous for the contractor – and for the customer if it leads the contractor into financial difficulties. Estimates should, therefore, always be checked as far as possible by a competent person who is independent of the estimate compiler. Comparisons with actual cost totals for past projects (for all materials and labour – not just engineering design) are valuable in checking that the new estimate totals at least appear to be in the right league.

Because the cost estimate is likely to prove the essential basis for many important commercial and management decisions, it is sensible to arrange for an authorizing signature from a responsible senior person, who is satisfied that all reasonable care has been taken.

Further reading

Kharbanda, O.P. and Stallworthy, E.A. (1989), *Capital Cost Estimating for the Process Industries*, Guildford: Butterworth Scientific.

Stewart, R. (1991), *Cost Estimating* (2nd edn), New York: Wiley.

5

Commercial management

Most project managers are appointed after the project's initial commercial environment has been established by others. Thereafter, the project manager's degree of involvement in commercial management must depend on the size and nature of the organization. Many large organizations expect their project managers to refer all matters requiring commercial decisions to their marketing, commercial or legal departments. Other companies will delegate all or most commercial authority to their project managers, so that they would (for example) be solely responsible for negotiating changes to the main contract or setting up subcontracts.

Apart from marketing activities, as far as project management is concerned the principal areas of commercial management are:

- financial project appraisal;
- funding;
- contracts and negotiations (including purchasing, for which see Chapters 12 and 13);
- accounting, invoicing and credit control;
- insurance.

Each of these subjects would justify at least one volume in its

116

own right. Many aspects of commercial management are highly specialized and, particularly for legal and insurance matters, these are areas where it can be dangerous for the lay person to venture without rigorous training or professional help. However, it is possible to outline some of the more important points. For study in greater depth there is a further reading list at the end of this chapter.

Financial project appraisal

Managers frequently have to make decisions on whether or not to authorize investment in a project, or decide between two or more different project options. The final decision will depend on many factors, including the answers to questions such as:

- Can the project be achieved technically?
- Are we confident that the claims of the engineers, designers, consultants or architects are valid?
- What are the environmental implications?
- Will the plant produce as much output as the experts claim?
- If we can produce it, can we sell it and at what price?
- Is the project likely to be finished on time?
- How much will it all cost?
- How can we raise the money?
- Is the return on our investment going to be adequate?

It may be necessary to commission one or more feasibility studies from various independent experts to answer many of these questions, and even their reports may be open to doubt or give rise to further questions. But, whatever the circumstances, a careful appraisal of the expected financial outcome is likely to have great influence on most project authorization decisions.

Assuming that sufficient finance can be raised, the remaining financial questions are all aimed at evaluating, for every different project option, the likely return on the investment (or, in the case of a project not conducted for profit, the likely financial outcome in terms of true overall cost or cost savings). Two methods of approach are in common use; the simple payback method and discounted cash flow. Whichever of these methods is chosen, the appraiser needs to have a good estimate of the amount and timing of each significant element of expenditure (cash outflows) and every item of revenue or savings expected (cash inflows).

The main cash outflow items include the acquisition cost (whether as a single purchase price, phased payments, or instalments against a leasing or rental plan), interest payable on loans, operating and maintenance costs, training costs, other expenses and fees payable, and any relevant duties or taxes.

Cash inflows can include savings in operating and maintenance costs compared with existing methods, revenue from resulting product sales, proceeds from the sale of existing plant, eventual proceeds from the sale of the new plant at the end of its planned life, and any relevant savings through tax concessions or other government financial incentives.

Simple payback

Simple payback is the appraisal method familiar to most managers. It seeks to answer the blunt question 'How long would this project take to pay for itself?' The method compares the predicted cash outflows and inflows relating to a new investment option against those of an alternative option (which in many cases means comparing the relative merits of proceeding with a project against the option of doing nothing). Costs and income or savings are analysed over consecutive periods (typically years) until a point is reached where the forecast cumulative costs of the new project are balanced (paid back) by the cash inflows that the project is expected to generate.

A simple payback example

A project is under consideration for the installation of new, more efficient central heating boilers for a group of industrial buildings, together with a new optimizing control unit and heat insulation for the buildings. Total installed cost of the project is estimated at £60 000, and the work could be carried out in mid-1995. Benefits claimed for the new system include a reduction in fuel costs from the current £90 000 per annum to £80 000 in each calendar year, although only £5 000 savings could be expected in 1995 because the project would not come on stream until July.

Year	1995	1996	1997	1998	1999	2000
Existing system:						
Fuel	90	90	90	90	90	90
Maintenance	10	10	10	10	10	10
Outflow	100	100	100	100	100	100
Cumulative	100	200	300	400	500	600
Proposal:						
New plant	60					
Fuel	85	80	80	80	80	80
Maintenance		6	8	10	10	10
Outflow	145	86	88	90	90	90
Cumulative	145	231	319	409	499	589
Expected saving or (loss) if project is authorized:						
Year	(45)	14	12	10	10	10
Cumulative	(45)	(31)	(19)	(9)	1	11

Note: all figures are £'000s.

Figure 5.1 Simple payback tabulation for new boiler project
This shows that payback (break-even) occurs at just about the end of 1999 or, in other words, the payback period for this project is between four and five years.

Maintenance of the new plant is free for the first year, under the terms of a guarantee. After that, maintenance costs are expected to be £6 000 for the second year, rising to £8 000 for the third year as the plant begins to age, finally reaching £10 000 per annum (which is the same maintenance rate as the old system).

The forecasts for each calendar year can be tabulated, as shown in Figure 5.1. In this case, it is seen that the project seems set to break even just before the end of 1999, so that the payback period is between four and five years. If greater accuracy is needed, a graph can be plotted of the cumulative net annual expenditure or saving to find the point in time at which the curve crosses zero.

Methods using discounted cash flow

The simple payback method is adequate provided that the total payback period is one or, at the most, two years. It is less satisfactory when looking ahead for longer periods. The reason for this is that any given sum of money earned or spent in the future has less real value than the same amount of money earned or spent today. The main cause lies in the notional earning power of today's money. If £100 is received today and invested for an annual net return of 10 per cent, that £100 should be worth £110 after one year. Put another way, £110 received or spent in one year's time is equivalent to receiving or spending only £100 today. Today's £100 is called the discounted or *net present value* (npv) of the future £110. Although cost inflation can also have a major effect, it is usually ignored for the purposes of appraisal calculations (partly because the amounts arising from inflation usually occur on both sides of the inflow/outflow equation and therefore tend to cancel out).

Tables can be obtained which list discount factors over a wide range of percentages and periods. Discounting is usually calculated for whole years, but shorter periods are sometimes chosen, especially where very large sums are involved. A short but useful table of discount factors is given in Figure 5.2. The discounting rate used for a particular project is a matter for management judgement, probably influenced by prevailing interest rates, certainly related to corporate financial objectives and preferably assessed with the advice of the company's financial director or accountants.

Example of a net present value calculation
The boiler project can be used to demonstrate the net present value concept. The example has been kept simple and does not include all possible cash flow items (especially taxation). A five year period has been used in this case, because management has considered this to be a reasonable life expectancy for the plant without further change. (In many appraisal calculations there is a future planned event that will set a finite limit on the project life, such as the expiry of a lease on a building, the planned discontinuance of a product, or the forecast exhaustion date of a mineral resource.)

Net present value calculations can seem a little strange at first but they are really quite simple, provided that all the inflows and outflows are carefully tabulated in their respective periods. In the boiler project example, the tabulation and calculation of

Year	1%	2%	3%	4%	5%	6%	7%	8%	9%	10%	11%	12%	13%	14%	15%	16%	17%	18%	19%	20%
0	1.000	1.000	1.000	1.000	1.000	1.000	1.000	1.000	1.000	1.000	1.000	1.000	1.000	1.000	1.000	1.000	1.000	1.000	1.000	1.000
1	0.990	0.980	0.971	0.962	0.952	0.943	0.935	0.926	0.917	0.909	0.901	0.893	0.885	0.877	0.870	0.862	0.855	0.848	0.840	0.833
2	0.980	0.961	0.943	0.925	0.907	0.890	0.873	0.857	0.842	0.826	0.812	0.797	0.783	0.770	0.756	0.743	0.731	0.718	0.706	0.694
3	0.971	0.942	0.915	0.889	0.864	0.840	0.816	0.794	0.772	0.751	0.731	0.712	0.693	0.675	0.658	0.641	0.624	0.609	0.593	0.579
4	0.961	0.924	0.889	0.855	0.823	0.792	0.763	0.735	0.708	0.683	0.659	0.636	0.613	0.592	0.572	0.552	0.534	0.516	0.499	0.482
5	0.952	0.906	0.863	0.822	0.784	0.747	0.713	0.681	0.650	0.621	0.594	0.567	0.543	0.519	0.497	0.476	0.456	0.437	0.419	0.402
6	0.942	0.888	0.838	0.790	0.746	0.705	0.666	0.630	0.596	0.565	0.535	0.507	0.480	0.456	0.432	0.410	0.390	0.370	0.352	0.335
7	0.933	0.871	0.813	0.760	0.711	0.665	0.623	0.584	0.547	0.513	0.482	0.452	0.425	0.400	0.376	0.354	0.333	0.314	0.296	0.279
8	0.923	0.854	0.789	0.731	0.677	0.627	0.582	0.540	0.502	0.467	0.434	0.404	0.376	0.351	0.327	0.305	0.284	0.266	0.249	0.233
9	0.914	0.837	0.766	0.703	0.645	0.592	0.544	0.500	0.460	0.424	0.391	0.361	0.333	0.308	0.284	0.263	0.243	0.226	0.209	0.194
10	0.905	0.820	0.744	0.676	0.614	0.558	0.508	0.463	0.422	0.386	0.352	0.322	0.295	0.270	0.247	0.227	0.208	0.191	0.176	0.162
11	0.896	0.804	0.722	0.650	0.585	0.527	0.475	0.429	0.388	0.351	0.317	0.288	0.261	0.237	0.215	0.195	0.178	0.162	0.148	0.135
12	0.887	0.789	0.701	0.625	0.557	0.497	0.444	0.397	0.356	0.319	0.286	0.257	0.231	0.208	0.187	0.169	0.152	0.137	0.124	0.112
13	0.879	0.773	0.681	0.601	0.530	0.469	0.415	0.368	0.326	0.290	0.258	0.229	0.204	0.182	0.163	0.145	0.130	0.116	0.104	0.094
14	0.870	0.758	0.661	0.578	0.505	0.442	0.388	0.341	0.299	0.263	0.232	0.205	0.181	0.160	0.141	0.125	0.111	0.099	0.088	0.078
15	0.861	0.743	0.642	0.555	0.481	0.417	0.362	0.315	0.275	0.239	0.209	0.183	0.160	0.140	0.123	0.108	0.095	0.084	0.074	0.065
16	0.853	0.728	0.623	0.534	0.458	0.394	0.339	0.292	0.252	0.218	0.188	0.163	0.142	0.123	0.107	0.093	0.082	0.071	0.062	0.054
17	0.844	0.714	0.605	0.513	0.436	0.371	0.317	0.270	0.231	0.198	0.170	0.146	0.125	0.108	0.093	0.080	0.069	0.060	0.052	0.045
18	0.836	0.700	0.587	0.494	0.412	0.350	0.296	0.250	0.212	0.180	0.153	0.130	0.111	0.095	0.081	0.069	0.059	0.051	0.044	0.038
19	0.828	0.686	0.570	0.475	0.396	0.331	0.277	0.232	0.195	0.164	0.138	0.116	0.098	0.083	0.070	0.060	0.051	0.043	0.037	0.031
20	0.820	0.673	0.554	0.456	0.377	0.312	0.258	0.215	0.178	0.149	0.124	0.104	0.087	0.073	0.061	0.051	0.043	0.037	0.030	0.026

Figure 5.2 Table of discount factors

Year	Cash inflow £	Cash outflow £	Net cash flow £	Discount factor @ 10%	Discounted cash flow £
0 (1995)	–	45 000	(45 000)	1.000	(45 000)
1 (1996)	14 000	–	14 000	0 909	12 726
2 (1997)	12 000	–	12 000	0.826	9 912
3 (1998)	10 000	–	10 000	0.751	7 510
4 (1999)	10 000	–	10 000	0.683	6 830
5 (2000)	10 000	–	10 000	0.621	6 210
Net present value					(1 812)

Figure 5.3 Net present value of new boiler project
An annual discounting rate of 10 per cent has been used in this example, using discount factors taken from the table in Figure 5.2. The significance of the result is explained in the text.

net flows before discounting has already been performed (see Figure 5.1).

The discounting calculation is illustrated in Figure 5.3. Using a discount rate of ten per cent, it is seen that this project has a net present value of minus £1 812 after five years. In fact it will not break even (the npv will not become positive) until the year 2001. This is a more pessimistic (but more realistic) result than that obtained from simple payback analysis. It suggests that the project can not be justified on purely financial grounds (although there might, of course, be environmental, welfare or other reasons for going ahead).

Calculating the expected rate of return on investment
Suppose that management want to know the expected rate of return on their company's investment in the boiler project over the five year period. The rate of return is equivalent to the percentage discounting rate that will give zero npv. The rate of return has to be found by repeating the calculation shown in Figure 5.3, testing with different percentage rates until one is found that yields the required zero npv. There are three possible ways in which this can be done:

1   One of the test calculations might, with good fortune, yield zero npv or a value which is sufficiently close to zero.

2　It is likely that no calculation using a whole number percentage rate will result in a zero npv. The calculation will probably have to be reiterated using fractional percentages, changing the discounting rate in small steps until zero npv occurs.

3　Instead of reiterations by trial and error, calculations can be made using a few whole number discounting rates that give a range of fairly small positive and negative npv values. These results can drawn on a graph, plotting npv against the discounting rates used. The point at which the line crosses zero npv will allow the forecast percentage return on investment to be read off.

Funding

Sources of finance

Project funding may not be of direct concern to every project manager – unless shortage of funds puts the future of the project (and its manager) in question. However, here is a list of possible sources from which an organization may be able to find the capital needed for investment in a project:

- Cash reserves (money held in the bank or in short-term investments, including profits not distributed as dividends to shareholders).
- Sale of assets (for example, the owner of a stately home sells a valuable work of art to raise capital for a building restoration project, or a company realizes cash on its real estate in a sale and leaseback deal).
- Mortgaging property.
- Borrowing from a bank or other financial institution, either as an overdraft or as a fixed loan.
- Borrowing through a lease purchase agreement.
- Renting or leasing (in which case the project will never be owned by the project user).
- Issuing debentures or loan stock.

- Raising share capital, either in a private or public company. The company may be specially set up for the project.
- Collaborating with other companies to set up a consortium or a joint venture company in which skills, resources and risk are all shared.
- Government sources at international, national or local level, through direct grants or fiscal incentives. It is often possible to borrow from a bank against security provided by a government's export credit guarantee scheme (see 'Pecuniary insurances' in the insurance section of this chapter).

A company will be able to reduce its borrowing requirement if it can improve its cash flow. Methods for consideration include:

- Reducing inventory (stocks and work-in-progress).
- Using trade creditors to advantage, negotiating longest possible credit terms for the payment of suppliers' and subcontractors' invoices.
- Keeping trade debtors to a minimum through prompt and accurate invoicing, asking for progress payments where appropriate, and applying rigorous credit control.

The contractor's viewpoint

Project funding considerations are not the sole concern of the purchaser. Contractors need to take a serious interest in the financing of projects for several reasons:

- In some cases the contractor may undertake to assist or advise the customer to arrange finance. Financing proposals may even feature in the project tender.
- The contractor must be assured that the customer is financially viable, and has access to sufficient funds to meet all project costs. Will the customer be able to pay the bills?
- The contractor may need finance to invest in new plant or to expand other facilities in order to be able to carry out the project.
- If the project size is significant compared with the contractor's other work, cash flow will have to be considered. The

contractor may have to fund costly work-in-progress until payment is eventually received from the customer. Invoices may be disputed, delaying revenue receipts. Some customers pay late, not just through innocent tardiness, but because of a deliberate policy to delay payment of every bill for as long as possible. The experienced contractor will attempt to minimize these effects by insisting on a contract that allows for progress payments, and by efficient invoicing and credit control methods.

- Money due from overseas customers can be particularly difficult to collect, with risk of serious delays or even non-payment (see the reference to export credit insurance later in this chapter). These difficulties can arise through any failure to observe the complex formalities and for other, less savoury, reasons. The major banks are excellent sources of advice for those new to importing.

Financial viability of participating organizations

A sensible contractor will take steps to try and investigate the financial viability of any new major customer. The contractor might start by asking for copies of the customer's audited annual accounts and reports for recent years. Organizations such as Dun and Bradstreet can provide useful information on a confidential basis. Conversely, customers often make similar enquiries of their new contractors and suppliers. Complementary processes exist, therefore, by which the contractor wants to be assured that his customer will be able to meet all proper claims for payment, while the customer takes steps to ensure that he does not employ a contractor likely to get into financial difficulties or even go bankrupt before being able to complete the project.

The contractor's project manager has a major role to play in protecting his organization's cash flow. Apart from the obvious job of managing the project itself to keep it on plan, the project manager must see that claims for payment are issued promptly. All claims for payment must be correct, supported by contractually agreed certificates, reports, or by accurate export/import documentation, to avoid any reason for dispute. Claims for payment must be followed up with polite but prompt credit control action if payment becomes overdue.

Contracts

Essential elements of a contract

Although there are many cases where a legally binding contract can exist between two parties on the basis of a verbal agreement, for project management purposes it is assumed that the contract between the customer and the contractor, and contracts between the contractor and his suppliers and subcontractors will be formal written documents. These should ensure that all aspects of each agreement are available for subsequent reference in order to administer the contract or to help in resolving any dispute. The document might be a purchase order, an exchange of letters, a specially drafted contract or a preprinted standard form. It is also assumed that any subsequent amendments to the contract will be recorded on suitable documents.

Several conditions must be satisfied in order for a legally binding contract to exist. The following notes are a summary, and do not list the exceptions:

1   *Intention*   The parties must intend that the contract shall be legally binding. In project contracts this intention will be assumed unless the parties have specifically declared otherwise, in which case the contract becomes only a formal version of a 'gentleman's agreement'. Project managers are not likely to be concerned with this question of intention, except perhaps when problems arise with collective agreements between management and trade unions.
2   *Offer and acceptance*   The contractor must make a definite offer stating that he is willing to contract on specified terms, and the contract becomes legally binding on both parties when the customer informs the contractor that he has accepted the offer without qualification. Acceptance must be communicated before the expiry of any offer time limit set by the contractor.

It may happen that the picture becomes blurred as to what

has been offered and what actually has been accepted. It is essential that the offer be properly defined by a specification that is as complete and up-to-date as possible, amended as necessary to take account of changes agreed during any negotiations.

Purchase order forms usually have the purchaser's conditions of purchase attached or printed as a standard list on the reverse side. The seller is asked to acknowledge the order and to accept its conditions by returning a tear-off acknowledgement slip. Many companies instruct their buyers never to return such slips, but to acknowledge receipt instead by returning the seller's own standard form. The seller's form might well carry a set of conditions which conflict with those offered by the purchaser. It might then be argued that no contract exists because neither party has formally accepted the other's offer, but many purchasing contracts are made in such circumstances. If a dispute should arise, it is possible that legal argument would favour the party who sent the last offer, provided that the other party has not actually rejected it.

3 *Consideration* A contract must result in each party promising the other a valuable benefit. In projects, this usually means that one party promises to deliver certain property or services by a specified date and the other promises to accept the property or services and pay for them. Failure of one party to keep its promise can lead to action by the other for breach of contract.

4 *Capacity* In general, if the offer made by a company falls outside the scope of its powers as set out in the objects clause of its memorandum of association, then the company has no power to make the offer and the contract is void (said to be *ultra vires*, or 'beyond the power').

Terms describing participants

In general this book refers to the two main parties in project contracts as the customer and the contractor, but many other terms are used in practice. Some people use the term 'owner' to mean the customer, but this can be misleading because there are often circumstances where the customer will not have legal title to the project until certain conditions regarding settlement of invoices, delivery and handover or credit finance have been fulfilled. At least one contracting company in the UK calls its own project managers 'owners' which, confusingly, means that the project managers 'own' responsibility for their projects within the company until they have been handed over. The terms in most general use are customer, purchaser or client, and 'customer' is used in most cases throughout this book. When a project passes through a customer to a third party, the expression 'end user' can be useful to describe the eventual recipient.

The organization carrying out the project may be described as the contractor, vendor or seller. The terms 'main contractor' or 'managing contractor' are often used to identify an organization which is directly responsible to the purchaser for a project but which uses subcontractors for some of the work. 'Managing contractor' is not the same as 'management contractor', the latter name being applied to a contractor who coordinates and oversees the work of other contractors on behalf of the purchaser. In this book, 'contractor' is used generally, and may mean a single company or a group or consortium of companies that have contracted jointly to carry out the work.

Independent consultants often figure in large contracts, and may be appointed to safeguard the interests of one party or the other (usually the purchaser). In most such cases the consultant is either a professional organization or a suitably qualified person, referred to contractually as 'the engineer'.

Contract scope

The contract documents should obviously specify, without ambiguity, the exact role that the contractor is required to perform. The purchaser and the contractor must both be clear on what is included in any quoted price or charging rate, and on what is excluded. At its lowest level, the contract scope might be limited to minor involvement by a company as a subcontractor. At the other extreme, a contractor could be completely in charge of a large project, with turnkey responsibility for all the works (that is handing the project over to the customer only after it has been fully completed and commissioned). Specifying the technical and commercial scope of a contract is part of the project definition process (Chapter 3).

Contracts with standard conditions

Professional institutions, trade associations and some large companies operate standard forms of contract. These may take the form of recommended model conditions or preprinted contract forms.

Model conditions of contract published by various institutions and international bodies are well described and compared by Professor Stephen Wearne (see Wearne, 1989). They include:

For UK engineering and construction contracts:
- *Conditions of Contract for Complete Process Plants* (Institution of Chemical Engineers).
- *Conditions of Contract for the Purchase of Mechanical or Electrical Equipment* (a joint publication of the Institution of Mechanical Engineers, Institution of Electrical Engineers and the Association of Consulting Engineers).
- *Conditions of Contract for Civil Engineering Works* (a joint publication of the Institution of Civil Engineers, the Association of Consulting Engineers and the Federation of Civil Engineering Contractors).
- *GC/Works/1 Conditions of Contract for Construction* (Property Services Agency).

International models
The following are among the many models published for engineering and construction contracts outside the UK:

- *General Conditions for the Supply of Plant and Machinery for Export* (United Nations Economic Commission for Europe).
- *Conditions of Contract (International) for Electrical and Mechanical Works* (Fédération Internationale des Ingénieurs-Conseils [FIDIC]).
- *Conditions of Contract (International) for Works of Civil Engineering Construction* (FIDIC).

and many others, including some for projects in developing countries published by the United Nations Industrial Development Organization (UNIDO).

Contract payment structures

There are many ways in which contractors and their customers set up pricing and payment arrangements for project work. The payment terms will depend on factors such as:

* risk, uncertainty and any other factor affecting the accuracy with which the project can be defined, estimated and budgeted;
* the customer's intention to set the contractor performance incentives. These are usually aimed either at completion on time or at completion below budget, but they can also have a bearing on the standard of workmanship and quality. A penalty clause may be included in the contract as an attempt to limit failure in performance, the most common form being a penalty payment calculated according to the number of days, weeks or other stated periods by which the contractor is late in successfully completing the project.

Pricing considerations

It can be assumed that any company worth its salt will be equipped with a well-defined general pricing policy. Profit targets and the relationship between estimated costs and selling prices may be laid down very firmly. Pricing decisions for any significant project usually fall within the responsibility, not of the project manager, but of the company's higher management. Companies typically have procedures for authorizing quotations, and it is usual for new proposals to be discussed and agreed at senior management or board level meetings before the firm allows any commitment to be made to a potential customer.

One might imagine that a fixed selling price could always be obtained by taking a set of project estimates and marking up the cost at the specified level. Life, unfortunately, is seldom quite so straightforward. Even where a project is to be quoted on the basis of a schedule of rates or on some other cost-reimbursable basis, setting the level of charges can be a matter for expert judgement rather than simple accountancy.

Under certain conditions a firm may be forced to submit a tender or accept an order at a price so low that any possibility of making a fair profit is precluded right from the start. Consider, for example, a company that is temporarily short of work, but which can confidently foresee long-term continuity and expansion of its business. It may be that a period of market recession is seen to be coming to an end. Perhaps the start of one or more new projects is being delayed while customers arrange funding, or for other commercial, political or technical reasons (such delays are common with new projects).

The contractor may be faced with a real dilemma: the choice between dismissing idle staff as redundant or keeping them on the payroll for no return. Specialists and skilled people are difficult and expensive to recruit. Their training and acquired experience in a company's methods is an investment which represents a valuable part of the firm's invisible assets. Disbanding such a team can be compared to the cutting down of a mature tree. The act of chopping down and dismembering takes only a few hours, but to grow a replacement tree of similar size must take many years. No one can tell whether the new tree will turn out to be such a fine specimen as its predecessor. In addition, of course, trying to ensure the survival of work groups can be argued as a moral or social obligation of employers, especially in the larger industries where entire local communities may be dependent on one company for employment and local prosperity.

Contracts taken on to tide a firm over a lean period are termed 'bridging contracts' for obvious reasons. The profit motive becomes secondary in these circumstances, but there are, of course, risks to be considered and accepted in adopting such a policy. The impact of an estimating error or any other problem that causes a budget to be overspent is always greater without the cushioning effect of a planned profit margin. There is also some danger that customers who return with requests for projects in the future might be disappointed or aggrieved when they discover that prices for the new work are not quoted at comparable, artificially low rates. A more likely risk is that an underpriced project will materialize far later than expected (as many large projects have a way of doing), so that the workload no longer falls in the business trough but hits the contractor just when more profitable work is materializing. This could put the profitable work at risk: it might even prevent the contractor tendering for or accepting new profitable work until the underpriced project has been completed.

It may be expedient to submit a tender at an artificially low price in an attempt to gain entry into a market not previously exploited. There are, of course, other proven ways of achieving this end, not least of which is to acquire a firm that is already well established in the chosen market sector. Underpricing (offering 'loss leaders') remains a common, less drastic alternative. It is hardly necessary to stress that any company which decides to adopt a deliberate policy of underpricing will soon suffer from badly burned fingers if it has not first done the essential marketing homework.

Market conditions generally dictate the price which can be charged for any commodity, service or project, although the exact relationship is not straightforward and can produce surprises. In certain cases sales can actually be increased by pricing high, contrary to normal expectations. Usually, however, the laws of supply and demand operate. Most project tenders must stand a better chance of acceptance if they are kept low compared with competition. Even when a firm boasts a market monopoly, with competition entirely absent, the intensity of demand can influence the prices that can be charged; if a price is too high the potential customer may simply decide to do without altogether.

Local government authorities and other public bodies under strict obligations as trustees of public money may be compelled to accept the lowest tender for a given project. If such an organization wishes to place an order at anything other than the very lowest price possible, they must have an overriding reason which they are prepared to defend.

Orders can be unwelcome and possess nuisance value under some circumstances. Suppose, for example, that a firm has been asked to tender for a project at a time when the order book is already full to overflowing. This firm knows that either a very long delivery time must be quoted or, in the event of receiving the order, it will have to put work out to subcontractors that it would prefer to keep in-house (this can apply particularly to conceptual engineering and design, for example). Overtrading can also lead to cash flow difficulties. Unless the company can foresee a continuing expansion of business, sufficient to justify raising new capital and increasing its permanent capacity, it may simply not want the order. In a case such as this the company can choose between quoting at a very high price or not quoting at all.

Accurate project definition and reliable cost estimates are essential to the pricing process: they provide the platform from which profits can be predicted relative to any price that may be set. Shaky estimates produce a tendency to increase the mark-up to cover the increased risk, possibly destroying any chance of gaining an order in a competitive market. Sound estimates are also vital as a basis for any subsequent price negotiations with the customer: a contractor must know as accurately as possible just how far he can be pushed into paring a price before any hope of profit dwindles to useless proportions.

Fixed (or firm) price contracts

A fixed price contract is the result of the familiar situation in which one or more contractors bid for work against a purchaser's clear specification, stating a total price for all the works. The purchaser understands that the contractor cannot, in normal circumstances, increase the price quoted. The offer to carry out a project for a fixed price demonstrates the contractor's confidence in being able to complete the specified project without spending more than its estimated costs.

In practice there are sometimes clauses, even in so-called fixed price contracts, which allow limited price renegotiation or additional charges in the event of specified circumstances that may arise outside the contractor's control (national industry wage awards are the most common cause).

Cost reimbursable contracts

There are, of course, many types of contract which do not start with the inclusion of a known total fixed price. Most of these are 'cost reimbursable' contracts, based on some arrangement where the customer repays the contractor for work done according to a pre-agreed measurement of cost or rate of working.

Fixed prices are usually avoided by contractors in all circumstances where the final scope of a project cannot be predicted with sufficient accuracy when the contract is signed, or where the work is to be carried out under conditions of high risk. Projects for pure scientific research where the amount of work needed and the possible results are completely unpredictable would obviously be unsuitable for fixed price quotations. Many construction contracts for major capital works or process plants are subject to high risk, owing to site conditions or to political and economic factors outside the contractor's control.

Even in cost reimbursable contracts, with no fixed prices to bid, managers have to decide the levels at which to set the various charging rates. It cannot be assumed that a contractor will charge all his customers the same rates. Some customers will demand details of how the direct and overhead charges are built up, and will expect to agree the final rates after negotiation.

In any contract where payment is related to agreed rates of working the customer will want to be assured of the veracity of the contractor's claims for payment. This might entail access to the contractor's books of account by the customer or by auditors acting for him. In construction contracts based on payment by quantities, quantity surveyors will act for the customer to ensure that the work being billed has in fact been done.

Estimating accuracy might seem less important where there are no fixed prices operating but, practically without exception, tenders for contracts with no fixed prices must contain budgetary estimates. If these are set too high, they can frighten a potential customer away, and the contractor stands to lose the contract against competitors. If the estimates are set too low, all kinds of problems could arise during the execution of the work, not least of which might be the customer running out of funds with which to pay the contractor. Any contractor wishing to retain a reputation for fair dealing will want to avoid the trap of setting budgetary estimates too low, especially where this is done deliberately in pursuit of an order. In any case, avoidable estimating inaccuracies must prejudice subsequent attempts at planning, scheduling and management control.

Summary of contract types

Quoted prices or rates do not always fall entirely into the clear category of fixed price or cost reimbursable, often because one of the parties wishes to introduce an element of performance incentive or risk protection. Some contracts (compound contracts) incorporate a mix of these arrangements. Others (convertible contracts) allow for a change to a fixed price arrangement at some pre-agreed stage in the project when it becomes possible to define adequately the total scope of work and probable final costs.

Some well known options are summarized below, and Figure 5.4 indicates the relationships between risk and incentives.

Fixed price

A price is quoted and accepted for the work specified in the contract. The price will only be varied if the customer varies the contract, or if the contract conditions allow for a price increase to be negotiated under particular circumstances (for example, a nationwide wage award in the particular industry).

Target price

Target price contracts are similar to fixed price contracts, but they are used where there is some justifiable uncertainty about the likely costs for carrying out the project as it has been defined. The contract allows for price adjustment if the audited final project costs either exceed estimates or show a saving, so that the risks and benefits are shared to some extent between the customer and the contractor.

Guaranteed maximum price

A guaranteed maximum price arrangement is a target price contract in which, although cost savings can be shared, the contractor is limited in the extent to which excess costs may be added to the target price.

Simple reimbursable

A simple cost reimbursable arrangement means that the contractor is reimbursed for his costs and expenses, but makes no profit. This type of payment sometimes occurs when work is performed by a company for its parent company, or for another company which is wholly owned within the same group of companies. A formal contract may not be used in such cases.

Type of contract	Basis for paying the contractor	Degree of control needed by the customer	Project definition needed	Contractor's risk	Contractor's motivation
Fixed price	Achievement	least	highest	highest	highest
Bill of quantities with scheduled rates					
Target price					
Reimbursable plus fee					
Simple reimbursable					
Cost-plus	Time and costs incurred	highest	least	least	least

Figure 5.4 Relationship between the type of contract and control emphasis

Cost-plus
Cost-plus is a common form of reimbursable contract. As in simple reimbursable contracts, the contractor charges for materials used and for time recorded against the project on timesheets. But the charging rates agreed with the customer are set at levels which are intended not only to recover direct costs and overheads, but are marked up to yield profit.

Schedule of rates
Contracts with scheduled rates are reimbursable contracts (usually cost-plus), charged according to the number of work units performed. A specific work unit charging rate will be agreed beforehand for each trade or type of work involved.

Reimbursable plus management fee
This is a form of reimbursable contract in which the contractor's profit element is charged as a fixed fee, instead of being built in as a 'plus' element in the agreed rates. Unlike cost-plus, the contractor's profit revenue does not increase with cost but instead decreases proportionally as total project costs rise, arguably providing an incentive for the contractor to keep costs low.

Bill of quantities with scheduled rates
A bill of quantities contract is reimbursable, operating with a schedule of rates, but the total number of work units expected in each trade or type of work is estimated and quoted beforehand.

Payment timing

Invoice timing for fixed price contracts
Many large projects, spread out over timescales that might extend to several years, could well involve the investment of large sums of the contractor's money. By the time the contract is completed and paid for, the resulting profit could be offset or nullified by the cost of capital employed. In other words, the contractor has had to bear the interest on all money tied up in stocks and work in progress. For these reasons, 'progress' or 'stage' payments are often agreed between the contractor and the customer. This enables the contractor to raise some invoices

during the course of the project, so that he is not called upon to carry the whole cost of the project until completion, when the final invoice can be issued.

The basis for making stage payment claims may be cut and dried contractually, being dependent upon completion of certain stages in the project, or on the deliveries of specified items of equipment to the customer. Standard contract conditions for various trade organizations may define the stage payment requirements. The arrangement might be made along the following lines:

Percentage of the total contract price payable	*When*
10	On signing the contract or placing the purchase order, before the contractor starts work
20	Upon design approval by the customer and the start of manufacture
30	On delivery of the main consignment to the customer's premises
30	On handover
10	A 'retention payment', due after six months of satisfactory use or operation
100	

In other cases, no such stages will be defined, and progress payments are made at regular intervals, the amounts being decided according to the measure of actual progress achieved, as certified by the contractor or an independent professional person. It is obviously important that such achievement can be accurately measured to ensure that invoicing is kept in step with real progress. The subject of relating achievement to costs is dealt with in Chapter 15.

Invoice timing for cost reimbursable projects
Payments for day works or casual work using temporary agency

staff may be invoiced at weekly intervals but most contractors will invoice their customers at regular calendar monthly intervals, either against certificates of work done or against cost records subject to independent audit.

Insurance

Every business organization has to face risks in its everyday life. Projects (which metaphorically or even literally always break new ground) tend to attract more than their fair share of uncertainty. Part of management's responsibility is to identify as many risks as possible and decide how to counter them. The first priority must be to manage the organization and the project in such a way that all foreseeable commercial and physical risks are minimized. But some risks are unavoidable and insurance is then an obvious option to consider.

Figure 5.5 demonstrates that managers do not have complete freedom of choice when deciding which risks should be insured. Every risk can be categorized according to its priority for inclusion in the organization's insurance portfolio. The remainder of this chapter is a brief summary of some of the risks and types of insurance that can apply particularly to project work.

Risks for which insurance can not provide an answer

There are risks which an underwriter will either refuse to insure, or for which the premium demanded would be prohibitive. Such circumstances arise:

- Where the odds against a loss occurring are too high or, in other words, where the risk is seen as more of a certainty than reasonable chance. Examples are losses made through speculative trading or because of disadvantageous changes in foreign exchange rates.
- Where the insurer is not able to spread his risk over a sufficient number of similar risks.
- Where the insurer does not have access to sufficient data from the past to be able to quantify the future risk.
- Where the insured would stand to gain as a result of a claim

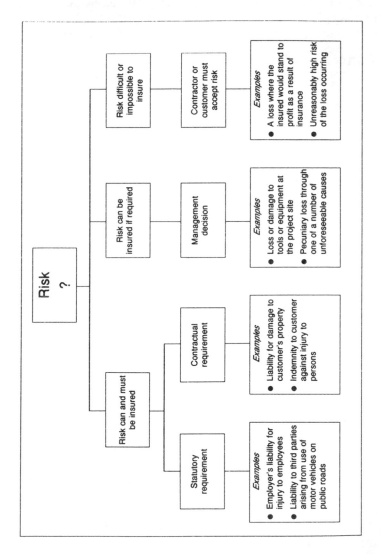

Figure 5.5 Risk and insurance in project management

(except in some forms of personal insurance, the principle of insurance is to attempt to reinstate the insured's position to that which existed before the loss event). A person cannot, for example, expect to benefit personally from a claim for loss or damage to property not belonging to him (property in which he has no *insurable* interest).

Any of these items, therefore must be excluded from the insurance portfolio. In some cases other commercial remedies may exist for offsetting the risks.

Risks which can be insured

There are four main classes of insurance. These are:

1 legal liabilities (payments to others as a result of statutory, contractual or professional commitments, compensation awarded by the courts, legal expenses, but not fines imposed by the courts);
2 protection against loss or damage to property;
3 cover relating to personnel;
4 pecuniary loss.

A policy may combine cover for two or more of the above classes of risk.

Statutory requirements

At the top of the insurance shopping list are those items which *must* be insured in order to comply with government laws and regulations. In the UK, these include the familiar minimum level of insurance (third party) required for motor vehicles used on public roads. UK employers are obliged to insure their employees, without limit, against injury or illness arising from their employment Employers' Liability (Compulsory Insurance) Act, 1969, and every employer has to display a valid certificate on its notice boards to show that such insurance exists. Other regulations cover the insurance of such things as lifts and hoists, boilers and other pressure vessels. Understanding and complying with statutory requirements and regulations is part of normal company administration, and is not confined to project management.

Care must be taken when working on construction contracts to ensure that national statutory liabilities pertaining to contractors, architects and consulting engineers are adequately covered by insurance. In certain countries 'decennial liability' covers the ten-year period following project completion, and is a separate insurance issue, in addition to any contract requirements mentioned below.

Contractual requirements and legal liabilities

In commercial and industrial projects, whether for construction or manufacturing, it is certain that some onus will be placed upon the parties (usually the contractor) to insure against several risks. All the model conditions of contract for engineering, civil and construction contracts embody such requirements. The project contractor will also wish to make certain that subcontractors employed by him are bound, in turn, by similar conditions.

Liability insurances are most likely to feature prominently in project contracts. The project purchaser will want to know, for example, that the contractor has adequate cover for legal liability in the event of personal injury, illness or death caused to anyone as a result of the project.

In summary, liability insurances may be required for:

- compensation to persons for bodily harm (employees of either party, others working on site, visitors and members of the public);
- any property loss or damage;
- financial loss;
- infringement of property rights;
- accidents;
- product liability (arising from use of a product);
- professional negligence;
- nuisance caused by the works;
- environmental damage.

Every organization or professional person with project responsibility (including architects, consultants, surveyors, designers and project management organizations) must make certain that they have professional liability insurance which is adequate to cover any liability which they might incur in the course of their work.

Insurance policies designed for projects

For civil engineering and construction contracts there are purpose-made 'contractors' all risks' (CAR) policies available. These cover not only liability risks, but also the contractor's property risks. Policies can be arranged for each specific project, or annually to cover most or all projects undertaken by a contractor. Similar all risks policies can be arranged for engineering and manufacturing projects.

Combined policies can be simpler to administer and less complicated in the event of a claim. Consider, for example, a policy which includes combined insurance for goods, plant or machinery, and which covers damage or loss of this property during loading, transport, unloading, handling and erection or installation at the project site. If some of these stages were to be covered by several different policies, disputes could easily arise in the event of a claim as to where fault for the loss lay, and as to which insurer was responsible for meeting the claim.

Other insurances for project work

In addition to the statutory and contractual requirements, there is a range of other risks against which a contractor may be required to insure, or for which a contractor may decide that insurance is prudent. Some of these are listed below.

Personnel
Provisions for personal accident, sickness and medical expenses insurances will need particular consideration when employees are required to travel, whether at home or abroad. Those working on projects in foreign countries will expect to be adequately covered for the higher risks involved, and such

cover will have to be extended to spouses and children if they are also allowed to travel.

'Key man' insurance offers various kinds of protection to an employer against expenses or loss of profits which result when illness, injury or death prevents one or more named key persons from performing the duties expected of them. Arrangements are flexible and policies can be tailored to suit particular circumstances.

Pecuniary insurances

These insurances are designed to protect a company against financial losses from a variety of causes. Risks which can be covered include embezzlement, loss through interruption of business, and legal expenses. Advance profits insurance may be possible in some limited circumstances to provide cover for delay in receiving return on project investment caused by late project completion.

Of particular interest to contractors where business with foreign customers is involved is export credit insurance. In the UK, the government's Export Credits Guarantee Department (ECGD) provides guarantees which can provide security against bank loans for large capital goods and long-term projects. Most industrialized companies have similar schemes. The contractor will be expected to bear some of the risk, although the proportion will usually be small. The security offered by credit insurance can be an important factor in obtaining finance for a project.

Where to obtain insurance

Insurance can be sought directly from an underwriter, or through a broker; preferably one with a good reputation and experienced in the insured's type of project activity (for example, in engineering all risks or in CAR policies). The insurer will need to be supplied with sufficient information for the risk to be adequately defined, and the contractor will be expected to inform the insurer of any change of circumstances likely to affect the risks insured. The insurer may wish to make investigations or even follow up the project work using his own experts.

Professional advice from insurers can often be of great benefit in reducing risks, especially in the areas of health and safety and crime prevention.

Further reading

Association of Insurance and Risk Managers in Industry and Commerce (1984), *Company Insurance Handbook* (2nd edn), Aldershot: Gower.

Carter, R.L. (ed.) (1973 (updated)), *Handbook of Insurance*, Brentford: Kluwer.

Carter, R.L. and Crockford, G.N. (eds) (1974 (updated)), *Handbook of Risk Management*, Brentford: Kluwer.

Carter, R.L. (1987), 'Insurance', in Lock, D. (ed.), *Project Management Handbook* (Ch. 7), Aldershot: Gower.

Duxbury, R. (1991), *Contract Law* (2nd edn), Andover: Sweet & Maxwell (a concise and well-written text in the Nutshells paperback series).

Franks, J.R. and Broyles, J.E. (1979), *Modern Managerial Finance*, Chichester: Wiley (inexpensive, comprehensive and includes much on financing and financial appraisal).

Marsh, P.D.V. (1987), *The Art of Tendering*, Aldershot: Gower.

Marsh, P.D.V. (1988), *Contracting for Engineering and Construction Projects*, Aldershot: Gower.

Sassoon, David (ed.) (1982), *Bidding for Projects Financed by International Lending Agencies*, Aldershot: Gower.

Scott, W. (1981), *The Skills of Negotiating*, Aldershot: Gower.

Taylor, T. (1985), *The Financing of Industry and Commerce*, London: Heinemann.

Treitel, G.H. (1984), *An Outline of the Law of Contract* (3rd edn), London: Butterworth.

Uff, J. (1991), *Construction Law* (5th edn), London: Sweet & Maxwell (for construction and civil engineering contracts).

Wearne, S.H. (1985), *Civil Engineering Contracts*, London: Thomas Telford Ltd.

Wearne, S.H. (1989), 'Engineering Contracts', in Lock, D. (ed.), (1989) *Handbook of Engineering Management* (Ch. 21), Oxford: Heinemann Newnes.

6

Planning the timescale

Whenever any job has to be accomplished according to a time or date deadline, then it is advisable to have at least some idea of the relationship between the time allowed and the time needed. This is true for any project, whether a dinner is being prepared or a motorway constructed. In the first case one would be ill-advised to tell guests 'Dinner is at seven – but the potatoes will not be ready until seven thirty'. Similarly, there would be little point in having an eminent personage arrive to open a new motorway if, by cutting the tape, the eager and unsuspecting traffic stream were to be released towards a bridge that still consisted of a few girders over a yawning chasm (complete with rushing torrent below).

So it is a safe assumption that a plan of some sort is always advisable if project completion is to be assured on time. In the culinary example the planning might be very informal, a mental exercise by the cook. Projects such as motorways are more complicated and have to be planned with more formal techniques.

Once a need has arisen to commit any plan to paper, a suitable notation must be chosen. Any plan, drawing or specification which is to be read by more than one person must be regarded as a means of communicating information. This information has to be expressed in a language which is understood by all recipients if effective communication is to be established and maintained. Several notational methods and 'languages' have been devised for timescale planning, and some of these will be examined in this chapter.

The planning time frame

Time scheduling can be considered from two opposite viewpoints. On the one hand, a set of estimates could be obtained and used to produce a plan that predicts a project completion date. Conversely, the end-date requirement might be predetermined by factors outside the planner's control. A delivery promise might already have been given to a customer in a sales proposal, or the project could have to be finished to meet a forthcoming exhibition or public event.

Neither situation is wholly good or bad. Schedules produced from estimates without the application of any external pressure to compress the timescale may predict an end date which is ludicrous from the customer's point of view, so preventing any possibility of gaining an order. Some incentive to complete a project reasonably quickly may not be a bad thing because time is money, and projects which are allowed to drag their feet tend to attract higher costs from fixed overheads and other causes. Giving planners complete freedom to decide the project timescale may not always be quite so advisable as it might at first seem.

If a plan has to be suited to a predetermined, inflexible delivery requirement, all the estimates must be fitted into the time available as best they can. A temptation is thus created for estimates to be shortened arbitrarily, without justification, and for no better reason than that the time available is too short. An honest person will admit that projects planned on this basis are not likely to be finished on time, although such plans may gain a temporary advantage by serving to pacify higher management or by deceiving a trusting customer into placing an order. Unfortunately the truth is bound to emerge sooner or later, bringing consequent discredit on the company.

If the time available is restricted, it is often possible to find a way of rescheduling the work, still keeping to the original estimates but simply changing the sequence of jobs or overlapping them to shorten the overall time. Of course it is sometimes possible to condense programmes by allocating more resources, but *never* must the project manager allow himself to be persuaded or coerced into trying to expedite a plan by 'marking down' estimates without any justification.

Another danger which might arise from a timescale dictated by arbitrary or external factors is that the overall period allowed is longer than necessary. This would be rather unusual, but not impossible. Such extended schedules are an ideal breeding ground for budgetary excesses according to Professor Parkinson's best-known law, where 'Work expands so as to fill the time available for its completion' (*Parkinson's Law or the Pursuit of Progress* (1958), London: John Murray).

The ideal project plan requires careful cooperation between the key participants in the proposed work, all striving to meet the needs of the customer and balancing these with the capabilities of the project organization. To be really effective, the constituent elements of the plan must be reliably estimated and arranged in their most logical sequence.

Timetables

Timetables are the simplest form of project plans. Although simple planning methods often have merit (and can be ideal for very small projects) the timetable method is really too simple. However, the method serves as a good 'how not to do it' introduction to the subject of project planning techniques. Here is an example.

A prototype for a small electromechanical assembly has to be designed and built. The company's chief engineer is asked to oversee the project, and has been given a total of 18 weeks in which to have a completed prototype ready for testing and appraisal. Asked to prepare a plan, the chief engineer comes up with the following timetable:

	Start	Finish
Engineering design	4 Jan 1993	19 Mar 1993
Purchase components	22 Mar 1993	16 Apr 1993
Manufacture	29 Mar 1993	23 Apr 1993
Assembly and inspection	26 Apr 1993	8 May 1993

At the end of January there is an informal meeting at which the chief engineer reports 'good progress'. After another four weeks, at the end of February, another progress meeting is told that engineering is 'running a little late, owing to unforeseen problems'. When pressed, the chief engineer estimates that the delay will amount to 'about a week'. At the next meeting, when the design should have been finished, the forecast is that three weeks' design work still remains. Eventually, on 23 April, the drawings are issued to purchasing and production, leaving the buyer and the production manager with no chance of completing the project on time. So, the prototype is going to be very late. So are the jobs on to which the design engineers should have moved.

A project manager must be able to answer two complementary questions at any time in a project:

- Where *should* we be on the plan now?
- Where exactly *are* we on the plan now?

Timetable plans are usually written down with insufficient care and thought. They are ineffective for day-to-day progress monitoring and control because they have inadequate detail, and display even that badly.

Bar charts

Figure 6.1 is a bar chart version of the timetable plan just described. Although this plan is really not made in enough detail it can be seen at once that the bar chart displays the programme more effectively. Notice that the plan is drawn up on a scale where the horizontal axis is directly proportional to time (calendar weeks in this case but days, months, years or other units are often used instead to suit the overall timescale).

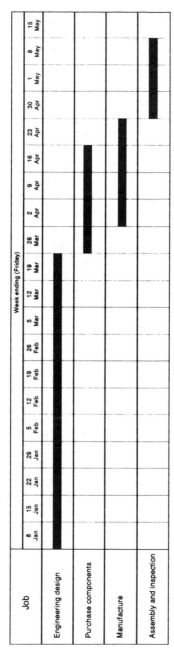

Figure 6.1 Bar chart for design and manufacture of a prototype electromechanical assembly
This is the same plan as that shown as a timetable in the text, but is visually more effective in this form.

Each horizontal bar represents a project task, its length scaled according to its expected duration. The name or description of each job is written on the same row, at the left-hand edge of the chart.

Bar charts derive from Gantt charts, named after their originator, the American industrial engineer Henry Gantt (1861–1919). These charts have long been in widespread use, and they continue to be very valuable planning aids. Not only are bar charts easy to construct and interpret, but they are also readily adaptable to a great variety of planning requirements. They are still to be seen displayed as wall charts for controlling many functions, such as development programmes, duty rotas, machine loading, computer room scheduling, training programmes and so on.

A bar chart's effectiveness can be improved by ruling a vertical line or by placing a cursor on the chart to coincide with the 'time-now date', highlighting the jobs (or proportions of jobs) that should have been done (to the left of the cursor) and those jobs which remain to be done (to the right of the time-now line).

On more complex charts the bars are often colour coded or (if colour is not available) given distinctive shading to denote the department, trade or individual responsible for each job. A word of caution is necessary here, however, since there is a real danger of destroying the effectiveness of any system by being too ambitious. A bar chart is above all a visual representation of a plan and it must be capable of easy interpretation. When more than about six different colours or shading patterns are used, much of the visual impact is lost and the coded chart becomes difficult to use.

Coded bar charts are the simplest method for scheduling resources on very small projects. It is only necessary to add the number of bars of a particular code that fall within each time column to aggregate the resources needed from that department or trade. If the bars are set up on an adjustable board, they can be moved sideways (that is rescheduled) so that unwanted peaks and troughs in the workload are smoothed out and allowing the project to be planned without exceeding the resources available.

Several office equipment suppliers manufacture their own proprietary brands of bar charts, which can be assembled from kits and hung on walls. Some use magnetic strips which cling to a sheet steel background, but these can suffer from the disadvantage that an elaborate schedule, painstakingly prepared, can be wrecked in a moment if a passer by happens to brush carelessly against the board. Other schemes use plug-in plastic strips (one system resembles Lego bricks) or cardboard strips dropped into slots. A typical arrangement uses strips about 4 mm wide which plug into holes arranged on a square 6 mm grid. A board only 60 cm high therefore has almost 100 rows. In the horizontal direction, a sizeable project timescale can be divided into columns depicting weeks or even separate days without the board becoming too long. A surprising number of activities can thus be accommodated in a small space, allowing the inclusion of a wealth of detail.

With the advent of more sophisticated planning methods, notably critical path network analysis, bar charts have tended to fall into undeserved disrepute. Although more modern techniques must be preferred in many situations, the older charting methods still have their valuable uses. Planning by bar chart is infinitely better than no planning at all. The visual impact of a well-displayed schedule can be a powerful aid to controlling a simple project. Bar charts are still preferred to other methods in some executives' offices, on project sites and in factories. All levels of supervision and management find them convenient as day-to-day control tools. Even when projects have been planned with advanced computerized techniques, the same computer systems are often used to translate the schedules into bar charts for day-to-day use.

Of course bar charts do have their limitations. For example, although it is possible to schedule more than 100 jobs using an adjustable bar chart, *rescheduling* is a different story. Setting a complex plan up in the first place might take a week. Adjusting it subsequently to keep in step with changes might prove impossible. Planners using over-complex bar charts find difficulty in casting their eyes along the rows without going off track and prolonged exposure to such work makes them easily recognizable by their sore eyes or 'planners squint'. When project planning requires this level of detail there are highly effective computer-based alternatives (discussed in later chapters).

Another problem with bar charts is that they cannot usually indicate interdependent relationships between tasks. Figure 6.2 is a simple project bar chart for a project aimed at developing a prototype desk and chair set. The chart gives no positive indication of the logical requirement that the anatomical study must be finished before design and drawing can begin. In such small charts these constraints can be dealt with mentally but with larger charts it is easy to make mistakes, with jobs scheduled to start before they logically can. The danger of such mistakes is increased when jobs are 'shuffled' on large adjustable charts to smoothe out workloads.

Vertical link lines can be added to bar charts to show constraints between jobs. Figure 6.3 is a linked version of the bar chart of Figure 6.2. Linked bar charts are, however, suitable only for relatively small projects. Critical path networks provide the more powerful notation needed to show all the logical interdependencies between different jobs in more complex projects (and they can also be used to good effect in small projects).

Critical path network analysis

Network analysis is a generic term for several project planning methods, of which the best known are critical path analysis (CPA) and programme evaluation and review technique (PERT). Although several methods are described in this chapter, CPA is widely used and is the basis for all the network planning and scheduling examples in this book.

Network analysis techniques can be traced back to developments in the UK and elsewhere, but their full exploitation was seen in the late 1950s, when they were used with great success and much publicity for the planning and control of US defence projects. The striking improvements demonstrated over earlier methods have since led to their widespread adoption in many industries far removed from either America or defence.

Several notation systems have emerged, and it is convenient to list these under two principal groups:

1   The activity-on-arrow system (often simply called arrow networks). These can be used for CPA or PERT. A very early

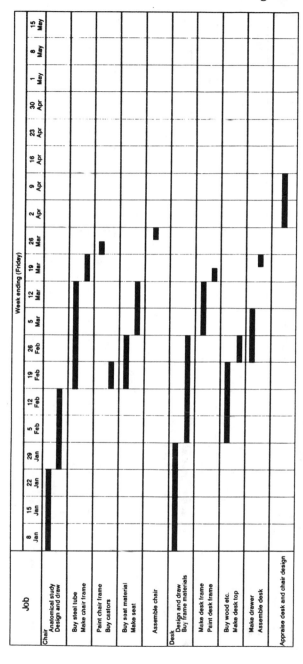

Figure 6.2 Bar chart for desk and chair project

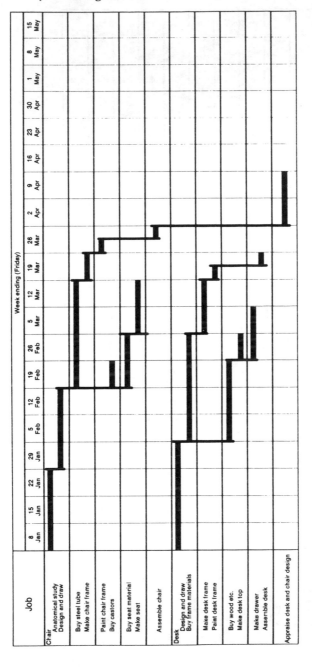

Figure 6.3 Linked bar chart for desk and chair project

Figure 6.4 The simplest network possible
Two project events are represented by the circles, while the arrow denotes the activity necessary to progress from the first event to the second.

version of the activity-on-arrow system was known as the link and circle method.
2 Activity-on-node networks, of which the precedence system is the most common. The method of potentials (MPM), also known as the Roy method, is a less well-known activity-on-node system that is very similar to the precedence system.

Whichever method is used is largely personal preference. Computer software is available for both groups.

Critical path analysis

The heart of any activity-on-arrow system is the arrow diagram, logic diagram, or 'network', itself. This differs from the more familiar bar chart in several important respects. Arrow diagrams, in common with all other network methods, are not drawn to scale. Every network is, however, constructed with careful thought to ensure that it shows as accurately as possible the logical relationship and interdependence of each activity or task with all the others in the project. Indeed, it is for this reason that networks are sometimes called logic diagrams.

Figure 6.4 shows the simplest arrow diagram possible. Each circle represents a project event, such as the start of work or the completion of a task. The arrow joining the two events represents the activity that must take place before the second event can be declared as achieved. Activity arrows are always drawn from left to right by convention. They are not drawn to scale and their length has no significance whatsoever.

(Although the intention is this book is to avoid the use of unnecessary jargon, readers may occasionally meet other terms that describe the event circles and activity arrows which make

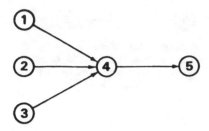

Figure 6.5 Network constraints
The activity leading to event 5 cannot begin until all activities preceding event 4 have been accomplished.

up networks. These strange terms have their origins in the mathematical theory of networks. In this alternative language, the circles are termed nodes and the arrows become arcs. The first event circle of an activity (the preceding event) is called the *I* node for that activity, and the end event circle (the succeeding event) is called its *J* node. Arrow networks are occasionally referred to as *IJ* networks. This jargon is not essential to the understanding and application of project network analysis, but the terms crop up occasionally in the literature and in such places as the specifications and instruction manuals for some computer software.)

In Figure 6.5 four activities are shown which link five events. The numbers written in the event circles are put there simply to label the events: they allow the events and their associated activities to be referred to without ambiguity. Thus the arrow from event 1 to event 4 can be described as activity 1 to 4. This labelling is convenient for all networks and essential for those which are to be processed by computer. The significance of the diagram in this example is that event 4 cannot be considered achieved until all three activities leading into it have been finished. Only then, and not before, can activity 4 to 5 be started. The dependence of activity 4 to 5 on all preceding activities is clearly highlighted.

Now, applying the method to an everyday 'project', suppose it is planned to plant a tree in a garden. If an arrow diagram were to be drawn, the result would look something like the sequence shown in Figure 6.6. The interdependence of activities

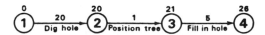

Figure 6.6 Tree project network
The addition of duration estimates to a network.

is clear in this case, and only one sequence of events is possible. The tree cannot be placed in the hole before the hole has been dug, and there would be little point in filling in the hole before before putting in the tree.

Estimates for the duration of each activity have been made for this example. They are:

Activity		*Estimated duration*
1–2:	Dig hole	20 minutes
2–3:	Position tree	1 minute
3–4:	Fill in hole	5 minutes

No one needs network analysis to tell that this project is going to take a minimum of 26 minutes to complete. Notice, however, that the estimated duration is written above each activity arrow, with a concise activity description written below. The estimated achievement time possible for each event (written above the event circles) is arrived at by adding up these activity durations from left to right along the arrow path. These estimated times for events are obviously the earliest possible times by which they can be achieved.

The network in Figure 6.7 represents a slightly more complex project. Now the configuration is actually seen to be a network of activities, and not just a simple straight line sequence. In this example there is more than one path through the arrows to project completion at event 6, which is usual for all project networks. In fact there are three possible routes here, one of which flows through the dotted arrow, or 'dummy activity' 4 to 3. Dummy activities (always called dummies for short) do not represent actual work and practically always have zero duration. Rather, they denote a constraint or line of dependence between different activities. In this case, therefore, the start of activity 3 to 6 is dependent not only upon completion of activity 2 to 3, but it must also await completion of activity 1 to 4.

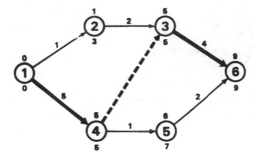

Figure 6.7 The critical path
In this simple network, duration estimates have been analysed to find critical path, shown here by the heavy lines.

Alternatively expressed, activity 3 to 6 cannot start until events 3 and 4 have both been achieved.

Numbers have, as for the 'tree project', been written above the activity arrows to show their estimated durations, but they represent weeks in this example. The earliest overall project duration possible has again been calculated by adding activity duration estimates along the arrows from left to right. However, this addition process has been somewhat complicated owing to the fact that there is more than one possible path, and the sums will depend on which path is followed. The earliest possible completion for event 3, for instance might be seen as $1 + 2 = 3$, if the path through events 1, 2 and 3 is taken: however completion of event 3 cannot really be achieved until week 5 because of the longer path through the dummy. Thus the earliest possible completion time for any event is found by the addition of all preceding activities along the longest path. By following this procedure through the network to the end of the project at event 6 it emerges that the earliest possible estimated project duration is nine weeks.

Now consider event 5 in Figure 6.7. Its earliest possible achievement time is week 6, three weeks before the earliest possible time for finishing the project at event 6. It is clear that activity 5 to 6, which is only expected to last for two weeks, could be delayed for up to one week without upsetting the overall timescale. In other words, although the earliest possible achievement time for event 5 is week 6, its latest permissible achievement time is week 7. This result can be indicated on the arrow diagram by writing the latest permissible time underneath the event circle. The result is found this time, not by addition from left to right along the arrows, but in exactly the opposite way of subtraction from right to left (9 − 2 = 7 for event 5). This subtraction exercise can be repeated throughout the network, writing the latest permissible times below all the event circles. Where more than one path exists, the longest must be chosen so that the result after subtraction gives the smallest remainder. This is illustrated at event 4, where the correct subtraction route lies through the dummy.

Although the earliest and latest times are written above and below the event circles, they can also be applied to the activities leading into and out of the events. Thus, for example, activity 5 to 6 has:

- duration: 2 weeks;
- earliest possible start: beginning of week 6;
- earliest possible finish (6 + 2): end of week 8;
- latest permissible finish: end of week 9;
- total float (9 − 8): 1 week.

The term 'float' indicates the amount of leeway available for starting and finishing an activity. The word slack is also used, although far less often and in connection with the times for events (rather than activities). There are different kinds of float, explained in Chapter 7, but for the purposes of this simple example these differences can be ignored.

When all the earliest possible and latest permissible times have been added to the diagram, there will always be at least one chain of events where the earliest and latest times are the same, indicating zero float. These events are critical to the successful achievement of the whole project within its earliest possible time. The route joining these events is not surprisingly termed the 'critical path'. Although all activities may be important, it is the critical activities that must claim priority for resources and for management attention.

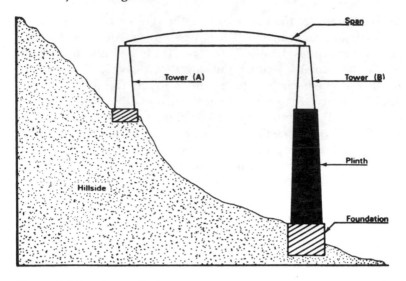

Figure 6.8 Gantry project
This is a sectional view of the hillside showing the outline requirements
of the gantry project.

A slightly more substantial project example will show how
this network notation and calculation works in practice. Figure
6.8 shows a steel gantry that has to be set up on the side of a
steep hill. The requirements of this small project are quite
simple, but one or two points have to be borne in mind about
the order in which the work is to be carried out.

The first step in erecting this gantry must be to mark out the
site and prepare the foundations. Assume that all other
preparations, including the delivery of plant and materials to
site, have already been carried out. Because of the asymmetry
the two tower foundations differ in size, because foundation B
will bear more weight than the other. Tower B has to be placed
on a prefabricated plinth in order to raise it to the same height as
tower A. A final levelling adjustment must be made at base A
after the plinth has been erected for B, and this is to be done by
taking a theodolite sighting from the plinth top. All these special
requirements are reflected in the project network diagram,
shown in Figure 6.9. Dummy 8 to 9 denotes the constraint
imposed on the start of levelling at base A, since if the plinth

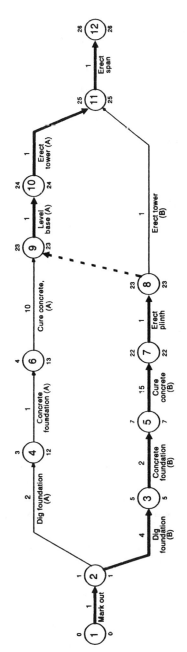

Figure 6.9 Gantry project network

were not erected no sighting could be taken. Estimates for the durations of all the activities, in days, are listed below:

Activity		Duration (estimated in days)
1–2:	Mark out site	1
2–4:	Dig foundation A	2
4–6:	Concrete foundation A	1
6–9:	Cure time, foundation A	10
2–3:	Dig foundation B	4
3–5:	Concrete foundation B	2
5–7:	Cure time, foundation B	15
7–8:	Erect plinth	1
8–9:	Dummy	0
8–11:	Erect tower B	1
9–10:	Level base A	1
10–11:	Erect tower A	1
11–12:	Erect span	1

When all the activity duration estimates have been written on the network, time analysis can begin. Addition of these duration estimates, working from left to right, gives the earliest possible achievement time for each event. Where there are alternative paths, with more than one activity leading into an event, the longer path must determine the earliest completion time possible for the event. This is evident at events 9 and 11. Remember that the earliest possible achievement time for an event is written above the event circle, and this time is also the earliest possible starting time for every activity leading out of the event. At event 12, project completion, the earliest possible time is seen to be 26, which means the end of the 26th working day. If this answer is desired as a calendar date, it is necessary to consult a calendar to take out non-working weekend days and public holidays, a chore made much easier when a computer is used (described in later chapters).

The critical path in the gantry project has been found, as in the earlier example of Figure 6.7, by subtracting activity durations through the network paths from right to left (with the latest permissible event times shown below the event circles).

The critical path in Figure 6.9 is seen to run through events 1, 2, 3, 5, 7, 8, 9, 10, 11 and 12. All activities on this path are critical, and any delay to one of them must delay project completion. There is a float of one day on activity 8 to 11, while activities 2 to 4, 4 to 6 and 6 to 9 all share a float of nine days.

Optimized crash action using critical path analysis (CPA)

Critical path analysis, by identifying critical tasks, helps to ensure that scarce resources can be allocated to best effect. Detailed scheduling of project resources is dealt with in Chapters 7, 8 and 9, but there is one specific application of critical path analysis with respect to resources which can be explained here. The resource in question is money.

Suppose that the predicted duration of 26 days for the gantry project is unacceptable to the project customer, and that the shortest programme possible must be devised (even if this increases the project costs). The project manager can consider several options, starting by re-examining the network logic to see if any short cuts are possible and questioning the original estimates. In this case, no improvement is possible and the project manager is left with the need to consider taking 'crash action' on some or all activities. These actions might include:

- hiring extra labour (which may lead to some inefficiency: doubling a work-force does not always halve the job duration);
- hiring heavier or more plant;
- working overtime on weekdays or at weekends (which will attract overtime payments);
- working all night (again attracting overtime payments plus additional expense in providing floodlighting);
- the use of additives to shorten concrete curing time (again adding cost).

Cost/time forecasts for crashing specific activities have been made according to the table below. Activities which are not capable of being speeded up (regardless of cost) are not included in the table.

Activity		Normal duration (in days)	Crash duration (in days)	Extra cost
Floodlight hire				200
2–4:	Dig foundation A	2	1	150
4–6:	Concrete foundation A	1	0.5	50
6–9:	Fast cure concrete A	10	5	100
2–3:	Dig foundation B	4	2	200
3–5:	Concrete foundation B	2	1	100
5–7:	Fast cure concrete B	15	8	200
10–11:	Erect tower A	1	0.5	80
8–11:	Erect tower B	1	0.5	80
11–12:	Erect span	1	0.5	80
Total cost of crashing all possible activities				———
				£1240

If all these crash times are substituted in the project network (see Figure 6.9) it is found that the total estimated project duration is reduced to 15 days, which now include weekends and holidays.

However, when the network is examined it is found that there is no point in crashing all the activities, because some have float and the original times can be tolerated.

In order to reach the optimum cost-time solution, the first thing to do is to crash all the critical activities. When this is done, it is found that the original critical path becomes shorter than the path through events 2, 4, 6 and 9. These events therefore now lie on a new critical path, and that too must be crashed until it either ceases to be critical or becomes just critical. Taken to its limit, this process can be reiterative, requiring much time and effort for a large network (although using a computer for time analysis removes a lot of the effort needed). True optimization will result in many activities being crashed until they become critical, producing multiple critical paths through the network. The procedure is not often followed to this extreme, but even applying the principle in moderation can save time and avoid wasting money on non-critical activities.

The solution for the gantry project is shown in Figure 6.10, where it is seen that most activities are now critical. It was not

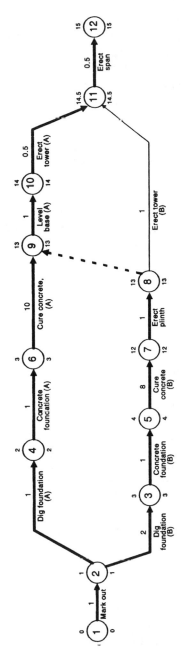

Figure 6.10 Gantry project network after optimized crash action

necessary to crash activities 4 to 6, 6 to 9 or 8 to 11, saving an estimated £230 out of the total possible crash costs of £1 240.

This is a very simple example, chosen to illustrate the principles of this application of critical path analysis. In a more complex network, the outcome could be far less obvious and save a great deal more unnecessary expenditure. But for whatever reason a network is drawn, attention and subsequent control usually concentrates along the critical activities. No time is lost worrying about occurrences or situations which the network demonstrates to be inconsequential. Any contingency which arises can be checked against the network to establish its relevance. Only those factors which deserve management attention need be reported to executives higher up the line organization. This is, of course, a practical case of management by exception.

PERT

PERT (programme evaluation and review technique) is very similar to critical path analysis, and the two methods are often confused with each other. Construction of the arrow diagrams is carried out in the same way for both methods, the main difference only becoming apparent when the time comes to estimate activity durations.

For PERT, three time estimates are required for every activity. These are:

t_o = the most *optimistic duration*
t_m = the most *likely* duration
t_p = the most *pessimistic* duration

From these quantities a probable duration is calculated for each activity, on a statistical basis, assuming that the errors will fall within a normal distribution curve.

$$t_e = \frac{t_o + 4t_m + t_p}{6} \text{ (where } t_e \text{ is the } expected \text{ time)}$$

This calculation is repeated on all activities in the network and used to predict the probability of completing the project within the scheduled time. When more than about a hundred separate activities are included in the network a computer becomes necessary to remove the drudgery from the calculations and enable the results to be made available in time for appropriate action to be taken. A computer is particularly needed when the time comes to make changes to networks or update them in line with actual progress.

Some authorities do not accept that a normal distribution curve is suitable for predicting the spread of estimating errors. It is well known that estimates are frequently too optimistic rather than too pessimistic. Allowance for this tendency can be made by skewing the distribution curve deliberately, using the following variation of the formula:

$$t_e = \frac{t_o + 3t_m + 2t_p}{6}$$

Whichever statistical basis is chosen, PERT will produce a critical path in the same way as the CPA method. The emphasis has changed slightly however, from cost-time analysis and concentration on the critical path to a more statistical approach, predicting the probability of completing the project by a given date. Although many users refer to their networks as PERT, the term is often misapplied because it is the more straightforward critical path analysis method, with its single duration estimates, that is most widely used. Possibly, with estimating accuracies leaving much to be desired and with contingencies popping up all over the place, the PERT approach is just a shade too academic and removed from practicability when compared with CPA. However, please see the section on risk analysis in Chapter 9.

Arrow diagram construction

Drawing a project network

When a project network is drawn, it has to be assumed that the person who actually commits all the working proposals to paper is sufficiently competent to do so.

The essential elements of network analysis are not difficult to learn and can be taught in a few hours. Complete mastery of the art of network logic takes a little longer and much practice. There are several pitfalls which can rob a potential network expert of accuracy and success. Although the basic logic uses only a few simple symbols, it is not always easy to assemble them in a way that avoids unintentional mistakes, to show a practicable way of completing the project. To some extent the degree of success depends on the aptitude of the individual. Getting the logic right can be compared with solving recreational puzzles, and some people see the challenge of drawing networks in that light. Networking can, indeed, be fun.

Give three different project planners the same data for a project and they would probably produce three different networks, each signifying each planner's personal vision of how the work should logically proceed. This does not necessarily mean that any of the networks is wrong. Each proposed method of working could be valid and lead to a satisfactory result. But it is, of course, important to avoid actual logical errors and task omissions as far as possible.

The number of people involved in drawing a network depends to some extent on the size of the project. At the smallest end, individuals will draw networks simply to plan and control their own activities. For larger projects it is customary, and desirable, to have at least one responsible person on hand who can speak for each department or organization involved. The individuals chosen should be of sufficient seniority to enable them to commit their departments to the plan, and to any specific methods of working or estimates upon which it depends.

The network should be drawn rapidly, as large as possible and in full view of all those who are contributing information. One early US defence project network was drawn in chalk on a hangar floor and photographed from an overhead gantry! For most projects a more down to earth method is to use a blackboard or whiteboard, or to hang or spread a roll of paper, either on a wall or on a table top around which everyone can gather. A useful kit comprises:

- a soft pencil;
- pencil sharpener;

- soft eraser;
- a long ruler, with a hole at one end for use as an event circle template.

Although initial networks can be drawn freehand, a ruler and template help to keep it neat and save it from sprawling over too large an area of paper (which can prove awkward when the paper runs out as the later stages are reached). Although the network can be taken away for tracing after the meeting, if it is produced without sufficient care in the first place it will soon become unreadable and vague because of all the erasures, corrections and additions during the meeting. It is as well to start the diagram using straight lines and with sensible spacing between events.

The person entrusted with the task of wielding the pencil for this initial network should be as skilled a network analyst as possible. The task of this expert will be made easier if everyone present has received some training and is able to grasp the meaning of the arrow diagram as it grows. The skilled analyst should be allowed to control the meeting (regardless of seniority). He will ensure that the logic develops along the right lines, asking check questions from time to time in order to prove the logic and avoid errors. Check questions can take the form:

- 'Isn't it necessary to check these drawings before issue?'
- 'Is customer approval needed before work can start on this activity?'
- 'Does this steelwork need priming or any other treatment before erection?'
- 'Can this tower really be erected as soon as the concrete base has been poured, or will it ooze slowly downwards into the wet cement? (There were two such mistakes in the gantry project logic – Figure 6.9 – in earlier editions of this book.)
- 'Does the start of this activity really depend on all these incoming activities?

If a diagram emerges from the initial meeting bearing the scars of several erasures and changes, this is a sign that active thought has gone into the logic. The analyst must never be too lazy or reluctant to erase and redraw parts of the network as the combined minds of the meeting agree on the correct logic.

It is possible to introduce logical errors unwittingly as the plan builds up. An example is shown in Figure 6.11, which is a classic trap well known to all experts. Imagine that a construction firm is drawing up an arrow diagram for the planning and control of a new building project. Figure 6.11(a) shows a fragment of this network at an early stage during the planning meeting. Notice that, rather obviously, the roof frame cannot be started until the brick walls have been erected and the necessary timber purchased. So far, so good. Now suppose that the next activity to be added is 'Point brickwork'. This can start as soon as the walls have been built, after event 22. The trap is to draw the logic as shown in Figure 6.11(b), simply by drawing the new activity as emerging from event 22. In fact, the correct logic is shown in Figure 6.11(c), since it is not necessary to buy the roof timbers before starting pointing. The planner must always question the logic when there are multiple input activities and output activities at an event, as in Figure 6.11(d).

Level of detail

A question often facing planners new to the art is 'How much detail should we show in the network?' In other words which activities should be included in the network and which should be left out or combined with others. To some extent this depends on the size of the project, the project duration, the size of the duration units chosen, the amount of detailed knowledge available and the purpose of the network. A project network containing 20 000 activities might sound very impressive, but smaller networks are more manageable. Also, very big single project networks can prove tiresome (to say the least) when they have to be considered along with plans for other projects in multi-project scheduling systems (see Chapters 8 and 9).

Some companies like to draw outline networks of the project, perhaps containing only 100 or 150 activities in fairly coarse detail. These are then used as higher level management controls, but they must be backed up later by more detailed networks produced for the various project departments or participants, and all these networks must be tied together in some way so that their corresponding events are scheduled on the same dates and have the same float. This correlation can be

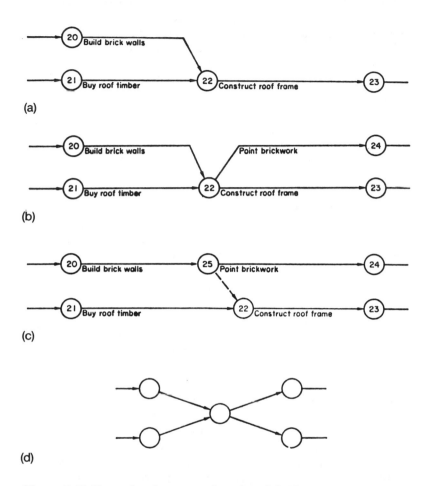

Figure 6.11 Example of an error in network logic
The network shown here, in (a), (b) and (c) is an extract from a larger network. At (a), the diagram is under construction, while at (b) another activity has been added. But this addition has introduced an error into the logic. Although the pointing of the brickwork does depend on the brick walls being built, it is not dependent at all on the purchase of timber for the roof. The corrected version is shown at (c). In fact, whenever a pattern is encountered like that shown at (d), where multiple activities enter and leave an event, the planner must ask himself 'Do all emerging activities depend on all preceding activities?' If they do not, then the logic must be corrected by the addition of dummies and isolating events.

achieved by designating all the detailed networks as sub-networks and by identifying events common to them and the master network as interface events. The procedure is complex however, and needs the use of a computer system.

There are several guidelines that can be given here which apply generally to the level of detail which should be shown in project network diagrams.

It is probably well to avoid showing jobs as separate activities if their durations amount only to a very small fraction of the expected overall timescale, especially if they do not require resources. Of course these activities cannot be ignored, but they can be included in the network as parts of other activities. An example might be the preparation of a group of drawings, where a single activity 'detail and check subassembly X' would be shown rather than including a set of separate activities for detailing every drawing, and another set of activities for checking them. In a short project lasting only a few weeks (for example the overhaul and maintenance of an electricity generating station during a planned period of shutdown) it would be reasonable to use network planning units of days or fractions of days, and to include activities lasting only half a day. For projects lasting several years the planning units might be weeks, with very few activities included that have less than one week's duration. As with all rules, however, there are exceptions. Some activities with very short durations may be so important that they must be included (for example, an activity for obtaining authorization or approval before subsequent work can proceed).

One way of looking at planning detail is to consider the network events rather than the activities. It can be argued sensibly that a network should include every event where an item of project work proceeds from one department or organization to another – in other words where the responsibility for work changes. This sets practical guidelines for the choice of events (and therefore for the activities which join them). Events highlighted by this approach typically include:

1   Work authorizations and formal approvals to proceed (including design approvals and financial authorizations from the customer).
2   Drawings passed over for checking (this usually means sets

of drawings for subassemblies or work packages rather than going down to the level of individual drawings).

3 Drawing releases for manufacturing or construction (again as sets rather than individual drawings).

4 The start of purchasing activity for each subassembly or work package, signified by the engineering issue of a bill of material, purchase specification or advance release of information for items which are known to have long delivery times.

5 Following on from 4, the placing of purchase orders with a supplier or subcontractor (again on the level of work packages and subassemblies rather than small individual purchases).

6 Material deliveries, meaning the event when the last item needed to complete the materials for a particular work package (or for a single item of capital equipment) is received on site or at the factory. For international projects, this delivery point may be to a ship or to an aircraft, with subsequent transit time shown as a separate, consecutive activity (when the change of responsibility rule applies, because an event is created when responsibility transfers to the carrier or freight forwarding agent).

7 The starts and completions of manufacturing stages (in large projects usually only looking at the entries into and exits from production control responsibility, and again considering work packages or subassemblies rather than individual small parts).

8 The starts and finishes of construction subcontracts, and important intermediate events in such subcontracts (see milestones below).

9 Handover events for completed work packages. This would include handing over the finished project, or major parts of it, to the customer but would also ensure that associated items such as maintenance and operating manuals were itemized in the network plan.

Milestone events

Bearing in mind that the purpose of the network diagram is to produce a schedule from which project progress is to be initiated and controlled, it is important to provide intermediate points throughout the network and any resulting schedules that can be used as benchmarks. This is done by choosing events that are considered to be particularly relevant and designating these as 'key events' or 'milestones'. Computer programs for project scheduling allow reports to be printed out relating to such milestone events, and these greatly help the assessment of progress against time and costs and are of value in reporting to higher management and to the customer.

Estimating activity durations

Either as the network is drawn, or as soon after as possible, it is necessary for all activity durations to be estimated. These estimates are for elapsed time and do not necessarily relate directly to cost estimates.

What units of duration should be used? This can depend on the duration of the project. It may be found convenient to use weeks. Days are often used. However, a very useful unit for general purposes is the half day (0.5), since many projects are conducted on a 5-day week basis and a week then becomes 10 units. Even when the duration extends to several years, the use of half or one day units is no problem when a computer is used for subsequent calculations. Resolution of estimates to better than 0.5 day duration is not usually required. Of course, once a unit of duration has been decided, the same unit must be used throughout the network.

The usual procedure is for the estimates to be added as the network is drawn. Another approach is for the network sketch to be carried from one department to another, each responsible manager adding estimates to the activities for which he is responsible.

Some people recommend that activities should be estimated at random rather than in a left-to-right sequence. They argue that estimating sequentially along network paths could lead to early awareness of possible critical activities or programme overruns. In other words, the impartiality of the estimators might become impaired, the estimates being influenced by project demands rather than by the true nature of each job and the time properly required to complete it.

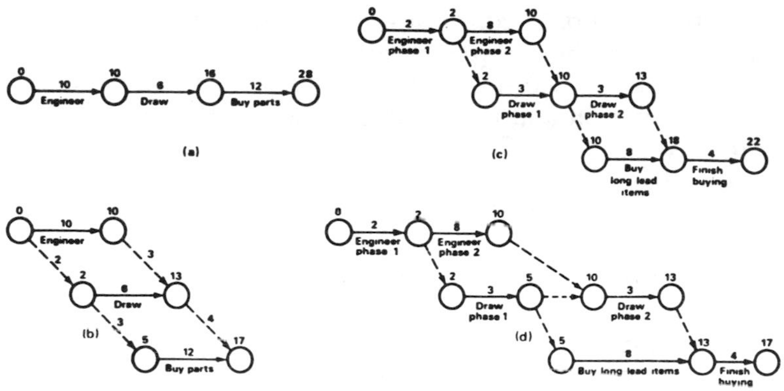

Figure 6.12 Ladder networks

Any temptation to assume that overtime will be worked should be avoided, and estimated durations should not be made with overtime working in view. While overtime can often be used to shorten the elapsed time of an activity, it should always be regarded as a reserve resource, to be held back for use as a corrective action against unforeseen contingencies.

Is the timescale shown too long?

The logic of a network must always be checked to ensure that it accurately reflects the most practicable and efficient way of working. It is often found, for example, that the network will at first predict a timescale that is longer than necessary because it shows constraints that do not really exist. Constraints must always be questioned to ensure that the network does show the practical working sequence. This is especially important when the planner is told that the timescale predicted by a network is too long, and that something must be done to shorten the plan. Of course crash actions can be considered, but the network logic must always be examined first.

It is often found that the start of an activity depends not on its immediate predecessor being completely finished (as depicted by the network), but only on the predecessor having been partly completed. An example is illustrated in Figure 6.12, where a small extract from a larger network is shown. Three activities are involved: design engineering, drawing and the procurement of materials. Figure 6.12(a) shows the network as it was originally drawn, with these three activities following each other and bound by rigid start-to-finish constraints. The activities lay on the critical path and contributed 28 weeks to the total project duration.

It would have been possible to shorten the duration of these activities by employing more people or by taking special procurement steps, but only at some additional cost. Is such expenditure necessary? Re-examination of the network uncovers a fundamental flaw in the logic. Does all the engineering have to be finished before drawing can start? Of course not. The activities can be allowed to overlap to some extent. Similarly, some of the long-lead purchase items can be ordered in advance, as soon as the designers can specify them: it is not necessary to wait for the final parts lists.

In Figure 6.12(b) an attempt has been made to indicate the permissible overlap of activities by redrawing the network. The start and finish constraints have now been relaxed by inserting dummies, each of which has been given a duration value. Drawing can start two weeks after the start of engineering, but cannot be finished until three weeks after the completion of engineering. Purchasing can begin three weeks after the start of drawing, at which time it is estimated that the long-lead items can be specified. Some purchased items cannot be ordered, however, until the parts list is issued along with the general assembly drawing, and delivery of these late bought-out items is not expected until four weeks after the completion of drawing. Although no crash action has been planned, the timescale for this small part of the main network has been reduced from 28 to 17 weeks – almost halved.

Overlapped activities, where one is dependent upon a flow of work or information from the other, are called 'ladder activities'. Strictly speaking the logic of Figure 6.11(b) would not stand up to close scrutiny. It might be assumed that drawing could start two weeks after week 0 even if no engineering had been carried out, and that procurement could start at week 5, whatever the state of engineering or drawing. Clearly this was not the planner's intention when the network was drawn, and alternative networks might be suggested.

In Figure 6.12(c) the same sequence of activities has been

depicted but, by splitting engineering into two phases and doing the same with drawing, the true relationships and constraints are more clearly defined. But a different, and wrong, answer has been obtained this time. The mistake lies in the start restriction imposed on buying, which is in fact dependent not on the completion of engineering but only upon phase 1 of the drawing. The true picture is obtained by drawing the network in Figure 6.12(d), where all the dummies are correctly placed.

By checking and correcting or rearranging the logic, therefore, it is possible to achieve realistic improvements in the timescale at no additional cost to the project. As illustrated in Figure 6.11, however, care must be taken to set out the correct logic, otherwise wrong answers will result. In practice, there is a convention which allows the simpler ladder network of Figure 6.12(b) to mean what was intended: this is sometimes denoted by drawing squares instead of circles for the end events.

If a project network diagram has to show many cases of overlapping activities, the use of ladder networks becomes tedious and the diagrams can become very complicated. In these circumstances the planner should consider using the precedence system, which is outlined later in this chapter.

Using dummies to improve clarity

Dummies can often be added to a network in order to clarify or extend its visual presentation. One example is shown in Figure 6.13, where the final stages of a project network are illustrated. In Figure 6.13(a) the earliest and latest completion times cannot be shown for each of the inspection activities because they all share the same end event. By inserting dummies, as in Figure 6.13(b), the separate end events can be drawn in and all their earliest and latest times can be written in. Now suppose that this project has reached its final kitting stage, and that a print of the network diagram is being used as a direct aid to progressing the work. In Figure 6.13(a), any one of the inspection activities might be holding up the final kitting stage, but it is not easy to see which. If dummies have been added, end events can be coloured in or crossed off as they are achieved. Uncompleted activities therefore stand out.

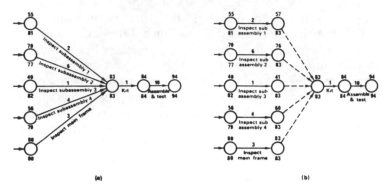

(a)   (b)

Figure 6.13 Using dummies to extend displayed information
In diagram (b) the activities preceding the kitting activity can be analysed
individually because their end events have been separated by the
addition of dummies. This argument is only relevant to small networks
which are manually calculated. Larger networks, needing the use of a
computer, should be drawn without the additional dummies, which
would only have the effect of complicating the input data and taking up
unnecessary computer memory, with no advantage in the output
reports.

These comments do not apply to networks processed by
computer, because the printouts will display the information
needed and unnecessary dummies only add to processing time
and cost.

Early consideration of resource constraints

Nothing much has been said so far about possible scarcity of
resources and the additional constraints that such problems
might impose on the network logic or estimated activity
durations. Consider, for example, the most simple case of a
resource constraint, where one particular individual is going to
have to perform several network activities. Assume that this
person cannot perform two activities at the same time. The
planner, knowing this, might be tempted to add dummies to the
network to indicate this constraint and prevent any two of these
activities from being planned as overlapping. But if all these
activities lie on different paths in a complex network where

should the dummies be placed? Before time analysis has been done the planner cannot know in which order all these jobs should be performed.

Similar worries about resources might attach to other activities where the resource requirements are more complex, when several can be allowed to run in parallel or overlap provided that the total resources needed do not exceed the total available.

Fortunately there is a simple solution to the problem of all such resource constraints. Ignore them! The purpose of drawing the initial network is to establish the logic of the most desirable work pattern (assuming no resource constraints). Time analysis follows to establish the amount of float available, which effectively allots priority values to all activities. All of this data provides a sound basis for subsequent resource scheduling, which is a quite separate procedure (described in following chapters).

Planning and scheduling has to be carried forward one step at a time, and consideration of resource constraints is a step that is not taken when the first network is drawn. However, the planner must use common sense in this respect. Suppose that an activity requiring skilled fitters has been estimated to require 150 man-hours, and that several people could work on the task if required without getting in each other's way. The duration for this activity would therefore depend on the number of people assigned:

- 1 fitter for 20 days;
- 2 fitters for 10 days;
- 3 fitters for 7 days;
- 4 fitters for 5 days;
- and so on.

The correct approach for the planner is to ask the manager of the department responsible (or his delegate) to say how many fitters would be best for this task, and write the corresponding duration on the network. The possible demands of other activities on these fitters are disregarded at this stage. However, if the company only employs two suitable fitters in total, the planner would be stupid to schedule more than two for this or any other activity. This is where common sense comes in.

A case for drawing networks from right to left

The example which follows illustrates how a skilled and experienced network planner can control and lead a meeting to extract a workable plan from a seemingly impossible situation. The example also points to a circumstance where it can be better to draw the network from right to left, from finish to start.

A project had been in progress for several months. Its purpose of was to develop a diverse range of products and have at least one representative prototype from each range made and presented on a stand at a national trade exhibition. The end date for the project was, therefore, fixed (and not very far off). But there had been no coordinated planning. Indeed there was no plan at all (let alone a network diagram). The situation had become completely out of control and the divisional manager called in an experienced network planner, arranged a meeting of all the managers responsible for the project, and put the network planner in charge.

The planner found that no one could say what the current state of progress was. There were so many loose ends that no one knew where to start making a plan. The planner asked everyone to concentrate on the end event, with the stand ready for the opening day of the exhibition. This event was duly drawn at the right-hand end of the network sheet. 'What', the planner asked, 'is the last thing to be done before the exhibition opens?' Slowly the answer came, 'Clean up the stand'. This activity was drawn in front of the final event. And so the questioning continued, going into more and more detail. The confidence of the members at the meeting grew, and so did the network – from right to left. Duration estimates were added as it went along.

The network continued to expand in a series of logical steps, working through each product to be exhibited in turn, until the diagram finally terminated at the left-hand side in a number of start events. Each start event represented, in fact, a particular aspect of the current state of progress or related to some activity that had not been thought of previously. Indeed, if the network had not been drawn backwards, the thought processes of the meeting would not have been directed to these forgotten activities, and they would otherwise have been remembered too late or not at all. At last, everyone knew where they had got to and what remained to be done. And there was now a detailed plan from which to control the remaining work.

By adapting the planning tactics to suit the particular project case order was retrieved from chaos. The exhibition did open on time, with all the products on the stand.

Precedence networks

Network analysis, and particularly the use of arrow diagrams, gave planners a valuable new tool with which they could express the logic of a proposed work plan for their projects. Coupled with the concept of the critical path and the use of float to determine priorities, these were major steps forward. But both the PERT and CPA systems still had their drawbacks. Not least of these was the difficulty experienced by early network analysts in trying to persuade their managers and others to accept the new and unfamiliar notation. Bar charts were still preferred. Networks could not (and still cannot) be used for resource scheduling without the use of computer systems: in this respect the earlier bar charts were superior and easier to understand, particularly for small projects. Moreover, although arrow diagrams could show many complex relationships between different activities and events, there were limitations – particularly where it was desired to show activities where starts and finishes could be allowed to overlap (see Figure 6.12).

The precedence system of notation is preferred by some because:

- The logic diagrams more closely resemble engineering flow diagrams or block schematic diagrams and are therefore claimed to be more easily understood by engineers who have had no network training
- Precedence notation allows clear illustration of activities whose starts and finishes do not coincide directly with the starts and finishes of their immediate predecessors and successors. In other words, precedence networks can show activities which should be allowed to overlap each other or which, conversely, must be separated by a time delay.

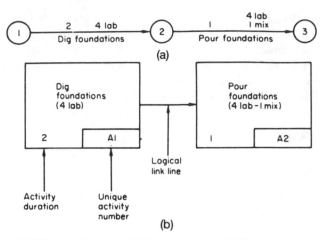

(a)

(b)

Figure 6.14 Precedence notation: normal activity constraint
Here, a small part of an arrow diagram has been reproduced at (a), and
its precedence counterpart is shown at (b). The connecting arrow in the
precedence version is assumed to have no duration where none has
been given. It is possible, however, to plan for delays that must occur
between activities by adding a duration to the linking arrow. This could
also be achieved in arrow notation by inserting a dummy between the
two activities and assigning a duration to it.

The resource scheduling problem still remains: as with arrow
diagrams, precedence networks cannot be used to schedule
resources without either conversion into bar chart form or the
use of a computer.

The most noticeable characteristic of precedence diagrams is
that the activities (not the events) are drawn at the nodes, and
rectangles (rather than circles) are used. The arrows no longer
represent activity or work, but are simply lines of constraint or
logical links (which may be given time values). The precedence
system is therefore known as an activity-on-node method. The
basic notation and relationships are illustrated in Figures 6.14
and 6.15.

A simple precedence logic diagram is shown in Figure 6.16.
Once duration estimates have been added to all the activities
and to some of the logical links, time analysis can be carried out
to determine float and find the critical path. Calculations are
similar to those for CPA, but more involved owing to the
various complex constraints.

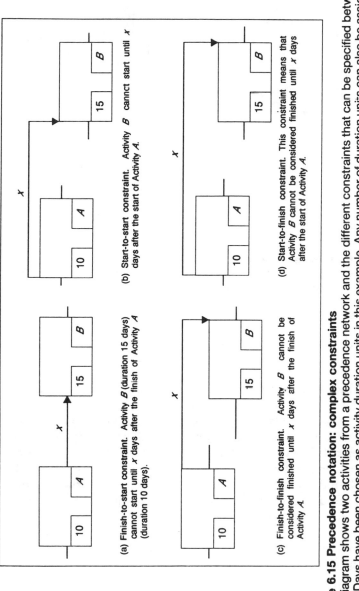

(a) Finish-to-start constraint. Activity B (duration 15 days) cannot start until x days after the finish of Activity A (duration 10 days).

(b) Start-to-start constraint. Activity B cannot start until x days after the start of Activity A.

(c) Finish-to-finish constraint. Activity B cannot be considered finished until x days after the finish of Activity A.

(d) Start-to-finish constraint. This constraint means that Activity B cannot be considered finished until x days after the start of Activity A.

Figure 6.15 Precedence notation: complex constraints

This diagram shows two activities from a precedence network and the different constraints that can be specified between them. Days have been chosen as activity duration units in this example. Any number of duration units can also be assigned to constraints, although zero duration is usual for the most common case at (a), equivalent to two consecutive activities in an arrow network. With the little-used Roy method, also known as the method of potentials (MPM), negative values may be assigned to constraints. Precedence networks are favoured by many computer software houses, but some programs may not be able to deal with all four types of constraint.

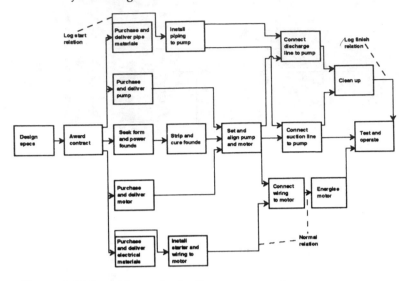

Figure 6.16 Precedence logic diagram example
Here is a simple construction network in precedence notation. Estimates
and resource requirements have not been added at this stage, but the
diagram does include some of the complex constraints that are not easy
to express with CPA or PERT networks.

Precedence versus activity on arrow

Difficulties of the more complex time analysis calculations for
precedence networks disappear when a computer is used. It is
claimed that precedence networks can be faster and cheaper to
run on computers when compared with their activity-on-arrow
counterparts. Generally there are no dummies in precedence
notation, and networks tend to contain fewer total activities.
This should mean less input to the computer, although the
amount of data is greater for each activity owing to the complex
constraints.

Some computer programs are able to accept and process data
allowing overlapping or lagging consecutive activities in
activity-on-arrow networks, without the need to use precedence
notation.

One apparent disadvantage of the precedence system is
illustrated in Figure 6.17. Whenever a significant number of

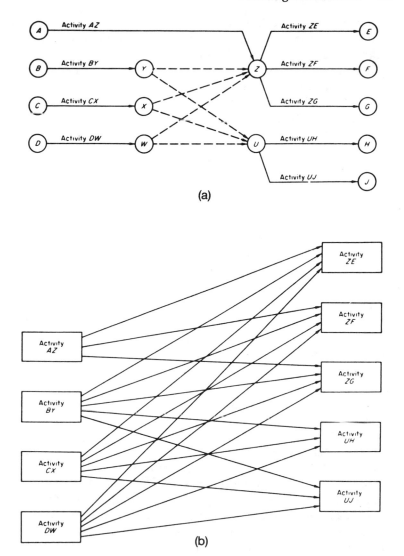

(a)

(b)

Figure 6.17 One disadvantage of precedence notation
Precedence networks can show complex relationships between activities very clearly (Figure 6.16) but there are occasions when arrow diagrams are easier to follow. Here is one example. Both networks show the same logic, but the arrow version at (a) is less complicated than its precedence counterpart (b).

activities have to be linked independently to several following activities, the use of dummies in arrow diagrams produces a clearer diagram than the precedence counterpart.

The author is not alone in preferring activity-on-arrow networks and has used them successfully over a wide range of big and small projects. But many others will disagree, and people use arrow diagrams or precedence networks largely as a matter of personal choice. Precedence networks are tending to supplant arrow networks, and some of the more recently introduced computer software packages will only accept precedence networks. Perhaps the best advice is that, if a planning method is in use and producing good results, then stick to it.

Network analysis as a basic tool

Network analysis demands the application of sound common sense and very little else. When the techniques were first introduced they were regarded with suspicion by many and tended to be protected by an elitist mystique. This was unfortunate and unnecessary. The basic elements of network notation are simple. Although a project network can contain thousands of activities, all the essential notation is demonstrated by the simple example (containing only about a dozen activities) that was shown in Figure 6.9.

No special degree of intelligence is required. Any individual endowed with a fair share of mental aptitude could be expected to acquire at least a working knowledge of logic diagram preparation in just one day. The method of teaching is, however, all important; the premature introduction of all but the basic bones of the system must be avoided. It is also sensible to start by practising, to gain competence in using the notation, getting the logic right, and time analysing small networks mentally. All of this should take place before going on to the use of a computer and more advanced procedures such as cost and resource scheduling.

Those who choose to go through project life in ignorance of the finer points of networking language may find themselves at some disadvantage if called upon to discuss network problems with their more erudite colleagues. Every profession has its own technical language, and without it communication must suffer. Nevertheless, the actual application of critical path techniques can be conducted very effectively, provided that the logical concepts are properly appreciated. Basic network analysis is a simple but valuable management tool which should never be regarded as a complicated and advanced technique reserved for the specialist.

There is always a danger of trying to be too clever by dotting every i and crossing every t. Planning is not a precise technique and networks will be more effective if they can be kept as simple as possible, consistent with incorporation of all the essential activities and constraints. It is very probable that attempts to improve existing techniques arise not because the techniques themselves are inadequate, but because the planners are not able to exploit them properly.

The benefits to be derived from drawing a network are in themselves often worthwhile, even if no duration estimates are made, no time analysis takes place, and the network is not used to control subsequent progress. Networking encourages a logical progression of thinking and planning. In fact a network meeting can be regarded as a productive form of brainstorming. Not only does the notation allow expression of all interactivity dependencies and relationships, but there is also the important possibility that activities may be brought to light that might otherwise have been excluded from schedules, estimates and (most important) pricing.

It would be unreasonable and unrealistic to expect the project manager to carry out network planning (or any other kind of planning) in isolation. He must be able to count on the support and cooperation of members from every department in the organization. This applies not only to the initial planning session, but also to all subsequent discussions and progress monitoring. This support will only be possible if suitable training has been provided. Most important of all, encouragement and support must come from the top, from the company's senior management. Once the idea of project planning and control by networks has been accepted throughout the organization, most of the battle will have been won.

Further reading

British Standards Institution, Milton Keynes:
   BS 4335: 1987 *Glossary of terms used in project network techniques.*
   BS 6046: *Use of network techniques in project management*
      Part 1: 1984: *Guide to the use of management, planning, review and reporting procedures;*
      Part 2: 1992: *Guide to the use of graphical and estimating techniques;*
      Part 3: 1992: *Guide to the use of computers;*
      Part 4: 1992: *Guide to resource analysis and cost control.*

Lester, A. (1991), *Project Planning and Control* (2nd edn), Oxford, Butterworth-Heinemann.

Lockyer, K. (1984), *Critical Path Analysis and Other Project Network Techniques* (4th edn), London: Pitman.

7
Scheduling resources

A network cannot normally be used by itself to demonstrate the volume of resources needed at any given point in project time. In fact, when the network is drawn no considered account can be taken of the resources which will be available. The start of each activity is usually assumed to be dependent only upon the completion of its preceding activities, and not on the availability of resources at the right time.

Naturally if a planning team knows that, for the sake of argument, a total of four pipefitters are employed in their project organization, they would not estimate the duration of any pipefitting activity at a level which demands the employment of more than four pipefitters on that activity. However, the chance of other pipefitting activities occurring elsewhere in the network at the same time is impossible to deal with. In any case, the timing of those other activities cannot be known before time analysis has been carried out. In general, therefore, network logic shows only those constraints between activities that are related to the actual work or working methods. Thus, although a network might be fine in logical theory, it is unlikely that all activities can be scheduled to start at their earliest possible times, and it might be impossible to carry out the project in the time indicated by the critical path owing to the additional constraints imposed by insufficient resources.

This is far from saying that work spent in preparing a critical path network has been wasted, even if resource limitations do cause the earliest possible start times of some activities to appear impracticable. Network construction and time analysis must be seen as the first essential step in the wider process of scheduling resources. Resource constraints are treated as a separate issue, requiring at least one more stage of scheduling after the determination of float and location of the critical path.

The results of time analysis are used to allocate priorities to activities. When different activities compete simultaneously for the same limited resources, priority rules can be applied so that the resources are allocated where they are most needed. Usually it is the activity with least remaining float that gets the highest priority. Management decisions can be based on these data, for example by planning to employ additional subcontract labour over a difficult period. All of these points will be discussed in greater detail later in this chapter.

Resource considerations can, for the purposes of scheduling, be extended to include not only labour, but also other resources such as bulk materials and money. The treatment of these other resources is generally similar to manpower scheduling, except that the names and units of quantity will change. There is, however, a section on cash flow scheduling at the end of the chapter because this introduces different concepts and requires its own methods.

Accommodation is one resource that may be impossible to schedule using the methods described in this chapter, because the shapes of floor areas or volumes are usually important and it is not possible to deal with these solely in terms of resource units. In these circumstances, the manager responsible for accommodation must resort to some other form of modelling, on paper, with a physical scale model, or using a computer-aided design system.

Case study: garage project

The principles of resource scheduling and some of the problems can be introduced by considering a very simple construction project. Clerical methods (as opposed to the use of a computer) are described first, because these provide a very useful introduction to the more advanced methods covered in Chapters 8 and 9.

A small firm of builders has been commissioned to erect a detached garage. The building is to be constructed of brick, with a corrugated sheet roof. This roof will incorporate some transparent sheets as roof lights instead of windows. The doors are to be timber framed and hung on strap hinges. No heavy lifting is involved in this project and no activity needs more than two people.

Figure 7.1 shows the network diagram for this project. All the activity durations have been estimated with a small labour force in mind, consisting of one skilled all-round craftsman, aided wherever necessary by a labourer. No consideration has been given in this network to the simultaneous occurrence of activities and the corresponding implications for manpower resource requirements. This plan also assumes that all necessary materials and plant will be on site when needed. Under these conditions, assuming that all the earliest possible dates can be achieved and ignoring any possible limitation of resources, the whole project should take 24 working days. But the network does not indicate how many people must be employed to achieve this result.

The first step in determining the labour requirements is to convert the network diagram into a bar chart. Figure 7.2 shows the result for this project. The scale used for the horizontal axis in the full-sized original version of this chart was 6 mm (¼ inch) to each working day. Every horizontal strip represents each activity on the network, with its length scaled according to the activity's estimated duration. Please picture this chart as having been set up on a wallboard, using strips that plug in, or are otherwise attached so that they can be moved easily to adjust the schedule if required.

The strips are coded using colours or patterns to indicate the type of labour needed. In this example, solid black has been used to represent a skilled worker and cross hatching indicates a labourer. Each strip represents one person. If more than one person is needed for a job, the required number of strips are laid alongside each other.

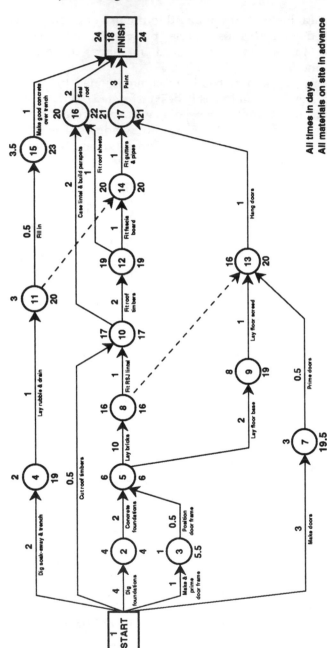

Figure 7.1 Garage construction network

Although this network indicates a project duration of 24 days, resource limitations could delay some activities and prolong the project. Also the network durations are all expressed in working days, so that interruptions caused by weekend breaks must extend the timescale to completion.

All times in days
All materials on site in advance

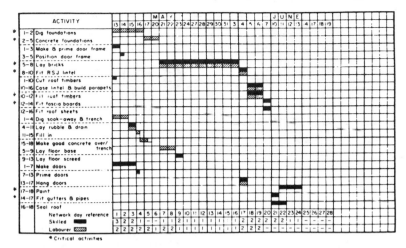

Figure 7.2 Garage project resource schedule before levelling
This schedule corresponds to the network of Figure 7.1, except that the plan has been converted to calendar dates, with allowances for weekend breaks. Each activity has been set to start at its earliest possible time as indicated by the network constraints, without any consideration of resource limitations. The figures at the foot of each column show the resulting unevenness of resource usage. This simple approach is termed resource aggregation and is not true resource scheduling.

The timescale has been arranged with weekend breaks taken into account. With five-day week working, Saturdays and Sundays are not shown. Public holidays have been ignored in this example but in real life they should obviously be taken out of the schedule too. The effect of taking out the weekends has been to extend the 24 *working* days of the network to a total project schedule of 32 *calendar* days.

If there are vital reasons for finishing this project on time, the contractor might decide that Saturday mornings (not shown on the chart) can be considered as time to be held in reserve against unforeseen contingencies. Similarly, evening overtime is another possible reserve resource.

Each activity on the bar chart is shown starting at its earliest possible time (as indicated by time analysis of the network). No thought has yet been given to the resources needed and it is now time to start putting that right. The resources needed each day to carry out this simple plan are easy to calculate. It is only

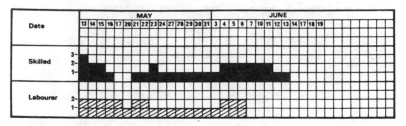

Figure 7.3 Garage project resource histogram before levelling
The histogram emphasizes the uneven resources which would be needed to achieve the schedule shown in Figure 7.2.

necessary to add up the number of times a strip of each colour occurs in each day's column. Where a half-day job is shown, this can be regarded as one person of the particular resource type for the day, but if two half-day jobs occur on the same day they can be 'paired', so that the requirement is still shown as one person for the day.

The daily resource usage totals are entered at the foot of the chart (as shown in Figure 7.2), but these are demonstrated more clearly in the histogram of Figure 7.3. The result is shown to be, to say the least, unsatisfactory. On some days the work-force is expected to be idle; on other days three people will be needed. The workload is unbalanced, showing too many peaks and troughs for profitable comfort. Either the contractor has to be able and willing to switch people around at short notice between different sites, or the unprofitable alternative of paying for idle time must be tolerated.

The reason for this uneven schedule is that the planner has shown every job starting at its earliest possible date, regardless of need or priority. Such a plan is known as 'resource aggregated' and it has little practical use except as a step towards obtaining a more practicable 'resource allocated' schedule. The important principle is that many of the jobs have been shown from time analysis to have float, and the starts of these activities can be therefore be delayed to smoothe the workload without pushing out the end date. Using the adjustable wallchart, therefore, it should be possible to reschedule non-critical activities to remove some or all of the unwanted workload peaks.

The approach to resource scheduling (otherwise called resource allocation or resource smoothing) must be governed by the most significant planning objectives (priority rules). These can be summarized as follows:

1 *Resource limited*: to produce a plan in which the known levels of available resources are never exceeded. This may mean accepting a project end date that is later than the earliest possible date predicted from network time analysis. In other words, working within available resource levels is seen as the first scheduling objective, with second place given to priority for completing the project in the shortest possible time.

2 *Time limited*: to assume that unlimited resources can be made available, using temporary or subcontract labour if necessary, so that the project can be scheduled with completion by a specified date. This date is often the earliest possible completion date indicated by network time analysis, but it might be some later date. The procedure followed is to attempt scheduling the project with the normally available resources, but to call on the additional resources (known among planners as 'threshold resources') when all the normal resources are busy. Even though resource constraints are seen as having secondary priority, the planner should still aim at a smooth resource usage pattern, avoiding unnecessary interruptions, peaks and troughs in the workload patterns of both the normal and the threshold resources.

3 *Compromise*: to adopt a compromise solution, agreeing to limited use of extra (threshold) resources in an attempt to satisfy the completion date requirement, but being prepared to let the project end date be extended if these limited additional resources prove to be insufficient.

To take first the resource-limited situation, suppose that the building firm engaged on the garage project is a very tiny outfit, comprising the not unusual father and son team. The father, no longer capable of sustained heavy work, is nevertheless a good all-round craftsman with long experience. The son, on the other hand, can best be described as a strong, willing lad, sound in

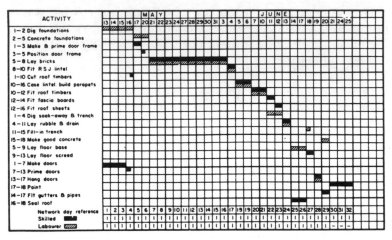

Figure 7.4 Garage project schedule levelled to use available resources
The garage can now be built with the limited resources available but the project duration has been extended. Network restrictions have still been observed.

wind and limb but lacking any special experience or skill. This firm's resource availability can therefore be listed as:

Skilled persons – 1
Labourers   – 1

If the project is to be carried out solely by this small team, it is obvious that the schedule displayed in Figure 7.2 is useless and cannot be implemented. The schedule must be rearranged so that the modest resources available are not 'double booked'. Using the adjustable chart, this can be done by shuffling the activities around until no column total exceeds the number of people available. When any such shuffling is carried out, the original constraints of the network from which the bar chart was constructed must be remembered and observed.

Figure 7.4 shows the resource-limited network for the garage project, and the resulting workload histogram is given in Figure 7.5. The resource constraint has extended the timescale by 12 calendar days, increasing the overall duration from 32 days to 44 calendar days. However, there is now a nice smooth schedule,

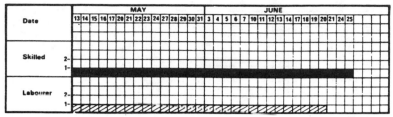

Figure 7.5 Garage project resource histogram with resource limitations observed
The histogram gives a clear display of the levelling achieved by the resource schedule of Figure 7.4. This result is usually termed a resource-limited schedule.

perfect for the firm because there are no idle days or unwelcome peaks.

The new schedule may not be so acceptable to the customer, who is expecting delivery of an expensive new car and wants to be able to garage it safely. If the new garage cannot be promised in time the customer may decide, not unreasonably, to use another contractor.

Under these circumstances, several courses of action are open to the small builder. These include the following:

1 Work to the resource-limited timescale of 44 days (Figures 7.4 and 7.5), but make a false promise to the customer that the garage will be ready after only 32 days. Lying and making false promises in this way can never be recommended, for commercial as well as for moral reasons.
2 Tell the customer that the project cannot be finished in 32 days – and lose the order as a penalty for telling the plain, unvarnished truth.
3 Revert to the original resource-aggregated schedule shown in Figures 7.2 and 7.3, and take on additional workers, regardless of cost, in order to finish the project in 32 days.
4 Plan to complete the project within the required 32 days, accept that additional workers will be needed, but review and adjust the resource-aggregated schedule in an attempt to smoothe the workload into a more cost-effective pattern.

Option 4 is one that is commonly taken in project scheduling,

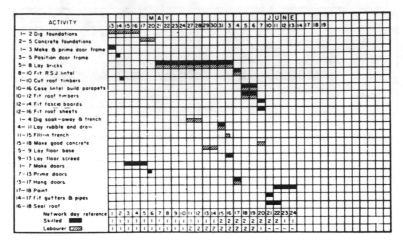

Figure 7.6 Garage project resource schedule levelled to achieve earliest finish
Here the project can be completed within the network's timescale. By shuffling activities around within their network limitations the undue peaks shown in Figures 7.2 and 7.3 have been removed.

and it will work well for the garage project. Remember that this rescheduling of activities can only take place within the constraints imposed by the network logic, so that no activity may be started before its preceding event has been achieved. Further, if the overall project timescale is not to be extended, no activity may be rescheduled to start later than its latest permissible start date, as determined by network time analysis. This means that non-critical activities can be delayed within the float which they possess. Critical activities have zero float, and must therefore always be scheduled to start at their earliest possible times. Figure 7.6 is the rescheduled bar chart, and the corresponding resource histogram in Figure 7.7 shows that it is in fact possible to reschedule the activities to obtain a resource-usage pattern which is far smoother and more acceptable.

Float

The concept of float and the specific definitions for its possible variations are sometimes difficult to comprehend. Since one of

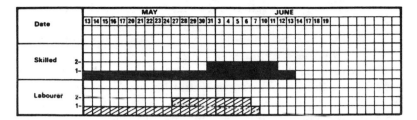

Figure 7.7 Garage project resource histogram levelled for earliest finish
Compare this histogram with that shown in Figure 7.3. The same project duration can be achieved but the benefits derived from resource levelling show up dramatically in the smoother requirement pattern. This result is known as a time-limited schedule.

the more practical applications of float is found during the resource scheduling process, it is convenient to illustrate and define float in some detail at this point. The network for the garage project (Figure 7.1) will provide a suitable case for study.

First consider activity 9 to 13, 'lay floor screed'. For clarity, this activity is shown as a separate detail in Figure 7.8. Although this diagram has isolated the activity from the network, all the data relative to float are shown. These include the earliest and latest times for both the preceding and succeeding events, and the estimated duration of the activity. A glance at event 9 shows that the earliest possible start for this activity is day 8. The latest permissible finish (event 13) is day 20. Allowing for the one

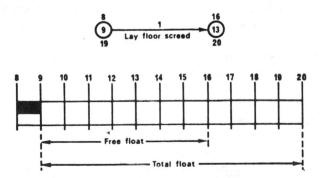

Figure 7.8 Garage project: float analysis of activity 9 to 13

day's duration of this activity, it is easy to see that its start (and finish) could be delayed by up to 11 days without causing delay to the activities which follow. This 11 days is the 'total float' possessed by the activity.

If, because of delays in the project or through intentional scheduling, the floor screed operation takes place later than its earliest possible time, some (if not all) of its float will be eroded. This will usually have a 'knock-on' effect through the network, robbing some of the float from activities which follow because they can no longer be started at their earliest possible times. In fact the float for any activity must always be seen in relation to how it is likely to affect, or be affected by, the float possessed by other activities in the network. Consideration of these effects gives rise to definitions for various types of float. These definitions follow, but it is not necessary to be conversant with all of them. Before the start of a project, planners and project managers are generally most concerned with 'total float'. From the time when resource scheduling starts, and throughout the active life of the project, the emphasis changes to consideration of 'remaining float'.

Total float

Total float is defined as the amount by which an activity can be delayed if all its preceding activities take place at their earliest possible times and following activities are allowed to wait until their latest permissible times.

Although the total float for activity 9 to 13 (Figure 7.8) happened to be equal to the difference between the earliest and latest start times for event 9, this cannot always be taken as a reliable guide to the amount of total float available for any activity. A study of the formal definition just given with reference to another activity from the garage network will show that other network restrictions can easily upset this simple situation.

In Figure 7.9, activity 10 to 16, 'case lintel and build parapets' has been isolated and subjected to special analysis. It is seen that event 10 has equal early and late times, which should indicate zero float and a critical activity. However, although event 10 lies on the critical path of the network, the path branches at this

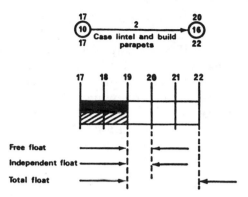

Figure 7.9 Garage project: float analysis of activity 10 to 16

event (away from activity 10 to 16). A glance at the whole network in Figure 7.1 shows that the critical path actually goes through activity 10 to 12. Activity 10 to 16 does indeed possess float.

The actual float conditions are illustrated best in the segment of bar chart included in Figure 7.9. It is apparent from this diagram that, using the formal definition, the total float for activity 10 to 16 is three days. It is not difficult to derive the simple mathematical expression needed to calculate this float when the bar chart segment and activity arrow in Figure 7.9 are compared.

> Total float = latest permissible end-event time
>   *minus* the earliest possible start-event time
>   *minus* the activity duration

Applying the data from Figure 7.9 to this formula:

Total float (activity 10 to 16) = (22 − 17 − 2) = 3 days

Free float

Returning to the network diagram, suppose that the floor screed activity (9 to 13) must be delayed owing to the absence of available workmen at the right time. The network shows that activity 13 to 17 (hang doors) can not in any case start before day

16 because of the restriction imposed by the dummy from event 8. This means that the start of the floor screed activity could be delayed as late as day 15 before any ill effects would be caused to activities following event 13. There is a float of seven days over which activity 9 to 13 is free to move without having any effect on the float possessed by following activities. This float is termed the free float of activity 9 to 13. However, although any change in this float cannot affect following activities, it will be eroded if any preceding events are allowed to run later than their earliest possible dates.

Free float is therefore defined as the amount of float available when all preceding activities take place at their earliest possible times and following activities can also take place at their earliest possible times.

> Free float = the earliest possible end-event time
> *minus* the earliest possible start-event time
> *minus* the activity duration

Applying the data from Figure 7.9 to this formula:

> Free float (activity 10 to 16) = (20 − 17 −2) =1 day

Independent float

Now consider activity 10 to 16 once again (as shown in Figure 7.9). Notice that it is possible to shuffle this activity around over a one-day period, whatever happens to the schedule for all other network activities. It matters not whether the preceding events are allowed to run up to their latest permissible times, or if the following events must start at their earliest possible times. This activity can still be moved backwards and forwards within a total amount of one day before any other activity is affected. This small amount of float, because it is entirely independent of all surrounding activities, is called 'independent float'.

Defined formally, independent float is the amount of float available when the preceding event takes place at its latest permissible time and all following activities are to take place at their earliest possible times.

Independent float = the earliest possible end-event time
minus the latest permissible start-event time
minus the activity duration

Using the data from Figure 9.7 once more:

Independent float (activity 10 to 16) = (22 − 17 − 2) = 1 day

The incidence of independent float is comparatively rare. Usually when the above formula is applied to any activity in a network the result is zero.

Remaining float

The total float possessed by any activity is at risk of erosion from the moment that project resource scheduling starts right up to the time when the activity is completed. Total float can be reduced, for example, as a result of a conscious decision to delay the planned start of an activity as part of the resource scheduling process (in order to plan a smoother workload pattern). There is also the obvious risk that preceding activities will run late, absorbing some or all of the total float.

For practical purposes, once a project is started the project manager is not interested in the total float that an activity had in the beginning, when the network was first drawn. If the project progress is being reviewed on 13 July 1995, it is the residue of the total float still possessed by each uncompleted activity on 13 July 1995 that should concern the project manager. This is the 'remaining float'.

Activities with zero remaining float
Activities which have zero remaining float have obviously become critical activities. They should claim priority for resources and for management attention to ensure that they are finished without delay. Otherwise the project completion must itself be delayed.

Activities with negative remaining float
Suppose that the critical path through a network has a total estimated duration of 100 weeks. The end event will therefore have an earliest possible completion time of 100.

Barring other considerations, the latest permissible completion time for the project end event will also be 100. Time analysis will, in the usual way, produce one or more critical paths back through to the start of the network in which all the critical activities have zero total float. Suppose, however, that those 'other considerations' include a promise to the customer that the project will be completed in 90 weeks. The latest permissible project end date is therefore 10 weeks before its earliest possible date. All activities that were previously on the critical path with zero total float will now have a total float of *minus* 10 weeks.

Negative total float can be caused whenever scheduled target dates are imposed on the end event, or indeed on any other event in a project network.

Negative remaining float will appear in any schedule (especially in computer printouts) where it is impossible to achieve scheduled target dates for events because:

1 The duration of the relevant path through the network is longer than the time allowed by the imposition of scheduled dates.
2 Delayed progress will prevent activities being started by their latest permissible dates.
3 Activities have to be delayed beyond their latest permissible dates because resources are inadequate.

Needless to say, activities with negative remaining float have become hypercritical. Prompt management action is essential in looking for all possible corrective measures that might be used to expedite progress.

Project resource scheduling in practice

When an attempt is made to implement a plan in which resources have not been properly taken into account, success or failure must depend largely on the size of the project and on the determination to succeed of those employed in its execution. In a very simple case, such as the garage project, there is little doubt that, even in the absence of any plan at all, common sense (plus possibly a little trial and error) would result in the job being finished within a reasonable time. Experienced managers of small projects are often able to rely on their memory of past work, which enables them to plan and schedule the work mentally. Formal planning methods and modern scheduling techniques are not always essential to the success of very small projects therefore (but they should still be considered, because they usually lead to greater efficiency).

Now suppose that instead of a tiny project aimed at the construction of one private garage, a contractor has undertaken to build a complex of shops, offices, industrial premises, roads and car parks. There is no question in this case that scheduling is essential. It might have to take into account bulk delivery and storage of materials, plant hire, cash resources, and many other factors in addition to direct workers and the supervision of subcontractors. No single person on this project could be expected to visualize all the planning detail mentally, or without the use of formal techniques. If these techniques are chosen sensibly from those available to modern industry, the planning and scheduling process itself can be efficient and cost effective. The resulting schedules should form a proper basis for project management, helping the contractor to work systematically and efficiently, impressing the customer and the market competition.

A computer would undoubtedly be needed to cope with the large volume of data to be gathered, filed, calculated, scheduled, edited, sorted and reported for most projects. Fortunately, suitable computer systems are readily available at comparatively low cost. Before moving to the subject of computer scheduling (Chapters 8 and 9) it is necessary to move the discussion beyond the basic techniques and simple examples outlined so far in this book and list some of the rules and matters of policy that must be considered if practicable schedules are to be produced for real-life projects.

Essential elements of a practicable schedule

To be practicable, every project work schedule must be based on a logical and feasible timescale. The level of detail chosen should be right for the purpose of the plan. The schedule should preferably be derived from a network, so that activities can be listed in a logical, achievable working sequence. A network-derived schedule also has the advantage that time analysis data are available, allowing the float for each activity to be taken into account when allocating scarce resources and for subsequent progress management.

Unfortunately these principles are not always understood or accepted. Project managers, engineers and planners can still be found drawing up complicated bar charts and histograms which purport to show working plans peering many months – even years – into the future, without the slightest logical justification and in incredibly fine depth of detail.

Here is an example of 'how not to schedule'. One engineering director known to the author called for a departmental plan, drawn on a sheet of paper covering a large reference table, which was supposed to allocate 30 engineers (actually identified by their names) to jobs from several projects (actual orders and possible orders) at weekly intervals covering a period of no less than two years ahead. The chart therefore needed about 3 000 entries. It cost several days of a highly paid engineering manager's time and involved detailed discussions with the engineering director and others. The schedule looked quite impressive when it was finished, but it was completely inflexible, impossible to adjust easily, and therefore totally useless. Even if the work plans had been soundly based (which they were not) it is ludicrous to expect to be able to allocate named individuals to specific jobs during any particular week so far in advance. Even if all the jobs did actually materialize in the particular weeks shown on the plan, there would be a question mark regarding how many of the original 30 engineers would still be employed by the company? In fact, that firm went into liquidation with big debts before the plan could run its course.

Schedules have to be flexible, capable of being recalculated whenever necessary to accommodate new work and changes. Manual scheduling systems only provide adequate flexibility in the very simplest cases. Much of the remainder of this chapter is based on the assumption that a computer will be used.

Choice of resources to be scheduled

In engineering design for major petro-chemical or construction projects it would probably be necessary to schedule work and manpower resources for each of the main engineering disciplines (civil, structural, mechanical, electrical and so on) for each work package or convenient group of drawings. This scheduling might be further broken down into engineering, drawing and checking (although the application of computer-aided design may blur these boundaries and reduce the need for such breakdown).

In engineering design for manufacturing projects, again confining the scheduling detail to subassemblies and groups of drawings rather than to individual drawings, it has been found sufficient to consider only three resource types during scheduling, designated as:

- Layout (engineers)
- Detailers
- Checkers.

It is recognized that this will not cover every grade of engineer. For example, many mechanical engineering design activities might also attract a proportion of lubrication and process control design. The common-sense approach here is to avoid getting into too much detail. If the company knows, from experience, that process control engineering always takes place alongside mechanical engineering, but typically requires only 10 per cent of the manpower level, then there is no need to include process control design specifically in resource scheduling. In such circumstances, process control design activities would not even have to be shown on the network diagram, unless they had particular individual significance. It is only necessary to schedule the mechanical design engineers. The process control manager can be left to schedule his or her department's work in line with the mainstream mechanical design schedule, and the process control engineering manpower requirements can be assumed as being 10 per cent of those calculated for the mechanical engineers. This approach may not appeal to the fastidious expert or the timid planner, but it saves considerable planning and scheduling effort and has been proved to be effective in practice.

For scheduling projects through a factory, it is again necessary to choose only one or two key resource types. This approach can be as crude as lumping all machine shop grades together as one resource type, and all assembly workers as another, giving just two manufacturing resource categories. If this sounds surprising, remember that the project planner and project manager are not concerned with the day-to-day detail of job scheduling in the factory, which is the separate function of production control. The project schedules simply ensure that project work is loaded to the factory at a rate consistent with its expected total capacity.

For similar reasons, it is not necessary to be concerned about the fluctuations in resource usage that would normally occur during the course of a single manufacturing activity (for example, an activity covering the production of all components needed for a project work package). In large manufacturing projects, or when several projects are being scheduled in a total, multi-project calculation, it is only necessary to specify an average rate of usage for each production resource, spread evenly over the duration of each production activity. The reason is that each activity is likely to be very small in relation to the total workload of hundreds of manufacturing activities. Workload peaks and troughs of individual activities are small in relation to the whole and tend to even out, especially since the activities have been scheduled so as not to exceed the total stated production capacities. Project resource allocation will therefore ensure that work is fed to the factory at a pace that does not overload the separate production control system, which can then break the manufacturing activities from the project schedule down into detailed factory work schedules.

These arguments concerning manufacturing activities, because they rely on statistical chance, need a fairly large sample. They are best justified when the total manufacturing workload for all projects is represented by at least a few hundred activities. All of this depends on the use of multi-project scheduling (described in Chapter 9).

Choice of resource units

Whenever resources are to be considered for scheduling, it is necessary to decide what units should be used. For most purposes, it is only necessary to work with simple units, so that a quantity of one indicates one person from the particular department or resource type. If 50 labourers are available for allocation to the project, then 50 resource units are entered in the computer or other system as the available strength. If eight labourers are estimated to be needed for a particular activity this is indicated on the network, computer input and subsequent schedules as 8L (where 'L' or some other suitable code identifies the resource as labourers).

Note that an activity can have two, three, or more different types of resource assigned to it. This was seen in the garage project, where some activities required both a skilled person and a labourer.

Factored units
It is sometimes necessary to factor resource levels in order to avoid getting involved in fractions or decimal quantities. For example, large projects sometimes impose a heavy and uneven workload on purchasing departments. So it might be desirable to schedule the buyers' activities in order to ensure that purchasing can be carried out in the correct sequence of priorities without causing health-threatening overloads. Buyers can therefore be specified as a resource, shown as a requirement on each purchasing activity. But an average purchasing activity may only involve a buyer intermittently throughout its total duration, because most buyers are handling several enquiries or orders at any given time. A department of five buyers might easily have 50 enquiries and orders in various stages of preparation. The planner could overcome this by reasoning that the average buyer only spends 10 per cent of his or her time on one order, so that a usage rate of 0.1B can be shown as the resource requirement for a purchasing activity. But the use of decimals here can give rise to errors, or cause difficulties when it comes to preparing input for the computer. A solution which has been found to be effective is to call each buyer 10 resource units. The total number of people declared to be available as buyers must then also be multiplied by 10. A department of 5 buyers might, therefore, be stated to have a resource availability of 50B. Now when a resource requirement of 1B is written against a two-week's purchase order activity on the network, this indicates one buyer spending 10 per cent of his or her time over a two-week period, and this will allow subsequent scheduling to produce realistic workloads.

Rate-constant and non rate-constant usage of resources

The usual convention is that the usage of any resource is assumed to be constant over the life of an activity. Thus if an activity is shown with an estimated duration of one week, needing 1B and 1L (where 'B' is a code for bricklayers and 'L' signifies labourers) this means that the job requires one bricklayer and one labourer working full time for one week. This is known in scheduling terms as a rate constant use of resources.

Planning for uneven resource usage within one activity is possible with some computer systems. For example, the activity just described might have needed no bricklayer or labourer for two days in the middle of its period, but two bricklayers and two labourers for the last two days. The total resource cost and requirement is the same, but the usage pattern is no longer rate constant. In practice, it is seldom necessary to be concerned with such fine detail in project scheduling, especially in large networks where the numbers of activities being scheduled should tend to smoothe out any small ripples. The use of most, if not all, resources in a project schedule can usually be considered as rate constant.

Specifying resource availability levels

If there are 100 people of one resource type in a department, it might seem reasonable to declare that 100 units of that resource are available to the project. There are, of course, complications. Some of these people will be needed for other projects. This problem can be overcome by scheduling all projects together in a multi-project system (Chapter 9).

There is also the fact that no department ever achieves 100 per cent efficiency. People take time off or work at reduced efficiency for a variety of reasons (illness, holidays, dentist, brief visits to the cloakroom, longer visits to the cloakroom, time waiting for work to be allocated, machine or computer failures, and so on). Some of these people will also be working on unscheduled jobs, including rectification work and the like. The answer here is to estimate the level of efficiency for each department or resource type, and to use a correspondingly lower figure as the level of that resource which is available to the project. If in doubt, start with 80 per cent efficiency, and amend this as experience builds up. So, although there might be 100 people of a particular resource category on the permanent strength of a department, 80 would be the total strength of this resource declared as available for scheduling across all projects.

It has to be recognized that the availability level for any manpower resource can change as the project proceeds, possibly increasing as a result of recruitment or decreasing if redundancy measures have to be taken. The extent and timing of such planned changes should be reflected in the organization's budgets and manpower plans, and it is obviously necessary to vary the resources declared as available for project scheduling accordingly. Computer scheduling programs do allow for such changes. The pattern for the declared availability of a manpower resource is therefore likely to be either a continuous rate-constant level, or a level which varies in one or more steps during the life of the schedule according to the relevant departmental manpower plan.

There is a special case where non rate-constant resource availability occurs. This is explained below in connection with the treatment of weekend working.

Weekend working

There is an application of non rate-constant resources that planners with sufficient experience and expertise sometimes find useful. This is when the usage, although not constant, conforms to a repeating pattern. Here is an example.

Suppose that some workers on a project work seven days per week, while engineering and other office staff only work five days. If the work-to lists and all other schedule reports from the computer are to include all calendar dates relevant to the project, it is obvious that weekend days must be included in time analysis. Saturdays and Sundays have to be regarded as work days. Yet the office workers cannot be scheduled as starting, completing or carrying out any activity on a Saturday or Sunday. There are several ways of solving this problem. One of these is to show the availability of all office resources as non rate-constant, with a repeating pattern of five days on, two days off (obviously starting the sequence on the first project Monday).

Most computer systems provide another (better) solution, which is to allow the planner to specify two or more different calendars for resource allocation. In our example, the seven-day workers be assigned according to one calendar (Calendar 1, which uses all seven days in a week), while the office workers would be assigned to another calendar (Calendar 2, in which weekends are not valid days for scheduling).

Shift working

It sometimes happens that a schedule must allow for a mix of single shift (normal) working with two- or three-shift working.

The simplest solution to this problem is to multiply the number of resource units shown as available by the number of shifts to be worked. If three fitters are to work on each of two shifts, then six fitters are the total available resource within each working day.

Holidays

Annual holidays of individuals, provided that these are not all taken simultaneously during a plant shut-down, are treated as a general reduction in the resources stated to be available. This contributes to the suggested 20 per cent reduction mentioned above in the section on specifying resource availability levels.

The dates for forthcoming public holidays, when all project work must stop, should be determined in advance using diaries or long-range almanacks. These dates must then be removed from the days available for scheduling. Computer programs usually allow such dates to be specified when the calendar or calendars are first set up. Complete plant holiday shut-downs and industry-wide holidays are treated in the same way.

Use of overtime as a resource capacity

Projects should not be scheduled with the intention of using resources during overtime. As work on the project proceeds, overtime may become a valuable additional resource, to be called upon in emergencies, when critical activities are in danger of running late. Overtime should normally be held in reserve against such contingencies, and the stated resource availability levels should be limited to the capacities present during normal working hours.

Threshold resources

Sometimes it is necessary to consider a second tier, or 'threshold' level of a particular resource, to be used in schedules only when all the normally available resources have been allocated to activities, and when the project timescale would otherwise be at risk. An example would be an engineering department with a declared resource strength of 50 permanent staff employees, where the engineering manager knows that an additional 50 engineers could be made available from various subcontract agencies.

When a computer is used for scheduling with threshold resources available, it first attempts to generate a schedule that only uses the normally available resources. The additional resources are only brought into play when the computer is unable to schedule an activity without exceeding the stated amount or 'threshold' of normally available resources. In the case of the engineering department, the engineering manager would receive a computer report showing how many of the 50 subcontract people are expected to be needed, with the dates. This would enable the manager to negotiate with the subcontract agencies well in advance for the supply of the additional engineering staff. It would also give the company time in which to arrange for the hire of any necessary accommodation and equipment for them. This is another example taken from real life, where the system worked efficiently, prevented last minute panics, and allowed plenty of time for seeking subcontracted staff and facilities from the most cost-effective sources.

Scheduling costs

It will certainly be necessary to schedule estimated expenditure, and computer resource scheduling programs can be used for this purpose. Project management computer programs usually allow unit cost rates to be specified for all the different resources, and also allow the planner the alternative option of stating an estimated cost for a whole activity.

The resulting schedules are very valuable because they set out the predicted project costs against the scheduled project timescale, providing one of the essential ingredients for cost control and cash flow management.

Using resource rates for labour costs
It is possible to declare a cost rate per unit network time for each resource category. It is further possible, in the best programs, to put in cost rates for threshold resources, recognizing the different costs that must be incurred for example in bringing in temporary staff. The computer will calculate the costs for an activity as follows.

Suppose that an activity has an estimated duration of 10 days (equivalent to two calendar weeks) and that its resource requirement is one engineer. The cost rate for this resource (engineers) has been specified as £200 per day using normally available staff, and £250 per day for the threshold level. The computer will multiply the normal rate by the duration, giving £(10 × 200) = £2 000 as the cost of the activity. If, however, the computer has to allocate resources from the threshold supply, it would use the threshold rate in the cost calculation and the cost of this activity would rise to £2 500.

If factored resource units are used, the cost rate for the full-scale resource unit must obviously be divided by the factor. In the case of the buyers (see 'Factored units' above), if the rate per buyer is given as £150 per day, and if each buyer is represented as 10B, then the rate specified in computer input must be £15 per 1B per day.

Using activity cost estimates for materials costs and subcontracts
The simplest way to put the costs of material purchases into a schedule is to identify all the purchasing activities on the network, add up the estimated cost for the collection of materials being purchased in each activity, and then specify the relevant cost for each appropriate activity.

The question now arises as to which is the appropriate purchasing activity, because the purchasing process for each package of materials might have more than one activity in the project network. There might be separate activities for:

1   preparing the purchase specification (which is usually an engineering activity, attracting only labour costs);

2   getting bids;
3   preparing and sending out the purchase order;
4   external manufacture or lead time;
5   transport and delivery.

If the materials costs are shown against the purchase order activity, the resulting schedules will be timed to show the expected rate at which money is committed for purchases. Later chapters will demonstrate that this information is invaluable for materials expenditure monitoring and cost control.

By putting the costs of materials on the delivery activity, the costs will be scheduled later, approximating to the time when invoices have to be paid. A schedule with this timing is useful for predicting cash flow requirements (discussed later in this chapter).

When familiarity is gained with the use of computer systems and the use of sorting and reporting codes it will be found possible to use both of these options, obtaining schedules and graphs for both committed costs and cash flow.

Planners who become familiar with a particular scheduling program will, provided they have sufficient aptitude, learn how to exploit its features to produce the schedules that they need. They will then be able to extend the methods outlined here to include the more complex problem of scheduling the expected timing of stage payments for capital equipment purchases and subcontracts. The approach must be to ensure that there are events in the network which can be identified with stage payments for these major purchases and subcontracts. Most programs will allow these events to be entered in the schedule, together with their relevant costs. Otherwise, the planner has to ensure that each such event is preceded by a short activity that carries the relevant stage payment.

The seven steps of project scheduling

It is apparent that a large number of factors may have to be taken into account before a workable schedule can be produced for a project. Some of these factors are depicted in Figure 7.10. A mathematician faced with a problem containing a number of

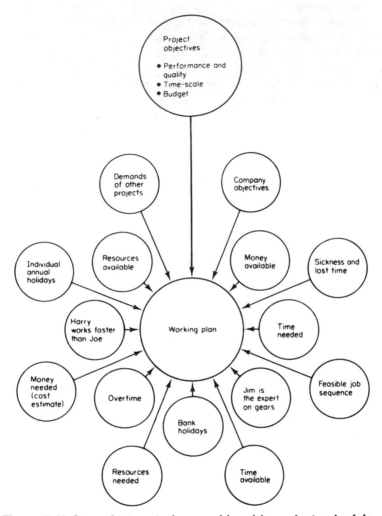

Figure 7.10 Some factors to be considered in project schedule preparation

The range of competing factors which influence the final working schedule is usually so extensive that the planning process can be regarded as an intuitive art. The job of the professional planner is to replace intuition with scientific reasoning. He does this by using appropriate techniques in a logical sequence, designed to eliminate the variables one by one. There are seven separate identifiable steps in this sequence, and these are listed in Figure 7.11.

unknown quantities would probably adopt a logical approach, and attempt to evaluate the unknowns by solving them one at a time. Project scheduling benefits from this approach, and there are seven recognizable stages leading from potential chaos to a practicable solution. The seven steps are listed and explained in Figure 7.11.

Project scheduling in the corporate context

The approach taken to scheduling must depend on what the schedule is to be used for. In any organization, planning has to be carried out at several levels. These range from the overall, strategic corporate long-range plans to the day-to-day allocation of tasks to individual people and machines. Project schedules generally lie on a stratum between these extremes, and they serve several purposes in the overall planning context.

Project schedules (combined with sales forecasts of possible work to come) provide the data from which manpower, financial and other long-range corporate plans can be formulated. These data are not needed in great depth of detail, but they should instead be summarized in quantities that will suit the broad corporate plans that they feed. This is the 'upward looking' purpose of project schedules, for which they should predict departmental manpower and facilities needed, the types of skills required, cash flows, and the like. If the organization is a joint venture or other company set up to handle a single major project, there is one level of planning less for the company because the overall project schedule doubles as the corporate plan.

The principal 'downward looking' purpose of project schedules is to list the jobs that all departments will have to carry out. These are sometimes known as 'work-to' lists. The aim of these lists must be to feed work to all the departments in correct sequence, timed to fit in with the needs of the project. Proper resource scheduling before the issue of work-to lists should ensure that work is fed to departments at rates that will not cause overloads. It should then be the job of the departmental managers to arrange the lowest layer of scheduling, which is the

Step	Method	See Chapter
1 Define the objectives – technical	Solution, concept or feasibility engineering, with the results documented in a technical specification	3
– financial	Cost estimates of the proposed solution, itemized and developed into cost budgets	4
– programme	Displayed on a simple chart, with the actual timescale derived from experience of past projects	6
2 Divide the project into manageable parts	By preparing work breakdown lists that define major areas of work and those departments or organizations primarily responsible. These areas of work are sometimes called 'work packages'	4
3 Decide, in detail, what has to be done and in what sequence	Bar charts for very simple projects, otherwise network diagrams	6
4 Estimate the duration of each separate activity	Consider the time that will probably elapse between the start of the activity and its completion. Do not take resources into account at this stage	6

5	Use the activity duration estimates to calculate the estimated project duration, and the relative significance of each activity to timescale objectives	For very simple projects a small bar chart can be used, but network analysis is usually the better method. For very large projects a computer can be used for the calculations. If results are unacceptable, either the network, the estimates or the timescale objectives must be changed	6
6	Reconcile the programme with the resources that can be mustered	For very small projects a bar chart can be used as a loading diagram. For larger projects, and for circumstances where more than one project is making demands on common resources, the computer is used to allocate resources, taking into account the data obtained from network analysis	7,8
7	Assign jobs to individuals by name	This is a supervision skill, outside the normal responsibility of project planners. It demands personal knowledge of each individual, including degree of technical competence, speed of working, accuracy and special attributes	–

Figure 7.11 The seven steps of project scheduling
From project definition to the establishment of a practicable work schedule there are seven distinct steps. These steps are listed here in sequence, together with appropriate methods. The figures in the right-hand column are the relevant chapter numbers in this book.

day-to-day allocation of jobs to individual people according to their availability or particular aptitudes.

The case studies and examples in this book have had to be kept simple for clarity. In real life, projects are likely to involve many more than the 50 or so activities used in our examples. Project networks with several thousand activities are not unusual. Worse still, a contractor may have to manage several such projects simultaneously, all in different stages of progress, and all making demands on common resources. It should be apparent that no project schedule can be considered in isolation from other projects being conducted within the same organization, especially when it comes to considering resources. At one time companies had to cope with all planning, even on this scale, using only bar charts on adjustable planning boards. Modern computer systems can do the job more accurately, and with far greater flexibility. The process, called multi-project scheduling, is described in Chapter 9.

Scheduling cash flow

Money is undeniably a basic project resource. Plans which show the expected cash 'outputs and inputs' throughout the life of a project are therefore an important aspect of project resource scheduling.

Any organization investing funds in a large project of several years' duration will want to know not only the amount of money required, but also when the money is likely to be required. The most obvious reason for this is so that provision can be made with bankers or other financial sources for the monies actually to be available at the various times when they are needed. There is, however, another important reason, which is that foreknowledge of the timing of every item of cost and every item of saving or revenue is an essential part of project appraisal (see the section on project appraisal in Chapter 5).

Project managers may be asked to arrange the preparation of cash flow predictions, either for their own organization or as a service to the customer. Whether for use in project appraisal, or for assembling actual project funds, cash flow schedules are necessarily bound up with project timescale planning. A cash

PROJECTS UNLIMITED LTD · Project number

Cash flow schedule for: LOXYLENE PLANT   Client: LOX CHEMICALS   Issue date: AUGUST 1983

QUARTERLY PERIODS – ALL FIGURES £1,000s

COST ITEM	COST CODE	1984 1	2	3	4	1985 1	2	3	4	1986 1	2	3	4	1987 1	2	3	4	TOTAL COST BUDGET EACH ITEM
ENGINEERING	A																	
DESIGN	A105	10	20	50	70	75	50	30	10									315
SUPPORT	A110			2	2	2	5	5	5	5	5	3	2	2	2	2	2	44
COMMISSIONING	A200													2	6	10	10	28
PROJECT MANAGEMENT	A500	4	5	7	8	8	8	8	8	7	6	6	6	3	2	2	2	88
EQUIPMENT PURCHASES	B																	
MAIN PLANT	B110				400		500		500				2200			400		4000
FURNACES	B150					60				480						60		600
VENTILATION	B175					20					160		10			10		200
ELECTRICAL	B200					5	20	25	25	140	5	2	2	1				225
PIPING	B300					10	5	5	20	20	40	40	50	20	20			230
STEEL	B400			20		80	200	200	200	200								900
CRANES	B180					50						400		50				500
OTHER	B900		5	25	5	10	20	20	50	5	5	10	5	10	5	2		177
CONSTRUCTION	C																	
PLANT HIRE	C800				2	3	10	10	8	6	4	2	1	1				47
ROADS	C105				10	20	40	80	60	5	5							220
EXTERNAL LIGHTING	C200				5				40			5						50
MAIN BUILDING	C050																	
LABOUR	C055				10	30	100	150	200	400	100	100	50	40	20	20		1120
MATERIALS	C080				2	10	30	100	200	220	200	100	100	10	5			977
STORES BUILDING	C300																	
LABOUR	C053					5	20	20	20	20	60	60	30	5				260
MATERIALS	C380					2	5	15	5	5	15	30	15	10	5			107
RACKING	C389						5						45					50
FORK TRUCKS	C600														120			120
CONTINGENCY SUM	X100				10	20	25	25	30	30	35	35	45	45	50	50		400
ESCALATION PROVISION	Y100				35	29	74	59	110	134	70	88	322	30	32	35		1070
QUARTERLY TOTALS		14	30	104	102	715	519	1132	800	1338	1496	711	827	2902	251	248	619	PROJECT TOTAL 11708

Figure 7.12 Cash flow schedule
This is a simplified example of a schedule prepared for a customer by the management team of a major project. Used on cost-plus projects, such schedules help the customer to marshal funds. The degree of breakdown shown is often agreed between the contractor and the customer, and each line may have to be cost-coded according to the customer's own capital appropriation coding system.

flow schedule for project appraisal can only be prepared after the timings of key project events have been forecast (probably using a bar chart or other simple plan). Detailed cash flow schedules for an active project must wait until after the project has been properly scheduled.

Suppose that a project manager is asked to prepare a detailed schedule of project cash outflows for a customer. All relevant items of expenditure will have to be divided up into their periodic elements and then set out in a table according to their due dates. Figure 7.12 is an example of a cash outflow schedule prepared by a project management team for a customer. In this illustration, the timescale is set out as annual quarters, owing to the limited space available on a page in this book. In practice, calendar months are more likely to be used. The project represented is for the engineering, purchasing and construction of a chemical process plant to produce the plastic 'Loxylene'. The customer has contracted to pay quarterly on a cost-plus basis, and has asked the contractor for a cash flow schedule (in this application, cash flow schedules are also known as phased budgets). The customer can use the information to assist with his own budgeting and in making arrangements with his sources of finance.

Where the cash flow schedule is prepared for a customer's use, each cost item is entered in the table in the period during which payment is expected from the customer. The customer will often want all the entries on cash schedules and other cost reports to be classified according to the customer's own code of accounts or set of capital appropriation codes. The following arrangements might apply to a project with cost-plus payment terms.

If the timescale breakdown is monthly, labour costs are shown as forecast monthly amounts, placed one month after the contractor's costs are scheduled to be incurred (wages paid). This typical arrangement assumes that an invoice for labour costs will be sent to the customer at the end of each month, and that the customer is expected to reimburse the contractor within 30 days of the invoice date.

Major purchases of equipment will be charged out to the customer as soon as possible after the contractor has been billed by the suppliers. Any interim stage payments agreed between the contractor and his suppliers or subcontractors would also be billed to the customer promptly. All of these payments should be itemized and shown on the schedule. Assuming again the the contractor's invoices are issued monthly and allow 30 days' credit, the customer's payments would be scheduled one month after the contractor had incurred the costs in each case.

It may be useful to provide those responsible for calculating cash flow schedules with guidelines applicable to the organization's customary experience. These should indicate the usual delays expected between various kinds of payments and their causal events. An example, for a company working with overseas clients, is given in Figure 7.13.

The concept of scheduling cash flow presents difficulty to some project staff, whose training and interests usually tend to be technical rather than commercial. To recapitulate, cash flow

Item	Key Date	Predicted payment delay	Notes
Head office man-hours including engineering, procurement and management	Manpower schedule	1 month	
Equipment, as follows: Suppliers' invoices, if lump sum	Planned f.o.b. delivery dates	1 month	
Suppliers' invoices, if deferred payments arranged	Contracted payment dates	Nil	
Shipping agents' invoices	Target f.o.b. delivery dates	3 months	
Local transport charges	Planned on-site date	2 months	
Port charges and customs duty	Planned on-site date	Nil	Usually payable before goods can be released
Construction subcontracts	Scheduled work rates	2 months	Delays expected owing to communications difficulties
Construction management	Manpower schedule	1 month	
Locally purchased site materials	Scheduled usage rates	2 months	
Locally hired site labour	Manpower schedule	2 months	
Commissioning charges	Manpower schedule	1 month	

Figure 7.13 Table of rules for timing a client's project cash flow
Companies asked to prepare cash flow schedules for clients' major projects can assist the project manager to achieve realistic predictions by compiling tables of simple rules for timing each item of expenditure based on relevant operating experience.

schedules can be required to show either expenditure, or a combination of expenditure and its consequent income. The essential feature of any cash flow schedule is that it must be compiled by placing each sum of money in the period when it falls due for payment or receipt.

8

Introducing the computer

Time analysis of the small garage project network in Chapter 7 can easily be carried out using pencil, paper and an average human brain. Subsequent resource scheduling should present no difficulty to a planner armed with an adjustable bar chart and all the relevant facts. Proprietary kits exist for such purposes, with colour coded bars that can be attached magnetically to a steel panel, or plugged into a grid-drilled baseboard. Projects with 100 activities, or even slightly more, can be planned with the aid of such adjustable systems. An initial schedule might take a day or two to set up and inflict some eyestrain on the scheduler, but an effective plan could be made, with well-smoothed resource loads.

The problem with any manual charting method, however, is that it is too inflexible. A change of plan to any except the very tiniest project can result in hours of tedious work in repositioning the coloured strips. This is always coupled with the risk of introducing logical or other errors. Most projects, of course, have many more than 100 activities, and manual resource scheduling becomes even more difficult (impossible altogether for really large projects). The job must then be given to a computer.

Those planners who use critical path networks but choose not to follow the planning process through to proper resource scheduling may be able to carry out time analysis of quite large networks without the need for a computer. It is not difficult to trace all the paths through a big arrow network (precedence diagrams are not so easy because of their complex constraint relationships), write the earliest and latest event times in by hand, and then highlight all the critical activities. But even if initial time analysis is relatively easy, updating the network to accommodate logic changes or progress information is a very different story. Without a computer, the planner is faced with the daunting task of having to erase large amounts of time analysis data from the network diagram and starting afresh. Even a change to the expected duration of one activity, or a simple alteration to the network logic can mean that most of the event times will have to be changed throughout the entire network.

Advantages of computer scheduling

The well-known advantages of using computers for many business applications apply equally to project management. These include the ability of the machine to process large volumes of data quickly and accurately, and to repeat the process just as quickly and accurately to reflect progress made or any change in the project scope or plan. This speed and flexibility is an important asset in project scheduling and control.

Another important feature of computer systems is that they allow management information to be produced and disseminated quickly and effectively. With a manual wall chart, the only practical fast way of spreading its information is to photograph the chart and distribute colour prints. If a bar chart or network diagram is drawn on a sheet of paper or film, the communication task is easier because photocopies or dyeline prints can be taken and distributed. But these charts and diagrams generally cover the whole project, so that prints taken from them are not specific to particular departments or managers. The ability of computers to sort, edit and print data will be found invaluable in overcoming this problem.

Computer systems allow reports to be generated that are up to date, detailed, and specific to the people or departments to which they are addressed for action. Activities can be listed in any desired sequence, with critical activities highlighted. Proprietary project management software usually contains a wide range of inbuilt report formats that can be used 'off the shelf', but many programs also give the project manager the option of creating new report formats to suit his or her own project needs. Plotters can be arranged to print network diagrams, bar chart conversions and all manner of other graphical displays, enhanced by the use of several colours. Work-to lists and scheduled resource requirements can be printed out on a day-by-day basis. Cost control data can be linked to the schedules, allowing budget cost curves, cost tables, and other presentations of planned and recorded expenditure to be printed.

It is also possible to schedule all company projects together, in one combined multiproject calculation. This will take account of the total demand made on the organization's resources, and balance this against the resources which can be made available. Using a computer in this way allocates all work according to critical path network priorities, should result in a smooth work pattern, and produces important input for the organization's forward budgets, manpower and other corporate plans. Such systems can also be used for modelling, with possible new projects or strategic decisions injected and tested in 'what-if?' calculations.

Many of these features will be explained and illustrated in this chapter and in Chapter 9.

Facilities required

Before any project can be scheduled by computer, the project manager has to ensure that appropriate facilities are available. These obviously include organizational factors, such as staff, accommodation, good project communications and adequate senior management support and encouragement. In the context of computing, the project manager needs:

1   computer hardware of sufficient speed and capacity;

2 suitable software;
3 maintenance and systems support for the hardware and software.

Hardware

Not many years ago, a computer with sufficient capacity to handle project network analysis and resource scheduling was a formidable piece of capital equipment, occupying a large area of costly, dust-free, air-conditioned office space. All of this needed a highly trained team of well paid (sometimes overpaid) data processing specialists to run the machine and its programs. The chances were that the project manager would not even have been allowed to enter the computer room. All the data had to be written out first on coding sheets and then translated into decks of punched cards. Processing was carried out on a batch basis, and the total interval between providing the input data coding sheets and the receipt of valid reports or a workable schedule could (after allowing for one or more error-correction runs) take one, two or even more weeks.

Now it is common for project management staff to run their own systems. Although mainframe and minicomputers are used, desktop personal computers are increasingly proving popular. The minimum hardware requirements will be specified by the software company's literature. Output devices are important: these should include a plotter capable of handling A3 size sheets, and able to do justice to the colour graphics that the modern software packages provide. Processing speed with such systems can be counted in seconds or minutes rather than hours (obviously depending on a combination of the hardware and software characteristics and the size of the project). Users will probably find that the limiting time factor for producing reports is the speed of the printer, especially where graphic reports are to be plotted.

Software

Early systems concentrated on time analysis, either using CPA or PERT. As early as the 1960s powerful programs became available that claimed to be able to handle large networks with the added features of cost reporting and resource allocation, but only one or two of these were truly successful (notably ICL PERT and the K & H Projects systems). Other programs (including some from 'big names' in the computer industry) either only produced resource aggregation or were too limited in capacity or too full of bugs to be of any practical use at all (even the early version of ICL PERT was said to crash every time the words 'coffer dam' appeared in an activity description).

For many years users were reluctant to grasp the opportunities provided by the few good systems that did exist. Most people were content to run time analysis, print out the results, and attempt to run their projects using the earliest possible dates with little regard for the consequences of resource constraints. It took decades for this state of affairs to change but in recent years a healthy improvement has taken place. A flourishing market has developed between the providers of practicable, very powerful project management software and users, who are able not only to appreciate and make effective use of what is on offer, but who also encourage further development by making their own suggestions or requests for new features.

Choosing a suitable program

Today the planner is spoiled for choice when looking for a suitable program. The starting point has to be a carefully reasoned specification of what the planner needs.

Without a certain amount of previous experience the intending user will probably not be competent to write a specification that accurately reflects the future needs of his or her organization. The user must be thoroughly familiar with the use of networks and resource scheduling principles (experience which is best achieved by starting with simple manual examples). Contact with organizations which already use computer systems successfully for project planning and management is important: their people should be able to discuss and demonstrate their procedures and so make the intending user more aware of what can be done. The unbiased views of these independent users are also important for outlining possible problems or limitations.

The intending user's specification must answer such basic questions as:

- Should we only try to find software that will run on our existing hardware?
- Are arrow networks, precedence networks, or both going to be used?
- What is the maximum number of activities that are ever likely to be needed?
- Is resource scheduling wanted?
- Are cost data to be included in processing and reporting?
- What kind of output reports are wanted?

Once all the basic factors have been listed, it becomes possible to read through the brochures provided by the program purveyors and eliminate those that are clearly unsuitable. The initial choice, therefore, is decided on a simple 'go' or 'no-go' basis. All the surviving contenders should at least be able to perform calculations on the size and type of networks to be used by the project organization.

It is best to plan for starting on a small scale, so that the user is not overwhelmed by all the features possible from a powerful project management package, but can start with modest aims that will allow confidence to be built up. However, the future must be borne in mind. The project manager may eventually wish to extend the use of computer scheduling to take advantage of planning and control through an integrated database, where scheduling data, progress and cost information, purchasing and drawing schedules, and other project management information can all be processed in the same computer, and with interchange of data between the various parts of the database. It could well be advisable to purchase a program which is sufficiently powerful and flexible to allow a small-scale start, while having the capabilities in reserve for more ambitious use later on. This is the 'think big, start small' approach.

Figure 8.1 is a checklist of the most significant factors to be considered when setting out to choose a program for the first time. This is a convenient starting point for any project manager who wishes to specify the project organization's requirements

Item	Program capabilities
Type of network	• Capable of arrow diagrams (also known as activity on arrow, I/J or ADM networks)?
	• Capable of precedence networks (also known as activity on node or PDM networks)?
	• Capable of both arrow and precedence networks?
Ease of use	• Is the system menu driven?
	• Are there useful help screens?
	• Is the procedure for entering data self-explanatory and simple?
	• How fast is the expected processing time using the hardware that is: (a) available (b) recommended
Event data	• Can event numbers be alphanumeric?
	• Maximum number of characters allowed for event number?
	• Maximum number of characters allowed for event description?
	• Maximum number of events allowed?
	• Can events be specified as interface events between different networks?
	• Can scheduled start or finish dates be imposed upon events?
	• Can events be specified as key events or milestones for report editing?
Activities	• Maximum number of activities allowed?
	• Maximum number of characters allowed for activity description?
	• What choice of duration units is possible?
	• Can activities be designated as splittable (i.e. interruptible) for resource allocation?
	• Can scheduled start or finish dates be imposed upon activities?
Calendars	• What is the maximum range of calendar allowed (the earliest and latest years)?
	• Can holidays and other dates be specified as non-working days?
	• How many different calendars can the computer accept to run simultaneously? For example, two different calendars would allow some activities or resources to be planned for 7 days per week, with others scheduled for 5 days per week.

Figure 8.1 Checklist for a computer program

Item	*Program capabilities*
Error detection	• How effective are the error-search routines? • Are loops analysed and specified? • Are error messages in plain language?
Cost data	• Can the cost of an activity be input? • Can the cost rate for a resource unit be input? • Can different cost rates be specified for threshold resources?
Resources	• Can resource allocation be carried out? (Check that claimed capability for resource allocation is not simply resource aggregation.) • How many different types of resource can be specified altogether? • How many different types of resource can be allocated to a single activity? • How may units for each type of resource can be specified? • Must resources be rate constant (continuous at the same level throughout an activity) or can complex patterns be specified? • What priority rules are available for allocating scarce resources?
Subprojects	• Can the system accept separate subprojects for resource allocation (can it handle multiproject scheduling in other words)? • How many subprojects can be accepted? • How many activities can be handled for each subproject? • Can event numbering be completely independent between subprojects (so that no error will result if the same number is used in more than one subproject)? • What resource priority rules are possible between competing subprojects?
Editing and sorting	• Can the computer skeletonize networks or accept hammocks for report editing? • On what data fields can the reports be edited and/or sorted?
Output reports	• Can the system produce all the tabulations required, either as standard reports or as user-specified options? • What graphics are available? Are these in colour or monochrome?

Figure 8.1 *continued*

Item	Program capabilities
Updating and rescheduling	• What method is used for reporting activities that have been started? • What method is used to report completed activities?
Hardware requirements	• Will it run on existing hardware? • If not, what will have to be purchased? • Is the new hardware necessary standard commercially available and compatible kit, or is it purpose-built and part of a total project management package? • Is more than one terminal needed? If so, how many? Or is the system to be part of a systems network? • Has the printing or plotting device been remembered?
Support and expected reliability	The following questions should be asked about the proposed hardware and software: • How good is the user's manual? • Is the software house well-established, reliable, and with prospects of a secure future? • How many systems have been sold and are in use? • Can we be put in touch with some of these users to seek their recommendations or comments? • What level of back-up support is available in the event of hardware operating difficulties or malfunctions? • How far away is the nearest source of servicing or other support? • Is there a users' hot line? • How often are system updates issued and how are these made available to users? • Is there an independent users' association? • What training is provided for each user? • How much training is free of charge?
Expansion	• Is the system likely to meet the company's future needs for (say) the next five years? • Is the system built round a relational database? If so, is it a proprietary database or is it a purpose-built affair with unfamiliar commands? • Is the program compatible with other systems which may need to be hooked in later? • Are the programs modular, allowing easy add-on facilities?

Figure 8.1 *continued*

Item	Program capabilities
System cost	• Can the hardware, software, or both be hired or borrowed for a free trial period?
	• How much will the new hardware cost to buy?
	• Would renting or leasing be better?
	• Is an annual maintenance contract likely to be necessary, and how much will that cost?
	• If service engineers' charges are expected, what is the rate quoted? (Some such charges are horrendous.)
	• How much will the software cost?

Figure 8.1 *concluded*

before approaching the software suppliers. Some of the more advanced possibilities open to the expert have been excluded, but this checklist should be useful for most practical purposes.

Network notation

Whether a network is going to be calculated mentally or processed by computer, the notation is almost the same. When a computer is to be used, however, the following points have to be borne in mind:

1   With arrow diagrams, events must be given unique numbers, so that they and their connecting activities can be identified by the computer. Alphanumeric numbers can be accepted by most programs. (If precedence is used, it is [of course] the activities which must bear the unique numbers.)
2   Parallel activities have to be avoided. These are two or more activities in an arrow diagram which share the same start and finish events. The computer would not be able to distinguish one from the other. The solution is to create new identifying events by inserting dummies.

Event numbering and the treatment of parallel activities in arrow networks are illustrated in Figure 8.2. This diagram represents a fragment of a network diagram. The first event in

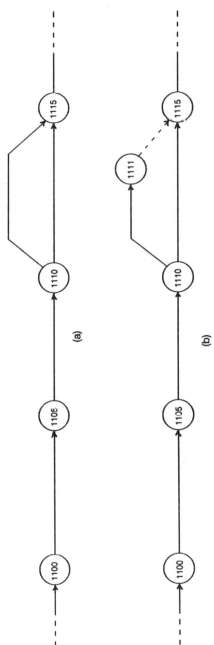

Figure 8.2 Identification of activities and events

The computer is programmed to recognize events by their serial numbers, which must be allocated by the planner and drawn on the network before data can be entered in the computer. It is customary to use an arithmetic progression for this numbering rather than a simple consecutive series, leaving gaps of 5 or 10 between successive event numbers in case further events have to be added later for network logic changes. Each activity is identified in the computer by its start and finish events, so that the first activity shown in this network fragment would be referred to as 'activity 1100 to 1105'. This diagram shows four activities from a larger network. Version (a) includes a deliberate mistake. Notice that the two activities drawn in parallel at the right-hand side of the diagram share the same start and finish events: they are both therefore identifiable as 'activity 1100 to 1115', and the computer would not be able to distinguish between them. The solution shown in version (b) must always be used to prevent such duplication. The dummy 1111 to 1115 has provided the two parallel activities with separate identities.

this fragment has been given the number 1100, and the computer will recognize the event by that reference. Any description or data pertaining to that event will always be fed to the computer with reference to the identification 1100. Similarly, the first activity shown in the diagram will always be associated with the numbers given to its start and finish events, namely 1100 and 1105. Whenever any data are added or changed for this activity, the input to the computer will always be accompanied by the activity identification 1100 to 1105. The activity can be referred to as 'activity 1100 to 1105'.

At the right-hand side of Figure 8.2(a) there is a pair of parallel activities which share the same start and finish events. Thus each activity could be described as 'activity 1110 to 1115'. The computer would therefore be unable to distinguish between them and would probably accept the first to be entered, and then report the second as a duplication error. The remedy is shown in Figure 8.2(b). The dummy 1111 to 1115 has been inserted to give each of the two parallel activities a separate identity. Now there is no confusion, and two distinct activity identifiers emerge (1110 to 1111 and 1110 to 1115). Of course the dummy must also be input to the computer. The addition of this dummy in no way upsets the logic.

In some of the earlier programs it was mandatory to have only one start event and one finish event for the whole network. Even with modern programs, this is a convenient arrangement. Dummies can be used to link multiple starts and finishes together, as shown in Figure 8.3. All activities with no preceding activities are identified and reported as 'dangling arrows' or 'start dangles' during error checking by the computer. Similarly, activities with no following activities will also be seen as dangling arrows by the computer ('end dangles' in these cases). All start and finish dangles must be accounted for by the user. Any unexpected start or end dangle reported may signify that an activity has been omitted from the input data, to leave a gap in the perceived logic surrounded by dangles. Time spent at the computer is greatly reduced if only one start and finish dangle have to be checked against the network diagram when the computer produces its first report.

With some systems it is possible to 'draw' networks directly on the computer screen, but only very tiny networks can be

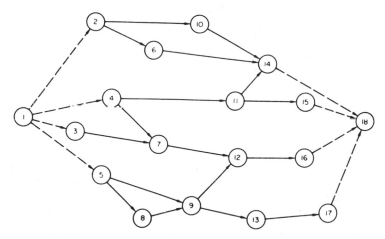

Figure 8.3 Multiple start and finish events
Although many programs can accept networks with more than one start or finish event, it is often convenient to work with only one start and one finish. If the original network has been drawn with multiple starts and finishes, dummy activities can be added to tie-in all the loose ends without altering the logic. This procedure may be preferable to extenᵈing the start and finish activities themselves into the first and last events because the use of dummies allows each start and finish event to retain its own identity. This is often important when the network is being time analysed by hand as a preliminary check. It is also useful when target start and finish dates are to be applied to different parts of the network.

displayed whole. Although a large network can be viewed by scrolling the screen or by producing interim trial prints from the plotter, this is not as practicable as starting from a network drawn on a single sheet or roll of paper or film, where the network can be viewed as a whole, and all the logic constraints can be checked through by running an inquisitive finger along them.

Preparing for a computer run

Assuming that the program has been installed and tested, the first step in setting up the computer schedule is to prepare and enter all the data. The way in which this is done will depend on the requirements of the particular program, but modern systems are very easy to use in this respect, with screen prompts provided at every step. As users become more familiar with their systems they will usually find that data can be entered in a number of different ways; a straight listing of activity data, for example, is quicker than entering the data as a series of responses to prompts.

Whatever the method chosen for entering data, the information can be divided into two main groups. These are:

1   Project control data, which means the data that sets all the project parameters according to which the computer must calculate and report.
2   Activity records, with one record for each activity or dummy activity in the network, together with its description, duration, and other directly relevant data.

For arrow networks, it may also be necessary to create separate records for some of the events, especially where they are to be designated as start or end dangles, key or milestone events, interface events, or events with imposed scheduled dates. Systems that can include management information data within a relational database may need a wider range of records, but these are not essential to basic project scheduling and will not be discussed in this chapter.

Project control data

Control data may be slightly more difficult to comprehend and remember than the activity record data. Some programs require several specialized commands and, because these do not crop up as often as the activity records, or indeed may not all need to be used for each run, it can take longer to become familiar with the exact nature of the commands and master their use. A menu-driven program with screen prompts is very useful in this context, especially where a help facility is included but, above all, the users' manual must be clearly written and set out so that the answers to likely problems can easily be found.

It is a good idea for the planner to prepare a checklist which includes all the factors that have to be considered and entered as control data. Some of these items may only occur once, when the network is first input to the computer. Others will have to be considered afresh at each schedule update. When enough experience has been gained with the program, standard forms can be produced to suit the control data requirements. These forms then act as checklists, presenting all the data in the sequence and format required by the program, ready to be keyed into the system.

Calendars and dates

The computer must contain a basic calendar that spans the total period over which projects are likely to be scheduled. At least one version of *ARTEMIS* (Lucas Management Systems), for example, can accept dates over the range 1 January 1901 to 31 December 2099, which should be sufficient for the practical purposes of most reasonable people.

Once it has been established that the total calendar period in the computer is adequate (which is almost certain to be the case), one or more special calendars will have to be defined and entered according to particular scheduling needs. The most important of these is the main or default calendar, which will include all dates except those days on which work may not be scheduled (such as public holidays). In many cases this main calendar will be the only one which is necessary.

Care always has to be taken when writing or entering dates in numerical form, to ensure that confusion between the American and other conventions does not cause errors. For instance, 01-03-95 means 3 January 1995 to an American and 1 March 1995 to an English person. It is better always to write dates in the form 3JAN95 or 1MAR95 to avoid confusion, especially where any part of the project business has to be conducted internationally. The convention used in the chosen computer program for numerical dates must be determined, especially if the software has been imported from abroad.

It is necessary to decide and enter the units of duration that will be used throughout the networks, and to specify how these will relate to each calendar. For example, a standard unit of 1 might be chosen to represent 1 day, to work with a calendar of five working weekdays within each calendar week. If this were to be the main (default) calendar used throughout the system, then an estimated activity duration of one calendar week would be written as 5 on the network diagram and entered as 5 units in the computer. Most systems allow the user a wide choice of units, even ranging from minutes to durations of one month or more.

Some project management programs allow hundreds of different calendars to be specified. Each separate calendar must be given its own identifying number. When the computer calculates schedules, it will work with the main or default calendar unless one of the special calendars has been allocated to an activity or a resource. Some examples follow to show why special calendars might be needed, and how they might be defined. Please note that the input requirements may vary from one program to another, and these examples are given only as a general guide.

Example 1   An organization works only on weekdays and all project work is contained within normal office hours, with no shift working. The project manager has decided that Saturday and Sunday working will never be required. The project manager would like to be able to schedule jobs with estimated durations as little as one half day.

Only one calendar (the main calendar) is necessary in this case. The solution chosen for dealing with units could be to specify the standard unit of duration as 0.5 day. This means that each working day will consist of 2 units (which, for practical purposes, can be taken as meaning 1 unit each for the morning and afternoon work periods). The computer will be told that the calendar comprises 10 units in one week, with only Monday through Friday as valid dates for scheduling. It is obvious that the same units must be written on the network diagram (so that an activity duration estimated at two weeks would have to be written as 20, for example).

The computer will count 2 units as a total calendar day for network time analysis (the two periods effectively occupying from 00.01 hours to 12.00 hours and from 12.01 hours to 23.59 hours). Work-to lists and all other reports from the system will then only show weekday dates, and Saturdays and Sundays will not be seen as permissible dates for scheduling. Note, however, that network time analysis using this calendar would remain valid for such activities as shipping delays (which do of course span weekends), although pickup and delivery dates could only be reported as taking place on weekdays.

Example 2 Most people in a company work only from Monday to Friday and they can not be scheduled as working on Saturdays or Sundays. However, one department does work on Saturdays.

The main (default) calendar in this case might be similar to that described in Example 1. A second calendar can then be defined, coded as 'Calendar 2', with six days available in the working week and with only Sundays excluded. Calendar 2 would be called into play whenever appropriate, either by specifying that this calendar is to be used when data are entered for each relevant activity or (preferably) by associating Calendar 2 with the labour category (resource type) affected.

Example 3 Activities for a project are to be carried out in two or more countries, some of which have different workday and public holiday arrangements. All the activities are contained within one network in complex logic, so that it is not desirable or possible to draw a separate network for each country. The whole plan is to be made and controlled from project organization headquarters.

One solution here is to start by deciding where most of the activities will be carried out, and create a main calendar to suit the holiday pattern of the relevant country. Then a special calendar must be created for each country which has a different set of workday and holiday conditions. Activities and resources would then be scheduled against the calendar relevant to the country in which they are planned to occur.

Example 4 A company has at least one department which operates more than one shift within each period of 24 hours. Some shifts operate continuously throughout weekdays and weekends.

A separate calendar can be assigned for each different pattern of shiftworking. For example, 21 work periods would be specified as being equivalent to one calendar week if three shifts are to be worked for all days including weekends. The planner must determine how this will affect the duration estimates written on the network diagram (according to the requirements of the particular computer program).

Another method for dealing with shiftwork is to use only one main calendar, multiply the number of resource units available to allow for all the shifts, and then specify the relevant usage pattern of each resource type affected (that is, declare the resources as non-rate constant).

Project start date

It is important to give the computer a datum point from which it will begin the project. This is usually done by imposing a scheduled start date on the first project activity or event. For subsequent updates, a 'time-now' date has to be specified (explained in Chapter 9).

Scheduled dates

The planner may wish to impose either fixed or target dates on events or activities anywhere in the network. In some systems it is possible to specify:

- an early date, which means that the computer must not schedule the start of any activity beyond the point in the network at which the scheduled date is applied (for example, the date when a project site is expected to be vacated by its previous owner);
- a late date, which is an imposed latest permissible date for an activity or event;
- A fixed date, which some systems allow by the imposition of the same date as both early and late dates on the appropriate event or activity.

Imposed scheduled dates will, of course, almost certainly conflict with the dates computed from time analysis, and so will affect float calculations. If an imposed date is logically imposs-ible, negative float will be generated and reported.

Resource data

Resource data must be entered if the computer is going to carry out resource scheduling or produce cost reports based on the cost rates of resources.

The planner has to start by deciding how many different resource types are to be considered and scheduled. It is not necessary, and is indeed a mistake, to attempt scheduling every possible department or type of labour employed by the project organization. For example, it is obviously not necessary to schedule canteen staff, cleaners, administrative office workers, and so on. There are usually some direct workers who do not need to be included in the resource scheduling, because their work is provided as a service, or follows automatically on from the work of others who must be scheduled. These aspects are described more fully in Chapter 7.

Mandatory resource data
The following data must be entered for each type of resource deemed necessary for scheduling:
Resource code: A simple identifier code, which often comprises one, two or three characters. Examples might be ENG for engineers, BKL for bricklayers, FTR for fitters.
Resource name: The name of the resource type as it will appear in reports.
Normal availability: The number of resource units normally available to the program for allocation to simultaneous project activities. In one or two cases it may be necessary to use artificial units, as described in the section headed 'Factored units' in Chapter 7.

Note that it is generally not advisable to declare a total department strength as being available for scheduling. If in doubt, start with either 80 or 85 per cent of the total level. Reasons for this are explained in Chapter 7, under the section 'Specifying resource availability levels'. If a resource is being used with a special calendar for two- or three-shift working, the declared availability level must be reduced even further, to allow for the people to be distributed over the various shifts, and also to take account of their rest days.

Optional resource data
The following optional data can also be entered with most systems for each type or resource specified:
Calendar: The code of any special calendar against which a particular resource is to be scheduled.

Cost rate: The cost expected to be incurred by using one unit of the resource in normal circumstances for one network unit of duration. For example, 1 BKL = £90 per day.

Threshold resources: These are resources above the normal availability level, which the computer may call upon to be used if the project cannot be scheduled using only normal availability levels. Examples might be extra hours available by working overtime, or additional staff that could be taken on as temporary or subcontract workers.

Threshold cost rate: The cost rate expected when one unit of a threshold resource is used during one network duration period – for example, an overtime rate payable.

Rate constancy: The program may allow the user to declare each resource category as rate constant or non rate constant. In the normal case of rate constant resources, scheduling takes place on the assumption that if two people are needed for an activity, they will be scheduled at the constant rate of two people throughout the activity duration. For non rate-constant resources a cyclical pattern of availability can be specified (for example, available for the first five days of every seven day period). This is not used very often, but it can offer an alternative to the practice of having special calendars, to give the planner another method for solving scheduling problems associated with departments that work different numbers of days or shifts.

Priority rules

If resource scheduling is wanted, certain priority rules will have to be defined. The main rules are:

- whether the schedule is to be time limited or resource limited;
- the priority rule for allocating resources to competing activities (a useful choice is to give priority to activities with least remaining float).

Activity records

Activity records comprise the bulk of the data to be entered before the initial run, and it is among these data that most input errors are likely to crop up. A sensible way of going about the task is to have a print of the network diagram on hand, and tick off each activity as it is entered into the keyboard. This will help to prevent errors of omission and duplication.

Dummy activities (arrow networks)
Dummies are usually very simple to enter, it being necessary only to enter the preceding and succeeding event numbers and designate the activity as a dummy. Zero duration is usually assumed.

Mandatory activity data
The following data must always be entered for every activity, otherwise the computer will not even be able to carry out basic time analysis. *For arrow networks:* the preceding and succeeding event numbers (otherwise called the *I* and *J* node numbers). *For precedence networks:* the activity number, and its preceding activity number, together with the type of constraint (for example, finish–start) plus the duration (if any) of the constraint. *For all types of network:* the estimated activity duration in the units applicable to the network calendar.

Optional activity data
Description: Although it is not strictly mandatory to provide activity descriptions, resulting schedules would not be much use without them. Modern systems allow activity descriptions to contain many characters but it will generally be found convenient to use sensibly abbreviated descriptions (containing perhaps about 30 characters) in order to leave more space in the columns of tabular reports for other data.
Alternative duration estimates: the addition of optimistic and pessimistic duration estimates, for use in PERT or risk analysis calculations.
Editing and sorting codes: A departmental sort code can usually be specified so that reports only contain those activities which are of interest to each manager or department. Some systems also allow various sorting and editing sequences on different parts of the activity data. It may be possible, for example, to use part of the description field as a sort code (perhaps by including a job number or cost code as part of the description for each activity).

Resource data: the code and average number of resource units estimated to be required for each resource type. Note that this input can be used for resource scheduling and (provided that cost rates have been specified for resources) also for cost scheduling and reporting.

Cost: the estimated or budget cost of an activity. This method of entering cost data is used for activities which use no declared resources, but which nonetheless incur costs. The most common use is for equipment and materials costs.

Special constraint rules: Some programs allow special logic constraints to be defined for an activity. These include tied activities, in which two designated activities must follow each other without delay. It is also possible to have lag or overlap constraints between the end of one activity and the start of its successor in arrow networks, which allows these networks to have some precedence-type constraints.

Is the activity splittable (applicable only to resource scheduling)? Activities may be declared as splittable if their progress can be allowed one or more interruptions. When this facility is activated, the program may interrupt an activity if its resources are more urgently needed elsewhere.

Event records

Although all the events in an arrow network will be entered in the system with the data for the activity records, it may be necessary to set up a special record for one or more events. The arrangement will depend on the program used but here are a few of the possibilities:

- the event number (mandatory);
- event description;
- designation as a project start event or as a finish event;
- designation as an interface event (that is, an event; which is shared by another subnetwork);
- designation as a key event or milestone (used for special management reports);
- an event cost;
- early or late scheduled date (as described above in the section on calendars and dates).

Report generation

It is likely that the system will give the user the option of choosing between either a range of standard output reports (tabular and graphic), or of reports that are adapted or specially designed to suit the particular needs of the project organization. The commands to be entered for generating reports will depend on the program used. One general word of advice can be given here, however, which is that the beginner would be well advised to start by using the standard formats provided by the system, and think about special report formats later as confidence in using the system is gained.

Data listing

When all the data have been fed into the computer it is helpful if the program can generate printed listings; for example a list of all activity records printed in ascending order of their identifying numbers. These listings will help in checking for errors and omissions, and may also be found useful when the plans are changed or updated.

Data errors

If all the data have been entered correctly there is a possibility that the first attempt at producing a schedule will work when the appropriate command is given. However, unless the network is really small, it can safely be assumed that something will go wrong.

Whether the computer is to be used only for time analysis or for sophisticated resource and cost scheduling, once it has digested all the data its first planning steps will be to make forward and backward passes through the network, recognizing the network logic by means of the relationship between event numbers in the activity records (or by the activity numbers and constraint data given for precedence networks). In addition to attempting time analysis, the program will also search for obvious errors.

All good network scheduling programs contain comprehensive error detection routines, designed to recognize particular types of mistakes and report them to the planner for correction (or for confirmation to be given that the relevant data are correct as entered). Errors might result from transpositions or other reading errors, keyboard mistakes, omitted data, entering non-valid control data (for example a date which lies outside the main calendar), or some basic flaw in the network diagram logic itself. Input errors can be divided into two categories:

1 Mistakes or apparent mistakes which the computer is able to recognize and report back as helpful error messages.
2 Mistakes which the computer cannot recognize, and which will lead to incorrect schedules. Examples of these are:

    • one zero too many on the end of an activity duration;
    • stating the wrong type of constraint for an activity in a precedence network;
    • forgetting to specify the cost of a materials purchasing activity;
    • entering the wrong resource or sort code for an activity.

Because there are so many ways in which undetectable mistakes can be made, it pays to be very careful when the data are first entered. It is useful if a second person can be on hand to check each item of data as it is entered.

It is not surprising that the most frequent source of input errors occurs in the activity records, since these represent by far the greatest amount of data to be entered. There are three particular types of input error for activities which the network program should be capable of identifying, analysing and reporting. Putting such errors right can sometimes prove to be an interesting exercise in detection, with the computer reports merely providing clues. The three main error types are as follows:

1 *Duplicate activities*, where two different activity records have been input with the same start and finish event numbers. It is almost certain that a modern system would report this type of mistake as soon as an attempt is made to enter the

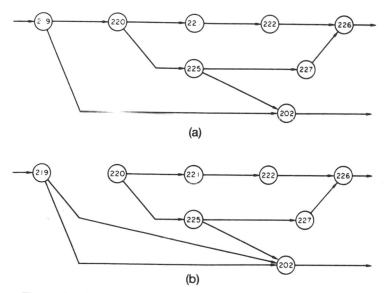

(a)

(b)

Figure 8.4 Error detection: duplicate activities
Duplicate activities can arise from several causes in both arrow and precedence networks, always through some mistake made by the planner. Here is one way in which this can happen with an arrow network. Suppose that activity 219, 220 in (a) were to be incorrectly entered as activity 219, 202. Such transposition of digits can occur easily when the person at the keyboard is tired. The network logic, as seen by the computer, must become that shown at (b). But two activities would now bear the same identification, namely 219, 202. In practice the computer would not allow the second activity to be entered, but would call the equivalent of 'snap!', leaving the planner to re-examine the network and trace the cause of the error.

second activity record at the keyboard (earlier systems made the unsuspecting planner wait until after the initial error run). The cause is likely to be one of the following:

- a real attempt to input the same activity twice, which might happen (for instance) if the person entering the data happened to be interrupted, and forgot that the activity had already been entered;
- a keyboard error in entering an event number (see Figure 8.4);
- an event numbering error on the network diagram;

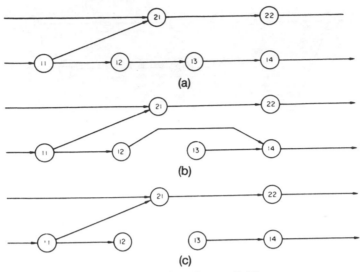

Figure 8.5 Error detection: dangling activities
Dangling activities are activities which lack either a preceding or a succeeding activity. They occur correctly at the beginning and end of all networks, and otherwise because of mistakes or omissions when data are input. In precedence networks an error dangle can happen if a constraint is wrongly specified or not specified at all. The illustration shows possible mistakes leading to dangling activities in an arrow diagram. At (a), if activity 12, 13 were to be wrongly input as 12, 14, the computer would interpret the logic shown in (b), and activity 13, 14 would be reported as a start dangle error. If the planner, instead, forgot to enter activity 12, 13 at all, the computer would 'see' the network shown at (c), and would report activity 11, 13 as an end dangle and activity 13, 14 as a start dangle.

- a network drawing error, such as that depicted in Figure 8.2(a).

2 *Dangling activities*, which occur whenever records have been created for activities with no preceding activities (start dangles) or no succeeding activities (end dangles). Obviously the activities connected to the first and last events in a network will be seen as dangling arrows: some programs allow these to be reported as such beforehand, to prevent their inclusion in error messages. The occurrence of unwanted dangles in arrow networks arrows is explained in Figure 8.5.

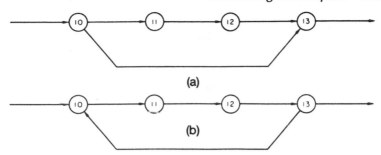

Figure 8.6 Error detection: loops
If activity 10, 13 in diagram (a) were to be input by mistake as 13, 10, the logic shown in (b) would result. There is now a complete loop, formed by activities 10,11; 11,12; 12,13 and the incorrect activity 13,10. The duration of an endless loop is infinite, which is of no use in a project schedule. The computer will report a loop error. The program should be able to list all the activities contained within the loop, in order to help the planner to find the cause of the mistake and put it right.

3 *Loops,* which can be caused by entering an incorrect event number or precedence constraint, or by making a mistake when the network is drawn. Figure 8.6 shows how a loop might be caused. A loop is impossible for the computer to time-analyse, because it creates a continuous, endless cycle of activities. The computer program should be capable of listing all the activities which comprise a loop (or all the events contained in the loop).

All computer programs contain many more error checking routines than the three just described. Error reports will be generated, for example, if the planner has tried to enter a target project-completion date which precedes the specified start date (not a very clever thing to do, but easily done at the end of a tiring day by putting in the wrong year). Other messages will arise if any of the program capacities are exceeded. This would happen, for example, if the network proved to be too large for the computer to handle. Another possibility is that the total project duration might be too long for the specified project calendar. However, in spite of this array of possible pitfalls, dangles and loops are most common errors, and they are the ones which are most likely to go unnoticed until the first schedule calculation is attempted.

The initial scheduling process

Suppose now that either all errors have been eliminated from the input data or, less likely, that there were no errors at all. There should be no further impediment to prevent the computer from producing a complete working schedule from which all the project activities can be initiated and controlled. Of course some unexpected event is bound to happen, sooner rather than later, to upset this plan (strikes, lockouts, fire, flood, tempest, earthquake or a customer's modification). Updating the initial plan to take account of such circumstances will be considered later in this chapter. First, it is necessary to concentrate on producing the project starting schedule. Routines may vary from one program to another, but the following sequence of procedures is typical.

Once the computer has digested and sorted the input data it will make forward and backward passes through the network and report any loops, dangles or other detectable errors (as already described). When the planner has corrected these errors, the computer will again make forward and backward passes through the network but, with the errors removed it can perform time analysis, determining the amount of float, and the earliest possible and latest permissible times for the start and finish of every activity. The system will observe any constraints imposed by scheduled dates attached to events anywhere in the network during this process. Calculations are made in terms of numbers, using the chosen standard units of duration, and conversion to calendar dates takes place as a subsequent operation.

If time analysis only is required, the computer can now be instructed to edit, sort and print out data in the required report formats. However, it will be assumed here that the computer system is expected to produce a complete schedule, with resource scheduling in addition to simple time analysis.

Unsatisfactory programs will simply schedule each activity at its earliest possible date, assign the estimated number of resources for the period of the activity, and then repeat this for all other activities. No attempt is made to schedule any activity other than at its earliest possible time, and the resource pattern that results for each type of resource is calculated by simple addition. This is resource aggregation, which is of very limited use because it takes no account of the actual resources available.

All the best programs will still attempt to schedule each activity at its earliest possible time, but will 'draw down' the estimated number of resource units from the amount available for the specified resource category (or categories), restoring the amount available as soon as the activity ends. If the residual resource level is too low for an activity to start at its earliest possible time, the computer will delay the activity's scheduled start until the earliest time at which enough resources become available. When the computer schedules an activity to take place later than its earliest possible date, it has obviously used up some of the total float originally possessed by the activity and by following activities. The amount of float left in each case is called the *remaining float*.

The planner is usually given some choice from a set of priority decision rules, which govern how scarce resources are to be allocated to activities. Perhaps the most important of these rules is to decide whether the schedule is to be resource limited or time limited. If the computer is operating under the resource-limited rule, it is instructed never to schedule any activity at a date which would cause more resources of any particular type to be needed than the quantity available for the project. This could mean that the project would have to be extended beyond the earliest possible completion date shown to be possible by the length of the critical path. It might also mean that any target completion dates specified for key activities within the network would have to be ignored. An example of a resource-limited schedule was given in the previous chapter (see Figures 7.4 and 7.5).

If the time-limited rule is chosen, the computer will schedule all activities at dates necessary to ensure that the project is completed within the timescale specified. Any target dates imposed on the starts or finishes of individual activities within the network will also be given priority. If necessary, the computer will exceed the number of resources stated to be available in order to meet the time obligations. But the computer cannot schedule any activity to start before the earliest possible time calculated from network time analysis, so that it will disregard any target dates imposed by the planner which are simply impossible to meet owing to the cumulative estimated values of preceding activities.

There are other decision rules, from which the planner is usually given a choice. For example, suppose that time analysis of the network shows that several activities could all start on the same day, and that several of these activities each require the employment of two electricians. If only four electricians happened to be available for the entire project, it is obvious that only two of the activities needing electricians could be started. How does the computer decide which two activities these should be? Such priorities can be decided in a number of ways, and the computer software manual should list the options. An arrangement which often produces the best schedules is to give priority to activities which have least remaining float. Other priority rules may exist to determine when threshold resources should be called into play.

It is recognized that resource allocation by computer may not necessarily produce the smoothest possible pattern of resource usage. Even when a resource schedule is calculated which never exceeds the stated capacity, there may be peaks and troughs that could be ironed out by further calculation. For example, if ten electricians are available, the computer could produce a schedule for a particular project that calls for the use of electricians along the following lines:

Day	Electricians needed	Electricians available	Electricians spare
1	3	10	7
2	2	10	8
3	8	10	2
4	10	10	0
5	2	10	8
6	4	10	8
7	10	10	0
8	9	10	1
9	8	10	2
10	4	10	6

. . . and so on

Although this table results from resource allocation, and never exceeds the total number of electricians available to the company, it is an inconvenient schedule because of its unevenness. This would be particularly true if the project site happened to be remote from the main company premises, in which case the ideal must be to schedule work smoothly to a resident group with a fairly constant strength. A better scheduler might have achieved a daily usage which did not vary much around the average (which is six electricians per day over this 10-day period). However, this example has been slightly exaggerated, and the problem is not usually serious. Some computer programs can go beyond resource allocation, to attempt *resource smoothing*, or *resource optimization*. These systems make multiple-resource allocation passes through the network, striving to remove preventable fluctuations from the usage pattern for each resource category.

All of the foregoing suggests a protracted succession of calculations, which might be thought to take considerable time. Indeed, with the old batch processing methods that was the case. However, modern computers (even desktop personal machines) can make the time analysis and resource scheduling calculations very rapidly, with no noticeable delay between the different operations. Once the errors have been removed, the whole scheduling process should be counted in seconds rather than minutes.

Output reports

After a big network has been processed, a very large volume of data is stored in the computer. The quantity of information usually far exceeds that needed for project management. Not only are there a lot of data, but computers are capable of producing output in many different forms, even from a small selection of data. If all possible reports were to be produced, the result might be an unmanageable pile of paper, impressive for its bulk, but not for much else. It follows that the project manager must manage the data carefully, ensuring that reports are concise, well presented and as effective as possible for their intended purpose.

The data content of every report must be carefully considered, to ensure that each recipient gets information that is particularly useful or relevant to him or her (preferably on a 'needs-to-know' basis). This is achieved by the process of editing, made possible by the provision of departmental report codes entered in the control data and activity records, or by specifying milestones or key activities. All unwanted data should be excluded (for example, the dummies used in arrow networks should not be included in activity reports sent to supervisors and managers).

Another important aspect of reports is the sequence in which data are presented. This is the process of sorting. For example, a manager responsible for issuing work needs a report which lists jobs in order of their scheduled start dates. A progress clerk or expeditor is best served by a report that lists jobs or materials deliveries in order of their scheduled completion dates.

Most project planning and scheduling programs are capable of producing reports that use colour to highlight critical activities, or to distinguish other important features such as the scheduled use of threshold resources.

There are several ways in which report formats can be described, but the most fundamental property is whether they are to be tabular (data printed in columns) or graphic (plotted charts). In many cases the same data can be presented by both methods. The following sections describe some, but by no means all of the possibilities.

Tabular reports

Simple activity listings
The most basic form of activity listing simply prints out all activity records, probably in numerical sequence of their identifier numbers. These lists are useful only for checking that data have been entered correctly into the system.

If resources are not to be scheduled, an activity listing produced after network time analysis will have to be used as the basis for issuing and progressing work.

Activity listings can be edited according to department codes, so that each department only receives lists of those activities for which it is directly reponsible. Reports for senior managers may be confined to milestones or key events and activities.

The sequence in which the activities are listed is important,

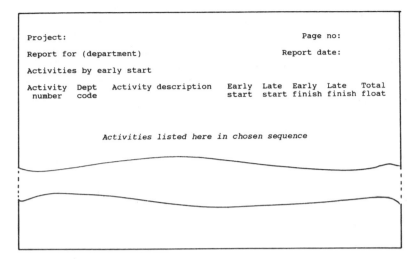

```
Project:                                    Page no:

Report for (department)                    Report date:

Activities by early start

Activity  Dept   Activity description   Early Late  Early Late  Total
number    code                          start start finish finish float


              Activities listed here in chosen sequence
```

Figure 8.7 Typical report format for an activity list
This type of report results from time analysis, with no consideration of resources. The column headed 'Activity number' would apply to the precedence system: for arrow networks this would be replaced by two columns headed 'Preceding event' and 'Succeeding event'. Activities can usually be listed in a choice of sequences, one of the most popular being in ascending order of earliest start date. Critical activities are often highlighted by an asterisk.

and the earliest possible start date is often favoured for these time-analysis-only reports. Critical activities are usually highlighted by an asterisk. A typical arrangement of headings and columns for an activity list is shown in Figure 8.7.

Activities reports as work-to lists
The work-to list (Figure 8.8) is another form of activity listing, similar to the activity lists just described, but with the important difference that activities are presented with their data after resource scheduling. Managers are able to use such reports for issuing work with some degree of confidence that departmental resources will be adequate to meet the schedule requirements. Scheduled start and finish dates are the main controls, but earliest start and latest finish dates can also be shown if required, to allow the manager some flexibility in issuing and progressing work. Remaining float is reported rather than total float, because some of the total float will have been used up by

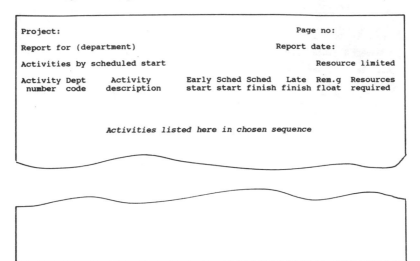

```
Project:                                    Page no:

Report for (department)                     Report date:

Activities by scheduled start                          Resource limited

Activity Dept    Activity        Early Sched Sched  Late  Rem.g  Resources
  number  code   description     start start finish finish float required



            Activities listed here in chosen sequence
```

Figure 8.8 Typical format for a resource-scheduled activity list
This type of report is far more useful than the simple time analysis listing shown in Figure 8.7 because the scheduled dates have been calculated after taking available resources into account. Listing activities in ascending order of scheduled start date is usual for the purposes of issuing work, but reports listed by scheduled or latest finish date are useful to progress chasers and expeditors.

the computer during the process of calculating the resource-scheduled activity dates.

Resource and cost tables
If the system has been used for resource scheduling it will be capable of printing tables of expected resource usage. When cost rates have been specified for resources, cost data can also be included in the reports, and this information will automatically be timed according to the resource schedule. A useful report arrangement is shown in Figure 8.9. Such reports can be produced for each type of resource, for each department, or for all activities in the project.

Reports from computer graphics

Early attempts at graphical reports used line printers, dot matrix or other printers that were not designed to produce diagrams or

```
INGERDALE MACHINE TOOL COMPANY                            Page no:
```

DATE	DESIGNERS				SUB-CONTRACT DESIGN				CUMULATIVE
	AVAIL	USAGE	REM'G	COST	AVAIL	USAGE	REM'G	COST	COST
01FEB93	3	3		240	4	2	2	140	380
02FEB93	3	3		240	4	2	2	140	760
03FEB93	3	3		240	4	3	1	210	180
04FEB93	3	3		240	4	3	1	210	1110
05FEB93	3	3		240	4	4		280	1630
08FEB93	3	3		240	4	4		280	2150
09FEB93	3	3		240	4	4		280	2670
10FEB93	3	3		240	4	4		280	3190
11FEB93	3	3		240	4	4		280	3710
12FEB93	3	3		240	4	4		280	4230
15FEB93	3	4	-1	320	4	4		280	4830
16FEB93	3	4	-1	320	4	4		280	5430
17FEB93	3	3		240	4	4		280	5950
18FEB93	3	3		240	4	3	1	210	6400
19FEB93	3	3		240	4	2	2	140	6780
22FEB93	3	2	1	160	4	1	3	70	7010
23FEB93	3	2	1	160	4		4		7170

Figure 8.9 Resource/cost table
This shows how resource usage and costs can be tabulated on a day-
by-day basis after a computer has carried out resource scheduling from
a project network. Two resource grades are depicted here. Although this
table has been simulated for clarity, and is only a fragment of a full
report, it is based on a real case.

graphs. Graphical effects had to be simulated by printing
suitable alphanumeric characters in blocks or patterns. The
speed of printing could be fast, and the results were reasonable
for bar charts and resource histograms. The charts were less
effective for showing any non-linear graph, mainly because the
resolution was too coarse, being about one tenth of an inch
along one axis and even worse along the other.

Current systems use plotters which are readily available, and
have typical resolutions of 300 dots per inch along both axes.
Moreover, many of these plotters are able to use colour. They
do, however, tend to be considerably slower than other
printers, largely because their vastly improved resolution calls
for far more data to be transferred during printing.

The range and design of reports available must depend on the software chosen, but most systems will support bar charts, resource histograms, cost curves and more advanced applications such as probability charts (see the section on risk analysis in Chapter 9).

Reports produced in bar chart form are particularly appreciated by supervisors, especially on construction sites. Their visual impact makes them far easier to understand and use for day-to-day control than the networks from which they have been derived. The bar chart in Figure 8.10 is a bar chart conversion from the arrow diagram of the garage project in Chapter 7. This version shows the project before resource levelling, with activities all positioned at their earliest start dates. It was produced specially for this book using the powerful *CRESTA* software, by courtesy of K&H Project Systems Limited. We can only show the black and white version of the graphics here – in colour these charts come to life vividly, with critical activities standing out.

A valuable graphics feature is the ability of computer systems to plot the project network diagram. With some packages it is possible for the planner to design the initial network diagram on the screen, although this has obvious size limitations from the practical point of view. A computer which can plot a network after logic changes have been made, or when progress data have been entered, can save the many hours of drawing or tracing time that used to be wasted in producing revised versions of a hand-draughted or traced network, especially when these had to be specially neat and tidy to impress the project client. Figure 8.11 is a computer plot of an arrow diagram, again specially produced for this book and featuring the garage project from Chapter 7. This illustration was prepared using Lucas Management Systems' acclaimed *ARTEMIS* system.

Updating

Updating is the process of producing a fresh set of schedules and other reports to take account of one or more of the following:

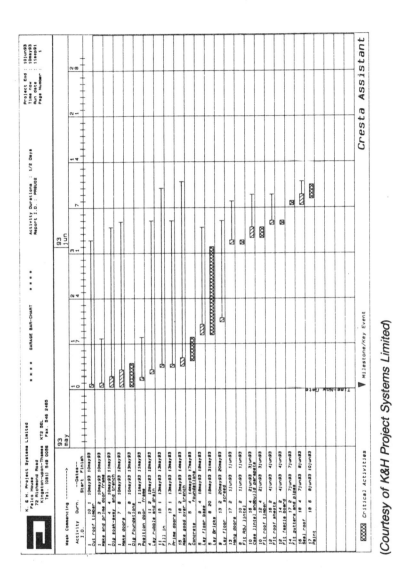

(Courtesy of K&H Project Systems Limited)

Figure 8.10 Garage project bar chart plotted by *CRESTA*

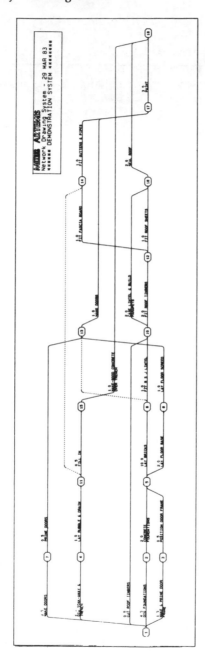

(Courtesy of Lucas Management Systems Ltd)

Figure 8.11 Garage project network plotted by *ARTEMIS*

number of resources available, cost rates, or an imposed target date.
2 A change in the network logic. This could arise, for example as a result of a serious technical problem and consequent change of design strategy, or a change in the project scope as a result of a customer modification.
3 A desire to produce new schedules that take into account progress made to date.

Updating frequency

If a schedule has been produced which proves to be totally practicable, and if everything goes according to plan, there is no need at all to return to the computer for a new schedule during the life of the project. This could very well be the case for a simple project, or for a schedule covering only a very short total timespan. Even a more complex project has been known to run entirely according to its original plan, where the plan was well made and the project particularly well managed. In most project situations, however, too many unknown factors lurk. Just when things appear to be on plan, a key supplier fails to deliver vital materials, a design error is discovered that will take weeks to put right, the customer puts in a late modification, or a site supervisor is horrified to see the scaffolding and formwork for a bridge gradually collapse into the shape of a graceful bow under the weight of much newly-poured and liberally reinforced quicksetting concrete (yes, it really did happen).

The integrity of a project schedule must be protected at all times. If anything happens that renders a schedule obsolete it must be updated as soon as possible; otherwise people will lose faith in the plans and disregard them. Updating frequency can be contemplated:

- on an *occasional* basis, which usually means that, owing to a specific event or change the existing schedules have either become inconvenient to use or are actually wrong;
- on a *regular* basis (which often means monthly). Regular updating may be needed if the project is very complex, with large volumes of progress data to be digested. For some projects, regularly updated schedules and their resulting

tabular and graphic reports provide an essential part of reporting to the project client.

A word of warning is necessary here. The ability of computers to produce tidy printed schedules at regular intervals is very convenient, and the schedules should be ideal for controlling the issue of work and for monitoring the subsequent progress of *that* work. But, as progress reports, the updated schedules are of historical interest only. In other words, the schedules are updated chiefly for the sake of controlling work yet to come. For the purposes of day-to-day management of project work in progress, it is the current schedule that counts. If only scrap is produced after six weeks of a manufacturing job, or if it is found that 100 metres of trench have been excavated along the wrong side of a road, the manager (after recovering his or her composure) can soon tell from the dates and float given in the current schedule how much time (if any) remains for repeating the abortive activity, and therefore how much effort needs to be put into corrective action. The manager does not turn immediately to the computer for help. If the activity was critical or nearly so, it is obvious that all the stops need to be pulled out at once to put things right. Of course the schedule must be updated, but that is a consequential process which follows once steps have been taken to sort out the immediate problem.

Updating method

Changes to network logic or to project parameters are simply a case of replacing data that were entered for the initial run. Some new steps must be explained, however, in connection with entering progress information.

The first thing to decide before producing a new schedule is the date from which the computer is to start calculations. There is no point in having a schedule printed out to start on 1 July if copies of the schedule will not be distributed for action until 15 July. So a datum point has to be chosen, and this is always referred to as 'time now'. All progress information must be collected or assessed with reference to time now. The time now date can be anywhere on the main network calendar, but is likely to be either the date on which the update is carried out or (often) a date which looks slightly into the future. A future time may be chosen to allow for delays in gathering progress information from the farthest outposts of a project. Supervisors and managers must be asked to report their progress as they forecast it to be at the future 'time now' (a 'future time now' really does sound like a contradiction in terms, and is a difficult concept for some people to grasp initially). Progress reporting for a future time now does, therefore, introduce a small element of uncertainty, but the degree of such risk is likely to be very small if all the managers are sufficiently competent and, more important, truthful.

For every schedule update the planner must enter the following data:

- time now date;
- the identifying number(s) for every activity that is in progress or will be started by time now, together with an estimate of its duration remaining after time now;
- the identifying number(s) for all activities which are complete, or which will certainly be complete by time now.

Methods for reporting the degree of progress achieved for activities which have been started may vary from one system to another. The better computer programs should not reschedule activities reported as being started or in progress. No one wants to receive an updated schedule that calls for work in progress to be interrupted.

Producing the first updated schedule will involve the planner in learning a few new commands or ways in which to operate the particular system. But the most difficult (and the most important) aspect of updating schedules for any complex project is the gathering of accurate and reliable progress information. This, however, is a problem common to many management systems, and is by no means peculiar to computer project management procedures.

Suggested programs

The following software systems, listed in alphabetical order, are versatile and powerful, and all are well proven, with good support offered by their respective companies and a large number of existing users. Each program can handle arrow and precedence networks, and all are capable of dealing with advanced applications such as those described in Chapter 9. UK addresses are given here, but these companies all have offices or agents in many other countries throughout the world.

ARTEMIS, from Lucas Management Systems, 23 Clayton Road, Hayes, Middlesex, UB3 1BR.

CRESTA, from K&H Project Systems Ltd, Felco House, 72 Richmond Road, Kingston-upon-Thames, Surrey, KT2 5EL.

OPEN PLAN, from Welcom Software Technology International, South Bank Technopark, 90 London Road, London, SE1 6LN.

9

More advanced procedures and systems

The three previous chapters described the principles of project planning and scheduling in some detail. This chapter begins with a case study by way of recapitulation and then continues by outlining some methods by which experienced planners can improve their effectiveness in drawing networks, or by exploiting more fully the computer systems available to them.

Case study

This case study is another scheduling exercise for the garage project which was introduced in Chapter 7. However, all the illustrations in Chapter 7 were calculated for the first edition of this book, in 1968, using pencil and paper. The reports in this case study were run on 12 November 1991 using a computer, with the project start date updated to Monday, 10 May 1993. Cost data have been introduced, but the project definition is otherwise unchanged.

Acknowledgement is due to Welcom Software Technology International for making computing facilities available at their offices, and for calculating all the schedules for this case study, using their *OPEN PLAN* system.

The project

Two people (one skilled person and one labourer) are to construct a small garage. The network diagram, shown in Figure 9.1, is effectively the same as that in Figure 7.1, but precedence notation has been used this time (simply to demonstrate the alternative method). The network has been kept simple for clarity: for example it does not show any plant hire, purchasing or materials delivery activities and the critical examiner will notice that no times have been allowed for concrete to cure.

The control data

It was necessary to augment or qualify the data written on the network diagram to set all the parameters needed for resource and cost scheduling. Here is a complete list of that data.

- *Project title*: Garage project
- *Calendar*: Duration units are half days
        10 units = 5 days = 1 week (Monday to Friday)
- *Project start date and time now*: 10 May 1993
- *Progress status at time now date*: Project not started
- *Scheduled (target) finish date*: None given, but please see the next item
- *Time and resource constraints*: A resource-limited schedule is required, held within the resource availability levels shown below. However, a time-limited schedule is also to be run, should the resource-limited finish date be unacceptable. The time-limited reports are to plan for the project being completed at its minimum possible duration (that is, the duration of the critical path)
- *Valid start dangles*: Activities 5, 10, 15, 20 and 25
- *Valid end dangles*: Activities 105, 110 and 115
- *Resource codes, availability levels and resource cost rates*:
    SK = skilled, only 1 available, cost rate £50 per half day
    LB = labourer, only 1 available, cost rate £30 per half day
- *Splitting rule*: All activities are non-splittable
- *Stretching rule*: No activity is to be stretched (that is, to be scheduled with a longer planned duration so that it uses fewer day-by-day resources). In any case, there is no oppor-

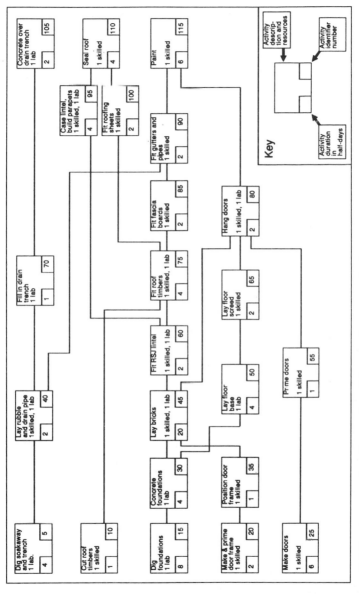

Figure 9.1 Garage construction network (precedence version)
This is the precedence equivalent of the arrow diagram that was shown in Figure 7.1.

tunity for stretching, because only one unit of each resource type is available.
- *Materials costs*: The activities listed below are expected to incur material costs at the levels shown:

Activity number	Cost £	Activity number	Cost £
10	250	65	25
20	50	80	50
25	120	85	15
30	40	90	25
40	40	95	45
45	300	100	230
50	40	105	20
55	10	110	35
60	50	115	25

Input errors

Even though this network was very small, no less than three data errors cropped up in the first attempt at time analysis. This indicates a little more carelessness than usual, but it does emphasize the point that human errors can be expected in most initial scheduling attempts.

The computer listed all the expected start and finish dangles on screen, but it also named one activity as isolated. This was caused by failure to key in a logic constraint leading out from one of the start activities.

Time analysis indicated a project duration of about four months, but a previous mental run through the network gave a critical path length of only one month (which was the result obtained in the Chapter 7 illustrations). Two separate data errors were responsible for this result:

1 The duration for Activity 60 had been input as 60 instead of 2, a clerical error. (This mistake was traced by calling up a list of all activities on the VDU screen so that the input data could be checked.)
2 The calendar instructions had been wrongly set, so that the computer was allowing a whole day's duration for every

duration unit, instead of one half of a day. (This error was deduced after comparing activity durations with the start and finish dates printed out in reports – it became obvious that all calendar intervals were twice what they should have been.)

These last two errors demonstrate the need for care, because they were accepted (quite reasonably) by the computer as valid data. It was only by performing independent manual checks that these mistakes were discovered. It always pays to make such manual checks as a matter of routine. For example, it is advisable to run through a network forwards by hand, just to get an idea of what the critical path duration ought to be.

The schedules

The errors noted in the previous section were soon put right, leaving the computer able to calculate and plot a wide variety of schedules. The reports illustrated here were chosen from a wide range of standard options available to *OPEN PLAN* users. Reports could also have been adapted or set up specially to cater for individual needs or quirks.

Some features of the reports illustrated have been edited or removed to preserve clarity in the small size of reproduction necessary in this book. For example, although the computer was able to divide the timescales into calendar days and print in all the dates, I have converted these to weeks and replotted the charts in order to use larger type.

Work-to lists
Figure 9.2 is a complete activity listing for the project, assembled in chronological order of scheduled starts after a resource-limited scheduling calculation. This is the document which should be used to control the sequence and timing of all work, provided that the calculated project completion date is accept-able to all concerned.

The following columns would also have been included in the standard version of this report, but have been removed for clarity of reproduction:

OPEN PLAN   ACTIVITY LISTING BY SCHEDULED START   PAGE: 1
REPORT: ACTRES   RESOURCE LIMITED REPORT   REPORT DATE: 12NOV91
PROJECT: GARAGE   Garage Construction Network   TIME NOW: 10MAY.12:00A

ACTIVITY	ORIG DUR	DESCRIPTION	RESOURCE CODE	QTY	SCHEDULED START	SCHEDULED FINISH	SCHED FLOAT
15	8	Dig foundations	LB	8	10MAY.12:00A	14MAY.12:00A	0
20	2	Make and prime door frame	SK	2	10MAY.12:00A	11MAY.12:00A	9
35	1	Position door frame	SK	1	11MAY.12:00P	11MAY.12:00P	9
25	6	Make doors	SK	6	11MAY.12:00P	14MAY.12:00P	30
30	4	Concrete foundations	LB	4	14MAY.12:00A	18MAY.12:00A	0
55	1	Prime doors	SK	1	14MAY.12:00P	15MAY.12:00A	30
10	1	Cut roof timbers	SK	1	17MAY.12:00A	17MAY.12:00P	23
45	20	Lay bricks	LB	20	18MAY.12:00A	01JUN.12:00A	0
			SK	20			
60	2	Fit RSJ lintel	LB	2	01JUN.12:00A	02JUN.12:00A	0
			SK	2			
95	4	Case lintel and build parapets	LB	4	02JUN.12:00A	04JUN.12:00A	6
			SK	4			
50	4	Lay floor base	LB	4	04JUN.12:00A	08JUN.12:00A	-4
65	2	Lay floor screed	SK	2	08JUN.12:00A	09JUN.12:00A	-4
80	2	Hang doors	LB	2	09JUN.12:00A	10JUN.12:00A	-4
			SK	2			
75	4	Fit roof timbers	LB	4	10JUN.12:00A	12JUN.12:00A	-12
			SK	4			
5	4	Dig soakaway and trench	LB	4	14JUN.12:00A	16JUN.12:00A	-16
85	2	Fit fascia boards	SK	2	14JUN.12:00A	15JUN.12:00A	-12
100	2	Fit roofing sheets	SK	2	15JUN.12:00A	16JUN.12:00A	-10
110	4	Seal roof	LB	4	16JUN.12:00A	18JUN.12:00A	-10
40	2	Lay rubble and drain	LB	2	18JUN.12:00A	19JUN.12:00A	-20
			SK	2			
70	1	Fill in drain trench	LB	1	21JUN.12:00A	22JUN.12:00P	-15
90	2	Fit gutters and pipes	SK	2	21JUN.12:00A	22JUN.12:00A	-20
105	2	Concrete over drain trench	LB	2	21JUN.12:00P	22JUN.12:00P	-15
115	6	Paint	SK	6	22JUN.12:00A	25JUN.12:00A	-20

Figure 9.2 Garage project, resource-limited work-to list

- *Scheduled duration*: Two columns compare the duration originally estimated for each activity with that determined by the computer after splitting or stretching during resource allocation. No stretching or splitting was allowed during this case study.
- *Code 1 and Code 2*: Columns which allow codes to be allocated for such things as editing and sorting for reports at different hierarchical levels.
- *Resource class*: Not used in this case study, but applicable (for example) when threshold resources are used.

Because half-day duration units were used on the network, each date in the schedule is suffixed by a time, indicating whether the activity is to be started in the first half of each day (12.00A) or from midday (12.00P). The use of half day units is unusual in project scheduling, but it illustrates the versatility of *OPEN PLAN*, which can deal with very small units of duration if required.

The most significant result shown in Figure 9.2 is the amount of negative float appearing in later activities (right-hand column). This is a result of the computer having to delay the scheduled starts of several activities owing to insufficient resources (while operating under the resource-limited rule). Figure 9.3 shows what happened when the schedule was run again using the time-limited rule, so that the project could be completed within the duration of the critical path, at the expense of having to deploy more resources.

Other standard reports are available which include the data already described for work-to lists, but which also allow actual progress data and a forecast of the remaining duration to be listed for each activity.

Resource histograms
Figure 9.4 shows two comparative resource histograms for the skilled resource category. (Histograms produced for the labourer resource were similar, and are not shown.) Figure 9.4(a) is the resource-limited version, and Figure 9.4(b) is time limited (so that it incurs overload peaks). Notice that weekends appear as gaps in the schedules.

```
OPEN PLAN                    ACTIVITY LISTING BY SCHEDULED START           PAGE: 1
REPORT: ACTRES                      TIME LIMITED REPORT              REPORT DATE: 12NOV91
PROJECT: GARAGE                 Garage Construction Network         TIME NOW: 10MAY.12:00A
```

ACTIVITY	ORIG DUR	DESCRIPTION	RESOURCE CODE	QTY	SCHEDULED START	SCHEDULED FINISH	SCHED FLOAT
5	4	Dig soakaway and trench	LB	4	10MAY.12:00A	12MAY.12:00A	34
15	8	Dig foundations	LB	8	10MAY.12:00A	14MAY.12:00A	0
20	2	Make and prime door frame	SK	2	10MAY.12:00A	11MAY.12:00A	9
25	6	Make doors	SK	6	10MAY.12:00A	13MAY.12:00A	33
35	1	Position door frame	SK	1	11MAY.12:00A	11MAY.12:00P	9
10	1	Cut roof timbers	SK	1	11MAY.12:00P	12MAY.12:00A	30
40	2	Lay rubble and drain	LB	2	12MAY.12:00A	13MAY.12:00A	34
			SK	2			
70	1	Fill in drain trench	LB	1	13MAY.12:00A	13MAY.12:00P	39
55	1	Prime doors	SK	1	13MAY.12:00A	13MAY.12:00P	33
105	2	Concrete over drain trench	LB	2	13MAY.12:00P	14MAY.12:00P	39
30	4	Concrete foundations	LB	4	14MAY.12:00P	18MAY.12:00A	0
45	20	Lay bricks	LB	20	18MAY.12:00A	01JUN.12:00A	0
			SK	20			
50	4	Lay floor base	LB	4	18MAY.12:00A	20MAY.12:00A	22
65	2	Lay floor screed	SK	2	20MAY.12:00A	21MAY.12:00A	22
60	2	Fit RSJ lintel	LB	2	01JUN.12:00A	02JUN.12:00A	0
			SK	2			
80	2	Hang doors	LB	2	01JUN.12:00A	02JUN.12:00A	8
			SK	2			
75	4	Fit roof timbers	LB	4	02JUN.12:00A	04JUN.12:00A	0
			SK	4			
85	2	Fit fascia boards	SK	2	04JUN.12:00A	05JUN.12:00A	0
100	2	Fit roofing sheets	SK	2	04JUN.12:00A	05JUN.12:00A	4
90	2	Fit gutters and pipes	SK	2	07JUN.12:00A	08JUN.12:00A	0
95	4	Case lintel and build parapets	LB	4	07JUN.12:00A	09JUN.12:00A	0
			SK	4			
115	6	Paint	SK	6	08JUN.12:00A	11JUN.12:00A	0
110	4	Seal roof	SK	4	09JUN.12:00A	11JUN.12:00A	0

Figure 9.3 Garage project, time-limited work-to list

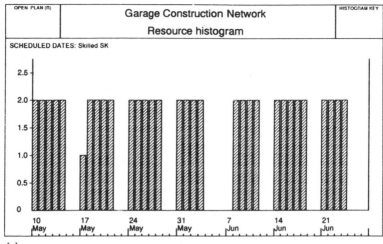

(a)

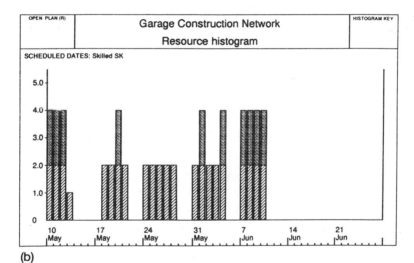

(b)

Figure 9.4 Garage project, resource- and time-limited load histograms

The units on the y axis are total resource units per day. Because all durations have been estimated in half-day units, it follows that one person occupied for one-half day is one resource unit, and one person needed for a whole day is two

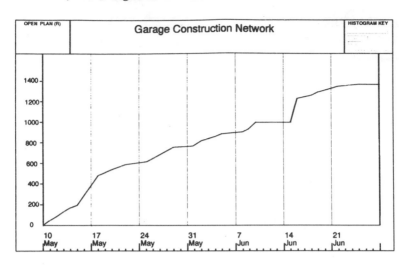

Figure 9.5 Garage project, materials expenditure estimates against time

resource units. So, halve the numbers on the y axes in both of these charts to arrive at the number of skilled people required.

A line on the original histograms traced the level of availability for each resource, but this was omitted when the charts were edited and redrawn for this book (for clarity).

OPEN PLAN has a number of other standard histogram reports available for indicating resource loads and costs.

Material costs

Figure 9.5 is a graph of the materials expenditure, as it is expected to accumulate against time. The results shown here are scheduled for the resource-limited option, timed to coincide with the actual use of the materials on site. The costs are those estimated for activities shown in the table in the 'Control data' section above. The total estimated cost of materials is £1307, a result which can be obtained by adding up the figures in the table or (very approximately) by looking at the graph.

If separate activities had been included in the network for ordering materials, their estimated costs could have been plotted as a graph of committed expenditure. When the graph is plotted at its usual full size (A4 or even A3) and in different colours, other features which *OPEN PLAN* provides are far easier to distinguish. These include actual costs, earned value and revised estimated cost to completion (subjects which are explained in Chapter 15).

Resource costs

The reports for resource costs are not illustrated, but *OPEN PLAN* has a number of standard reports which can produce tables, S–curves, or both combined on the same chart. For those interested, the total cost of resources calculated for this project was £4860 which, combined with the materials cost of £1307, indicates a total cost for this modest garage of £6167.

Standard networks and library modules

It is likely that, if a company looks over the plans of its past and current projects, a broad common pattern of working will be found, regardless of project size. It is even more likely that those project plans will contain common elements, identical work patterns or subplans that occur at various stages in most of the company's projects. By analysing past project plans and by carefully considering current working methods it is often possible to identify and use these common patterns, either to produce complete standard network diagrams, or to isolate standard network elements (network modules) for use as 'building bricks' in larger networks.

It can be argued, with some justification, that the concept of 'standard' networks is a contradiction in terms. Networking is, after all, supposed to inspire logical thought. It was never intended to regiment planning into a stereotyped routine, devoid of creative thought or constructive imagination. Nevertheless, standard networks have proved their worth. When the time allowed for planning is short, standard networks can sometimes prove to be such timesavers that they will be used when the networking process might otherwise have been ignored altogether. Standard networks which have been developed as a result of experience gained over a number of suitable projects can also represent a valuable way of capturing knowledge, ensuring that lessons learned in the past are not forgotten.

Some companies fight shy of standard networks and network modules, and either continue to draw a completely new bar chart or network for each fresh project or skimp the planning process. The excuse most often heard is 'We are a special case. It can't be done here because we are different from other companies and all our projects are different too.' Of course these standardization techniques cannot be applied to all projects, but failing even to consider their possibility is a blinkered approach, sometimes causing potential benefits from greater planning efficiency and effectiveness to be lost.

Standard networks

The easiest type of standard network to envisage is a complete network that can be applied directly to two or more identical projects, with no need to change any part of the logic or data. Not surprisingly, this condition seldom arises in real life. There are, however, many cases where a standard master network can be devised that will at least act as a general pattern for planning similar projects. The technique is carried out by first drawing up a master network covering all activities required for a project which is judged to be typical of a range of projects carried out by the organization. It is valuable if as many suitably experienced people as possible are consulted, or better, are actually on hand in a brainstorming session when the master network is sketched. The aim must be to plan the most efficient and practicable work sequence that can be devised.

Many companies sell projects that can be designed and built with a range of options. In these cases the standard network should be drawn to include all the options, or at least all the more common options. If, for example, the network is produced for a range of houses to be built with or without a garage, the standard version should include the garage. It is a simple matter for the project manager to strike out the activities not needed for houses ordered without garages.

The master standard network can be stored as 'hard copy' (on paper or polyester film) or in an electronic data storage and retrieval system. When each new project materializes, a secondary master is produced from the master network. This is then discussed with the project manager or other responsible person, who:

- deletes activities relating to options that the customer has not ordered;
- edits the network in the light of any possible retained engineering (designs from earlier projects that can be used directly or adapted for the new project);
- adds any special constraints or new activities needed for the particular project (for example, *A* must be designed before *B*);
- adds estimated duration, resource and cost data to all activities according to project complexity.

The secondary master is then adopted as the network plan for the new project.

Standard networks: a house construction example
A number of identical or very similar detached houses are to be built by a construction company on different sites and at different times. Here is an obvious case where a network diagram drawn for the erection of the first house must have relevance to all subsequent houses of the same design.

However, although the network configuration (logic) may be identical throughout, it might be necessary to review all the duration estimates for each house according to its particular environment and ground conditions.

Standard networks: an engineering company example
A company making special-purpose heavy machine tools to individual customer orders used the same standard project networks very successfully in its engineering plants on both sides of the Atlantic. The simplest of these was used solely as a logic diagram, without time estimates. It served as a sequenced checklist for the start-up activities needed every time a new order for a transfer line machining system was received. That standard network is illustrated later, in Figure 11.4.

The same company made full use of project standard networks for its range of adjustable rail milling machines (also known as plano-mills) and scalpers. Machines varied greatly in size, but a typical machine weighed hundreds of tonnes and was built on a bed about 20 m in length. Although each of these projects could last up to 18 months, and might be valued at over

£1 m, the network planning cost was measurable in only hundreds of pounds because one standard network was devised that could be applied to all machines of this type. When a new order was received, it was only necessary for the chief engineer or project manager to spend a 1 hour or so in marking up a copy of the master network with appropriate estimates and logic changes. The result in each case was a network whose logic embodied all the lessons learned on similar previous projects, yet was 'customized' for the particular project in hand.

Standard subnetwork modules

A search through networks from past projects should reveal several small repeating network elements, perhaps occurring more than once within each network and common throughout all the projects. Two examples follow which show how these can be exploited, either in a manual system or stored in a computer.

Standard subnetwork modules: an engineering company example
The machine tool company mentioned above reviewed its network diagrams for several special transfer line machine projects. As a result, it was able to break down those networks into areas that could be represented by small, standardized modules. Summarized briefly, this company's breakdown approach was first to divide the main project network into three consecutive subnetworks, comprising:

1 Engineering design and drawing.
2 Procurement and machining.
3 Assembly.

Within each of these three main areas, small network modules were identified which could be used for every subassembly and main assembly. Two examples of these modules are illustrated.

From the design subnetwork, Figure 9.6 shows the module used for the design of any machine along the transfer line that required manufactured (as opposed to purchased) machining heads.

The module used for machining all the components needed for any mechanical subassembly is shown in Figure 9.7. This

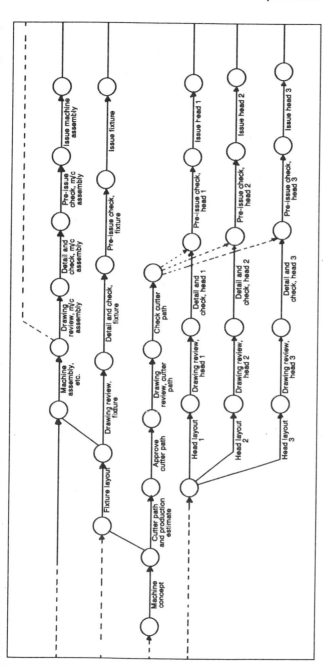

Figure 9.6 A standard subnetwork module for the design of one machine in a transfer line

This example includes all the mainstream design activities necessary to produce a set of manufacturing drawings for a machine in a transfer line, complete with its specially manufactured heads. The module caters for a machine with up to three heads. If only one or two heads are specified the unwanted activities are simply crossed out and ignored. Other standard subnetworks in this system were developed to cover machines with purchased heads and for project start-up activities. These design modules lead into purchasing and manufacturing modules (see Figure 9.7) which lead in turn into the assembly network modules (not illustrated). By compiling a 'library' of all these modules, printed in quantity on self-adhesive film it is possible to assemble complete project networks with great speed and very little effort by sticking the appropriate subnetworks on a large sheet of drawing film. Each network is completed by the addition of linking dummies, event numbers, resource and duration estimates and a final project manager's review of the overall logic.

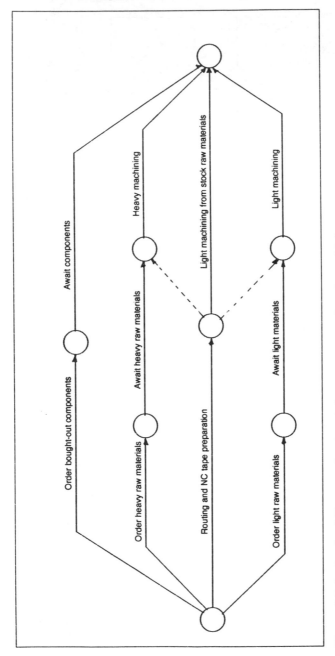

Figure 9.7 A standard library subnetwork for procurement and machining
Used with the engineering design standard network shown in Figure 9.6, this module includes all the project network activities necessary for purchasing and machining any subassembly.

would be linked into the network by interface events or dummies so that it fitted in between its relevant design engineering and assembly activities (from the preceding and succeeding subnetworks).

The whole system only needed about 12 different modules. All of these were printed in suitable quantities on transparent, self-adhesive film and kept as a 'library' for use in the small planning department. Whenever a new project had to be planned, the network was 'drawn' by sticking all the appropriate modules on a large piece of polyester film or translucent paper. This process could be carried out by relatively junior staff, using the sales specification block schematic drawing for the transfer line machine as the guide. Standard start, interfacing and finish modules were available for sticking at the front and back ends of the three subnetworks. The project manager was then called in to modify, edit and approve the network before computer scheduling.

Event numbers were partly preprinted on the modules, the planner simply having to complete each number by prefixing two digits from each module's relevant cost code. This procedure made it impossible to duplicate event numbers by mistake.

Using the company's well-documented past cost records, standard tables were later developed for the duration, resource and materials cost estimates, based on a few simple rules about machine size and complexity. The network plan could then be fed into the computer to produce work-to lists, resource and cost schedules. The system was fully multi-project across the whole company and the resulting resource schedules and work-to lists were very effective. The cost estimates produced were within ± 5 per cent overall of those calculated separately by the company's cost estimating department.

Standard subnetwork modules: a construction company example
A construction company discovered that the network planning for every one of its very different building projects could be speeded up using subnetwork modules. Modules were devised to cover all trades and commonly occurring processes. These were stored as 'library modules' in the computer, and had only to be shown on the hand-drawn network as single activities.

For example, an activity on the main network for plastering a wall would cause the computer to find and substitute a plastering subnetwork, comprising activities for ordering materials, preparing the surface, and rendering with two layers of plaster. Figure 9.8 illustrates the principle. The upper part of the figure shows a small part of a main network for a construction project. The lower portion of the figure shows the library module that the computer would substitute for activity 140 to 150 in the main network. Activities 130 to 140 and 150 to 180 would also generate their own associated modules.

Hammocks and skeletons

Project networks may contain only a few hundred activities, but networks comprising several thousand activities are not uncommon. It is obvious that the level of detail shown in the full project network is not required in plans and reports given to everyone in the project management structure.

The editing and sorting of network-derived information for computer output reports was described in the 'Output reports' section of Chapter 8. There is, however, the additional possibility of viewing the network itself as a document which can exist at two or more levels of detail for different management strata. A typical approach is to regard the main, detailed network primarily as the tool of the planner, from which all activity and resource scheduling is performed. The main network is then summarized to produce an upper level network which contains far fewer (but proportionately larger) activities, scaled to the reporting level which is more appropriate to senior managers.

One way of summarizing a network is to use the process of skeletonization. The planner must name particular events throughout the network as key events (similar to milestone events), chosen because they occur at significant stages in the project which are easy to identify and which are likely to be of particular interest in controlling and reporting progress. The computer then produces a summary network which is constructed upon only the key events. Because all non-key events are excluded from this summary network so, therefore, must be

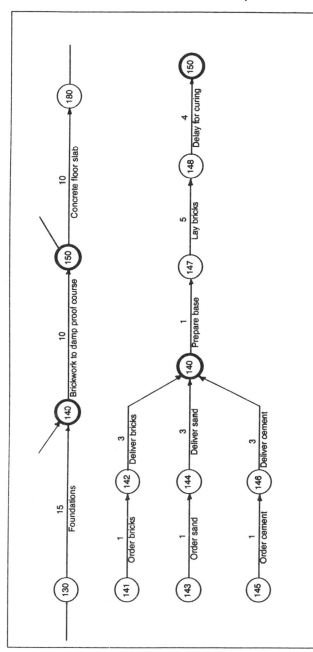

Figure 9.8 Example of a standard library subnetwork for a construction project

Here is a use of library subnetworks that was developed by a construction company. The upper illustration represents part of a network for a construction project. When this network is presented to the computer some of the activities are replaced automatically by more detailed subnetworks. In this example, activity 140 to 150 in the upper diagram would generate the stored subnetwork shown in the lower diagram, and all the additional activities would be analysed and printed out in the work schedules. Events 140 and 150 are shown bold to emphasize the relationship of the module with the main network diagram. Events 141, 143, and 145 are start dangles.

the activities which previously joined them. The resulting network logic is skeletonized, with new activities put in place (by the computer) to link the key events. Each of these new activities summarizes the group of activities which it replaces from the original network.

Another way of reaching a similar result is to introduce hammock activities. Again, key events are chosen throughout the network. The planner adds a new hammock activity to straddle all the activities linking any two key events. The network can either be run to report on all the detailed activities, or to report only on the higher-level hammock activities.

Some organizations find the use of skeletonized or hammocked networks particularly useful when large amounts of data are being handled in multi-project or relational database systems.

Multi-project resource scheduling

Any organization which handles projects using common resources should obviously not schedule one without considering the resources needed by all the others. The organization's managers must therefore look for a way in which to allocate resources over the total company workload, while respecting the priority of each project and, indeed, the priority of every activity within each of those projects. This can present a serious planning problem. The planning system has to digest a large amount of data, conflicts must be resolved, all logical constraints need to be observed, and the result has to be dynamic and responsive to sudden changes in project circumstances (such as design modifications, technical problems, work cancellations or the introduction of new projects).

In the past such planning had to be carried out using adjustable bar charts but, as in the case of single project scheduling, computer systems are now available to everyone for this job. The process is called multi-project scheduling. There is nothing difficult in the application of the method, provided that the principles of single-project scheduling by computer (described in the two previous chapters) are understood. Multi-project scheduling is largely a matter of common sense, although the amount of data to be handled is greater.

The case for multi-project scheduling

Every company which handles more than one project at a time can derive some advantage from multi-project scheduling. A multi-project schedule has benefits for an organization far beyond the planning and control of existing work. The schedule, if properly prepared, is a model of a company's total operational workload. As such, it is a powerful aid to manpower and corporate planning. It is even possible to run 'What if?' trial schedules, testing possible new projects to see what effect these might have on the company's future workload and capacity requirements. It is only necessary to draw a very simple summary network (comprising only a few activities) for each new sales opportunity.

Many companies, however, choose to do without multi-project scheduling using network analysis. Construction companies which rely mainly on subcontractors for their site work, for example, will be able to leave most manpower resource scheduling to the individual firms. Only head office design and supervision staff will have to be scheduled, and primitive scheduling methods will often suffice for that limited purpose.

It is in those organizations which employ their own direct labour, such as the engineering and manufacturing industries, where multi-project scheduling is more likely to be seen as necessary throughout the organization (although it has to be remembered that manpower is not the only resource that can be scheduled using computer techniques).

How multi-project scheduling works

Preparation for multi-project scheduling is very similar to that required for single-project scheduling. A separate network must be drawn for every project in the organization. Estimates for durations, costs and resources are made in the normal way and prepared for input to the computer. All of this follows the methods explained in Chapters 7 and 8. In multi-project scheduling, however, there is an important difference of scale, so that the total organization's load must be regarded as 'the project'. Each of the former individual projects becomes, effectively, a 'subproject' within the new total project. Terminology varies from one system to another. OPEN PLAN refers to the total workload as the 'group of projects', for example, with each separate network called a 'project' in the normal way. In other multi-project systems (and in the remainder of this section) the term 'subproject' is used to refer to each separate network which contributes to the corporate plan.

Thus a continuous overall project is created, with a life that can be expected to last as long as the organization exists, containing a changing number of subprojects with different durations and finite lives.

The computer will carry out time analysis of each subproject and then attempt to allocate resources to all the activities, drawing on the total corporate resources which have been declared by the planner as available.

Output reports can be sorted for each subproject, so that (sub)project managers will not be inconvenienced by receiving data referring to other subprojects being handled by the organization. Apart from the possibility of a manager seeing the multimillion pound venture for which he is responsible being described as a 'subproject', all project managers' reports should be indistinguishable from those that the computer system would produce from a single, separately scheduled project network. Now, however, each manager can have added confidence that the resources needed to meet the schedule are more likely to be available on time, because the organization's total needs have been taken into account.

Priority rules

Planners are always able to choose from a number of priority rules for allocating resources to activities within each subproject, just as in single-project scheduling. In the multi-project case, however, there is a further level of priorities to be decided, namely the allocation of resources between subprojects. The planner will need to ask the relevant software company how the particular system deals with this aspect. It may be necessary to designate a scale of priorities for the subprojects. I have always relied on the use of imposed target start and finish dates for each subproject, without encountering any difficulty (using a K&H Project Systems package similar to *CRESTA*).

Reserving resources needed for non-project work

Any requirement for the use of common resources on non-project work must obviously be taken into account when the total, multi-project, schedule is calculated. Such requirements might include the manufacture of customer spares items for stock, or the setting aside of direct staff to provide a general enquiry, consultancy or other commitment under a service contract with a major customer. The general level of such miscellaneous non-project work must first be forecast for each resource, after which there are two ways in which it can be allowed for:

1 The total level for each resource in the organization that is declared as being available for projects can be reduced by an amount equivalent to the miscellaneous work (see the section 'Specifying resource availability levels' in Chapter 7).
2 The non-project work can be introduced into the scheduling calculations as if it were a continuous 'project'. This would require a 'network' (which might need only one activity) having a duration spanning not less than the life of the whole schedule, and carrying the forecast non-project usage level for each category of resource.

The second of these approaches must be used if the organization wishes to use the results of multi-project scheduling in any corporate manpower studies.

Subproject and activity identifiers

There is a probability that the same event or activity numbers will crop up on different subproject networks (although this can be avoided at the expense of using a larger number of digits for each identifier). The confusion and number of errors generated by having what the computer might perceive as the same event or activity cropping up in more than one subproject can be imagined, with all sorts of complex constraints and paths being created across all the subprojects by mistake.

Fortunately most, if not all, modern computer systems do not demand that every number in the overall project is unique. It is only necessary to make certain that, in the usual way, every identifier is unique *within its own subproject*. The vital point is that each subproject must then be given its own identifying subproject code (which can be a simple one-, two- or three-digit number in most cases).

Interface events or activities

There may be a few instances where it is necessary for one or more subproject networks to share the same event or have a linking constraint. In such cases the common events must bear the same identifier, and be designated as interface events. On arrow diagrams interface events can be highlighted by drawing the event as a pair of concentric circles on each of the subprojects concerned.

The incidence of interface events in multi-project scheduling should be rare. It is not good practice, for example, to use them in an attempt to control priorities between different subprojects (where reliance on remaining float relative to scheduled target dates is the sensible option). There are, however, exceptions. One example is in the allocation of final factory assembly space for large items of plant or machinery, where one subproject cannot be assembled until another has cleared the area. Assembly space for large engineering projects is very difficult, if not impossible, to specify and allocate as a resource using project management programs because it involves area shape and can even mean considering headspace and overhangs. In such cases the sequence in which projects arrive in the assembly bay will have to be decided by the planners, and forced into the computer schedules by the use of interface events or the insertion of constraints between subprojects.

In addition to their use in multi-project scheduling, interface events are of course also needed whenever any large network is split into a series of smaller subnetworks for the purposes of clarity or ease of handling.

A program for probability and risk analysis

Whenever investment in a new project is contemplated, the sponsors or managers will obviously want to quantify the predicted results as far as possible before making any commitment. Financial aspects of project appraisal were covered in Chapter 5. In some cases, however, there may be particular concern about an element of risk or uncertainty, possibly concerning the scale of likely total costs, or the timescale, or both.

Computer programs exist which, using statistical methods, can help planners to evaluate the extent of such risks. One of these is *OPERA*, part of the *OPEN PLAN* project management system. The procedure outlined below explains how *OPERA* can evaluate the chances of a particular activity or an entire project being finished by a particular date.

In order to use the system, the planner has first to consider every network activity and decide how much confidence can be placed in the estimate made for its duration. Then, the duration estimate for each activity is expressed as two alternatives, the most optimistic and the most pessimistic. This is superficially similar to the PERT approach (see the PERT section in Chapter 6) except that only two estimates are needed for each activity, not three.

During network time analysis, the *OPERA* program causes the computer to allocate either the optimistic or the pessimistic duration estimate to each activity. The choices are random (based on a random number generator), so that whether or not the optimistic or pessimistic estimate is used for any activity is chance. If the time analysis calculation is repeated, chance will again decide the estimates used, and a different overall project duration will almost certainly result. Processing speed is so rapid that time analysis of the network can be repeated many hundred times in less than one or two minutes.

This technique, known as a Monte Carlo simulation, produces a large sample of results that can be analysed statistically to predict the most likely completion date for any selected activity. Naturally the activity of most interest is likely to be the last in the project, which will give the completion date for the whole project.

An output report from *OPERA* is shown in Figure 9.9. The report comprises two main elements, a frequency histogram and a graph.

On the scale used in this particular example, each bar in the histogram has a width equivalent to two project days. The height of each bar is proportional to the frequency of results, which is the number of times the computer calculated a completion date lying within the two-day period covered by the particular bar. Because the estimates were allocated according to pure chance, the results are statistically likely to conform to a normal distribution curve, although the degree of smoothness and conformity to this curve depends on having a network comprising more than just a few activities, and on a substantial number of time analysis reiterations (in order to provide a statistically significant sample size). For the plot in Figure 9.9, 500 trials were performed on a precedence network of about 130 activities.

In addition to the histogram, there is a graph plotted by the system, called the cumulative curve. This shows the calculated percentage probability of achieving the particular trial result against each date on the timescale.

The version shown in Figure 9.9 has been simplified for the purposes of clear reproduction in this book: the original version also included text giving the following information:

- report title: Early start histogram for Activity A00130 (Project complete);
- project title;
- report name (RISKACT);
- run date;
- number of trial calculations performed (500 in this case);
- arithmetic mean for the early start date of activity A00130 (20 September 1995);
- standard deviation from the mean (11 days);
- a statement that each bar width represents two days;

plus the proprietary titling of Welcom Software and *OPERA*.

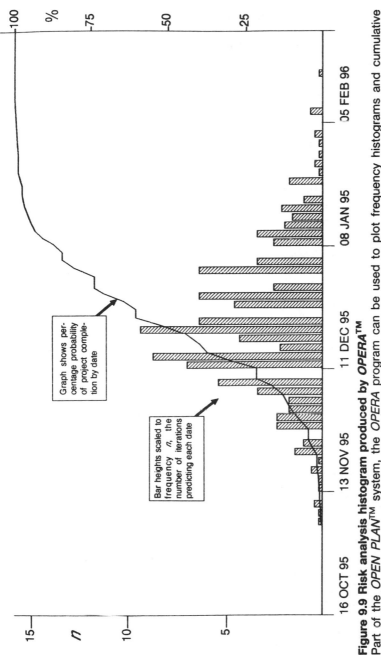

Figure 9.9 Risk analysis histogram produced by *OPERA*™
Part of the *OPEN PLAN*™ system, the *OPERA* program can be used to plot frequency histograms and cumulative probability graphs to show the probability of a project running early or late. Please refer to the text for a description of the method and an explanation of the above plot, which has been slightly adapted and redrawn in simplified form to preserve clarity at this greatly reduced size. (*Based on original material provided by Welcom Software Technology International*)

The *OPERA* system allows statistically proficient planners to instruct the computer to allocate estimates so that the distribution curve is skewed, or conforms to some other shape (such as triangular).

Simulations can also be performed to analyse probable project costs, using methods similar to those outlined here for time analysis.

Integrated databases

One of the problems facing the managers of large projects is keeping all the various administrative systems in step with change and progress, and with each other. For example, it has long been the practice in the mining engineering, civil engineering and construction industries to maintain and distribute project drawing and purchase schedules, which contain not only lists of all drawings and significant project purchases, but which are also intended to convey schedule and progress information. The amount of work involved in keeping these and other documents up to date can be prodigious. Copying and redistributing schedules to managers, the client and other organizations is a costly and time consuming business, sometimes involving many hundreds of updated pages.

Part of the problem lies in the separate nature of all these systems. A project manager may have to deal with many sets of records, covering such things as cost estimating, cost control, drawing schedules, purchase schedules, work-to lists, manpower plans, modification schedules, build schedules, and so on. Even one simple change in the project schedule (network plan) can mean changing many of these records. In 'traditional' project administration practice, there is the paradox that all these systems share some common data, but all are maintained separately from each other, and separately again from the company's corporate information systems.

Consider, for example, what could happen if just one important event date for a project were to be changed. Perhaps a problem at site means that all materials deliveries (and the activities dependent on them) have to be delayed by four weeks. Using the 'traditional' separate systems, the planners would first have to update and re-run the network schedule. Then, a series of separate, laborious clerical exercises would follow to update each of several project administration systems. The revised dates would have to be written on many pages of purchase schedules and purchase order control schedules. All cost curves would have to be redrawn to fresh scales. Cash flow schedules would need to be restructured. And so on, throughout all the project administration systems, and beyond into the company's general management systems.

By putting all the project administration records systems into a computer which uses a common relational database, the problems of wasted clerical effort, slow response to change and high risk of errors can be avoided. All three programs listed at the end of Chapter 8 (*ARTEMIS*, *CRESTA* and *OPEN PLAN*) are database systems.

Database elements

Figure 9.10 illustrates four main elements of a database. A useful starting point is to consider data records. One of these might be, for example, a drawing record (which is analogous to the drawing record card used in a traditional clerical system, where one card would be kept for each drawing).

The data items held on each record are located in data fields, equivalent in this case to the rows and columns of the clerical card. Figure 9.10 illustrates this principle, using items that might feature in a typical drawing record.

All the drawing records taken together constitute the drawings dataset, equivalent to the complete file of record cards. In the clerical system there would be a separate drawings register but, in the computer, the drawings dataset can perform this dual role.

Datasets can be compiled for any other groups of records in the project administration or company management systems. All these datasets, together, comprise the database.

Typical datasets in a project management system

The number of datasets held in the database is decided by the system user, but the following list is a useful guide based on experience with *ARTEMIS* (condensed from, Palmer, 1987):

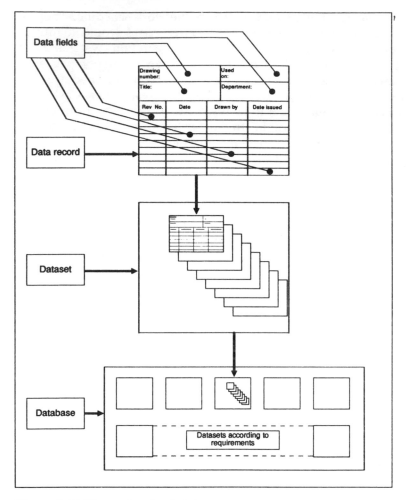

Figure 9.10 Elements of a database

Network dataset, which represents the project plan and includes all the network activities.

Drawings dataset, which, as already described above, contains drawings records in the form of a drawings register.

Materials dataset, listing purchase requisitions and orders and effectively acting as a purchase control schedule.

Vendor dataset, which is (at its simplest) a mailing list of all relevant suppliers. However, in addition to the usual name and address details, other information or comments can be recorded. For example, facts relevant to performance rating can be included. It may also be useful to list the range of products or services offered.

Job cards dataset, where each record describes a job to be performed. 'Fixed' information will include the task description plus the department and trade(s) involved. With information imported from other datasets, these can form the basis for preparing work-to lists and gathering progress control information.

Cost dataset, which lists the code of accounts used on the project together with relevant budgets. A logical structure for this dataset is essential (see the sections on work breakdown and cost coding in Chapter 4).

Resources dataset, includes a record for each type of resource needed for the project. It can include, for example, normal and threshold availability levels with respective cost rates.

History dataset, contains a series of archive records pertaining to different project dates. Each record carries significant data (project scope, cost, progress and so on) relevant to the record date. Thus, for example, the earliest of these records should show initial project budgets and milestone dates. Any of these records can be chosen as a comparison source for data used in current cost and progress reports.

The database approach in practice

An example of a project management information structure is shown in Figure 9.11. Using a database facility means that nominated categories of data held in the database can be related in some way across all the different datasets. Thus, if a date or some other item in a particular record should be changed, that item can automatically be related to other records in the system which need to include it.

Reports produced by the computer can be designed to include information from more than one dataset. It is possible, for example, to provide a materials expediter with combined information from the network schedule and the purchase order files, resulting in a report that lists all orders due for expediting

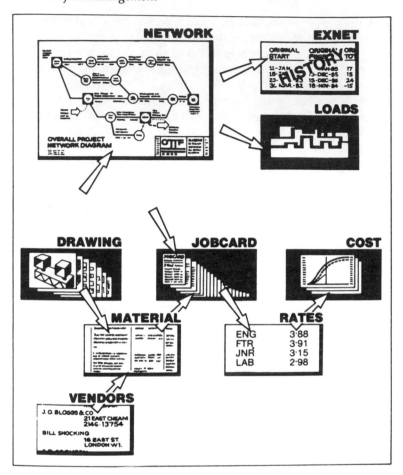

(*Lucas Management Systems*)

Figure 9.11 A typical project information database structure

together with the latest information on available float and other schedule status items.

A database system allows far more detail to be included in the system and linked to the network schedule. For example, provided that network activity descriptions include suitable codes (again demonstrating the need for a good work breakdown and coding system), groups of drawings can be identified from the drawings dataset as being relevant to a particular activity. This means, for example, that the system can generate a list of drawings required by a site construction team or a manufacturing organization for each network activity, together with all relevant schedule and budget data as required.

Designing the system is, however, never simple. If the distribution of data into fields and datasets is not right for the organization, realization that a system change is necessary can be embarrassing when many thousands of data items have been entered. More fundamental still is the choice of computer, whether it should be one micro, several micros, a minicomputer or a mainframe, and how any or all of these should be connected. For further reading and a clear general explanation of this subject, see Palmer, 1987.

Reference

Palmer, Ray (1987), 'Integrated Systems for Planning and Control' and 'An Integrated Project Management System in Action', in Lock, Dennis (ed.) (1987), *Project Management Handbook*, Aldershot: Gower.

10

Scheduling parts for manufacturing projects

This chapter deals with the scheduling of components for projects which finish up as one or more manufactured assemblies. Materials and parts are obviously just as much part of the resources for those projects as money and labour, so that this chapter continues the project resource scheduling theme of previous chapters. Problems associated with parts scheduling are, however, quite different from those met when scheduling other project resources. Solving these problems can involve much tedious hard work, and specialized techniques are necessary.

The scheduling framework

All the techniques described in this chapter assume that the project manager knows when each assembly or subassembly is required for the project. That information must be derived from the overall project schedules (using critical path networks or bar charts as described in the preceding chapters). Then, provided all the labour forces are scheduled sensibly, and provided also that the supporting raw materials are made available in accordance with immediate manufacturing demands, the production of piece parts and assemblies should generally fall into line with project needs.

However, the overall schedules can not usually be made to show a depth of detail much smaller than main assemblies, or at least large subassemblies. Within each of these assemblies there might be a number of subassemblies, and each of these might contain a mixture of specially purchased components, items manufactured within the company's own works, and other parts which are held in stores as general stock.

The parts scheduling task is usually complicated further because some of the parts for one assembly are also used on other assemblies, so that provisioning must take all of these different uses into account. Suppose that a project needs 100 cam-operated electrical switching subassemblies, all slightly different but each containing a particular type of microswitch in varying quantities. Someone obviously has to find a way of discovering how many of these switches are needed in total for the project, and make sure that 100 separate purchase orders for microswitches are not placed. The switching units might easily have other components which must be investigated to discover their total requirements as common items (the cams, for example).

Another complication arises if a project has to result in more than one output batch. Consider, for instance, a defence contractor who is working to produce a 'state of the art' weapons guidance system. The initial contract might be for the design and manufacture of six identical 'Mark 1' prototype units, to be delivered at two-monthly intervals. An improved version (Mark 2) could be under development before all the prototypes have been delivered, so that Mark 1 and Mark 2 systems are both in different stages of production in the factory at the same time, with some parts common to both batches. While all this is going on, engineering changes can of course be expected to affect one or both batches, or even individual units within a batch.

When parts scheduling becomes particularly complex, the project management administration office can provide help to the purchasing and production departments by collating all the known parts requirements, and issuing detailed schedules which show when all the parts are needed and on which

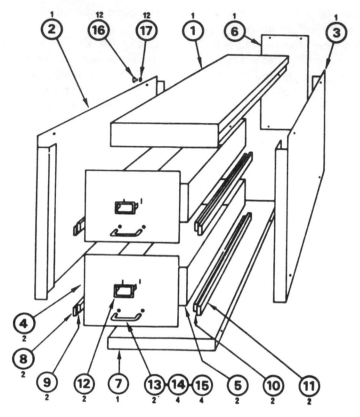

Figure 10.1 Filing cabinet: exploded view

assemblies they are to be used. Some of the forms which this help can take are outlined in the remainder of this chapter. A very simple manufacturing project is analysed first, in which only one item has to be made. Then the circumstances are deliberately complicated by making these items in different quantities for customers who need them on various dates.

Case study: single filing cabinet project

A company has designed a steel two-drawer filing cabinet, an exploded view of which is shown in Figure 10.1. In the first

ITEM NO	PART NUMBER	DESCRIPTION	QTY	REMARKS
1	FC/1001	Top plate	1	
2	FC/1002/L	Side plate, L/H	1	
3	FC/1002/R	Side plate, R/H	1	
4	FC/1003	Drawer front	2	
5	FC/1004	Drawer chassis	2	
6	FC/1005	Rear plate	1	
7	FC/1006	Plinth	1	
8	A 502-A	Runner, outer, L/H	2	Bought-out. Smiths Ltd
9	A 502-B	Runner, inner, L/H	2	" "
10	A 503-B	Runner, inner, R/H	2	" "
11	A 503-A	Runner, outer, R/H	2	" "
12	A 209	Title card holder	2	" Carter & Coy Ltd
13	A 350	Handle	2	" Epsom & Salt Ltd
14	S 217	Screw	4	" Acme Screw Co Type 347M-F
15	W 180	Washer, shakeproof	4	" Acme Screw Co Type 459SP
16	S 527	Screw, self tapping	12	" Acme Screw Co Type 1003ST-X
17	W 180	Washer, shakeproof	12	" Acme Screw Co Type 459SP

Iss	Mod No	Date	Sig	Iss	Mod No	Date	Sig	Iss	Mod No	Date	Sig
1	First	8-5-84									

Drawn by EFP	Checked AJP	Approved OL Lock	Date 1-5-84	

ROBINSON'S OFFICE FURNITURE COMPANY LIMITED, BIRMINGHAM

Title		Sheet 1 of 1 sheets	Assembly number FC/1000
Filing cabinet–Elite series–2 drawer without lock			

Figure 10.2 Filing cabinet: simple parts list

This list was produced by counting the parts shown in the exploded view, with no regard to the sequence of production subassemblies.

instance, only one cabinet is to be made. All the parts needed for the cabinet can be seen in the exploded view, and these could easily be listed on a parts list or bill of materials. This might be done using a computer-aided design (CAD) system or clerically, as shown in Figure 10.2. The item numbers on the parts list correspond with those on the exploded view. Armed with this parts list, the company's purchasing and production control clerks would be able to provision all the materials by drawing available items from existing stocks, and either buying or making the remainder. There is no ambiguity about the total required quantity of any item and no complicated calculations are needed.

Given a target completion date for the single cabinet, it would also be fairly simple to decide when each item must be ordered. Obviously any part which has a very long purchase or manufacturing lead time must be ordered first.

The best sequence of manufacture for the filing cabinet would be for the various subassemblies to be made first, and then for these to be brought together later for final assembly. In practice, therefore, the parts list arrangement shown in Figure 10.2 is not very convenient for the production department because, ideally, they need a separate parts list from which to issue the kit for each subassembly. In order to produce these separate parts lists, it is usual for the design office to start by drawing a family tree or 'goes into chart' showing how all the subassemblies and individual parts come together for the final assembly. The family tree for the filing cabinet is shown in Figure 10.3. This includes four subassemblies in addition to the final assembly, so that five parts lists are needed altogether. The contents of these five parts lists are summarized in Figure 10.4.

While the arrangement of parts lists in this family tree grouping is ideal for manufacturing purposes, it is not so convenient for the purchasing of parts, or for the scheduling of manufacture for parts common to more than one subassembly. For example, the shakeproof washer, part number W180 is common to two assemblies. It appears twice on the simple parts list of Figure 10.2, where it is an easy matter to add up the quantities to find the total number of washers needed to make one filing cabinet (4 + 12 = 16). On the family tree however, and on the parts lists derived from it, this result is not quite so obvious.

Anyone glancing at either the family tree or at the five separate parts lists might be forgiven for assuming that only 14 washers type W180 were needed (12 on the main assembly and two on the drawer assembly). On each of the separate parts lists

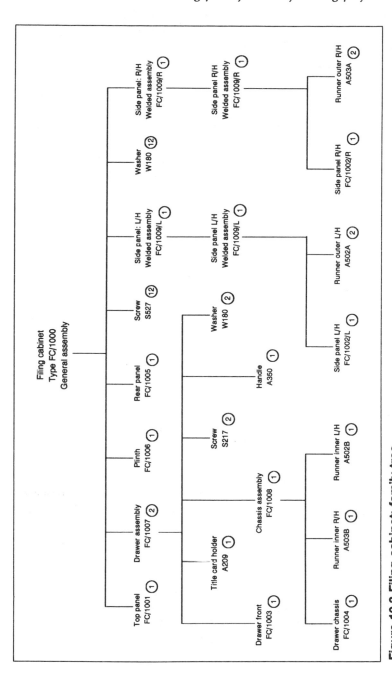

Figure 10.3 Filing cabinet: family tree

The family tree or 'goes into chart' shows how the various components and manufactured subassemblies come together to make the finished main assembly. Encircled numbers are the quantities needed for each subassembly or assembly on the next higher branch of the tree.

FC/1000 Filing cabinet Parts list for final assembly			Rev. 1
Part number	*Description*	*Qty*	*Remarks*
FC/1007	Drawer assembly	2	
FC/1009/L	Side panel welded assembly, left hand	1	
FC/1009/R	Side panel welded assembly, right hand	1	
FC/1001	Top panel	1	
FC/1006	Plinth	1	
FC/1005	Rear panel	1	
S 527	Screw, self-tapping	12	Acme Screw Company, Type 1003ST-X
W 180	Washer, shakeproof	12	Acme Screw Company Type 459SP

FC/1007 Drawer assembly parts list		Used on filing cabinet FC/1000	
FC/1008	Chassis subassembly, welded	1	
FC/1003	Drawer front panel	1	
A 209	Title card holder	1	Carter and Company Ltd
A 350	Handle	1	Epsom and Salt Limited
S 217	Screw	2	Acme Screw Company Type 347M-F
W 180	Washer, shakeproof	2	Acme Screw Company Type 459SP

FC/1008 Chassis subassembly parts list		Used on drawer FC/1007	
FC/1004	Drawer chassis	1	
A 502B	Runner, inner, left hand	1	Smiths Ltd
A 503B	Runner, inner, right hand	1	Smiths Ltd

FC/1009/L Left-hand side panel assy. parts list		Used on filing cabinet FC/1000	
FC/1002/L	Side panel, left hand	1	
A 502A	Runner, outer, left hand	2	Smiths Ltd

FC/1009/R Right-hand side panel assy. parts list		Used on filing cabinet FC/1000	
FC/1002/R	Side panel, right hand	1	
A 503A	Runner, outer, right hand	2	Smiths Ltd

Figure 10.4 Parts lists for filing cabinet arranged in family tree order of subassemblies

the washer (and every other item) only appears in the quantities needed to make one of the particular subassembly, regardless of how many subassemblies are needed. The catch is, of course, that two drawer assemblies are needed for one filing cabinet, so

STOCK COLLATION CARD							
USED ON ASSEMBLY OR MOD NO	PER ASSY	NO OF ASSYS	TOTAL QTY	USED ON ASSEMBLY OR MOD NO	PER ASSY	NO OF ASSY'S	TOTAL QTY
				TOTAL B/F	/////	/////	
TOTAL C/F	/////	/////					
Description					Part number		

Figure 10.5 Single batch stock collation card

that the total number of washers needed is $12 + (2 \times 2) = 16$. In order to find out how many of any item must be provisioned in total, therefore, it is necessary to work up through the family tree, multiplying the quantities as necessary.

This problem used to be solved (and probably still is in some places) using a card index system. The best of these systems have the cards fitted to lie flat in shallow trays, overlapped so that the bottom edge of every card is visible. One card is provided for every assembly, subassembly and separate item, and the cards will probably be laid out in ascending order of part numbers. A suitable card layout is shown in Figure 10.5. Bearing in mind that a manufacturing project might have hundreds of pages of parts lists, the work needed to set up the system can be considerable. It is made easier, however, if it is properly organized. One approach is as follows:

1   A complete set of parts lists is printed and split into smaller piles of sheets.
2   A technical clerk scans all the parts lists and crosses out all the obviously common parts (such as screws,).
3   A team of typists is organized, either within the company or employed as outworkers.

4 Each copy typist is given a pile of parts lists and asked to type the description and part number of every listed item on the foot of a card (except the crossed out items, which would otherwise have resulted in many duplicated cards).
5 The cards are collected, sorted into part number sequence and fitted into the trays, leaving generous gaps to allow extra cards to be inserted.
6 Technical clerks then read through and analyse the complete parts list, which allows all the 'used on' information to be added to the cards.
7 The first clerk to come across any common item with no card in the system will have to arrange for a new card to be typed immediately and inserted in the appropriate filing.

When all the parts list information has been transferred on to the card index, it is possible to work out the total usage for each item by studying all its 'used on' entries on the appropriate card.

The amount of work involved in setting up such a card system is tremendous, especially for a large project. When an engineering change is introduced additional, very tedious work is needed to find or replace all the cards affected and change the relevant entries and totals. This problem of family tree analysis or 'parts list explosions' has been recognized by the computer industry, resulting in a method known as material requirement planning (MRP). The system still requires the input of much data, and accuracy is vital. However, with MRP the family tree analysis and calculation of total quantities is automated, and engineering changes can also be dealt with far more easily.

Parts listing and collation for multiple batches

An extension of the parts scheduling and collation problem occurs when more than one project is being undertaken at the same time, especially when parts or assemblies used on one project are also required for some or all of the others. The form shown in Figure 10.6 was designed to help one company overcome this problem. The projects were for the supply and erection of modular prefabricated hospital operating theatres. The supply and erection scope varied considerably between

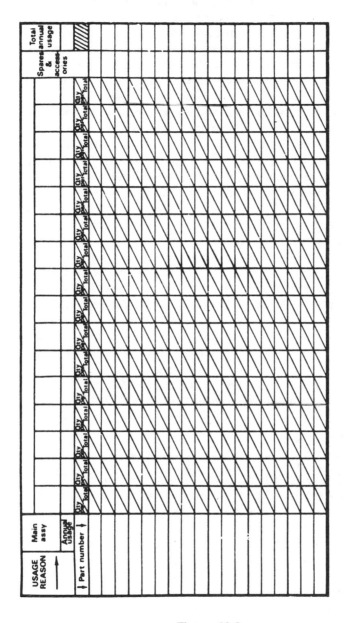

Figure 10.6 Multi-project stock collation card

Figure 10.6

projects but, because of the modular construction, many building elements were common to all sizes of theatre.

These collation forms proved invaluable in the control of manufacturing stocks for components such as steel door frames, wall panels, various items of wall-mounted equipment and so on. Naturally the company's usual stock-control methods sufficed for small items such as nuts and screws.

Each column headed main assembly in Figure 10.6 represents a common assembly used on the operating theatres. Each row is devoted to one of the parts needed for the assemblies, many parts being common to more than one assembly. The annual usage forecast for each main assembly is written in the space provided at the top of the column. The numbers of parts or subassemblies needed for one main assembly are written in the top left-hand corners of the boxes at the appropriate intersections. These numbers are multiplied to give the total quantities required for the estimated annual usages, and the results are entered in the bottom right-hand corners of the boxes.

The total estimated annual usage for each part is found by adding along its row (using the totals from the bottom right-hand corners of the squares lying along the row.

Although this example predated the use of computers, it is useful in demonstrating the essential principles of parts collation across several projects. With a computer system to list, edit, count, multiply and report on each item, careful watch can be kept on stocks to minimize shortages or excess stocks.

Line of balance

There remains one further aspect of parts scheduling which can affect project work and give rise to difficulties. Suppose that a number of identical units have to be produced according to some imposed timetable which does not allow manufacture to take place in one complete batch or at a constant flow rate. The fact that quantities and lead times are bound to vary from one item to another means that it may not be a simple matter to determine just how many of any one part should be in stock or in progress at a given time. The line-of-balance technique can be useful in such circumstances.

Line of balance is a method for scheduling and displaying the progress of repetitive manufacturing programmes. (There is also a variant of the system which is useful for repetitive construction projects, for example when a number of identical houses are to be built consecutively.) The age of the method is variously described by different authorities, so that the origin is given in one case as 'in the 1950s' and in another as 'before the Second World War'.

Case study: multiple filing cabinet project

The subject of this case study is the same filing cabinet that was illustrated in Figures 10.1 to 10.4. Assume this time, however, that the manufacturer has received a series of purchase orders for these filing cabinets, and that these are to be manufactured according to a small series of spaced delivery commitments. There is no possibility of making them all as one batch because there is insufficient production capacity and space. The total quantity to be made will be about 60, and orders for 50 have already been received. The delivery rate for these orders is tabulated in Figure 10.7.

The first step in a line-of-balance calculation is to obtain a family tree for the parts build-up. A family tree already exists for the filing cabinet (Figure 10.3) but for line-of-balance purposes it

Date promised	Customer	Quantity	Cumulative quantity
7 October	Jones	5	5
11 October	Jenkins	5	10
29 October	Griffiths	10	20
4 November	Morgan	10	30
14 November	Edwards	10	40
26 November	Williams	5	45
2 December	Preece	5	50

Figure 10.7 Filing cabinet delivery schedule

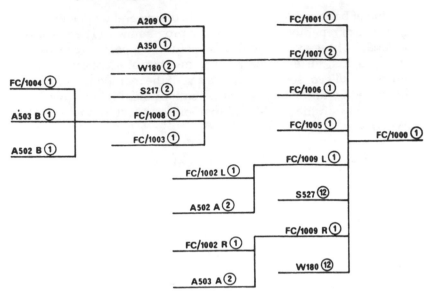

Figure 10.8 Filing cabinet: family tree redrawn for line of balance

is more convenient to redraw the tree laterally, so that the sequence runs from left to right. The revised family tree is shown in Figure 10.8.

The numbers written in the small circles alongside each part number show the quantity of that particular part which must be provided in order to construct one of the assemblies on which it is used. This quantity is, therefore, the same quantity as that shown on the parts list.

In order to arrive at the total quantity of any item needed to complete one main assembly (one filing cabinet) it is necessary to multiply the numbers in sequence along each path from left to right. Thus, for example, one A503B is needed to make one FC/1008, one FC/1008 is contained in each FC/1007, but two FC/1007s are used for every FC/1000. The total number of A503Bs is therefore $1 \times 1 \times 2 = 2$ for every complete filing cabinet.

In Figure 10.9 the next developments are shown. Circles have been added at every intersection and at the ends of the tree branches, rather in the fashion of events in a network diagram. Indeed, the following steps bear some resemblance to network time analysis.

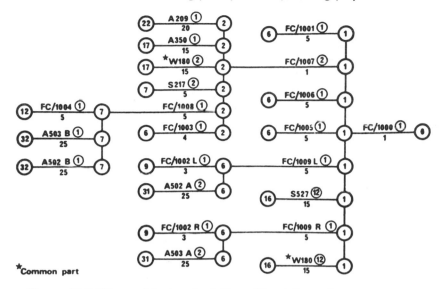

*Common part

Figure 10.9 Filing cabinet: calculation of lead times for parts

An estimate must be made for the time expected to pass between placing an order (purchase order or factory order) for each item and the day when that part becomes available for use. These are total duration estimates, which means that all activities such as preparation and issue of orders, machine setting times, suppliers' lead times, shipping times and stores kitting times have to be included. In this example each estimate has been written below the branch to which it refers. Estimates are in working days, with figures rounded up to the nearest whole day.

Now the total project lead time for any part can be found, by adding up the individual lead times backwards through the tree, working through every path from right to left. The results are shown inside the 'event' circles.

The family tree, set up and annotated as in Figure 10.9, tells us all we need to know about the provision of parts for one filing cabinet. Again taking part A503B as an example, we now know that two of these must be provided, and that they have to be ordered at least 32 days before the filing cabinet is wanted. If they are not received by the seventh day before completion is

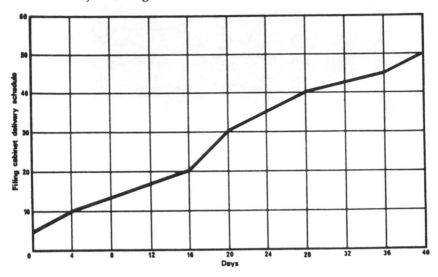

Figure 10.10 Filing cabinet: delivery commitment graph

due, the programme is bound to run late. Notice that, unlike an arrow network diagram, everything on this family tree is critical. No float exists anywhere.

If, instead of just one filing cabinet, a batch of 20 had to be manufactured, the family tree could still be used to work out the quantity/time relationships for all the parts and assemblies. The planner would only have to calculate the results for a single cabinet, and then multiply all the quantities by 20. All the time estimates would need to be checked, just in case the larger batch size caused some of the production processes to take a little longer.

Before a series of repetitive batches can be considered, it is necessary to draw a graph showing the cumulative quantities to be delivered against time. Figure 10.10 shows the graph for the filing project (drawn from the cumulative quantities given in Figure 10.7). The time axis is scaled in working days, allowing five days to each calendar week. All the calendar dates listed in Figure 10.7 have been converted into day numbers, starting with the first delivery of five cabinets on day 0.

Now suppose that day 4 of the programme has been reached and that the current status of production has to be checked against the delivery commitments. Again taking the drawer runner, part number A503B as an example, the lead time for ordering this part is known to be 32 days (Figure 10.9). Two of these runners are needed for each cabinet. By projecting forward along the delivery graph from day 4 by the lead time of 32 days, day 36 is reached. The graph shows that 45 cabinets should have been delivered by day 36. This means that at day 4 all the runners needed to make these 45 cabinets should either be issued, available or on order. In other words 90 parts number A503B must have been ordered.

Not only is it possible to calculate how many parts should be on order, but it is also possible to work out the quantities which must actually be available in stock or already used. This is done by considering the end event for the relevant part or subassembly in each case instead of its start event. For part A503B, the result would be based on a lead time of seven days, which takes the projection on the delivery graph up to day 11. A sufficient quantity of this part must therefore be in stock or issued by day 4 to make 16 cabinets (32 parts).

In the table of Figure 10.11 similar calculations have been performed for all the filing cabinet parts. The quantities all relate to day 4 of the programme, and the start events have been used in this example (so that the total quantities include the parts which should be on order, in progress, in stock or already dispatched in completed cabinets).

Now refer to Figure 10.12, where the data from Figure 10.11 have been converted into chart form. Each separate item has been allocated a column to itself, and the total minimum quantity required is shown as a horizontal line drawn at the appropriate scale height across the relevant column. These quantities are the necessary balance quantities for the programme, and the stepped graph which they form is known as the line of balance. Remember that this whole chart has been calculated with respect to day 4, and is only valid for that single day of the programme.

The last step is to find out what the actual progress is and plot these results on the same line-of-balance chart. The chart should take on an appearance similar to that shown in Figure 10.13, where some imaginary progress results have been assumed and plotted. The fruits of all the calculations and planning labours

Part number	Quantity (1 cabinet)	Total lead time (days)	Number of cabinets	Total quantity
W180	4	17	31	} 484
W180	12	16	30	
S527	12	16	30	360
A502A	2	31	45	90
A502B	2	32	45	90
A503A	2	31	45	90
A503B	2	32	45	90
A209	2	22	38	76
A350	2	17	31	62
S217	4	7	16	64
FC/1004	2	12	20	40
FC/1008	2	7	16	32
FC/1003	2	6	15	30
FC/1007	2	2	12	24
FC/1002L	1	9	18	18
FC/1002R	1	9	18	18
FC/1001	1	6	15	15
FC/1006	1	6	15	15
FC/1005	1	6	15	15
FC/1009L	1	6	15	15
FC/1009R	1	6	15	15
FC/1000	1	1	11	11

Figure 10.11 Filing cabinet: calculation of balance quantities at day 4

should now become obvious, since it is clearly seen that any achievement which falls below the line of balance indicates that the delivery schedule cannot be met.

In the example, parts W180, S527 and S217 have been purchased in total quantities from the start, because these are inexpensive items and they take up little storage space. Part A350 is seen to be below the line of balance, indicating that more should have been ordered.

Remember that the chart in Figure 10.13 has been based on quantities that should have been ordered or delivered by day 4. A different chart would have to be drawn if the planner wanted to know the quantities that must be in stock or used by day 4.

The vertical scale can prove troublesome because of the wide range of quantities that might have to be accommodated. This was true to some extent in the filing cabinet example. If the problem is particularly acute, a logarithmic scale can be considered.

Although line-of-balance charts can not, of course, show the reason for any shortages, they are very effective visual displays

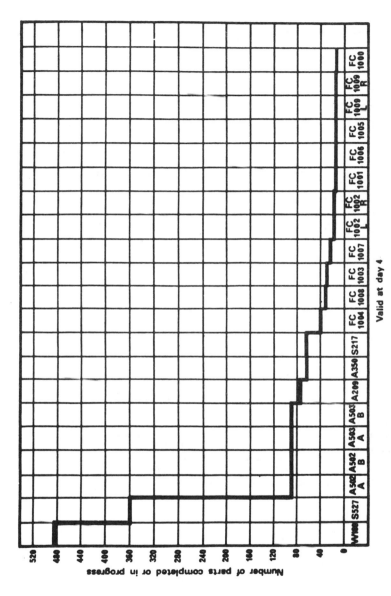

Figure 10.12 Filing cabinet: the line of balance at day 4

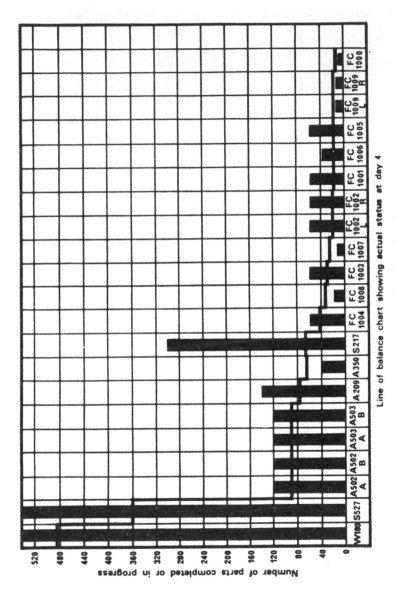

Line of balance chart showing actual status at day 4

Figure 10.13 Filing cabinet: completed line-of-balance chart for day 4

and particularly good at highlighting deficiencies. As such they are useful for showing to higher executives at project meetings, where they save time by satisfying the principle of management by exception.

In fact it is possible, although even more laborious, to split up the family tree and all the charts into more detail, not just into parts and subassemblies but also into the manufacturing operations needed to make the individual parts. All of these operations would then be allotted columns on the line of balance chart. If this is done, a very informative display can be produced, but it is a high price to pay for a chart which is only valid for one day.

The line-of-balance principles become more useful when the results are used not to draw charts but actually to plan and generate orders. Although still requiring much accurate and dedicated data preparation work, line-of-balance-type calculations and order generation can be carried out by computer, using MRP (material requirements planning).

11

Implementing the programme

Once an order has been received, the project ceases to be merely an object for planning and speculation and becomes instead a live entity, to which the contractor is fully committed. For the purposes of achieving all the project objectives, whether technical, budgetary or timescale, the appropriate project organization has to be set up. All participants must be made fully aware of the particular role they will be expected to play.

Project authorization

The first step towards project implementation in any well-run company is the issue of an authorization document. Entitled 'project authorization' or perhaps 'works order', this document carries essential data that define the levels of expenditure authorized (the departmental and purchasing cost budgets), planned start and finish dates, details of the customer's order, pricing information, invoicing and delivery instructions, and so on.

Project authorizations are usually summarized, to the extent that all information is contained on one side of an A4 page. This remains true even for large capital projects. Precise project definition is achieved by listing the relevant technical and commercial documents on the authorization form. If, for example, the project has been won after in-depth negotiation of a detailed contract, coupled with the discussion of technical and commercial sales specifications, the project authorization must identify these documents without ambiguity by giving their serial numbers and listing any agreed amendments or revision numbers.

Project authorizations typically announce the project number which, depending on the procedures of the particular contractor, will be used henceforth as a basis for drawing and equipment specification numbers, cost codes and other important project documentation.

The most important item on a project authorization is the signature of a member of the contractor's senior management. This is the signal that the project is properly authorized and that work can begin.

Project authorizations are generally issued to all company departments for general information, but the supporting technical and commercial documents are only handed over to the project manager. It becomes the project manager's responsibility thereafter to ensure that all other managers in the organization are made aware of project requirements in detail, and sufficiently in advance to enable them to make any necessary preparations.

Figure 11.1 shows a works order form of the type which has been used for many years in manufacturing companies handling special projects. The information on budgets and schedules is necessarily brief, and is only provided on the form to allow outline planning and to place overall limits on the amount of expenditure authorized. In practice, such works orders would be followed by the issue of detailed budgets and schedules.

Figure 11.2 shows a project authorization form used by a mining engineering company to initiate and authorize projects ranging from small feasibility studies and minor plant extensions to very large capital projects. Again, the form only summarizes the essential points, although this company did issue detailed budgets on the reverse side of the form. A fairly comprehensive management information system was in use (built round a computer database) and the form was designed to

WORKS   ORDER

| Project number

CUSTOMER

Delivery address (if different)

PROJECT DESCRIPTION

Title/description

Specifications and drawings defining this project	Number	Revision

BUDGETS

	Hours
Engineering	
Layout	
Detail	
Check	
After issue	
Works	
Assembly	
Inspection/testing g	
Installation	
Commissioning	
Materials/bought out services £	

SCHEDULE SUMMARY

Authorized start date :

Promised delivery date:

Detailed schedules by:

The following dates are issued provisionally pending issue of detailed schedules by the planning department

	Start	Finish
Manufacturing drawings		
Installation drawings		
Purchasing		
Manufacturing		
Assembly		
Inspection and testing		
Installation		

COMMERCIAL

Sales ref: _____ Sales engineer: _   Total value £

Contract reference:

AUTHORIZATION

Work is authorized to start as detailed above, subject to any limitations specified below.   The project manager assigned is:

Authorized by

Notes/limitations:

DISTRIBUTION

Project manager ☐ Engineering director ☐ Works director ☐ Chief engineer ☐ Purchasing manager ☐ Materials controller ☐ Chief inspector ☐ Admin manager ☐ Planning department ☐

Figure 11.1 Works order form
Example of a form used to authorize a manufacturing project.

PROJECT AUTHORIZATION

Client _____

Scope of work _____
_____
_____
_____
_____
_____
_____

Source documents _____
_____

Project number (Entered by accounts department) ☐☐☐☐☐☐

Project title (For computer reports) ☐☐☐☐☐☐☐☐☐☐☐☐☐☐☐☐☐☐☐☐☐☐☐☐☐☐☐☐

Project manager (Name) _____ Staff number ☐☐☐☐

Project engineer (Name) _____ Staff number ☐☐☐☐

Project start date (Enter as 03-APR-88) ☐☐-☐☐☐-☐☐

Project finish date-anticipated (Enter as 03-APR-90) ☐☐-☐☐☐-☐☐

Contract type
Reimbursable ☐   Lump sum ☐   Other (Specify) _____

Estimate of manhours

Costing categories	11	21	22	31	41	51	52	61	TOTAL
Manhours									

Notes

....
Authorisation

....
Authorisation

Proj manager	Man circ	Proposals	Proj services			
Accounts	Central file	Commercial	Cost/planning			

Figure 11.2 Project authorization form
A form used by a mining engineering company to authorize new projects.

open the project file and provide the basic input data to the system (as well as informing departmental managers about the new project).

Preliminary organization of the project

Even when a clear technical specification has been prepared there are often many loose ends to be tied up before actual work can start. The extent and nature of these preliminary activities naturally depend on the type and size of project.

One of the very first tasks is to appoint the project manager. A sensible procedure in large projects with a high degree of complexity is to seek out the senior sales engineer who spearheaded all the conceptual engineering studies during the proposal phase, and allow that person to take the actual project through to completion. In most cases this is not practicable, and another method must be found to ensure that the project is handed over from the sales organization to the fulfilment end of the business in such a way that there is no ambiguity about what has to be done, when and at what cost. For this purpose the sales engineers must prepare a definition package, detailing all the technical and commercial commitments in the contract. This package is handed to the new project manager and helps to ensure that he or she is well briefed from the start.

When the project manager has been named, an organization chart should be drawn up and published to show all key people concerned with the project. It must be extended to include senior members of all external groups who are to have any responsibility in the project. If the organization is large, the usual arrangement is to produce an overall chart and to draw a series of smaller charts which show some of the groups in more detail. Depending, of course, on the actual arrangements, an overall project organization chart might have to show:

1   External purchasing agent (if employed) together with any outside groups responsible for arranging expediting, equipment inspection and shipping arrangements.
2   Management teams working away from the contractor's head office (especially site teams on construction projects).

3 Major subcontractors.
4 Independent consultants, acting either for the customer or the contractor.
5 Government or local government departments (if relevant).
6 The customer's own project management group.

Setting up project communications

Document transmission between project locations

It is necessary to ensure that positive steps are taken to deal with the routing of documented information within and between all project locations. It is good practice for each organization to nominate one of its senior members to act as a control point for receiving and sending all written communications and technical documents, whether these are transmitted by mail, airfreight, courier, facsimile or telex. These individuals then become responsible for seeing that everyone within their own organization is kept correctly informed, by the direction of incoming documents for action, or by arranging for the sensible distribution of correspondence copies.

International projects, where the contracting organization is overseas from the customer, construction sites or other project groups demand careful attention to document transmission routes. If normal mail and airmail services are too slow or otherwise inadequate, a specialist postal service (for example Datapost) or the use of an international courier company can be considered. Airfreight can be used for particularly bulky consignments of drawings. When valuable documents have to be sent quickly to any overseas location, the use of regular courier or airfreight services has the advantage that the agent responsible can monitor each consignment throughout all stages of the journey, with all movements and aircraft changes under the control of the agent and his network, reducing the chances of delays and losses.

Good liaison between the company's travel department and the mailroom will ensure that travellers can be identified who might be persuaded to carry documents in their hand baggage, but this arrangement is often abused and individuals expecting to visit a site for a meeting or a short inspection can find themselves weighed down with an alarming heap of excess baggage.

At some overseas destinations the customs authorities can delay release of documents, and the contractor should always seek the professional advice of a carrier or courier familiar with the required route. Local industrial disputes can cause complete hold ups or frustrating delays. In other cases customs authorities have been known to be awkward for no apparent reason – in one case known to the author a consignment of drawings for a project site was held at a US airport while the customs authorities demanded payment of duty based not on the intrinsic value of the drawings but on the value of the whole project! The solution in that case was to abandon the drawings (they are probably still in the customs shed to this day) and send a duplicate set through another route.

The contractor will be well advised to take project correspondence seriously – he could find himself in a difficult contractual position if he were to lose vital letters or other documents. If a large amount of regular correspondence is expected, all the parties likely to correspond with each other can agree to use letter-reference serial numbers, prefixed with their own codes. Serial numbers should also be arranged for outgoing telexes and facsimiles, at least where these are between significant project locations.

Consignments of drawings and other documents which are not accompanied by a serially numbered covering letter must be given consignment numbers, and this is best achieved by the use of standard 'document transmittal' forms. These are little more than packing lists, but each is given a serial number and copies are retained on file as a record of what was sent. In the case of the US customs problem mentioned above, for example, the file copy of the relevant document transmittal form listed all the drawing prints in the impounded consignment, enabling a duplicate set of prints to be made and sent.

As an example, here is a set of correspondence codes which might be agreed by a project contractor, Alternative Engineering Limited, with its client Quaint Smelters PLC. All serial numbers run 0001, 0002, 0003 and so on.

	From AEL to QS	*From QS to AEL*
Letters	AQL 0001	QAL 0001
Telexes	AQT 0001	QAT 0001
Facsimile	AQF 0001	QAF 0001
Document transmittal forms	AQD 0001	QAD 0001

Apart from making consecutive filing and later document retrieval easier, the use of serial numbers means that any gap in the sequence of letters received at either end indicates a possible loss in transit that should be followed up.

Internal document routing

There is always a risk that documents will be received safely by a company, only to be lost or misrouted within the organization. There is a useful discipline which can be imposed to help prevent this problem, and to ensure that every document reaches the person who should take appropriate action. This procedure is based on the concept of two levels of distribution, the primary distribution and the secondary distribution. The following description explains how this concept operated successfully in one organization handling international projects of various sizes. The procedure described is for incoming project documents, but copies of outgoing correspondence were distributed in similar fashion.

Primary distribution
The original letter is date stamped on receipt and placed in central files. Sufficient copies are sent to the project manager, together with any enclosures from the original letter, to allow him to arrange for secondary distribution.

Secondary distribution
The project manager (or delegate) considers who should take action and answer the incoming letter. An action copy, with enclosures is passed to the individual. One copy is placed in project office files, and the project manager may decide to direct copies to other managers or staff for information. The copy intended for action must be clearly marked, to ensure that action is not duplicated.

Correspondence progressing

Most companies with a large volume of project correspondence arrange for a clerk or coordinator to ensure that every letter that requires an answer is dealt with without undue delay. The same person will also follow up any possible losses in transit, apparent from gaps in the sequence of serial numbers received. Companies sometimes set up correspondence registers for this purpose.

Establishing procedures

Companies accustomed to carrying out large projects may have at their disposal a considerable range of planning and control procedures. At the start of each new project these can be reviewed to determine which should be used. Factors affecting this choice are the size and complexity of the project, the degree of difficulty and risk expected in meeting the end objectives, the number and locations of outside organizations and the wishes or directions of the customer.

Most projects generate lots of paper. Once the planning, control and administrative procedures have been chosen, all the associated forms, expected reports and other types of documents can be listed. It is then possible to consider each of these document types in turn and decide who needs to receive copies as a matter of routine. The result can be drawn up as a matrix, with the names of the recipients along one side and document names along the other. In the square at each grid intersection a number is written to show how many copies of the relevant document each person should receive (if any). Letter codes can also be introduced if desired, so that 'O', for example, might indicate an original document, 'P' a paper print and 'S' a submaster or reproducible print of a drawing. Figure 11.3 illustrates the principle.

The contractor will have to investigate whether or not the project calls for any special design standards, safety requirements, or compliance with government or other statutory regulations.

It is often agreed that the drawings made for a project are the

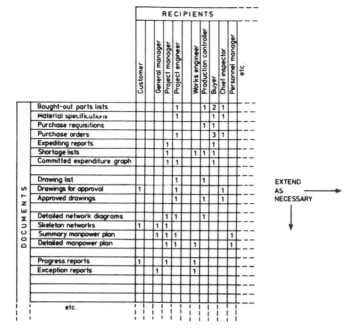

Figure 11.3 Document distribution matrix

property of the customer, who will expect to take possession of all the original drawings at the end of the project and file them in his own system (the contractor would, of course, retain a copy of the data as reproducible prints or on the appropriate computer storage medium). In such a case the contractor will probably have to discuss and agree the drawing numbering system to be used for the project (common practice is to number each drawing twice, using the customer's system and the contractor's normal standard, and then cross-reference these in the computer or drawing register).

The drawings may have to be made on the customer's own standard drawing sheeting, in which case the contractor must obtain supplies before drawing can start. If the sheets are of a non-standard size this might also mean purchasing new filing equipment.

Every contractor obviously develops his own expertise, according to the particular industry in which he operates. He is able to learn the sort of preliminary activities which must be carried out to establish procedures and design standards before one of his typical projects can start. If he is sensible, the contractor will write these into a standard checklist. One company designed such a checklist in the form of a network diagram, a copy of which was used at the start of each new project. Time estimates and time analysis were never used on this standard network. It was used only as a checklist, but its value lay in the fact that it listed all likely preliminary activities in their logical sequence. This particular standard network is shown in Figure 11.4.

For some projects contractors will compile a procedures manual. This will list the particular procedures that will apply to the project, and include such things as the names of key personnel, organization charts, document distribution matrix, the names and addresses of all key organizations with their relevant incoming and outgoing correspondence prefix codes.

Authorizing work without an order

A well-established rule of business, accepted without question by most sensible companies, is that no expense shall be committed on any project unless the customer's written authority to proceed (and promise to pay) has been obtained. The risks taken by disobeying this rule should be obvious. Once the customer knows that the contractor has already committed himself to actual costs, the contractor's bargaining position in any contract negotiations has been weakened. Worse still, if the customer changes his mind altogether and does not go ahead with the expected contract for any reason, all the contractor's committed costs may be forfeit. Thus the project authorization document (see the beginning of this chapter) will not normally be issued unless the customer's written authority to proceed has been obtained.

In spite of convention, there may be occasions when a very limited amount of work can be authorized before receipt of a firm order from the customer. This obviously poses a risk. Indeed, to some it may sound like heresy. But, provided the risk can be quantified and contained within controlled limits it is often possible to gain several weeks' progress in the project

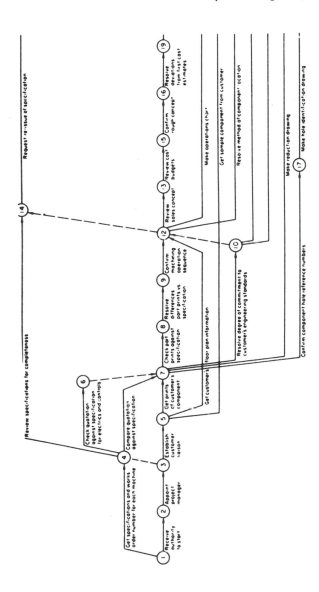

Figure 11.4 Standard network of preliminary activities
Network used by a machine-tool company at the start of each new project. Used primarily as a checklist, activities are crossed off the network as they are achieved or if they are not needed for the particular project. (*Ingersoll Milling Machine Company, USA*)

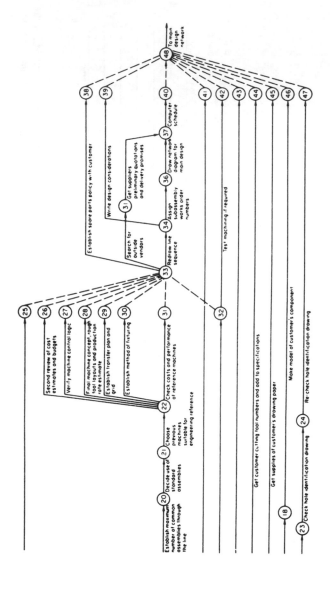

Figure 11.4 *concluded*

calendar for the expenditure of only a very small fraction of the total project costs. Of course no orders for supplies can be placed, but it may be possible to carry out many activities from the preliminary checklist, such as those in Figure 11.4, without committing more than one or two people over the period concerned.

Of course, such advance work in the absence of a customer order will only be authorized where this strategy has some advantages for the contractor. These advantages may include the avoidance of possible trouble later on, if the overall project timescale is seen to be particularly tight. If the contractor foresees a trough in his planned workload, it may suit him to carry out preliminary work that will enable full-scale work to start as soon as the order is received, thus pulling work for the new project forward to help fill the gap. Conversely, doing absolutely nothing and waiting until the official order is received from the customer could mean that the main project workload will be delayed until it interferes with work for other projects.

Graphs of project expenditure plotted against time display a characteristic *S* shape (see Figure 15.7, for example). The rate of expenditure starts very slowly, increases during the height of a project, and then falls off again as the project nears completion. Any talk of authorizing advance expenditure must be limited to the first few weeks, when the rate of expenditure is slow, and steps have to be taken to ensure that the rate remains low. Any decision to allow advance work is always risky, and this must be reflected in the conditions listed in the authorizing document. A preliminary issue of the project authorization can be used but, where such authorization is given:

- authorization should be limited to allow only named individuals to do the work;
- no materials or equipment must be ordered;
- there must be a total budget allocation for this work, regarded as the 'write-off' value of the risk;
- the work to be done should be defined by a checklist or schedule;
- progress and costs must be reviewed frequently, at senior level, with the provision that work can be stopped immediately at any time.

Making the project commitments known

The kickoff meeting

When the newly appointed project manager has collected his or her wits and absorbed the contents of the project specification (which will probably entail some candle-burning), the most urgent job is to mobilize all the project resources and tell the key participants what is expected of them.

This process takes place in different stages and by a variety of methods. The first executive action of the project manager is usually to call an initial meeting, often called the 'kickoff' meeting, which gives the project manager the opportunity for outlining the main features of the project to managers whose departments will work on the project, and to the most senior design staff and other key people. If the project is organized as a team, the project manager will have the advantage of talking to people who are directly responsible to him or her. If the organization is a functional matrix, the task is more difficult – even getting people to attend the meeting becomes a question more of invitation or persuasion rather than a direct summons.

Whatever the circumstances, the skilled project manager will make the best possible use of the initial meeting to get the project off to a good start. Everyone who attends the meeting should leave with a clear picture of the project's objectives, the part that they are expected to play in achieving them, and a sense of keenness and motivation to get on with the job.

Issuing overall plans

It must be assumed that some degree of work planning has been carried out, either in advance or immediately following the receipt of an order. The resulting plans and schedules will do no good at all if they are merely hung on a wall and regarded thereafter as objects to be gazed at and admired. The project manager must make certain that the contents of these schedules are made known to every key person in the organization.

If a networking session was held, in all probability many of these key participants would have been present. Therefore, each must have had some share in formulating the plan. This is just as it should be, because no plan can be imposed successfully in isolation. It must carry the acceptance and support of those who are to be bound by it. There are, however, many cases of projects which do not materialize as a firm order until several months after the creation of initial plans at the tendering stage. During such intervals many aspects of the plans and the discussions leading to them can be forgotten, and memories must be refreshed.

One sound idea is to send a copy of the original network diagram or project bar chart to every department as soon as the order is received. Possibly a table of activities with their scheduled dates can be issued instead, a more likely procedure if a computer is being used. Naturally, whenever any such information is distributed to project members it must be reissued as soon as any changes to the schedules are made. Even provisional or preliminary plans must be kept up to date.

Activity lists

As soon as detailed planning and scheduling has been carried out, work can be allocated to departments in a systematic and regular fashion. Dissemination of programme information must be made far more effective than the simple blanket distribution of common schedules to all and sundry. Instead each department should receive a list showing only those tasks for which it is responsible. The project manager can arrange this by having the overall schedule scanned periodically, either clerically or by computer, and for data to be edited, sorted and entered in lists that are relevant to each of the departments.

Lists need only be provided in detail to cover a few weeks ahead, but longer-term summaries may have to be given to help departmental managers to recruit or reserve the necessary people.

Figure 11.5 shows a suggestion for a detailed, short-term departmental activity list. The intervals between updating and reissuing such lists must depend on the nature of the project and the number of activities which are expected to start and finish each week. In many cases issues at two-weekly intervals will be adequate, and monthly issues may be all right. Each new list must be issued on or before the expiry date of its predecessor.

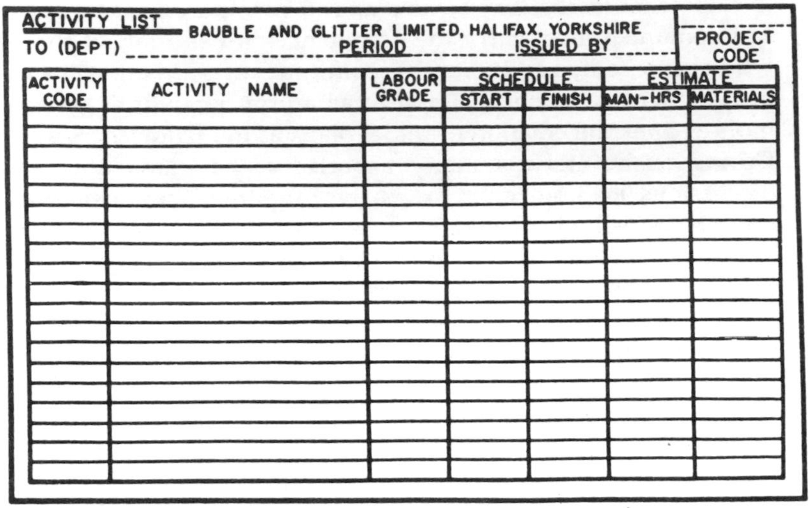

ACTIVITY LIST BAUBLE AND GLITTER LIMITED, HALIFAX, YORKSHIRE

TO (DEPT) ____ PERIOD ____ ISSUED BY ____

PROJECT CODE

ACTIVITY CODE	ACTIVITY NAME	LABOUR GRADE	SCHEDULE		ESTIMATE	
			START	FINISH	MAN-HRS	MATERIALS

Figure 11.5 Activity list
A list, edited from the schedule of all project activities, to give each departmental manager a list of immediate commitments.

Only the barest essentials need be listed, in order to keep the information crisp, concise and readable. In the example shown, the departmental manager is told the scheduled start and finish date for every activity which is either in progress or scheduled to start within the next period. Also shown are the estimates and the cost codes against which all time and materials must be charged. Any other details, such as technical information or manufacturing instructions, would be shown on drawings or in specifications in the usual way.

Activity lists can be regarded as departmental orders or as planning reminders, depending on the department to which they are sent. The exact interpretation must depend on the other documentation arrangements in force within the organization. Activity lists for manufacturing would be sent to the production manager or production controller, who would continue to issue works orders, job tickets, route cards or any other form of document demanded by the customary procedures used throughout the manufacturing organization. In engineering design departments, however, the activity lists are more likely to be used for controlling day-to-day work without the need for additional documents.

In many engineering design offices and other software groups, highly qualified staff may be found whose talents are not being exploited to the full. While technical and scientific aims might be well defined and understood, there is always a danger that the associated commercial aspects of time and cost are not sufficiently well known or appreciated. The issue of activity lists which include estimated costs and scheduled dates can contribute to the more effective use of highly trained specialists in this type of environment by making them aware of their time and cost responsibilities.

The instructions or reminders contained in activity lists should in no way detract from the personal authority vested in each departmental manager. Although the source of each instruction is the project manager's office, activity lists are intended to be implemented through the company's normal line management system. Authority, far from being undermined, will actually be reinforced. Each manager effectively receives a list of the work required of his department, but is free to allocate the work to individuals within the department and to direct and control it. These managers are in fact provided with more effective tools with which to control the activities of their particular groups.

Instructions are often ignored simply because they are issued to too many people, instead of only to the person who is expected to arrange for action. If an instruction is issued in a document that goes to more than one department, each may do nothing and rely instead on the other to carry the instruction out. This risk exists when project networks or other schedules are distributed to a wide number of departments or people without any explanation or precise instructions. Activity lists possess the advantage of being specific to their addressees, so that management responsibility for each item on each list is the clear responsibility of the recipient.

Activity lists are also known as 'work-to' lists in some companies, which is an apt title that sums up their purpose succinctly. When a computer has been used for critical path scheduling (and preferably also for resource scheduling), sensible report editing and sorting can result in the automatic production of activity lists (see Figure 8.8, for example). However, networks are not always drawn with sufficient breakdown detail for the day-to-day allocation of work, and it may still be necessary for managers and supervisors to arrange for very detailed activities to be listed by clerical means. For example, drawing and purchase control schedules are documents which can start their lives as activity lists, and these are usually required to show a greater level of detail than is possible on the project network diagram. A network activity usually summarizes a group of drawings needed for a small work package or subassembly, and it is not usually desirable or possible to have a separate network activity for every individual project drawing. A similar argument applies to purchases and purchase schedules.

Drawing and purchase control schedules

Drawing schedules show all the drawings which have to be made for a project. They are similar to a drawing register, and can be used for the allocation of drawing numbers provided that such numbers are contained within blocks of numbers reserved in the company's central drawing register. Drawing schedules are specific to the project, whereas the central drawing register is a general company record, listing all drawings made for all purposes.

Purchase schedules list all items of equipment to be purchased for a project, and are used to allocate technical specification serial numbers (and possibly enquiry, requisition and purchase order numbers too). They are to the large project what the parts list is to a small manufacturing project.

Drawing schedules and purchase schedules were prepared clerically before the age of computers and they also had to record the progress made on each item listed. But they were really too inflexible for this purpose and the use of erasers was called for when new revisions were issued or when progress information had to be updated. The schedules should be set up in a computer system, either used as a straightforward word processor or in a relational database system linked to the network schedule.

When the project is finished, the drawing and purchase control schedules must be updated to show all the final drawing numbers with their correct revisions, and all the purchase specification numbers and their final revisions. The schedules then define the 'as built' condition of the project. They are similar to the build schedule documents described in Chapter 14, the principal difference being that build schedules are particularly useful for defining manufactured products that can exist in two or more different versions.

Clerical versions of purchase and drawing schedules are shown in Figures 13.3, 13.4 and 14.8 (computerized versions can use the same column headings).

Monitoring progress

One prerequisite for any control system is a method for measuring the effect of any command given. The information so derived can then be fed back to the command source so that any errors can be corrected by modifying the original command. An artillery commander watches the placing of his shots and uses the results of each hit or miss to correct the aim of his gunners. In electrical circuits, signals can be generated which are relative to the position of moving parts or the amplitude of output voltages, in order that the system can be made self-correcting. Project management, as a control system, is no exception. For every instruction which is sent out, a resulting feedback signal must be generated, otherwise there will be no way of knowing when corrective actions are needed.

With any system of control feedback, it is the errors that are significant, because these are the factors that generate corrective action. In the management context these errors or divergencies are called 'exceptions' and the sensible approach of concentrating reports and attention on such exceptions is known as 'management by exception'. There *is* an alternative management approach that relies only on outgoing instructions, with no feedback: this is called 'management by surprise', because the manager feeds in work at one end of the system and is surprised when it doesn't come out at the other!

PROGRESS RETURN FROM (DEPT) _ _ _ _ _ _ _ _	BAUBLE AND GLITTER LIMITED, HALIFAX, YORKSHIRE PERIOD _ _ _ _ _ _ _ _ ISSUED BY _ _		PROJECT CODE
ACTIVITY CODE	ACTIVITY NAME	PERCENTAGE ACHIEVED	CAN NEXT ACTIVITY START?

Figure 11.6 Progress return form
This is the complement of the activity list shown in Figure 11.5. For every command there must be some means for feeding back the result.

A routine method

If instructions are to be conveyed from the project manager to participants by way of activity lists, there is no reason why the same procedure should not be applied in reverse to feed back progress information. When any project is in progress, therefore, it is necessary to imagine a two-way system of communication between the project manager and every departmental manager. The only missing item is a document complementary to the activity list. This gap can be filled by a progress return form, an example of which is shown in Figure 11.6. An alternative document, which will save much time and effort, is a copy of the relevant activity list itself, which the manager responsible can simply annotate to show the progress state of each item.

Progress feedback should be arranged at more frequent intervals than activity lists. Weekly intervals are suggested.

Whatever the document used for progress feedback, care must be taken to avoid either ambiguity or undue complication. The simpler the method, the more likely will be the chances of persuading all the managers involved to return them regularly on their due dates. Even so, training all key participants to adopt the regular routine of progress reporting often provides project managers with a real test of their mettle. Many attempts at project control break down because this particular process cannot be reliably established.

In the specimen progress return form shown (Figure 11.6), the feedback information requested is limited to that which is essential to progress status. Only two questions have to be answered for each activity:

1 What percentage of this activity has been achieved?
2 Can the next activity start?

A variation of the first question is to ask instead how much work remains, estimated as a duration.

The second question is particularly important, and refers to the activity or activities which the network show to be start-dependent on the reported activity being finished. A simple 'yes' or 'no' answer must be given. This is obviously vital to the sensible compilation of following activity lists and to the updating of the project network diagram. The answer has particular significance where activities can overlap each other in ladder fashion. For example, an activity, although not complete, may be sufficiently advanced to allow the release of procurement lists for long-lead items. A network diagram may not always indicate such possibilities, and very often these opportunities for speeding progress would be missed by individuals who had not regularly been asked the right questions.

An alert project manager will recognize the danger behind a progress return which says that the percentage progress achieved is 99 or 100 per cent, but that the next activity cannot start. This could mean that the progress claimed has not in fact been made. This anomaly also occurs when a design engineer has completed a batch of drawings, but keeps them hidden in a drawer and refuses to release them for issue through lack of confidence in the design, because he feels that, given time, he could make them more perfect, or for some other non-essential personal reason.

In organizations which have their project schedules and

activity lists computerized it has become practicable for departmental managers to have access to the computer files through
their own terminals. These managers can, therefore, report
progress by this direct, 'real time' method. Thus the project
schedule and progress information are updated continuously,
and interrogation of the computer by any manager with
authorized access should always show the current state of
progress. The project manager will want to be assured that
progress information fed directly to the computer in this way,
without first being subjected to critical examination, emanates
only from reliable and reasonable senior staff. False statements
could lead to subsequent errors in network analysis, future
resource allocation and activity lists.

The non-routine approach

The routine method just described for collecting progress
information can work properly only in an ideal world. It paints a
picture of the project manager working entirely from behind a
desk, issuing instructions and receiving reports while the
project proceeds smoothly on to its successful finish. While the
establishment of efficient routine systems is a commendable and
necessary aim, more is needed. The project manager must be
prepared to depart from the routine and his desk from time to
time, making visits and spot checks, giving praise or encouragement where due, and viewing progress for himself. This process
has been called 'management by walkabout'.

Visits to sites or production areas are particularly useful when
two or more visits are made some little time apart, so that any
difference in progress (or lack of progress) can be noted.
Construction site photographs should be taken on such visits,
for checking progress and as a permanent record of the project
as it develops.

One very useful occasional check is to ask how many people
in a department or of a particular grade are actually working on
the project at the time. This figure should then be compared
with the project resource or manpower schedule. For example,
suppose that 35 design engineers are supposed to be working
on scheduled activities on a given date. If only 18 people can be

pointed out, something is obviously very wrong somewhere. Although routine progress returns might indicate that everything is more or less on course, the 'head count' shows that work on the project in the design department is not taking place at the required rate. When action is taken, it may be found that the project design is held up for lack of information, that other work has been given priority, or that the department is seriously under-staffed. Comparison of scheduled and actual cost curves can also show up such deficiencies, but the head count is quicker, more positive, and produces the earlier warning.

Priorities in manufacturing projects

Occasions will arise when work cannot be issued within manufacturing departments in a sequence that suits project schedules. If the production control department were able to pick up all orders and load them sequentially, or according to their own machine and manpower schedules, no serious problem need arise. Sooner or later, however, an order is going to be placed which is wanted urgently, and the production controller will be asked to displace other orders in favour of the newcomer.

Some organizations attempt to allocate order priorities, labelling their works orders with the letters A, B or C (for example) to indicate the degree of urgency attaching to each order. It is not difficult to imagine why such systems break down. Delayed 'C' orders will eventually become wanted urgently but will continue to be labelled and treated as 'C' orders. In the end, everyone will label their orders as 'A' priority, so that everything is wanted at once and nothing in fact receives special attention. In the words of W.S. Gilbert, 'When everyone is somebodee, then no one's anybodee'.[1]

A preferable arrangement is to schedule orders by 'wanted by' dates. The production controller can then attempt to schedule to meet these dates, and inform those who are likely to be disappointed. If any project item is expected to be delayed beyond its critical date, the possibility of subcontracting the work can always be considered.

Special project work often has to take its place in the production organization alongside routine work or jobs for other projects. Conflicts can often arise between jobs with conflicting priorities, and it is indeed a brave person who attempts to intervene between two rival project managers who are fighting for the same production resources. Of course, multi-project resource scheduling, either manually or by computer, is the logical way for removing most of the risk of such conflicts. No matter how good the resource schedules are, however, occasions will always crop up when really urgent action must be taken on a particular job, to the exclusion of all others.

Immediate action orders

One solution to the handling of really urgent priorities relies upon the use of special 'immediate action orders'. These are printed on highly distinctive card or paper, either brightly coloured or covered with vivid red or bright orange stripes. Several essential features are necessary to ensure that a proper degree of urgency and respect is always afforded to these immediate action orders.

1   Immediate action orders must be designed so that they stand out easily from all other documents, and cannot be ignored.
2   Each order must be authorized at very senior level (for example, the managing director).
3   Only one immediate action order may be in force at one time.
4   Immediate action orders must be hand-carried from department to department, and from work station to work station, with the date and time of entry and exit stamped against each operation.
5   Every department named for action on the immediate action order must give the specified work absolute priority and interrupt other work if necessary.
6   All possible means are to be taken to achieve the work specified, which may mean incurring high expense. For example, a vehicle or aircraft may have to be sent to collect

vital components or materials. Special prices may have to be paid to suppliers to compensate them for any urgent action.

An example of an immediate action order is shown in Figure 11.7.

An immediate action order case history

A project for a complex defence weapons system was under way, part of which was a rocket-borne radar unit. One of the components was a miniaturized high-voltage transformer and, at the time of this incident, a single prototype was being made. The transformer was highly specialized, and required intricately machined parts, very careful winding, and awkward assembly. Because of the combination of small size and high voltages, the transformer had to be encapsulated in epoxy resin before it could be used or even tested. This meant that, in the event of failure, none of the components could be rescued and used again.

During final testing the transformer flashed over and burned out. This left the project without a key component, and with an obvious design problem regarding this transformer. The prototype had taken six weeks to produce, with rigid inspection routines imposed throughout because of the requirements of HM Government. The idea of having to wait a further six weeks for a replacement, on top of the delay while the engineers sorted out the design problem, was simply out of the question. The project manager accordingly raised an immediate action order to cover all the actions necessary for producing a new fully tested transformer. The order was authorized, but only after the project manager had convinced the company's general manager that the transformer really was critical, and desperately needed.

The first result of issuing the immediate action order was to preclude the possibility of any further immediate action orders being issued. Only one was allowed to be in force at any time. A progress chaser was assigned full time to the order, and he started by taking it to the chief engineer, placing it on his desk, and stamping the date and time of arrival against the 'investigate failure and modify design' operation. The failure of the

	Form No 35

IMMEDIATE ACTION ORDER

Job number:

Project number:

Work required:

Department/ work station	Task / operation	Date/time IN	Date/time OUT

Authorized by: Date: Time:

Reproduced from *ProjectPlanner* by Dennis Lock, Gower, Aldershot, 1990.

Figure 11.7 Immediate action order

first unit was considered to be due to the presence of bubbles in the encapsulating resin, and the engineers decided to modify the assembly slightly to reduce the risk of air being trapped during the moulding process. The presence of an impatient progress chaser with a time stamp in his hand, the general manager's signature, the vivid design of the order sheet, and the knowledge that a post-mortem examination would be carried out afterwards to look at all the in and out times, caused such a flurry of activity that modified drawings were issued within about one hour of the order being issued.

By removing another job from a milling machine, work was started at once on the manufacture of a new bobbin, and all the other small components were made ready within a very short time. The inspection department had been warned in advance, and they inspected and passed the work without delay, although they did ensure that the required quality standards were maintained. The progress chaser stayed with the job, and continued time-stamping the order in and out of each department or work station. The modification proved successful, and the new transformer was successfully encapsulated and tested.

Without the impetus given by the immediate action order, this job would undoubtedly have taken at least six weeks. It took only three days. Of course the cost was high, and might have been higher still had any special actions been necessary to get materials. But the programme was saved. In total terms, the cost of crashing all the transformer activities was far outweighed by the cost saving made by preventing a six-week slippage of the whole project.

The reasons why such success was achieved should be appreciated. In the first place, the order was sufficiently rare to command attention from all concerned. It was not 'just another high priority order'. Further, the high level of authorization carried on the document, together with the sense of urgency created by time-stamping the start and finish in every department, left no doubt in any mind regarding the genuine nature of the crash action request.

If special cases for priority are to be allowed, these must be strictly limited in number. But, once any job has been given top priority status, then all the force and weight of management must be used to back up that decision and ensure that the job is carried right through without interruption. There must be no half measures.

Haste versus quality

When a project is at risk of running late, there is always a danger that corners will be cut at the expense of accuracy or quality.

A high quantity of changes and 'after-issue' work arising from design errors could be the result of undue haste or crash actions. In normal circumstances all drawings, specifications and design calculations would be carefully checked, and design integrity is often proved by means of a prototype or laboratory model. It has to be accepted that occasions will arise when risks have to be taken, but these must never be at the cost of ultimate performance and safety.

A common result of attempting to increase the rate of working is to create a short-term work overload, leading to increased use of subcontractors. For work that is accurately specified in manufacturing or construction drawings, the quality control function has clear parameters against which to control the work. If, however, there is undue pressure on the design engineering department, this could lead to a demand for subcontract augmentation of the design function at a level normally considered to be unacceptable. It could become necessary to engage subcontractors or temporary staff at higher rates than usual, and with insufficient or no time available in which to investigate their background and proficiency. Subcontract design staff cannot be expected to identify themselves with the project or with the company's design philosophy and corporate image to the same degree as permanent employees. The motivational factors of these people must be different because their career aims lie elsewhere, and their performance may be at higher risk because they are unaccustomed to the regular practices and standards of the firm into whose activities they have suddenly been thrust. Guidelines are given later in this chapter for supervising subcontractors under normal planned conditions: the real danger comes when the organization is seriously overloaded.

When an engineer has to make a conscious choice between speed and design accuracy, the decision must be based on careful consideration of the possible consequences of error in the particular circumstances. Suppose, for example, that a small electronic package had to be produced in a great hurry for an urgent project and that, because design information was still awaited from engineers working on another part of the system, the values of certain components could only be guessed within fairly broad limits. The designers might feel justified in issuing the drawings and allowing production to proceed, knowing that any necessary component or simple wiring changes could be made during final testing and commissioning. The small risk involved would easily be justified if the project were to be running very late. If, however, the circuit changes envisaged would mean changing the layout of a printed circuit panel which was difficult to design, expensive to manufacture, had a long purchase lead-time, and was needed in significant quantities, then the engineers would need to be very certain of their design accuracy before releasing the drawings. Similarly, if a huge metal casting or weldment had to be purchased at considerable expense and then subjected to many hours of accurate machining by skilled operatives, a design error could be disastrous.

Pressures other than project delivery dates can also cause undue haste and put quality at risk. An electronic engineering company was once carrying out a project for the design and manufacture of a prototype system comprising a number of electronic units. The customer was a major aircraft company and the work was being performed to rigorous defence contract quality requirements. Divisional managers in this company were always put under pressure to achieve preset monthly billing targets and, on civilian projects, invoices were sometimes mailed early, before the goods were quite ready for dispatch, simply to beat the end-of-month billing deadline. Provided that dispatch followed within a few days, no great harm was done.

For the defence project in question, invoices could only be mailed when they were accompanied by final test certificates, and these had to be signed by the company's chief inspector. On one memorable occasion, the chief inspector allowed himself to be coerced or 'pressurized' into signing a test certificate for a piece of equipment before its final testing, so that an invoice for several thousands of pounds could be mailed before the end of the month. Of course the inevitable happened. The unit failed its test in spectacular fashion, with clouds of expensive smoke.

It had been the only one of its type, with no replacement in the production pipeline. The company had no option but to ask for the invoice and test certificate to be returned, explain why, and apologise.

Subcontractors

Most companies use subcontractors for major projects. They may be used in a variety of ways, the most common of which include the following:

1 To undertake tasks which require expertise or facilities that lie outside the main contractor's own capabilities (for example, heat treatment, plating and anodizing, gear cutting, chemical analysis, certification testing). This form of subcontracting is typically handled through the contractor's buyers and standard purchase order system and will not be discussed further in this chapter.

2 To provide additional 'temporary' staff to work in the contractor's own premises to cover work overloads.

3 To undertake specified tasks on the subcontractors' own premises, where the main contractor's accommodation, plant or work-force would otherwise be overloaded.

4 To work on a construction site, carrying out the various trades or specialist services. In such cases the contract situation is not dissimilar from that described in Chapter 5, but with the main contractor taking the role of client or customer for each subcontract. A brief account of construction site organization is given later in this chapter.

Temporary staff working on the contractor's own premises

The supply of temporary staff for all kinds of duties has become accepted practice in recent years and many agencies exist, some specializing in the particular trades or professional skills offered.

Some companies regard the employment of agency staff as a temporary expedient, to be undertaken to cover staff shortages caused by holidays, sickness or sudden work overloads. There are companies, however, who plan always to keep a proportion of their total work-force as temporary staff, because this provides flexibility in the event of workload fluctuations and reduces the possibility of having to make permanent staff redundant.

Whenever agency staff have to be used, especially if the numbers are significant, the search for suitable agencies and ensuing negotiations should take place as early as possible in order that manpower can be reserved at reasonable rates and with some guarantee of adequate performance. Project disasters excepted, the use of project resource scheduling techniques, such as those described in earlier chapters, should provide adequate and sufficiently accurate forewarning. The project manager also needs to ensure that the selected agencies are themselves given sufficient notice in which to mobilize the resources. Care should be taken, however, to avoid long-term commitments and the payment of retaining fees – a request sometimes made by subcontractors on the grounds that they cannot otherwise guarantee to have people available when required. The writer's experience has been that such retainers are unnecessary.

From the project control point of view, although the use of short-term agency staff may be unavoidable, there are risks of errors and inefficiency in all cases where the tasks require initial training or induction into the company's procedures and practices. Longer-term temporary staff can settle into an organization and acquit themselves well, becoming indistinguishable from the permanent employees until the fateful day arrives when there is no more work for them.

All temporary employees working on the contractor's own premises should normally come under the day-to-day supervision of the company's own departmental managers and their work should be issued, progressed and measured according to the same project-management procedures that govern permanent staff. The only additional feature is to ensure that invoices received from the various agencies claim for the hours actually worked, and at the agreed rates.

Temporary staff working in outside offices

An extra dimension of risk is added when tasks are entrusted to staff who cannot be accommodated within the contractor's own premises. In those cases, work allocation and day-to-day supervision is usually delegated to the subcontractor's own management. The main contractor will want to take steps to ensure that design quality does not suffer, and that the hours claimed by the subcontractor equate to the hours actually worked. The outside offices may be situated many miles from the main contractor's offices.

One way of overcoming these problems is to place a supervisor in the external office, which of course will require the agreement of the subcontractor. A more usual approach is to appoint one or more of the company's permanent engineering staff as 'subcontract liaison engineer'. The liaison engineer's task is to visit the external offices at very frequent intervals, making certain that the project design standards are known and followed, taking out new work, collecting completed work, monitoring progress and answering routine technical queries on the spot.

One company set up a simple procedure for ordering each new design task from any external subcontractor. The basic agreement for hourly rates and billing arrangements and working was first agreed and documented in an exchange of letters. Thereafter, each new task was delivered by a liaison engineer, who also presented a simple order card of the type shown in Figure 11.8.

Tasks authorized by each of these cards usually had durations of two to four weeks. The liaison engineer kept copies of the cards as records from which to follow up the work. The illustration of an activity arrow was a ploy to impress upon the subcontractor that the whole project was carefully planned by network, and that the subcontractor's task was an essential part of the plan. The company in question believed in telling the subcontractor the amount of float available, because this could be used for deciding priorities and also as the main factor in deciding whether or not overtime working (and therefore overtime premium costs) should be justified.

If major design packages are subcontracted to external offices, there is a danger that the results might not properly match the project concept, or that the solutions adopted would differ from those normally preferred by the company. This can be overcome by nominating one or more of a subcontractor's senior design staff as a 'key engineer'. Each key engineer can be invited to work in the contractor's main design office for a few weeks,

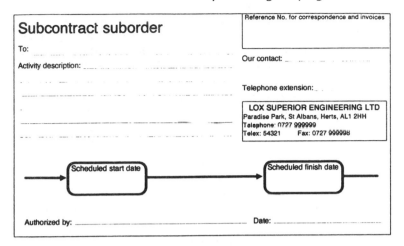

Figure 11.8 A subcontract suborder
Suborders of this type have proved very effective as a means for issuing relatively small items of work on a day-to-day basis under the blanket cover of a more formal subcontract or purchase order document. They can be used for engineering design and drawing or for any other project work subcontracted on a blanket order basis. They simplify clerical work but help keep costs and progress under control by the issue of work in small, controllable quantities. The top right-hand reference number is the activity cost code, and the inclusion of a network arrow highlights that this is part of a project which is planned and controlled by critical path network techniques – a ploy which has been found to impress subcontractors with the need to take time and costs seriously.

working under competent supervision and absorbing the company's standards and practices. A package of work is then selected for the external design office. The key engineer carries out the basic design and layouts in the contractor's main office and, when this has been approved, returns to the external office, where he or she supervises other subcontract staff in the detailing and checking of all the drawings needed for the work package.

Site organization

The management of a construction site obviously depends on the size and duration of the project and on the location of the site.

For a small project, located at a site within easy reach of all modern communications and facilities, the project manager's main responsibilities are to coordinate the activities of subcontractors, watch their quality and behaviour and measure progress.

The need for planned coordination is obvious. Otherwise bricklayers might arrive to start building walls before the footings had been finished, electricians would turn up early to install lighting and have to wait for ceilings to be installed or the roofing contractor would arrive after the scaffolding had been removed.

The need for watching quality should also be obvious and, where the site is within the jurisdiction of a local authority, the local building inspector might be one of many who would be watching the quality of workmanship, materials and building methods. In addition to the main contractor's engineers, the subcontractors' own managers should obviously be supervising the work, and architects, surveyors and even the client could be expected to take more than a passing interest. With all these people bearing and sharing responsibility for quality, why should anything ever go wrong? When it does, some months after the building has been occupied, the main contractor might have quite a problem in deciding where to lay the blame and how to pass on the costs of rectification. Adequate records of all site meetings, subcontract documents, inspection reports, site incidents, photographs, and so on should all be filed safely back at head office for subsequent retrieval.

The monitoring and measurement of progress has to be carried out not only to maintain the programme, but also to enable subcontractors to generate claims for payment and have these certified by an independent quantity surveyor. The main contractor, in turn, will probably be billing the client for progress payments on the total project, and these claims too must be supported by certificates.

The main contractor will have to ensure that adequate site office provisions are made, with the usual facilities such as furniture and filing cabinets, telephones, possibly telex and facsimile equipment, stationery and a photocopier, all probably housed in a site hut or other temporary accommodation.

All of the above is routine, established practice which no

competent main contractor or site manager needs to be told. However, the situation becomes far more complex when the project is very large and the site is remote. There may be no communications, power or water supplies. Setting up the site facilities and arranging for subcontractors then becomes a major project in itself, requiring very detailed planning well in advance. The main contractor may have to coordinate the provision of roads, temporary accommodation for site management and workers, secure stores, catering facilities, hospital, banking arrangements, and much more. This is yet another case where the value of a checklist developed from previous experience is likely to be invaluable.

An organization for a site with no special communications or location difficulties is shown in Figure 11.9.

Meetings

In project work, responsibilities often fall between two or more departments, one of which can usually manage to lay blame at the other's door for any shortcomings or apparent negligence. Manufacturing problems or delays, for instance, might be blamed on poor design or on unwarranted rejections by inspectors. On some occasions these criticisms will h ive some foundation. At other times they will not.

When conflicts arise they must be resolved quickly. Unprofitable stalemate conditions must not be allowed to persist and disrupt team harmony. The project manager has a clear duty to discover the true facts which underlie any interdepartmental problems, not so much to apportion blame as to ensure the continued progress of the project for which he or she is responsible. Often an impasse is reached where two departmental managers give separate and conflicting accounts of the reasons for a common problem.

There is only one way in which to overcome such arguments. The opposing individuals must be confronted with each other, in the presence of a responsible mediator – who logically should be the project manager. Each individual should now be more reluctant to make excuses which vary from the exact truth, because he or she knows that instant denial of any unjust

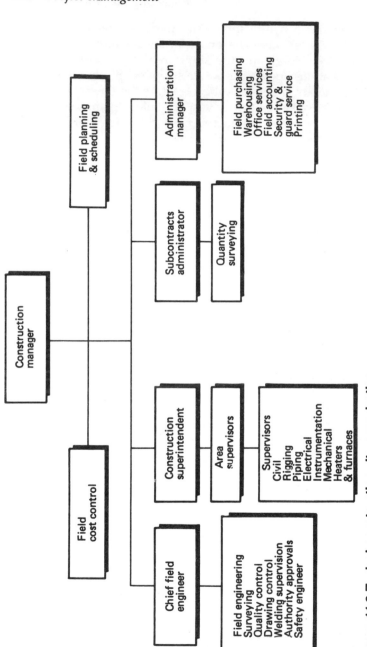

Figure 11.9 Typical construction site organization
Other functions would have to be added to make this team self-sufficient in accommodation, catering, welfare and other facilities if the site were to be located far away from a main centre of civilization. (*Reproduced from Stallworthy and Kharbanda, Total Project Management, Gower*)

criticism will be forthcoming from the other department. More constructively, the person-to-person discussion removes the communication delays that can exist between impersonalized departments, often allowing solutions or compromises to common problems to be worked out on the spot. This is one way in which the project progress meeting can be born.

Progress meetings

Any project manager worthy of the title will want to make certain that whenever possible his or her tactics are preventative rather than curative. If a special meeting can be successful in resolving problems, why not pre-empt trouble by having regular progress meetings, with senior representatives of all departments present?

Regular progress meetings provide a suitable forum where essential two-way communication can take place between planners and participants. The main purposes of progress meetings emerge as a means of keeping a periodic check on the project progress, and the making of any consequential decisions to implement corrective action if programme slippages occur or appear likely.

The frequency with which meetings are held must depend to a large extent on the nature of the project, the size and geographical spread of its organization, and its overall timescale. On projects of short duration, and with much detail to be considered, there may be a good case for holding progress meetings frequently, say once a week, on an informal basis at supervisor level. For other projects monthly meetings may be adequate. Meetings at relatively junior level can be backed up by less frequent meetings held at more senior level. Project review meetings, which can cover the financial prospects as well as simple progress, can also be arranged: the company's general manager may wish to attend such meetings and for some capital projects the customer might also want to be represented.

If meetings are held more frequently than is necessary there will be some danger of creating apathy or hostility. Departmental supervisors and managers are usually busy people whose time should not be wasted. For the same reason meetings must be kept short, not exceeding two hours on any occasion. It may be possible to arrange meetings to start mid-afternoon, so that there will be some incentive for members to get through all the business before the end of the working day. Discussions should be kept to key topics and irrelevancies swept aside.

There are certain dangers associated with the mismanagement of progress meetings. For instance, it often happens that lengthy discussions arise between two specialists which really concern technical issues that should be resolved outside the meeting. Such discussions can bore the other members of the meeting and cause rapid loss of interest in the proceedings. Although it is never possible to divorce design considerations from progress topics, design meetings and progress meetings are basically different functions which should be kept apart.

Arguments may break out during meetings. These may not be altogether undesirable because meetings must be kept alive, with enthusiasm encouraged (provided always that any heat generated can be contained within extinguishable limits). However, arguments must be resolved within the meeting, so that agreement is reached before the members disperse. If this is not done, continuing friction can result, which is an entirely different condition from healthy enthusiasm and team co-operation.

The chairperson bears responsibility for the conduct and arrangement of meetings – this will often be the project manager, but this is not always the case. On manufacturing projects it is possible that some progress meetings will be chaired by a production manager. Architects often chair progress meetings for construction projects.

As with any meeting, proper administrative arrangements should be made. These should ensure, for example, that:

- a meeting room has been reserved;
- visiting members are met and conducted with courtesy to the meeting room;
- messages and incoming telephone calls are not allowed to interrupt the proceedings;
- necessary visual aids are in place and functioning;
- there is adequate ventilation.

When a meeting breaks up, it will have been successful only if all the members feel that they have achieved some real purpose and that actions have been agreed which will have practical effect on project progress. Demands made of members during the meeting must be achievable, so that promises extracted can be honoured.

Publication of the minutes must be undertaken without undue delay in order that they do not become outdated by further events before distribution. Minutes should be clearly and concisely written, combining brevity with clarity, accuracy and careful layout, so that each action demanded can be seen to stand out from the page. If the document is too bulky it may not even be read by everyone. Short, pointed statements of fact are all that is required.

No ambiguity must be allowed after any statement as to who is directly responsible for taking action. Every person listed for taking action must receive a copy of the minutes (although this sounds obvious, the point is sometimes overlooked). Times must be stated definitively. Expressions such as 'at the end of next week' or 'towards the end of the month' should be discarded in favour of actual dates.

Progress meetings abandoned

The above account of progress meetings adheres to the conventional view that progress meetings are an accepted way of project life. Here is some food for less conventional thought.

A heavy engineering company had long been accustomed to holding progress meetings. Depending on the particular project manager, these were held either at regular intervals or randomly whenever things looked like going badly adrift (most readers will have encountered such 'firefighting' meetings). Several projects were in progress at any one time, and the permanent engineering department of about 60 people was often augmented by as many as 80 subcontracted staff working either in-house or in external offices.

Meetings typically resulted in a set of excuses from participants as to why actions requested of them at previous meetings had been carried out late, ineffectually, or not at all. Each meeting would end with a new set of promises, ready to fuel a fresh collection of excuses at the next meeting. This is not to say that the company's overall record was particularly bad, but there was considerable room for improvement and too much time was being wasted at too many meetings.

Senior company management, recognizing the problem, supported a study which led to the introduction of critical path network planning for all projects, using a computer to schedule resources on a multi-project basis (at first confined to engineering design and drawing activities). The computer printed out detailed work-to lists. Two progress engineers were engaged, one to follow up in-house work and the other to supervise outside subcontractors. Both engineers had the benefit of the work-to lists, which told them exactly which jobs should be in progress at any time, the scheduled start and finish dates for these jobs, how many people should be working on each of them, how many people should be working in total on each project at any time and the amount of remaining float available for every activity.

By following up activities on a day-by-day basis in accordance with the work-to lists, these two progress engineers succeeded in achieving a considerable improvement in progress and the smooth flow of work. If a critical or near-critical activity looked like running late, stops were pulled out to bring it back into line (by working overtime during evenings and weekends if necessary).

After several months under this new system it dawned on all the company managers that they were no longer being asked to attend progress meetings. Except for kickoff meetings at the introduction of new projects, progress meetings had become redundant.

Project progress reports

Internal reports to company management

Progress reports addressed to company management will have to set out the technical, fulfilment and financial status of the project and compare the company's performance in each of these respects with the scheduled requirements. For projects lasting more than a few months, such reports are usually issued at regular intervals, and they may well be presented by the project manager during the course of project review meetings.

Discussion of a report might trigger important management decisions that could lead to changes in contract policy or project organization. For these and many other reasons it is important that data relevant to the condition and management of the project are presented factually, supported where necessary by carefully reasoned predictions or explanations.

Information in these reports may contain detailed information of a proprietary nature. They might, therefore, have to be treated as confidential, with their distribution restricted to a limited number of people, all within the company management.

Exception reports

There is another type of internal management report in addition to the detailed management reports just described. These are the reports of 'exceptions', and are confined in scope to those project factors which are giving rise to acute concern, and which must receive immediate attention if the project is to be held on course. If the report is to do with costs, the exceptions will probably be listed as 'variances', but variances are so-called whether they are adverse or advantageous divergences from plan.

Exception reports can range from documents such as adverse cost reports, materials shortage lists or computer printouts of late jobs to a frenzied beating on a senior manager's door by a distraught departmental manager who feels that his or her world has just fallen apart.

Before allowing any exception report to be passed to more senior management, the project manager must first be certain that some remedy within his or her own control cannot be found. Once it has been established that events are likely to move out of control, however, the project manager has a clear duty to appraise senior management of the facts without delay.

All of this is, of course, following the sensible practice of 'management by exception'. This seeks to prevent senior managers from being bombarded with large volumes of routine information which should be of concern only to supervisors and junior managers. The intention is to leave executive minds free to concentrate their efforts where they can be employed to the best advantage of the company and its projects.

Reports to the customer

The submission of formal progress reports to the client or customer could be one of the conditions of contract. If the customer does expect regular reports then, quite obviously, these can be derived from the same source which compiled all the data and explanations for the internal management reports. Some of the more detailed technical information in the internal reports may not be of interest to the customer or relevant to his needs. Customer progress reports, therefore, are to some extent edited versions of internal management reports.

Whether or not financial reports of any type are to be bound in or attached to customers' progress reports will depend on the main contractor's role in each case. Under some circumstances cost and profitability predictions must be regarded as proprietary information, not to be disclosed outside the company. In other cases, the project manager may have to submit cost summaries or more detailed breakdowns, possibly in the form shown in Figure 15.8.

Although customer reports may have to be edited in order to improve clarity and remove proprietary information, they must never be allowed intentionally to mislead. It is always important to keep the customer informed of the true progress position, especially when slippages have occurred which cannot be contained within the available float. Any attempt to put off the evil day by placating a customer with optimistic forecasts or unfounded promises must lead to unwelcome repercussions eventually. Nobody likes to discover that they have been taken for a ride, and customers are no exception to this rule.

Notes

---

1. From *The Gondoliers* by W.S. Gilbert.

12

Purchasing and materials management

Efficient purchasing and management of materials is essential to avoid delays through shortages, the acquisition of goods unfit for their intended purpose, or serious over-expenditure. In addition to the issue of purchase orders, the materials management function generally includes the provision of inspection and safe storage of goods received. It extends beyond the boundaries of the purchaser's premises to embrace supervisory expediting and inspection visits to suppliers, packing and transport arrangements, port and customs clearance for international movements, and involvement whenever special provisions have to be made for insurance, credit guarantees and other commercial arrangements.

Perhaps a good way to emphasize the importance of purchasing and materials control is to remember that purchased goods and services are likely to account for over half the total project costs. Competitive buying, therefore, is important to the financial success of projects, and overspending on material budgets can easily wreck profits.

Another aspect of materials management is bound up with the question of capital investment. If materials are bought long before they are needed, funds which might have been used more profitably elsewhere are tied up unnecessarily. If the contractor is relying on loan capital, idle materials represent waste in terms of avoidable interest or overdraft charges.

On the other hand, delays caused by materials shortages are likely to be more damaging than premature purchasing. There is the obvious fact that work may have to stop until the shortages have been made good, even though the project continues to attract wages and overhead costs during the idle period. Even if the workers can be found other temporary fill-in jobs, disruption to the scheduled smooth flow of project activity will cause man-hour estimates to be overspent. If materials shortages delay project completion, final billing will also be held up, putting back revenue receipts and damaging cash flow. There could also be contractual penalty payments or other expenses to put profitability at risk.

This chapter deals with some of the general principles of project purchasing and materials management. Purchasing complex equipment for construction and other capital projects differs in some important respects from manufacturing projects: appropriate procedures are given in Chapter 13, but many principles and some procedures are common to all purchasing, so that Chapters 12 and 13 are not mutually exclusive.

The purchasing cycle

Some people regard a purchasing department as an office staffed with individuals whose only function in commercial life is to type and send off purchase orders. Unfortunately this concept may sometimes come too close to the truth for comfort. Where this is the case any attempt at materials control is condemned to death before birth. Mainstream purchasing activities start long before an order is placed, and do not end until the materials have been delivered and put to use. Secondary purchasing tasks are even wider, including the establishment of purchasing records (including lists of preferred vendors, together with performance assessments or 'vendor ratings') and follow-up activities in the event that goods fail to match their specification upon delivery or in service.

The normal sequence of events for a single project purchase is not unlike that of the project cycle (shown in Figure 2.2). In fact,

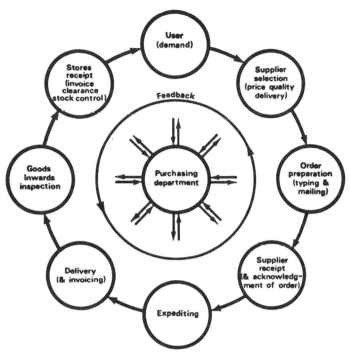

Figure 12.1 The purchasing cycle
A purchase can resemble a mini-project. Compare this chart with the
project cycle shown in Figure 2.2.

procurement of any item can be regarded as a mini-project in
itself. The project manager is replaced in this analogy by the
purchasing manager or project buyer, around whom all buying
activities revolve. Activities in the cycle vary slightly according
to the type of goods or services involved, but Figure 12.1 is fairly
typical of goods which must be ordered specially for a
manufacturing project.

The purchasing cycle is initiated by the discovery of a need for
raw materials or components. The origin of this discovery may
lie in stock control, stores, engineering design or production
control, depending on the type of goods and organization of the
firm. Once the need has been recognized, action must be started
by a request to the company's purchasing department. This
request specifies the goods and usually starts as an enquiry,

which asks the purchasing department to obtain details of suppliers, their quoted prices, delivery promises, and their reputation or expected performance. The buyer may recommend or help to choose the preferred supplier.

When the time comes to order goods, a requisition document is sent to the buyer which authorizes the purchase and gives all necessary details. This requisition, duly signed by a responsible person, can be:

1   A purchase requisition form.
2   A bill of materials or parts list, with items to be purchased clearly highlighted, and with the total quantities required made clear.
3   A stock replacement requisition, produced by stores or stock control personnel whenever replenishment of items stocked for general use is required.

The buyer's first responsibility is to select a suitable source of supply. Occasionally only one supplier can be found, or one may be specified on the requisition. Limitation of choice usually arises when goods are highly specialized but, even where there is only one manufacturer, there may be a choice between different stockists. In all other cases, the supplier must be chosen after the collection and perusal of several competitive quotations. The buyer would normally be expected to buy from the lowest bidder, provided that quality, performance and delivery date were all acceptable.

Moving one more step round the cycle, the order has to be prepared and sent to the supplier. This is the most routine and obvious part of the purchasing cycle, usually consisting of typing the order, signing it and popping it into the post. What has this to do with project management? The answer lies in the time taken. Several days or weeks of valuable project time can be consumed by this mundane, simple activity. Procurement lead times on the critical path network must always be estimated to allow for such delays. In fact, unless emergency measures are contemplated, two weeks should be regarded as a minimum estimate for purchase lead time, even for items that can be supplied from stock.

When the chosen supplier has received the order, he will be

expected to return an acknowledgement accepting the terms, or at least confirming details of quantity, description, price and delivery. Naturally these details must be compared with the supplier's original quotation, and the buyer will question any discrepancy. As far as the purchaser is concerned, the period which follows will be one of waiting, and a great deal of reliance will have to be placed on the supplier to meet his obligations. That is not to say that the purchaser can do nothing. This is the time when the company's expeditor can earn his money by keeping the supplier reminded of his obligations. Expediting also provides an early warning system, soliciting advance notice of any difficulties which the supplier might experience.

Receipt of the goods is not the end of the story. The consignment must be examined on receipt to check for possible loss or damage in transit. There may also have been some mistake, either in the quantity supplied or in the nature of the goods. Goods inwards inspectors may wish to examine the goods more thoroughly to ensure that they comply with requirements although, in recent years, the tendency has been to place more reliance on the suppliers' own quality procedures. If the goods are accepted, the goods inwards personnel will record the consignment, usually by distributing copies of a goods inwards certificate. One copy of the certificate will go to the accounts department, who need it before they can allow payment of the supplier's invoice. Another copy will go to the buying department, to cut short any further expediting action and close off the file on that particular order. Routeing of other copies might include other departments such as the stores, but this depends on the nature of the firm and the goods.

If the consignment is not received in satisfactory condition for any reason, it will be sent smartly back whence it came accompanied by a goods inwards rejection note. Distribution of rejection notes generally follows that of acceptance certificates, but will produce opposite reactions from the various recipients. For example, the accounts department will not pay any resulting invoice, and the purchasing department will redouble its expediting efforts.

When the correct goods have been received they will be passed into stores to await withdrawal for actual use. At the same time, the stock records must be updated to show the addition of the new arrivals into the company's stock holding or 'inventory'. If the consignment was ordered for stock used in repetitive production, there will be a gradual depletion of stock as usage takes place, until the stock records indicate the need for a fresh purchase order. Then the whole purchasing cycle is set in motion again.

The purchase order

The purchase of an item has already been referred to as a mini-project. It follows that, just as a project needs to be provided with a complete specification, so does a purchase order. There are two main parts to this particular type of specification: a statement of the relevant commercial conditions and a description of the goods.

The most obvious information to be given on a purchase order is:

1 a purchase order serial number, for identification, filing and possible subsequent information retrieval;
2 the name of the goods to be supplied;
3 the quantity required;
4 the agreed purchase price, as quoted by the supplier and accepted by the purchaser;
5 the delivery date required;
6 the reference number and date of the supplier's quotation or catalogue (if any);
7 the address to which the goods are to be delivered;
8 the terms on which delivery are to be made (liability for transport, packing, insurance costs, and so on);
9 invoicing instructions;
10 an authorizing signature.

A standard purchase order form should normally be used, an example of which is given in Figure 12.2.

Commercial conditions of purchase

It is customary for companies to standardize many of their commercial conditions of purchase and print them on the

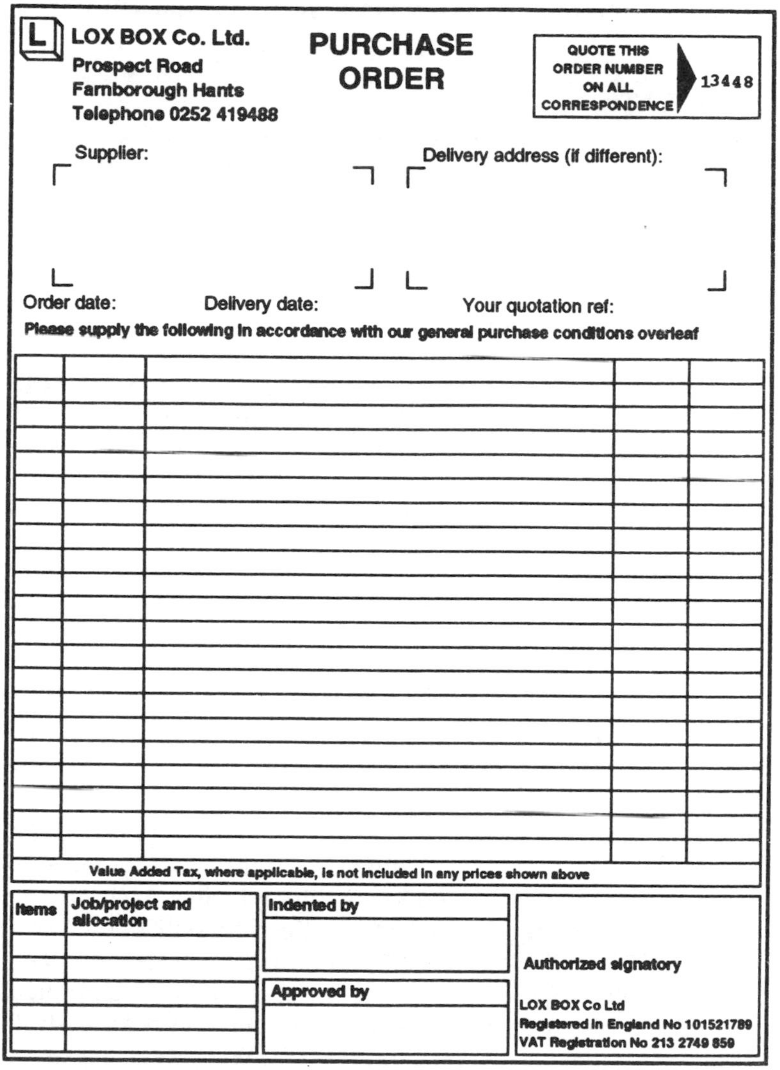
LOX BOX Co. Ltd.
Prospect Road
Farnborough Hants
Telephone 0252 419488

PURCHASE ORDER

QUOTE THIS ORDER NUMBER ON ALL CORRESPONDENCE 13448

Supplier:

Delivery address (if different):

Order date: Delivery date: Your quotation ref:

Please supply the following in accordance with our general purchase conditions overleaf

Value Added Tax, where applicable, is not included in any prices shown above

Items | Job/project and allocation

Indented by

Approved by

Authorized signatory

LOX BOX Co Ltd
Registered in England No 101521789
VAT Registration No 213 2749 859

Figure 12.2 Purchase order form
Example of a general purpose purchase order form.

reverse of their purchase order forms. The set of conditions which follows is based on those used by an actual company, but each firm must seek its own legal advice and draft its conditions of purchase according to its own experience, circumstances and needs.

1   DEFINITIONS:

Company — means Lox Box Company Limited.

Seller — means the person, firm or company to whom the company's order is addressed.

Goods — means the supply and delivery of the goods, materials or equipment in accordance with the company's order together with any subsequent modifications specified by the company.

Contract — means the agreement between the company and the seller for the supply of goods.

2   PAYMENT: Net cash against shipping documents or other proof of delivery unless otherwise agreed (subject to any deductions and retentions authorized in the terms of the order, and subject to the seller carrying out all his obligations).

3   PRICES: All prices are fixed for the duration of the contract and, unless otherwise agreed, are not subject to escalation charges of any description.

4   QUALITY AND DESCRIPTION: The goods shall conform to description, be of sound materials and quality, and be equal in all respects to any specification given by the company to the seller.

5   INDEMNITY: The seller shall at his own expense make good by repair or replacement all defects attributable to faulty design and/or workmanship which appear in the goods within the period of 12 months from date of delivery. The seller shall also indemnify the company in respect of all damage or injury occurring before the above-mentioned period expires to any person or property and against all actions, suits, claims, demands, costs, charges or expenses arising in connection therewith to the extent that the same have been occasioned by the negligence of the seller, his servants or agents during such time as he or they were on, entering on to or departing from the company's premises for any purpose connected with this contract.

6   INTELLECTUAL PROPERTY: The seller will indemnify the

company against any claim for infringement of letters patent, trademark, registered design or copyright arising out of the use of sale of the goods and against all costs, charges and expenses occasioned thereby except in so far as such infringement is due to the seller having followed the design supplied by the company.

7 LOSS OR DAMAGE: All responsibility for any loss or damage, whether total or partial, direct or indirect from whatsoever cause, shall lie with the seller until full and complete delivery in terms of the order shall have been made by the seller. But it is agreed that the company will take all necessary steps to ensure that it does not in any way invalidate any claim which the seller may have against the carrier.

8 CHANGES IN THE WORK: No variations of, or extras to the order shall be carried out by the seller unless specifically authorized by the company on its official amendment form.

9 SUBSUPPLIERS: The seller shall provide a list of all sub-contractors or subsuppliers when requested by the company.

10 EXPEDITING: The company's expediting staff shall be given access at all reasonable times to the seller's works or offices or those of any subcontractor in order to view or discuss work in progress.

11 REJECTION: The company may at any time, whether before or after delivery, reject (giving reasons therefor) any goods found to be inferior, damaged or if the seller commits any breach of the order. This condition shall apply notwithstanding that the goods may have been inspected or tested by the company.

12 ARBITRATION: Any dispute or difference arising from the contract shall, on the application of either the seller or the company, be submitted to arbitration of a single arbitrator who shall be agreed between the parties or who failing such agreement shall be appointed at the request of either party by the President for the time being of the Law Society. The arbitration shall be in accordance with the Arbitration Act 1950.

13 TIME FOR COMPLETION: The seller's promised delivery date must be firm, but if delivery is delayed through any cause beyond the control of the seller and immediately such

cause arises the seller notifies the company in writing giving full particulars then a reasonable extension of time shall be granted. If delivery is not made within the time stipulated or within any extension of time the company shall be at liberty to cancel the contract without prejudice to any right or remedy which shall have accrued or which shall thereafter accrue to the company.

14 TITLE TO GOODS: Title to the goods passes to the company on delivery to the specified place of delivery as requested by the company.

15 LAW OF THE CONTRACT: Unless otherwise agreed the contract shall be subject to the laws of England.

Terms of trade used in international business (INCOTERMS)

When a project proposal involves shipping goods to an overseas customer, or the purchase of goods from abroad, it is important that the boundaries of responsibility for transportation are clearly defined in proposals, contracts and on purchase orders. INCOTERMS, defined and published by the International Chamber of Commerce, are accepted worldwide as the succinct and definitive method for setting out these boundaries. A revised set of INCOTERMS came into force in 1990. The terms are listed below, in ascending order of the sender's scope of responsibility. Full definitions of these terms are given in ICC Publication 460 (see ICC, 1990 in the further reading list at the end of Chapter 13).

Group E INCOTERMS (departure)
EXW   Ex works

Group F INCOTERMS (main carriage unpaid)
FCA   Free carrier
FAS   Free alongside ship
FOB   Free on board

Group C INCOTERMS (main carriage paid)
CFR   Cost and freight
CIF   Cost, insurance and freight
CIP   Carriage and insurance paid to

Group D INCOTERMS (arrival)
DAF   Delivered at frontier
DES   Delivered ex ship
DEQ   Delivered ex quay
DDU   Delivered duty unpaid
DDP   Delivered duty paid

Specifying the goods

Bought-out parts, equipment and materials can often be specified by reference to a manufacturer's catalogue or part number.
This would appear to be a sufficiently rigid description of the
goods. It has to be remembered, however, that most manufacturers reserve the right to modify their designs. If goods are
ordered through stockists or factors, then even the company of
manufacture might be liable to change. Such a change could be
slight and insignificant to most users of the item concerned,
while rendering the product utterly useless for a particular
project. An example of this would be where a manufacturer
changed the material of a component: the catalogue description
and illustration might be identical for both versions of the item
but the strength, weight and other physical properties would
change.

Sometimes a relevant national standards specification (for
example, a British Standards Specification) exists which can be
quoted to specify the requirements. There are also many
specifications provided by other official bodies, including the
armed services. Some companies, however, take no chances
and produce their own drawings and specifications and allocate
part numbers themselves. This practice costs a considerable
amount of drawing time, but has much to commend it. Apart
from removing any ambiguity about what is being ordered,
provision is thus made for a common part-numbering system,
which simplifies stock-handling and purchasing procedures and
eases the burden of the cost office.

This subject of purchase specifications is continued in Chapter
13, with particular reference to procedures used by companies

working on complex construction, petrochemical, mining and civil engineering projects.

Case history

An example from the author's own experience will emphasize the pitfalls of inadequate purchase specifications and point to the type of circumstances where the preparation of special drawings for bought-out components is justified.

A company manufacturing apparatus for hospital operating theatres had a product which had been in very low volume production over a number of years without significant design change. This unit used three water taps of the elbow-lever action type; these enable surgeons to operate the taps without contaminating their gloved hands. Each tap had a threaded hose outlet. The operating direction of the tap lever and its on and off positions were critical to the correct assembly and operation of the equipment.

No drawing of these taps existed, but for several years the small stock was replenished from the same reliable supplier, who manufactured them specially each time according to a mixture of written instructions on the order form and the manufacturer's memory of past orders.

For various reasons a time came when orders for these taps had to be placed with a succession of different suppliers. A written description of the taps was given with each order, but there was still no drawing. Every conceivable error arose in the subsequent supply of these items. Taps arrived with the wrong hose connecting thread, or with no thread at all. Levers came as wrist action instead of elbow lever. Taps were discovered with the levers set at right angles to the required position and, on one occasion, the taps had anticlockwise rotation instead of clockwise. Sometimes consignments were accepted into stores without the errors being discovered until the taps were withdrawn for use.

Eventually a drawing of an ideal tap was produced. This defined the outline dimensions, general shape, hose connection and the lever operating direction and positions. Thereafter, one copy of this drawing was sent with every purchase order, while a second copy was sent to the goods inwards inspectors to enable them to check each new consignment. Very few mistakes occurred subsequently and, when they did, the goods inwards inspectors were able to spot them immediately and have them rectified by the manufacturer.

The improvement was dramatic, immediate and permanent. All the previous trouble could have been prevented if only the correct procedure to specify the goods had been followed all along.

Purchase order amendments

Should it become necessary to change any aspect of a purchase order after issue, the supplier's agreement should be sought in order to determine the effect on price and delivery, and to ensure that the proposed change is within the supplier's capability. Once these facts have been successfully established, an amendment to the original purchase order must be issued.

Each purchase order amendment should bear the same reference number as the original purchase order, suffixed by an identifying amendment number (amendment 1, 2, 3 and so on). Purchase order amendments should be prepared on official forms, and these must be given the same distribution as the original purchase orders.

The amendment procedure is often used to add one or more items to an existing order. If, however, the introduction of a new item is likely to jeopardize the timely completion of any other item on the order by its due delivery date, the best policy is to issue a fresh order for the new item, so leaving the supplier to carry on unhindered and with no excuse for failing to meet his existing commitments.

The practice of adding a succession of new items to an existing order can result in a number of partial deliveries, none of which completes the order, so that administration becomes messy. The need to wade through a purchase order plus a pile of amendments in order to discover its total extent and the balance outstanding is time-consuming and irritating.

Timing of orders and deliveries

Engineers and others responsible for initiating project purchases have a duty to identify those items that are likely to have long lead-times and ensure that ordering instructions are passed to the purchasing department as soon as possible. This may mean issuing advance information on such things as special bearings, motors and other bought-out components, although the relevant assembly drawings and final bills of material remain unfinished or even unstarted. It is sometimes desirable to issue advance information even when the goods cannot be specified in exact detail, because this gives the purchasing department the chance to get started on obtaining provisional quotations and (in a really urgent case) on reserving capacity in a manufacturer's works by issuing a letter of intent. Any company with sufficient project experience will attempt to follow such practices as a matter of course. If a project has been planned using a critical path network any need to issue advance purchasing instructions will almost certainly be highlighted.

On the other hand, there are often reasons why deliveries of project materials should not be called for too early. Materials which are ordered so as to arrive long before they are needed will have to be paid for earlier than is necessary, inflating the amount of money tied up unprofitably in inventory and work in progress. There are also possible problems of storage that can arise for items delivered prematurely.

As a general rule, it is late or incorrect deliveries (and the shortages which they cause) that will always produce the biggest headaches, and any decision to delay the issue of a purchase order must be tempered with caution, allowing time for unforeseen contingencies. What would happen, for example, if an important consignment arrived just in time, only to be rejected as being damaged in transit or was otherwise unfit for project use?

The phrase 'just-in-time', used in the previous paragraph, has taken on a more specific meaning in recent years with the adoption by some companies of the Japanese approach which attempts to reduce stockholding to zero and, among other things, relies on suppliers to deliver direct to the workplace 'just-in-time'. This system relies heavily on establishing a great deal of trust, and the suppliers are expected to be fully responsible for delivering the supplies in the right quantities, at the right time and of the right quality without day-to-day supervision from the purchaser. But these ideals cannot be achieved overnight and cannot be expected to operate for project purchasing where regular use of suppliers and repeat orders are not the norm.

There are other methods for ensuring that goods will be available on the required date without the need to accept early deliveries or premature suppliers' invoices. Possibly the best way is to warn all suppliers of the intention to purchase as soon as possible. This can be taken to the extent of issuing the purchase orders early, but with written instructions specifying that the goods are not to be delivered or invoiced until the required date.

If an order is for a large quantity of parts, deliveries can be arranged to take place in batches, at an agreed rate over a specified period. Of course the suppliers must be willing to accept such arrangements, but the practice is widely used. The manufacturer can either store the balance of the order or manufacture to suit the schedule. This is known as a 'call-off' procedure, because the items are called off as they are needed according to the purchaser's project. It is older than, but not too far removed from, the just-in-time approach.

Although the deliveries of items in large, repeating quantities brings batch or mass production to mind, some single projects do consume large quantities of materials. For instance, one would hardly consider the building of a large office block as mass production, but enormous quantities of building supplies may be involved. There would be very obvious difficulties if all the supplies were to be delivered before work had begun on site clearance. Chaos would reign, with cement, sand, ballast, bricks and other supplies strewn all over the area. Access for site work would then be impossible, and those supplies which survived without being pilfered or ruined by the elements would have to be moved before work could start. By indicating the total quantities required for the project, the contractor can gain the benefits of quantity discounts, but the deliveries must be called off only when they are needed.

Now consider a project requiring 10 000 tiny identical electro-mechanical components, perhaps costing £10 each, a total expenditure of £100 000. These components are small and present no storage problem. But are they all needed at once? Most likely they are to be used over a period of several months. Again, a call-off order is indicated, allowing the contractor to delay expenditure, keep inventory down and improve cash flow, while still reaping the benefits of any discount that can be negotiated because of the large quantity involved.

Having established that materials should be ordered to a project plan, there remain one or two questions regarding the common-sense application of that plan. Returning to the case of the 10 000 components, there is no question that the order for these items should be arranged on a call-off basis if possible. But what about the inexpensive items such as screws, nuts, washers, solder tags and so on. It would be nonsensical to attempt ordering these items to any plan. Rather, one would see to it that the whole quantity was ordered in advance, and with a generous supply to spare. Rigid control would not be necessary. The application of planning and control would probably cost more than the total value of the materials themselves, and might attract ridicule from the suppliers into the bargain.

Some items will therefore be controlled strictly from the plans while others will not. Where should the line be drawn? The following section describes one approach but, first, it has to be said that ordering to a plan is not likely to be one of the project manager's chief worries. The more likely problem is one of trying to obtain urgent materials in an impossibly short space of time. When slips occur early in a project, and no let-up of delivery time can be allowed, the remaining part of the work will resemble an incompressible object being squeezed between two irresistible forces. The procurement activity stands a high chance of being trapped in such a squeeze, owing to the tendency of engineers to provide their purchase specifications too late.

The Pareto principle and the ABC system of materials control

Firms which order many varied items for general production and for manufacturing projects have at their disposal a useful method for deciding which materials can be ordered in bulk without special controls, and for designating those purchases which justify rigid authorization, planning and control procedures. This is the ABC system, which is based on the Pareto principle.

Vilfredo Pareto (1848–1923) was an Italian sociologist and economist whose studies included the distribution of wealth among the population. His findings led to the 'Pareto principle', otherwise known as 'Pareto's law' or the '80/20 rule'. In its generalized version, used in several areas of management decision-making, the assumption made is that, in any 'population' of items, 80 per cent of the total value will be spread over only 20 per cent of the items. The converse is, of course, that 80 per cent of the items account for only 20 per cent of the total value. In its materials control application, the Pareto principle means that 80 per cent of items purchased or held in stock can be expected to account for only 20 per cent of the total inventory. The implication is that management control should not be dissipated on these less expensive items, but should be concentrated instead on those items where it will do most good, namely on the more valuable 20 per cent.

If a company cares to take the time and trouble, it can list its purchased goods (usually confined to general stock items) in descending order of their inventory value, analyse the ranking, and allocate each item into either the 20 per cent or 80 per cent groups. A more common variant is to have three groups, with the items contained in them labelled as category A, B or C. A typical choice of ratios would put the 10 per cent highest-value items into the A category, the lowest 70 per cent into the C category, leaving 20 per cent of the items in the moderate value B category. Reordering of these items would then be controlled as follows:

A items: Stores issues have to be properly authorized. Each fresh order must be justified against specific requirements and the purchase must be authorized by a senior manager.

B items: Stores issues must be properly authorized. Stock replenishment orders are triggered when stock records show that the stockholding has fallen to a predetermined minimum level, and the reorder quantity is calculated to restore the stock level to a predetermined maximum. This is called the 'max-min' system of stock control.

C *items*: This group typically includes items such as small screws, nuts, washers and consumables. Stores issues are less rigorously controlled, and some items may be left out in open bins or racks. The two-bin method is commonly used for re-ordering. Two bins are held in stores. When the stock in one bin has been exhausted, the second is brought into use and fresh stocks are ordered automatically.

Purchase of small quantities

Purchase orders for small quantities of materials or components are often a specific feature of projects where the work is non-repetitive and confined to the completion of only one end product. In these cases the purchasing department will be faced with appreciable handicaps when they attempt to achieve short-term deliveries and low costs. A single small component may be vital to the success of a project but, although this component assumes important dimensions in the eyes of the project manager, for the manufacturer it has only nuisance value, yielding small profit and disrupting work on larger orders for more valued customers.

If the contractor is a large company, or part of a big group, there is always a possibility that the supplier may give good service in the fond hope of larger, follow-up orders. Although the supplier's optimism may be completely groundless, only a foolish project manager would set out deliberately to discourage him. Similar motives sometimes prompt suppliers to proffer free samples of their wares. Items obtained in this way not only cost nothing, but also can usually be obtained by return of post, or out of a sales representative's brief case. Small stocks are sometimes reserved by suppliers for this purpose, and if the paperwork and formal ordering formalities are circumvented in this way much valuable project time can be saved. Project managers would obviously be ill advised to consider planning a project on the basis of materials supplied from free samples, but it should be remembered that some projects have been given the kiss of life by items procured in this way after all other methods have been tried and found wanting.

Items ordered in very small quantities will usually be priced higher than they would be if bought in larger, price-discounted amounts. Other penalties of small quantity orders include higher costs per unit for packing, transport, documentation, and general handling. These are some of the factors which can induce suppliers to charge higher prices for very small purchases.

Quantity discounts or other inducements offered by suppliers have led purchasers to buy well beyond their immediate needs. Some cases have been spectacular. To take a modest example, suppose that seven special instruments are required for a project, and that the unit price is quoted as £20 000 each for quantities of one to nine, and £17 500 each for quantities of ten or more. The buyer might be tempted to buy ten to take advantage of the discount, although only seven are required immediately. The saving on unit cost, however, will not be worth the cost of three surplus units left on the shelf at the end of the project. Instead of costing £140 000, the units have cost a total of £175 000. The only possible justification for buying above the net requirement would be to offset expected breakages (in which case a budget must exist) or against a *certain* follow-up order from the customer for spares. Any such unjustified inflation of order quantities must be vetoed by the project manager. Surplus stocks can accumulate with embarrassing speed if restraint is not exercised.

Materials purchased for use in continuous or batch production are also liable to become overstocked through the lure of quantity discounts. Overstocking leads to a reduction in the inventory turn ratio (annual sales value divided by the value of stock and work in progress inventory), which increases the amount of investment required in the business compared with the profits generated.

Textbooks will advise the purchaser in a company which regularly buys materials for production stocks to pitch the quantity of an item ordered on each occasion at or near its optimum economic level. Graphs can be drawn which relate the estimated or known costs of the various factors against batch quantity. The curve for purchasing costs falls as the quantity rises, and the curve for inventory holding rises. Adding these two curves to give the total cost of purchasing and inventory holding produces a shallow 'U' shaped curve, the minimum point of which indicates the economic quantity (which corresponds to the intersection of the purchasing and inventory curves). The alternative mathematical approach uses the formula:

$$Q = \sqrt{(2DS/VI)}$$

in which Q is the economic order quantity (units), D is the predicted annual usage (units), S is the administrative cost attributable to each purchase order (or the set-up cost if the formula is used for sizing a manufactured batch), V is the price paid per unit, and I is the estimated annual cost of carrying the items in stock, expressed as a fraction of the value of these items held in stock. (A similar approach can be used to calculate an economic batch size for parts manufactured for stock within the contractor's own factory.)

Anyone wishing to calculate the economic quantity need not be too precise, since the rate of change in total costs about the calculated minimum is not great and any penalty for a moderate variation in the quantity purchased is likely to be insignificant. In any case, the variables cannot all be evaluated with precision.

Project purchasing versus stock purchasing

Imagine a large factory, churning out a varied range of products in quantity, and suppose that this company did not operate the just-in-time system but held comprehensive stocks of all possible materials requirements. If a special manufacturing project were to be handled in this environment it is just conceivable that it could be completed entirely from stock materials and components, with no need for any special project purchasing whatsoever. An unlikely possibility, certainly, but not absolutely impossible if the project happened to be in the firm's customary line of business. This kind of stock purchasing provides cost advantages from the point of view of a project manager. There is no need to buy any materials in small quantities, but rather one could order in economic batch sizes. No special arrangements for materials storage need be contemplated, although the project manager would be well advised to see that the storekeepers reserved or 'pre-allocated' the essential materials.

Now consider a company which carries no stocks. Every time a new project appears on the scene each single item must be ordered, right down to the last nut, bolt and washer. This is an example of 'project purchasing' which for manufacturing projects might seem just as improbable as the stock purchasing case (although it is the norm for other types of project). There are definite advantages to be gained by adopting a project purchasing policy but, before moving on to discuss these, one or two of the disadvantages should be mentioned.

The most serious drawbacks of project purchasing in manufacturing projects occur when a company is running more than one project at a time in the same factory. With project purchasing in operation, any parts common to two or more of these contracts must be ordered and stored separately. Individual order quantities are therefore smaller, so that quantity discounts are forfeit or reduced. Such purchases tend to increase the company's total inventory (reducing the inventory turn ratio) because safety stocks to allow for losses, breakages and scrap have to be held in more than one place. Two or more separate stores occupy more floor space than one combined store of the same total capacity, and administration costs (including security) must be higher. Why then should project purchasing ever be considered?

Of course the situation is different for construction and other projects which have sites remote from the company's premises, where materials have to be delivered to site by the suppliers. All materials handling and storage is specific to each project, and project purchasing is the obvious and usual method.

Several very good reasons exist, however, for advocating project purchasing and storage for manufacturing projects wherever this can be arranged conveniently. One of these reasons arises from a weakness inherent in most factory stock pre-allocation systems. The only safe method for pre-allocating materials for use on forthcoming project work is to withdraw them from general stock and place them in a separate project store. If this is not done it is certain that, pre-allocation or not, some of the stock will be used on other work, so that it is not available for the project when needed. Cheery assurances from the storekeeper that the deficient items are 'on order' or 'expected any day now' will not be well received. A project cannot be completed with promises.

Another advantage afforded by project purchasing over stock purchasing, for any type of project, is the improved cost and budget analysis that it allows. This is illustrated in Figure 12.3, which compares the cost data obtained by three different methods for the same project materials. All the curves have one thing in common; each has been drawn by adding together the materials expenditure on a week-by-week basis as soon as the data are known. The only difference between the curves is the information route through which the cost data have been obtained for each curve.

Curve (B) in Figure 12.3 is the only graph which could be derived in all circumstances, whether stock or project purchasing had been adopted. In this case, the materials costs have been found by valuing all the items listed on stores requisitions or similar paperwork as the items have been withdrawn from stores for use on the project. Errors can arise owing to discrepancies between the amounts listed and the amounts actually issued or used. Valuations can also be inaccurate if outdated standard costs have been applied. These errors ought not to be significant, however, unless there are serious shortcomings in the stores or costing administration. The real disadvantage of this most usual form of costing only becomes apparent when the results are compared with those obtained from alternative methods.

Project purchasing (or 'contract purchasing') allows the material costs to be picked up as each purchase order is issued, which is when the costs are committed rather than when they actually occur. Plotting data obtained in this way gives a good indication of the expenditure committed well in advance of the time when the materials will actually be used. Any items already available from general stocks, and which are not to be ordered specially for the project, must of course be allowed for and included in the total commitment. This is easily accomplished: all that is necessary is to withdraw these stocks from production stores in advance and pre-allocate them by transfer into the project stores. The requisitions used to withdraw these mater-

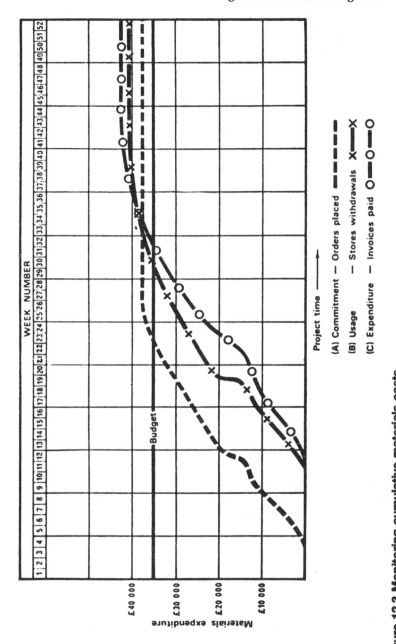

Figure 12.3 Monitoring cumulative materials costs
There are three basic ways in which materials costs can be collected but the earliest information is obtained by summing the value of purchase orders committed.

ials from production stores can be costed at their standard cost, and the costs added to the total project commitment.

Curve (A) of Figure 12.3 shows how data from committed materials expenditure can give the earliest possible warning of the need for action when budgets are in danger of being overspent. Once again, discrepancies from valuation errors can intrude if allowances have to be made for materials used from general stocks but, as before, these errors should be too small to destroy the validity of any trend indicated. Analysis of committed expenditure is the most effective method for monitoring the amount spent on equipment and materials and for predicting the approximate project total. The method is not, however, the most accurate and is of less use in measuring the amount actually spent in the final event, for reasons which will become apparent on considering Curve (C).

Payments against suppliers' invoices provide the most accurate account of purchased materials costs for a contract. Project purchasing is an essential condition, otherwise invoices cannot easily be related to the project being costed. Curve (C) in Figure 12.3 shows the way in which this type of cost information builds up as the project progresses. Note that this curve lags behind both the other two curves by an appreciable period. Most invoices will be paid only after the goods have been received. In fact, the customary office procedures for invoice checking and approving payment must mean the lapse of another week or two before the cheques are raised and signed. Suppliers do not always submit their invoices promptly, or they make mistakes, which can introduce further delays before payments are made. All these time lags provide some useful free credit for the purchaser, but they retard the date when the true project costs can be assessed. The significant fact which emerges here is that the information is far too late to be of use in budgetary control. By the time these facts are known, the money has long since been spent and nothing can be done. This emphasizes the importance of keeping tabs on committed expenditure. None of this can be possible, however, unless project purchasing is adopted.

Before leaving Figure 12.3, observe that all three curves attain different final levels. In this example the differences have been exaggerated deliberately, and in practice no more than about 5 per cent of the total material costs should separate the highest and lowest asymptotes.

Curve (A) (committed costs) did not quite reach the true final cost value (Curve (C)) owing to slight differences between suppliers' quotations (the amounts shown on the purchase orders and used to compile Curve (A)) and the total prices actually invoiced. These extra costs arose because one or two purchase orders were placed after the quotations were time-expired, and because of incidental expenses, such as freight, packing, insurance, and port and customs duties.

Curve (B) (materials actually withdrawn from project stores) also fell slightly short of the real total as shown by Curve (C). This could imply that some over-ordering took place (leaving some goods in stock at the end of the project). Project changes might also have led to materials being left unused in stores. When surpluses are accumulated in this way these must be accepted as a charge against project profits, unless they can be returned to the suppliers for full credit or used elsewhere on other projects. Otherwise the surplus materials will only have to be written off at a later date.

Project purchasing as a condition of contract

Some projects where reliability and safety are paramount (for example, in the aerospace, defence and nuclear industries) demand that all items are purchased against certification of fitness for use. Even raw materials will be included, and samples may have to be tested in independent laboratories. An external inspectorate body would be appointed to supervise and administer inspection procedures, both on the contractor's own premises and at the establishments of at least some of the suppliers. As each consignment receives its inspection clearance, a release certificate is issued specifically for the batch, naming the project on which the materials are to be used. Apart from the immediate quality aspects of these procedures, they also ensure 'traceability'. Suppose that a component fails in an aircraft in service: traceability means that the original source and batch of the failed component can be traced. This, in turn, will allow other components from the batch to be found and replaced to avoid problems in all the other aircraft that might be affected.

Under these conditions where all materials must be inspection-released, stores input, keeping and withdrawals must also be supervised closely. In order to achieve this it is usually necessary to set up special 'bonded' stores, where materials for a specific project can be kept apart from all general stocks. This procedure is intended to prevent any possibility of goods of normal commercial quality being mixed in with the controlled items. This is an example where the choice between stock purchasing and project purchasing has been taken out of the contractor's hands; project buying has, in effect, become a rigid condition of contract.

Incidentally, the additional inspection and documentation required for this specialized materials handling can inflate the cost of project purchases and materials handling and must be allowed for in the contract price.

Expediting

First reliance on the procurement of goods in time to meet the project schedule must be vested in the purchasing department. Once each order has been placed, responsibility shifts from the buyer to the expeditor, although in some smaller organizations the buyer will fulfil both roles.

Expediting, contrary to popular belief, is not just a process for chasing up goods which are overdue for delivery. It seeks instead to prevent lateness. It should be regarded as a routine procedure for monitoring the progress of each order, so that suppliers can be encouraged to deliver on time, and to allow adequate warning of any possible delay.

One common expediting method consists of arranging purchase order records in a file (card index or computer) with a flag attached to each record to signal the date when a reminder to the supplier would seem propitious. As each reminder becomes due, a standard message can be sent, tactfully asking the supplier to confirm that he is on course for meeting the delivery commitment. Obviously, if a satisfactory reply is not received, considerable activity is needed from the purchasing department, and their special efforts should not stop until the supplier has either shown the necessary improvement or has actually delivered the goods.

Sometimes a new method of approach to the supplier can produce the desired result. An offer to arrange collection of the goods from the supplier's premises will, for instance, make the supplier aware that the purchaser is willing to put himself out and that, on this occasion at least, there is genuine urgency.

Possibly the design engineers can suggest an alternative item that can be obtained more quickly. The solution may instead mean finding another source of supply. If the original order does have to be cancelled because the supplier has failed to make the agreed delivery, there should be no kick back, because the supplier has broken the contract by failing to perform.

A carefully composed letter, explaining why a particular item was urgently wanted for a vital export order once reduced a quoted delivery time from 16 weeks to an achieved 14 days, even though the component was a single small flexible drive shaft which had practically no profit value to the supplier and, because it was of a non-standard length, caused the supplier to interrupt his main production run and machine set-ups. Similar letters were sent to two other suppliers on that particular project, and they achieved almost the same degree of success in getting the parts on time. Incidentally, these were all cases where the purchasing department's routine procedures had failed to improve the suppliers' promises, and the project manager refused to accept defeat and wrote letters to the suppliers himself. Perhaps the written word in general carries more weight than telephone calls (which are easily forgotten). Letters are tangible objects that remain under the eye as a constant reminder and, if properly addressed, will reach senior managers in the suppliers' organizations. Telexes and facsimiles can be equally effective.

The purchasing department will not usually be directing all their attention to one project, unless it is very big. Quite understandably, each purchasing order which passes through their hands could be regarded by the expeditors as just another routine job. Projects of sufficient size, however, can justify the allocation of a team of buyers and expeditors to the project, and this can improve the motivation and control (especially when they report directly to the project manager rather than to the materials or purchasing manager).

If the supplier definitely cannot deliver on time, the project manager must be brought into the picture. He or she can then decide on just how important the delay is likely to be, and authorize emergency measures if these appear to be justified. In the last resort the project manager must feel free to intervene in the expediting process, even if this brings accusations of interference from the purchasing manager. A project manager should be motivated by a sense of personal involvement with the success of the project. He will perhaps realize that his own career prospects can be closely linked to those of the project in his charge. This realization should spur him on to exercise all his initiative, perseverance, tact and (in the last resort) guile. For these reasons the project manager can sometimes be successful in clearing a shortage which has been accepted by others as inevitable. He refuses to accept defeat and explores every avenue until a solution is found.

Shortages

Jobs are sometimes delayed because of materials shortages or have to be started before all the necessary materials have been assembled. This can happen if, in spite of expediting, a supplier has failed to deliver on time. Shortages also arise through breakages, theft, inadequate general stock levels, purchasing mistakes and a variety of other reasons.

Obviously no project manager likes to see any job delayed because of shortages, and no one wants to start a task before being assured that all the materials are available to carry it through to the finish. Shortages do, however, occur commonly in projects and the method often used to deal with them depends on the issue of shortage lists. These documents can be used on any project – for factory materials or for shortages on a construction site.

The aim of a shortage list system must be to:

• be quick and simple for the manager or supervisor of the job affected to use;

- provide precise information to the person responsible for purchasing in order that immediate steps can be taken to remedy the shortages;
- tell the manager or supervisor when delivery can be expected.

The essential elements of a shortage list are illustrated in Figure 12.4, which is a general purpose form.

In practice the storekeeper, foreman, supervisor or manager who discovers that there are shortages on a job will fill out a shortage list and despatch it to the relevant buyer by the quickest available means (facsimile or telex if necessary). Depending on the type of project, other copies of the list might be given to shop floor progress chasers, site foreman, storekeeper and, of course, the project manager.

The form should be designed so that a copy can be annotated by the buyer and returned to the originator to report back on what is being done to clear the shortages.

Stores

With the exception of just-in-time systems or the clearance of shortages, a decision usually has to be made about where incoming materials should be stored. The solution could be a very simple matter of placing a consignment of components in a bin on a vacant rack. On the other hand, the problem could be a large truck, taking up all the space in the goods inwards bay, and crammed to overflowing with bulky goods which cannot be unloaded because there is nowhere to put them. Problems of this type differ from purely mental worries. They possess a sickening and grotesque physical reality that can raise blood pressures and inflame human passions to dangerous levels. If the truck driver has travelled overnight on a long and tiring journey he is hardly likely to be disposed to offer any suggestions about where the goods can be put – at least none which might prove constructive.

Most problems arising out of the physical storage of goods can be resolved into a few well-defined categories, which are:

Shortage list	To Purchasing Manager: The items listed are critical to progress. Please expedite and report urgently.		Project:	Date issued:
			Department:	Issued by:
Purchase order number (if known)	Description of materials or equipment	Quantity needed	When needed	Reply from purchasing manager

Figure 12.4 Shortage list form

This shows a typical arrangement for a shortage list. Shortage lists are a splendid example of management by exception. They provide at a glance a summary of any materials or equipment shortages which are impeding the progress of a project.

1 Accommodation: requirements for floor space, racking and shelving, stockyards, etc.;
2 Labelling: marking the goods to identify them without ambiguity;
3 Location: recording the place where the goods have been stored in order that they can be found when they are needed;
4 Preservation: paying attention to possible deterioration, limited shelf-life, cross contamination between different materials and the storage environment generally;
5 Handling methods and equipment;
6 Health and safety;
7 Clerical routines (whether manual or computerized);
8 Security: prevention of theft, wilful damage or misallocation.

Space problems are generally brought about by lack of foresight and inadequate planning. This is one failing which the project manager should be well-equipped to put right. Space is just as much a project resource as labour. It might seem feasible to include these space requirements in the project resource allocation planning, but this is particularly difficult and seldom done in practice, because the problem is three dimensional and not suitable for the usual project management computer software. A simpler, and effective, alternative is to provide the manager responsible for materials control with a schedule of project purchasing activities, derived from the critical path network or bar chart (whichever is in use) and sorted according to their expected delivery dates.

Correct labelling of stored items is essential, otherwise mistakes in issuing are bound to arise. Stores staff cannot be expected to identify all the varied items needed for a project by their appearance alone. Parts must be given numbers so that ambiguities are not possible. A standard part numbering discipline, originating from the design office, is a necessary basis for a stock identification system. Each consignment will be marked with the correct part number on receipt into stores and, provided that the number and the goods do not become separated, identification is then made simple. Raw materials can be given the specification number as identification, in some cases backed up by dimensions. Commonly used materials can be painted with colour codes.

Location is a problem proportional to the size and layout of the stores. Valuable project materials have been known to vanish, causing urgent and expensive reordering, only to reappear at the back of a dusty shelf long after the project has been finished. The remedy is to give every rack, shelf, and bin an identifying 'address', which is usually a simple alphanumeric code. Stock records will show the stores address code (often called the bin number) against every item held. This is, of course, the common procedure in any well-run store or warehouse.

Any materials which are particularly susceptible to deterioration through mechanical shock, heat, cold or damp must be suitably protected. Some articles will deteriorate under any conditions, and must be used within a short time. Heat-developed photographic materials and some dry batteries are examples, and these must be issued in a first-in, first-out sequence. Certain raw materials are not suitable for storing in close proximity to each other because of the risk of damage through cross-contamination. No sensible person would dream of storing soap and biscuits on the same kitchen shelf.

Safe custody and security of stock demand that the storage area can be locked up outside normal working hours. At other times stores entry will usually be restricted to authorized stores personnel. Regulations such as these are designed not only to prevent theft, but also to minimize the possibility of irregular or unrecorded withdrawals. Irregular removals might arise from surreptitious attempts at making good losses, scrap or breakages on the site or workfloor. Over-zealous activity to clear shortages on one project could lead to unauthorized taking of stock pre-allocated for others. Site stores are particularly vulnerable and may need special protection, which can include a full-time watchman, dogs, patrols, high fencing, alarms, closed circuit television, security lighting and so on.

Information systems in a factory store must be designed and implemented to provide accurate feedback of all material movements (arrivals and withdrawals) to stock control. Withdrawals have to be reported against job numbers to the cost office. Stock control will rely on this information to maintain its records as accurately as possible, and re-order where appropriate. Stores receipts are documented by goods inwards notes or, in the case of items manufactured within the works, some form of completed job ticket, inspection ticket or stores receipt note. Items put back into store for stock because they are no longer required for any reason must be similarly documented. Issues from stores are usually authorized and documented by stores requisitions, bills of materials, stores issue schedules or parts lists.

Materials control as a common service

Unless a project store has been set up specially within the project organization, project managers generally have no direct control over the stores operation. The usual arrangement in a manufacturing company is for stores to operate as a common service, often combined organizationally with other materials functions such as goods inwards and despatch under the overall command of a materials manager. The project manager is usually entirely dependent on the materials manager and the stores organization for all materials handling aspects of the project. The project manager may even be denied access to secure stores areas.

Reliance on common services can always cause problems for a project manager, where there might be a clash of priorities, and with any attempt at random independent checking regarded with suspicion – even hostility – by the common services manager, who regards the project manager's interest in his department's performance as unwarranted interference. In fact, the project manager might actually have less direct access and control over a common services department within his own company than he has over an external supplier of goods and services where, at least, the purchase contract will probably give right of access for expediting and on-site inspection purposes.

Here is a true story to illustrate how reliance on common services can let a project manager down. A company in the UK was carrying out a project to manufacture and install two prefabricated operating theatres in a Scandinavian country. The parts for these theatres were derived from common stocks and shipped by common services to the project site, using containers sent by sea and road transport. The highly experienced installation team, which reported to the project manager, was flown out to the site as soon as the materials reached their destination. The hospital authorities arranged for the media to be present to give full publicity to the erection of the main frames. Each frame comprised a number of upright legs, bolted to a welded top frame (so that the basic theatre structures resembled spiders). Having marked out the floor accurately for the first theatre, members of the site team stood holding the legs in position while, watched by the expectant media and officials, the top frame was lowered gently into position by a hoist. Of course, it didn't fit: common services had packed the wrong frames. If there is anything worse than getting egg all over one's face it must be suffering that indignity under the bright lights of publicity. The project manager and the company had suffered acute embarrassment because of a failure by a common services department over which the project manager was not able to exercise control.

The immediate remedy in that case was for common services to airfreight two correct frames to site – an expensive operation because the frames were heavy and bulky. The longer-term remedy in such cases is usually more difficult, but involves motivating common services to improve their service to the project through a mixture of education, persuasion and (if necessary) mobilizing support and action from the company's senior management.

Further reading

A further reading list for purchasing is given at the end of Chapter 13.

13

Purchasing for major construction projects

Chapter 12 dealt with general principles of purchasing and materials management, with examples of procedures applicable to manufacturing projects. The subject of project purchasing is continued in this chapter, but with more emphasis on obtaining equipment for major construction projects (such as civil engineering projects or projects for the engineering, design and construction of petrochemical and mining plants). Some of the procedures described (such as the specification documents and bid summary procedures) are applicable to the purchase of high value equipment for any kind of project.

The purchasing organization

Figure 13.1 shows some of the important elements which might be found in a project purchasing organization. It has to be stressed that there are many ways in which such elements can be organized, and the arrangement in Figure 13.1 is deliberately drawn in very general terms for the purpose of discussion. Some elements have been omitted in order to keep the diagram simple: for example the suppliers might employ specialist export packing companies and (organized by the shipping agent) there

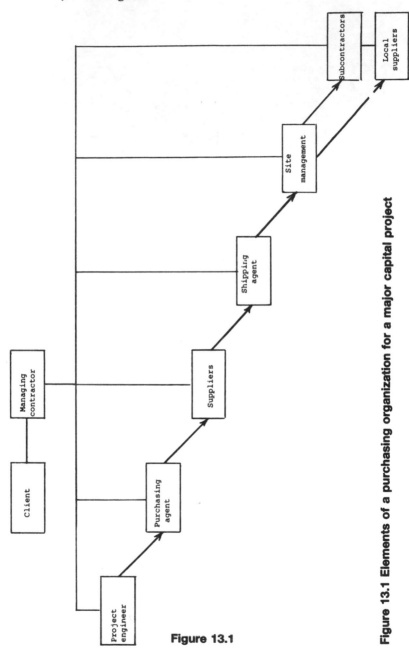

Figure 13.1

Figure 13.1 Elements of a purchasing organization for a major capital project

may be shippers, road hauliers, airlines, insurers and many others. It is also possible that the project client or the financing organization which is advancing funds for the project might wish to safeguard its own interests through the services of an independent consulting engineer.

In Figure 13.1 the client (often called the owner) is shown as dealing through a managing contractor, with all the other elements shown as separate entities. Among the many possible organizational variations, some of these elements could be part of the managing contractor's own company. In another case the managing contractor might be a professional project management organization, employing or controlling a main contractor which owns and operates some or most of the elements. Variations could be listed *ad nauseam*: it is only necessary to appreciate that it would be unwise here to include any diagram that purported to show a typical purchasing organization.

One particular organizational variation must be mentioned before passing on to a more detailed description of purchasing procedures. This concerns the identity and location of the purchasing agent. The purchasing agent could be an independent organization, the contractor's purchasing department, or even the client's own purchasing department. There can also be various combinations of these arrangements. In international projects the client's purchasing department might issue purchase orders to local suppliers, with the contractor's head office purchasing department dealing with other suppliers worldwide (possibly operating through purchasing agents overseas where their location and local experience provides for greater efficiency). Throughout the remainder of this chapter the term purchasing agent is used to mean the purchasing authority which happens to be responsible, irrespective of where it happens to be in the project organization or who owns it.

Figure 13.2 will serve to introduce the principal procedures needed to obtain project equipment (and other supplies, such as steelwork and piping) and transport it to site. The organizational functions shown in this diagram are based on an actual international project.

Process	Listing	Timescale planning	Provisional Specification	Enquiry request	Enquiry issue	Bid preparation	Bid summary preparation	Bid summary evaluation	Authorization	Purchase specification
Client									Authorize expenditure and endorse the project engineer's recommendation	
Project manager	Responsible to the client for planning, scheduling, monitoring and overall supervision of all project activities, and for the collection and interpretation of cost and progress data for submission to the client in the form of formal periodical cost and progress reports									
Project engineering	Identify requirements and list them by preparing a set of PURCHASE CONTROL SCHEDULES. Use these schedules to allocate purchase specification serial numbers	Alter critical path network scheduling add all programme dates to the purchase control schedules. Use a computer database system if possible to provide flexibility in case of programme changes	Write a provisional purchase specification (known as the ENQUIRY SPECIFICATION) for each item to be purchased	Send an ENQUIRY REQUEST to the purchasing agent together with the enquiry specification and a list of recommended suppliers	Technical support to the purchasing agent throughout the enquiry phase, including discussions with potential suppliers and assessment of any suppliers' suggestions for specification changes			Analyse and evaluate the bid summary and recommend the most suitable supplier		Review the enquiry specification in the light of discussions with the supplier and amend as necessary to produce the PURCHASE SPECIFICATION
Purchasing agent					Issue a PURCHASE ENQUIRY to each recommended supplier plus other possible suppliers. Include the enquiry specification		Receive suppliers' bids and tabulate them on a BID SUMMARY FORM			
Equipment suppliers						Prepare bids. Possibly discuss alternative specification details with project engineering				
Freight forwarding agent										
Site materials controller										

Figure 13.2 Summary of steps in the purchase of equipment for a major project

Process	Purchase requisition	Purchase order or issue	Order fulfilment	Export preparation	Documentation	Transport and shipping	Port and customs clearance	Site receipt and storage	Final payment release
Client									Pay supplier direct or reimburse main contractor according to particular project arrangement
Project manager	Responsible to the client for planning, scheduling, monitoring and overall supervision of all project activities, and for the collection and interpretation of cost and progress data for submission to the client in the form of formal periodical cost and progress reports								
Project engineering	Issue a PURCHASE REQUISITION to the purchasing agent authorizing him to proceed. Attach the purchase specification	Technical support and liaison throughout, including assisting if required during inspection and testing. Later, support to the site management during installation and commissioning of the equipment							
Purchasing agent		Issue a PURCHASE ORDER and the purchase specification to the supplier and make certain that it has been received and accepted by the supplier	Arrange expediting and inspection as appropriate. Monitor progress for the purpose of agreeing and certifying valid claims for stage payments		Monitor movements and progress of transport and shipping through contact with the freight forwarding agent, and report to the project manager regularly or on demand. Also keep in touch with the site materials controller.				Certify final payment
Equipment suppliers			Fulfil the order requirements in accordance with the purchase specification. Provide facilities for inspection and witnessed testing	Provide packing and crates suitable for journey and mark boxes according to specification to allow identification en route and at site	Issue test certificates, drawings, installation instructions, recommended spares list and operating and maintenance manuals	Make preparations, if required in the purchase order, for the installation and commissioning at site, and for training the clients' operators			
Freight forwarding agent				Arrange documents for shipping or other carriers, and for port and customs clearances. Arrange for a vessel or aircraft		Monitor the progress of each consignment through all stages of shipment or air freight and transport, by keeping in regular telex contact with carriers and overseas agents and representatives. Keep the purchasing agent informed of all movements, and of any loss or damage reports			
Site materials controller							Liaise with local representative of freight forwarder to progress movement of goods from port of discharge to site	Ensure that suitable lifting equipment is available, and provide secure space for storage. Inspect for signs of damage and start claim if necessary. Otherwise certify safe receipt to clear payment	

Figure 13.2 *concluded*

Purchase control schedules

Purchase control schedules list all the major items of equipment required for a project and are used as registers from which to control the serial numbering and preparation of equipment specifications. Preferably controlled and printed by computer, and linked with critical path network data, purchase schedules specify target dates for each major phase of the procurement cycle for every item on the list. An example of a purchase control schedule (a clerical version) is shown in Figure 13.3.

An effective arrangement for the preparation of purchase control schedules is to ask each project engineering discipline group (civil, structural, mechanical, piping and fluids, electrical, process control and so on) to prepare a separate schedule of the equipment for which it is responsible. Apart from the obvious common-sense technical advantages of this approach, it can greatly simplify the allocation of purchase specification serial numbers. If the project is of any significant size, or if the company procedures so demand, the schedules can be further broken down into subsets according to the various project plant sections. Thus the total set of purchase control schedules for a project could be arranged as shown in Figure 13.4 (which also shows how serial numbers might be allocated).

During the project execution, it is usual to arrange for a coordinating clerk to collect and assemble all parts of the purchase control schedule into the complete schedule for the project. This complete version is then distributed to all the engineering discipline groups (along with the drawing schedules), to the purchasing agent, and possibly to the client. Once the site management team has been set up, it too should receive the schedules to allow pre-planning of storage facilities and to assist in the planning of work on site. Purchase control schedules contain much information which is liable to considerable change from various sources as the project proceeds. These changes will affect both the equipment content of the schedules and the scheduled progress dates. It is important that the purchase control schedules are amended and reissued at suitable intervals to ensure that they incorporate all such changes. Clerical updating is very tedious, especially when a

Figure 13.3 Purchase control schedule
Purchase control schedules are used by engineers to coordinate the preparation of purchase specifications. After project completion the schedules are retained in archives, where the list of specifications with their correct revision numbers form part of the 'as-built' project record.

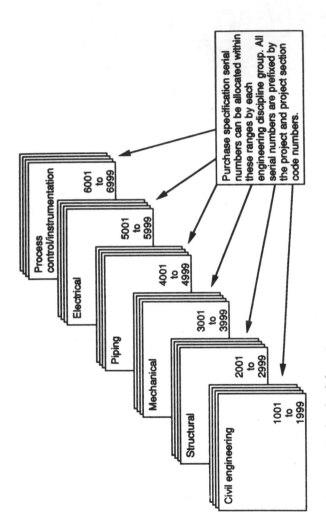

Purchase specification serial numbers can be allocated within these ranges by each engineering discipline group. All serial numbers are prefixed by the project and project section code numbers.

Figure 13.4 A purchase control schedule set

This illustration shows how purchase control schedule sheets can be grouped for a small project, or for a section of a larger project. The engineers within each discipline are free to allocate purchase specification serial numbers from batches of numbers assigned to them. If, for example, the project number is 1028, and the plant or project section code is 55, then the 100th specification listed by the mechanical engineers would be given the unique serial number 1028–55–100. The purchase control schedule could be compiled on sheets such as that shown in Figure 13.3, or (preferably) in a word processor or computer.

project timetable is changed and many scheduled dates have to be altered. The same argument applies to drawing schedules, which are usually updated and reissued at the same time as purchase schedules. These problems can be overcome if all the schedules are set up in a computer database which is linked to the project critical path scheduling program. It then becomes possible to change, reprint and re-issue the schedules with greater efficiency and less risk of error.

When the project is finished the purchase control schedules, because they list all the purchase specifications, become part of the essential documentation that records the 'as-built' state of the project.

Purchase specifications

The importance of defining purchases properly was stressed in the previous chapter and illustrated by an actual case history concerning the purchase of a simple component (a tap for use on operating theatre equipment). In that case, the technical purchase specification consisted of one small drawing. It was only necessary to supply a print of the drawing with each new purchase order and to quote the drawing's serial and revision numbers on the purchase order form to define the component properly.

Quite obviously the physical requirements for many project materials, components and equipment cannot be expressed on a single drawing. It is often necessary to prepare a full written specification, which might take many hours of a professional engineer's time to design and compile. In many cases, these specifications start life in provisional form, and are developed as other design work proceeds. It can also be expected that, when potential suppliers are approached, they might make suggestions that could further influence the final content of some specifications.

It is therefore convenient to identify two stages in the preparation of a purchase specification. These are:

1 *The enquiry stage*: the purchase specification starts life as an enquiry specification. This is issued by the project engineer-

ing department to the purchasing agent under cover of a 'request for enquiry' or similar letter. The purchasing agent sends the enquiry specification to potential suppliers along with a standard 'invitation to bid' or 'enquiry letter'.

2   *The order stage*: when a supplier has been chosen, the enquiry specification is reviewed and updated to include all changes resulting from discussions with the supplier. The enquiry specification has now become the purchase specification, which is re-issued to the purchasing agent by the project engineering department together with a purchase requisition. The purchasing agent then issues a purchase order to the chosen supplier, with the purchase specification attached.

There is no difference in the method of preparing enquiry and purchase specifications, and the same forms can be used for both. An example of a set of specification forms is shown in Figures 13.5, 13.6 and 13.7.

A possible numbering system for enquiry and purchase specifications was illustrated in Figure 13.4. Since the final purchase specification is derived from (or may be identical to) the initial enquiry specification, the serial number first allocated should be retained throughout all stages. This seems logical and straightforward, but there are pitfalls for the unwary. These are mentioned later in this chapter.

When a specification is first issued (say at amendment 0) all the individual sheets should also be labelled as amendment 0. Then the whole specification can be referred to confidently, without ambiguity as serial number so and so, at amendment 0.

When changes occur, it is not likely that every sheet of a multi-page specification will be affected. Some sheets may need changing, while others remain unaltered. It may also be necessary to insert additional sheets. The condition can then easily arise where the amended total specification contains some sheets which are still at amendment 0, while others will bear different amendment numbers. A sensible way in which to define the correct composition of an amended specification is to attach a contents list at the front, which shows the correct amendment number for every sheet. The amendment number of the contents list itself will be the same as the highest number

SPECIFICATION

SHEETS

At the latest amendment as shown below, this specification consists of all the sheets listed in the following table, assembled in ascending numeric - alphabetic order, and with each sheet carrying the amendment number stated. When this specification is amended normally only revised or additional sheets will be issued with this front sheet.

Sheet	amd't	Sheet	amd't	Sheet	amd't	Sheet	amd't	Sheet	amd't	Sheet	amd't	Sheet	amd't	Sheet	amd't
1															

ATTACHMENTS

The following attachments form a part of this specification

AMENDMENTS

No.	Date	Purpose of issue ie g. enquiry, purchase - requisition no.) and technical details

APPROVALS

Originated by	Checked by	... engineer	Project engineer

Client	—				
Project	—		Project No —		
Plant	—				
Disclosure	—				

TITLE	Specification number	Sheet number	Amendment number

Figure 13.5 Purchase specification – front sheet
Example of a form used by one company to head up every enquiry and purchase specification. The schedule at the top lists all sheets comprising the complete specification, which is particularly important when changes result in additions, deletions, substitutions and sheets with different amendment numbers.

SPECIFICATION

DRAWINGS AND DOCUMENTS

1. SCOPE OF SUPPLY. Complete engineering drawings, installation, operating and maintenance manuals, parts lists, recommended spares lists and other documents for all equipment/services covered by this specification, all in accordance with the following requirements
2. QUANTITIES.
   Drawings for approval   —   3 prints
   Final drawings   —   1 transparency
   Other final documents   —   6 copies
3. LANGUAGE. English
4. QUALITY. High quality suitable for microfilming. Final certified drawings full size on good quality plastic film and not folded.
5. IDENTIFICATION. Drawings and documents shall bear the purchase order number under which this specification is issued appropriate equipment and tag numbers as given and purchaser's drawing numbers when supplied.
6. REVISIONS. Drawings which are revised after initial submission shall be resubmitted immediately showing details of the changes and the new revision number.
7. CERTIFICATION. Final drawings shall be certified as accurate.
8. "AS BUILT" DRAWINGS. Where the specification includes installation and erection, "as built" drawings reflecting any site changes shall be supplied as soon as possible after completion of the work.
9. DATE OF SUBMISSION. Shall be within the number of weeks from order placement specified in the tabulation.
10. APPROVAL. All drawings for equipment specially designed to meet the specification shall be submitted for approval prior to manufacture, unless otherwise agreed.
11. TEST CERTIFICATES. Shall indicate the British or other national standard or code in accordance with which tests were performed and be identified as paragraph 5. The original and five copies, all signed, shall be supplied.
12. LUBRICATION REQUIREMENTS Shall specify recommended lubricants and quantities required for one year's operation.
13. RECOMMENDED SPARES LISTS. Shall be based on (one)(.....) years operation under specified conditions and shall include for each item
    – Identification, part or serial number
    – Maker's name and reference
    – Quantity recommended
    – Unit price and delivery

SPECIAL REQUIREMENTS

SCHEDULE OF SUBMISSION TIMES

Drawing/document	Shall be submitted			
	if ✓ with bid	WEEKS (see para 9)		
		for approval	final certified	
Arrangement drawings				
Foundation outline drawings				
Foundation loading details				
Engineering flowsheets P & ID's				
Electrical schematics				
Electrical termination and connection diagrams				
Shop details				
Calculations				
Data sheets				
Performance data				
Drawing schedule				
Test certificates				
Parts and materials lists				
Recommended spares list				
Lubricant requirements				
Erection instructions & drawings				
Operating & maintenance instructions manuals				

EQUIPMENT MARKING AND IDENTIFICATION

Each item shall be identified by its mark, equipment or tag number as given in the specification by the method indicated thus ✓

☐ Type stamping & painting	☐ Wired on metal tags
☐ Stamped nameplate	☐ As specification section ....

INSPECTION AND TESTING

Documented tests and inspection as indicated thus ✓ below are required

Inspection by purchaser	Required	Testing	Witnessed	Not witnessed
During manufacture		Standard works		
Final inspection		No load running		
Of packing		Full load performance		
As specification section............		As specification section............		

NOTES

TITLE		Specification number	Sheet number	Amendment number

Figure 13.6 Purchase specification – second sheet
This form is used to list various standard project requirements and schedule times. The main technical description follows on continuation forms (Figure 13.7).

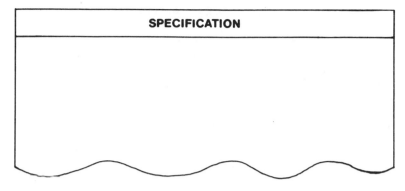

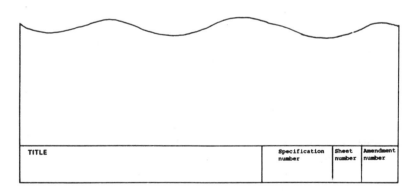

Figure 13.7 Purchase specification – continuation sheet
As many of these forms as necessary are attached to the first and
second sheets to carry the full descriptive technical text of each
specification. For regularly purchased items (such as valves, pumps,
motors and so on) it is good practice to store standard texts for the
relevant specifications in a word processor or computer.

amendment to be found among the sheets. Figure 13.5 shows a design used by one company for such a front sheet.

Each amendment should be issued to every person in the project organization who received the original issue, and relevant suppliers must also be included. Some companies only re-issue sheets that have changed (always including a fresh front sheet, of course). Others re-issue the whole specification each time. Total re-issue may have to be considered where the clerical proficiency of recipients is in any doubt (in other words, for those not directly supervised by the project manager and who cannot be relied upon to incorporate amended sheets or discard obsolete sheets correctly in their specification copies). These remarks on issuing amendments apply to any multi-page documents that are subject to change and re-issue, such as drawing and purchase control schedule sets.

For equipment which is purchased often, such as pumps, valves, piping, motors and so on, an experienced project engineering organization will avoid the chores and risks associated with preparing a new specification for every occasion by developing a library of standard material and equipment specifications. The texts of these can be held on file in a word processor or computer system, to be extracted, adapted as necessary, and used to prepare the specification for each new requirement.

Purchase enquiries

In order that the enquiry process can be put in hand, the project engineers will send copies of the enquiry specification to the purchasing agent, asking him to issue a formal purchase enquiry. The project engineers may have a good idea of which suppliers should be asked to bid and, indeed, they may already have discussed the requirements with some possible suppliers in advance. It is also likely that provisional quotations were obtained from suppliers for some of the more expensive items when the project cost estimates were first prepared.

The project engineers can use a form similar to that shown in Figure 13.8 to convey their instructions and suggestions to the purchasing agent. Some of the information on this form may be

PURCHASE ENQUIRY REQUEST

To:

Date:
Our ref:
Your ref:

Please obtain bids for the equipment, materials or services detailed in the attached specification from

☐ Only those vendors listed below

☐ Those listed below plus suitable vendors of your choice

☐ Suitable vendors of your choice

☐ Please supply a commercial bid summary

☐ Please forward bids as received

☐ Please forward all bids together after closing date

Bids are required by (date)

The recommended standard packing category will be
The order will be required on site by (date)

Your technical contact is   telephone   ext.

Notes a) Please ensure that tenderers are instructed to itemize in their quotation any items which they would buy - in or any work which they would sub-contract. The names of potential sub-contractors should be quoted.

Project engineer

Client	—	
Project	—	Project No —
Plant	—	
Discipline	—	

TITLE	Specification number	Sheet number	Amendment number

Figure 13.8 Purchase enquiry request form

This form is used by the project engineering organization to request action from the purchasing agent in seeking bids from potential suppliers. The project engineer would attach several copies of the relevant purchase specification. This often includes private commercial information, and the agent would detach this form and substitute his own letter of enquiry when sending out the invitations to bid.

commercially confidential, not to be disclosed to bidders, and the purchasing agent will substitute his own covering letter or form when he sends out the enquiries to bidders. The purchasing agent would usually have the authority to add potential suppliers of his own choice to any list put forward by the project engineers.

Enquiries should always be conducted in such a way that they encourage suppliers to submit their quotations according to a common format. Then all the bids can be compared with each other on a like-for-like basis.

In the relatively simple organizational arrangement where the purchasing agent is part of the main contractor or project engineering company, and where the purchasing and project engineering departments are located in the same building, then there should be no problem with the distribution of enquiry instructions and in communicating quotations and subsequent progress. Circumstances become a little more difficult when the purchasing agent is part of an external organization, and more difficult still if that external organization happens to be located far away from the project engineers or overseas. Matters can become very complicated where a project requires more than one purchasing agent, perhaps with one in the client's country, one in the country of the main contractor, and others operating in other countries to provide local expediting and inspection services.

It is sometimes necessary to keep purchasing agents informed by sending them copies of enquiries and specifications which are intended for initial action by another purchasing agent in the project organization. Although each such enquiry (and any subsequent requisition) bears the name of the purchasing agent with prime responsibility for taking action, there could be a risk of another agent taking action as a result of receiving a copy that was only intended to keep him informed. The project engineering company should consider colour coding each batch of documents (by printing or photocopying them on coloured paper stock), with a different colour chosen to represent each of the purchasing agents. Then everyone on the project would know, for example, that a pink set of enquiry documents was for the action of the agent in Lagos, yellow sets were for the agent in Buenos Aires, while plain white sets were always intended for action by the purchasing department in the contractor's head office. This measure, especially when followed through to the purchasing stage, can help to prevent unfortunate and expensive mix-ups where two different purchasing agents follow up the same enquiry and, in the worst case, place duplicate orders for the same goods.

Bid summaries

Companies which have to make high-cost purchases as a regular part of their project operations develop standard procedures for evaluating competitive tenders. The method typically used requires that information received from bidders is tabulated on a summary form which allows direct comparison of prices and other critical factors. An example of a bid summary form is shown in Figure 13.9.

Estimated packing, carriage, insurance, port and customs costs arising from foreign bidders have to be included, and all cost estimates and prices must be converted into the same currency. These steps ensure that the total delivered costs are compared in every case. Promised delivery dates are also compared on the bid summary, again not forgetting that the critical factor is the expected arrival date at site, and not simply the suppliers' ex-works dates.

Technical evaluation of quotations must, of course, be a matter for the relevant project engineer. Sometimes this has to be done in collaboration with the client's own engineers. The bid summary form illustrated is not suitable for making a detailed technical analysis (although it may be possible to devise other summary forms that could help). Once a technical preference has been identified, however, this can be noted on the bid summary form, where it must count heavily towards the final choice of supplier.

Recommendation of the successful bidder is usually the responsibility of a senior member of the project engineering staff, but in many cases the client will wish to have sight of the bid summary analysis and approve the conclusions reached (even in cases where the project engineering staff belong to a main contractor with complete contractual management auth-

BID SUMMARY					
SELLERS					
Country of origin					
Bid reference					
Bid date					
Period of validity					
Bid currency					
Project exchange rate					
Item	Qty	Description	Price	Price	Price	Price	Price

| Quoted price ex-works |
| Discounts |
| Inspection-testing |
| Packing-export prep. |
| Fob charges |
| Fob cost |
| Est transport to site |
| Customs duty tax etc. |
| Est.total cost on site |
| Quoted delivery ex-works |
| Est. transport time |
| Est. total delivery to site |
| Conditions of payment and notes- |

RECOMMENDED BY PURCHASING AGENT—
Reasons: lowest price ☐   acceptable delivery ☐   (tick for yes)

....
For purchasing agent

RECOMMENDED BY ENGINEER —
Reasons: meet technical requirements ☐   (tick for yes)

....
Project/senior engineer

RECOMMENDATION TO CLIENT —

| Delivery required | Delivery quoted | Planning Engr | Reason: |
| Budgeted cost | Price quoted | Cost Engr | |

....
Project manager

Project title   _____   Project No.   _____

Specification title   _____   Specification No.   _____

Figure 13.9 Bid summary form
Bid summaries are essential for comparing bids on a like-for-like basis.
Price comparisons should be on the basis of total delivered cost to site,
and all foreign currencies must be converted to a common currency for
this purpose.

ority). Whenever the final decision has to be made, the task will be easier if all the quotations have been set out carefully on a bid summary form to which sensible recommendations have been added.

Much time and effort are devoted to procedures and computerized systems for collecting and reporting the costs of material and equipment purchases. Although cost reporting is an essential part of project management, in the case of materials expenditure it is nothing more than reporting. It is not cost control. It is in the project engineering, enquiry and bid summary stages where the expenditure die is cast, and if over-expenditure is detected after the costs have already been committed in the shape of a requisition to the purchasing agent and his issue of a purchase order, the only remedy left to the project manager is to crawl into a quiet corner and have a good cry.

Sealed bids

Bid summary forms can be used by a purchaser to help evaluate bids for very high-value purchases and for letting valuable contracts and subcontracts, but it is likely that this would be done within the overall control of a more formalized sealed bid procedure.

In its strictest form, the procedure requires each bidder to submit two packages on or before a set date. One of these packs contains a specified number of copies of the technical proposal, but no price details. The other pack is the sealed commercial bid, which must include all prices, cost rates, and other commercial details.

The purchaser opens the technical bids first and evaluates these carefully, eliminating all bidders whose proposals appear to fall short of the technical and quality requirements and disqualifying any others who have contravened the rules of the game. The commercial bids are returned unopened to these unsuccessful bidders.

The short-listed survivors are then invited to attend a presentation meeting at which all their sealed commercial bids are opened and laid bare, after which the successful bidder is chosen.

Purchase requisitions and orders

When recommendations from the bid summary have been approved and the expenditure authorized, a purchase requisition can be issued to the purchasing agent by the project engineers (Figure 13.10). Again, a correct purchase specification must accompany each requisition. As, in the case of the case of the purchase enquiries, the requisition contains specific instructions for the purchasing agent and, as before, some of the commercial information on the requisition might be confidential between the project engineers and the agent, not to be passed on to the supplier. The agent will remove the requisition from the specification, and attach in its place a purchase order (which might be similar to that shown in Figure 12.2).

The distribution of requisitions will probably be similar to that for enquiry requests and, if a colour coding convention has been used to indicate which of several purchase agents must take action, the same convention can be followed through to this requisition stage. But then comes an important difference: the enquiry documents were only requests, but the purchase requisition actually vests authority in the purchasing agent to issue the official order and sign it on behalf of the contractor, with the intention of binding both supplier and purchaser to a contract.

Purchase requisitions must, therefore, be authorized at a suitably senior level in the project. There may be a case for grading the level at which various individuals can sign, according to the levels of committed expenditure (a system which can be abused by anyone smart enough to split an order that exceeds his limit of authority into a number of smaller orders which do not). It is not unusual to require the project manager's signature on all significant requisitions: for some particularly important or sensitive items the client's authorization may also be needed.

Specification, enquiry and order numbers

The filing, retrieval and general handling of purchase documents would be a great deal simpler if the initial enquiry, the

REQUISITION

To   Date:
                                            Our ref:
                                            Your ref:

☐ Please issue a purchase order and arrange transport etc as appropriate
☐ Please amend the purchase order
for the equipment materials or services detailed in the attached specification (at the amendment number given below) in accordance with the following

VENDOR   (name and address)

QUOTATION   (reference and date)

CONSIGNEE   (name and address)

Please instruct the vendor to confirm his arrangements regarding sub-suppliers or sub-contractors

Inspect in accordance with   - specification ☐   notes below ☐
The recommended degree of expediting is   - intense ☐   normal ☐   none ☐
The recommended standard packing category is
The order is required on site by (date)   -
The recommended method of transport is   -
Client's charge account   -
Client's authority reference   -
Your technical contact is   telephone   ext.

Notes

PRICE DETAILS	
Basis	-
Original quote	-
Total previous amendments	-
This amendment	-
LATEST TOTAL PRICE	-
Budget allowance	-

DELIVERY DETAILS	
Original delivery	-
Current delivery	-
Required delivery	-

APPROVALS			
Originated by	Senior engineer	Project engineer	Project manager

Client   --
Project   -
Plant   -
Discipline   -
TITLE

Project number:

Specification number	Amendment

Requisition number	Amendment

Figure 13.10 Purchase requisition
When properly approved, and supported by a purchase specification, the purchase requisition instructs and authorizes the purchasing agent to issue a purchase order.

specification and the resulting purchase order could all be arranged to have the same reference number.

Although it is often possible to use the specification number as the enquiry number, various events can intervene which prevent the same number being carried through to the purchase order. Not least of these is that each particular purchasing agent (and there could be more than one for the project) might wish to use his own standard order numbering system.

It is also very likely that the supply of materials listed in several specifications might be consolidated into one purchase order. It might be advantageous, for example, to collect all the requirements for pumps together and order them all from one supplier on a single purchase order. In that case several specifications would have to be attached to the purchase order, all with different numbers. An even more difficult complication arises when it is decided to order materials defined in one specification as two separate orders, placed with different suppliers (which means that the original specification must be amended or split to suit the different suppliers, and will generate two requisitions as well as two orders).

The authority responsible for project procedures must ensure that all these factors are considered and that, if a common numbering system is impossible, the system adopted allows all the related documents to be adequately cross-referenced. The organization which provided the forms that illustrate this chapter used the following procedure:

1 Enquiry specifications were allocated serial numbers from the purchase control schedules in the manner indicated by Figure 13.4.

2 Purchase enquiries were given the same numbers as the specifications which accompanied them.

3 A completely different series of numbers was used for requisitions, allocated from registers, and with a different series for each purchasing agent. These series were distinguished from one another by the use of a different letter prefix to denote the agent responsible. Every requisition also carried a cross-reference to the specification or specifications which accompanied it.

4 The purchasing agents were persuaded to use the requisition

numbers as their own purchase order numbers. This acceptance by the agents was made easier because each had been allocated his own continuous series of requisition numbers, which automatically meant that a purchase order system using the same numbers would also have no awkward gaps left in the sequence of numbers issued. As with the requisitions, each purchase order also carried the number or numbers of all attached specifications.

Thus several numbering systems were agreed and used, but there was full cross-referencing between all the vital documents.

Inspection and expediting

The purchaser may wish to arrange visits to a supplier's premises to check on progress, inspect workmanship or witness tests. Such visits could be linked to the certification of stage payments. The project manager and the client may expect to receive formal inspection and progress reports from the relevant purchasing agent following such visits.

The manufacture of special capital equipment is itself an industrial project, demanding (on a smaller scale) project management techniques similar to those used on the main project. A modern feature of project equipment purchasing is that the buyer will take a detailed interest in the vendor's own project management and quality procedures. Several large companies and government departments insist that those who supply them with project equipment or carry out subcontracts at least use critical path analysis, and it is likely that they will be expected to show that their quality policy and procedures satisfy the requirements of the international standard IS0 9000 (equivalent to British Standard 5750). It is not unknown for purchasers to offer advice to vendors in establishing their own internal systems.

There are several ways in which responsibility for carrying out inspection and expediting visits can be delegated. Where suitable engineers are available to the purchase agent concerned, it is often convenient for him to arrange visits which combine the inspection and estimating functions. Where specialist engineering attendance is needed for inspection or to witness tests, the project engineering organization might send one or more of its own engineers to assist the purchasing agent. To avoid expensive overseas travel when foreign suppliers are involved, it is sometimes possible to engage a local professional engineering company to undertake the inspection and expediting visits.

Whatever the arrangement for staffing the inspection function, the project engineers must make arrangements (usually through the purchasing agent) for the inspectors to receive all necessary drawings and specifications, the purchase order, and all revisions and amendments to these documents. Some companies are also able to provide the inspecting engineers with checklists, to help ensure that no vital point is overlooked.

Following each visit, the results must be fed back to the project engineer or project manager. The inspectors will probably be asked to use a convenient standard summary form for this purpose, an example of which is given in Figure 13.11.

Vendors' documents

Provision must usually be made for the project engineers to receive and approve documents from the supplier for items which are manufactured specially for the project. (The term vendors' documents is usually applied, although the providers of the goods might be referred to as manufacturers, sellers, suppliers, subcontractors or vendors.)

The first step in ensuring the timely receipt of vendors' documents is to make certain that the obligations for providing them are always spelled out clearly on the purchase orders or purchase specifications.

In addition to general design layouts, there is usually a requirement for early notification of installation instructions. With heavy plant and machinery, for example, foundation drawings, power supply requirements and overall weights and dimensions are all vital information, the lack of which could

INSPECTION/EXPEDITING REPORT

This report No	Sheet 1 of _____	Date of this visit	Last report No	Date of last visit	Inspector / Expediter
_____		_____	_____	_____	_____

MAIN SUPPLIER DETAILS

Supplier _____

Location _____

Suppliers reference _____

Personnel contacted _____

Telephone No _____ Telex No _____

Equipment _____
_____
_____
_____

Agreed delivery
Week number _____
Date _____

Latest delivery
Week number _____
Date _____

Next visit. week _____
To expedite ☐
To continue inspection ☐
For final inspection ☐
To inspect packing ☐

SUB-SUPPLIER DETAILS

Supplier's order No _____ Date _____

Sub-supplier _____

Location _____

Sub-supplier's reference _____

Personnel contacted _____

Telephone No _____ Telex No _____

Equipment _____
_____
_____
_____

Agreed delivery to main supplier
Week number _____
Date _____

Latest Delivery
Week number _____
Date _____

Next visit. week _____
To expedite ☐
To continue inspection ☐
For final inspection ☐
To inspect packing ☐

ORDER STATUS SUMMARY (For details see attached sheets)

Progress ahead of target	Slippage	Tests witnessed as specified	Complies with specification	Released for packing	Released for shipping
Yes _____ Weeks	_____ Weeks	Yes	Yes	Yes	Yes
No		No	No	No	No

Action by	Action required

Client	Project number
Purchasing agent's order number
Date of order	Specification(No's) amendment
TITLE	REQUISITION No amendment

Figure 13.11 Inspection and expediting report

Forms such as this can be convenient for summarizing the findings of inspecting or expediting engineers after their visits to equipment manufacturers.

hold up work on the project. Obtaining such information, and progressing any necessary approvals, is all part of the essential expediting process.

When the equipment is delivered, a final set of drawings, certified test results, installation instructions, operating and maintenance manuals and a recommended spares holding list will probably be needed. In some cases, suppliers may be required to supply documents translated into a foreign language, according to the nationality of the project end user.

The project engineering company will have obligations in providing a back-up service to the client after project handover. These obligations usually extend beyond the initial guarantee period, and can involve the provision of advice or services in maintaining, repairing, replacing, operating, modifying or extending the plant. Since much of the plant will rely on purchased equipment, the company must be able to refer to any relevant vendor document for many years after project completion. The contractor will therefore need to keep a complete project set of vendors' documentation safely in his own files or archives (either in their original state or on microfilm). It is not sufficient to rely on being able to obtain additional or replacement copies from all the various suppliers in the future: some of them might lose or destroy their records, be swallowed up in mergers or takeovers, or simply cease trading.

A great number of vendors' drawings and other documents can accumulate in a large project, and the project engineering company has to make certain that it will be able to find any of these quickly if the client reports operating difficulties, or if the documents are needed again for any of the other reasons already listed. For this reason, copies of vendors' documents are usually serially numbered and recorded in registers before filing. To ensure that any of these documents can easily be found again in the future (location and retrieval are the buzzwords) the files must be arranged in some recognizable and logical sequence. This might be based on specification numbers, requisition or purchase order numbers, or the project work breakdown code numbers. It may be necessary to provide a cross-referenced index so that, for example, a file can be found if only the equipment specification number or the supplier and approximate date of supply is known.

Shipping, port and customs formalities

It is best to entrust arrangements for long-distance transport, shipping, airfreight, seaport and airport and international frontier formalities to a specialist organization. The purchasing agent will undoubtedly have considerable experience and expertise, but the employment of a reputable freight forwarding agent will be invaluable.

Freight forwarding agents operate through worldwide organizations, They have their staff or representatives stationed at most of the world's ports and airports and, through telex or other communication networks, are able to monitor the progress of every consignment through all stages from initial loading to final delivery.

The purchasing agent must ensure that every consignment is properly marked before it leaves the supplier's premises. The marking method required should be stated on the purchase specification and will usually involve suppliers stencilling easily recognizable markings on packing crates so that each item can be clearly identified through all stages of its journey and, not least, by the site personnel when it finally arrives. The purchase order is usually required to feature in all markings.

Collaboration between the purchasing agent and a freight forwarding agent can achieve benefits from the economy of scale obtained when different consignments are consolidated to make up complete container loads.

The combined expertise of the purchasing and freight forward agent can be a great comfort to project staff confronted for the first time with the need to deal with the formidable array of documents associated with the international movement of goods. Failure to get the documentation right first time can lead to delays, the impounding of goods, and to legally-imposed penalties.

Local knowledge provided by the forwarding agent's contacts in the countries along the delivery route can yield important information about the type and capacity of port handling facilities, warning of any unusual congestion or industrial disputes (with suggestions for alternative routes), and details of inland road and rail systems (including size and weight restrictions). For example, the agent in one case was able to prevent an expensive mistake by pointing out that a local railway company operated an unusually short restriction on the maximum length of loads, because the route included tunnels with unusually sharp curves. At another port, the local agents were able to warn about a peculiar security problem, where the local shanty-town inhabitants were always on the lookout for fresh supplies of building timber. If such timber happened to exist in the shape of well-constructed packing crates protecting expensive project equipment standing on the dockside – well who could blame them?

Purchase order status reports

The purchasing agent is usually required to keep the project manager informed of the progress status of all current purchase orders. This responsibility, in addition to the inspection and expediting reports already described, extends through all stages of the journey to the project site. This reporting can be done by means of regular order status reports, which list all purchase orders in progress, giving outline details of shipping and delivery dates, and highlighting any problems and corrective actions.

Order status reports duplicate, to a large extent, the information contained in the purchase control schedules prepared by the engineers, but the listing sequence will be different. Only active orders are included and these will probably be listed in sequence of their purchase order numbers rather than their purchase specification numbers.

If a common computer database facility can be made available simultaneously to the project engineers and the purchasing agent, the purchase schedules and order status reports can be integrated to save much clerical work. What tends to happen in practice is, however, that no matter how cleverly the computer system or clerical method has been devised, much of the progress data (especially from overseas) simply doesn't get into the system in time to be of any use.

Efficient communications and dedicated, regular reporting by all the purchasing agents and freight forwarders involved on the project are essential if purchase order status reports are to be of any value.

Case history

A UK-based company was engineering and managing several projects for an African client. There was a requirement to coordinate all the order status data from several purchasing agents, one in the British Home Counties, one in South Africa and another in Zambia. Computer equipment was purchased specially on the recommendation of the company's computing manager (who, no doubt, meant well). The intended purpose of the system (its only declared purpose) was to coordinate the progress data contained in weekly reports from the three purchasing agents and various freight forwarding agents, and process this information to update and print one integrated weekly purchase order status report for distribution to the client and throughout the project organization.

The system never got off the ground and was a complete failure, simply because it was starved of data. With the communications existing at that time it was not practical to expect agents overseas to deliver comprehensive reports on the movements of materials and the progress of purchase orders, all supposed to arrive at company headquarters reliably, accurately, and on the same day of every week. Further, the company did not have direct authority over all the agents involved, and so was not able to insist on such reports.

The company tried for over a year to sell the system but, in the manner of computing equipment, it quickly became obsolete. It had cost about £8000. Eventually the company sold it to me for £10 as scrap, and I used it to provide components for making an electronic organ. By then the computing manager had left the company, so he did not have to face the music.

Further reading

Baily, P. (1991), *Purchasing Systems and Records* (3rd edn), Aldershot: Gower.

Baily, P.J.H. and Farmer, D.H. (1990), *Purchasing Principles and Management* (6th edn), London: Pitman.

Croner's Reference Book for Exporters, New Malden, Surrey: Croner Publications (by subscription: updated monthly).

Croner's Reference Book for Importers, New Malden, Surrey: Croner Publications (by subscription: updated monthly)

ICC (1990), *INCOTERMS 1990*, Paris: ICC Publication 460, International Chamber of Commerce (also available from ICC National Committees throughout the world).

Lysons, C.K. (1989), *Purchasing*, London: Pitman.

14

Changes, concessions and build schedules

No commercial project can be expected to run from initial order to final completion without the introduction of at least one change. The exception to this rule might exist as a project manager's dream of Utopia, but is unlikely to take on any more tangible form.

Classification

Whenever changes arise, they can usually be recognized as belonging to one of two principal commercial categories. One way of defining these categories is to ask whether the request for a change has originated within the project organization, or if it has come from the customer. There are, however, some borderline cases which cannot be put into either of these classifications but which contain elements of both. A more useful way of classifying changes from the commercial point of view is to label them as funded or unfunded. For a funded change the customer must take responsibility for the change and pay for it. For unfunded changes the contractor will have to carry the costs himself, with consequent risk to budget limits and expected profits. Whether or not a change is to be funded or unfunded will determine to a very large extent how it is handled and considered for authorization.

Funded changes

Changes requested by the customer to the specified project automatically imply a corresponding change to the contract, since the specification forms part of the contract documentation. If, as usually happens, the modification results in an increase in the contractor's costs, a suitable change to the contract price must be negotiated. The delivery schedule may also be affected and any resulting delays must be predicted, discussed and agreed.

Customer-funded modifications may possess nuisance value and can disrupt the smooth flow of logically-planned work, but they do, nevertheless, offer the prospect of compensation through an increase in price and possibly even an increase in profits. When a customer asks for a change, the contractor is in a strong price-bargaining position because there is no competitor and he has a monopoly.

Customer-funded changes are usually documented as purchase order amendments or contract variation orders (otherwise known as project variations).

Unfunded changes

If a contractor finds it necessary to introduce changes himself, he cannot expect the customer to foot the bill unless it arises from some contingency for which provision was made in the contract. He must be prepared to carry the additional costs himself, write off any work which has been scrapped, and answer to the customer for any resulting time delays. For this reason contractors have to be particularly wary about allowing unfunded changes to proceed.

Unfunded modifications are usually generated internally by documents called engineering change requests, engineering change orders, modification requests, or some permutation of these terms. In manufacturing projects, questions referred to the engineering design department by manufacturing or inspection personnel can result in design changes and the relevant documentation is described later in this chapter.

Permanent and temporary changes

Changes can be further classified as permanent or temporary. Permanent changes are those which are carried out with the intention of leaving them permanently embodied in the design and execution of a project, and which will remain recorded in drawings and specifications after the project has been finished to show its true as-built condition.

Temporary changes may be needed for expediency in getting a project finished, but they are carried out with the intention of either removing them or converting them to some alternative permanent change at a later, more convenient time. Temporary changes are often authorized when a manufacturing department wants permission to deviate from drawings or specifications in order to expedite progress, on the understanding that such permission is temporary and will not apply to the subsequent manufacture of similar items.

Authorization procedure

The effects of any change, whether customer-requested or not, may be felt far beyond the confines of the project area that is most obviously and directly affected. This could be true of the technical, timescale or cost aspects. A project has to be regarded as a technical and commercial system, in which a change to one part can react with other parts of the system, bringing about consequences that the change's originator may not have been able to foresee. For these reasons alone it is prudent to ensure that every proposed change is considered by at least one key member of each project department, in order that the likely overall effects can be predicted as reliably as possible. Naturally these considerations should take place before any change is put into practice.

The change committee

In many companies engaged on project work a regular panel of experts is appointed to consider changes and decide how they are to be handled.

Departmental managers should be included in or represented on the committee. These must include those who are able to answer for the likely safety, reliability, performance, cost and timescale consequences of changes, the effects on work-in-progress, and the practical feasibility or otherwise of introducing the change into manufacture or construction.

In some cases, especially in projects involving the nuclear industry, aviation, defence or other cases where reliability, safety or performance assume great significance, two key members of the committee represent:

- the *design authority* (typically the chief engineer);
- the *inspecting authority* (a chief inspector or quality control manager, who may be acting under authority delegated from and supervised closely by an external government or industry-appointed inspecting authority).

Committee meetings

Change committees often meet on a regular basis, dealing with change requests in batches. Others avoid meetings by circulating requests around the committee members, so that each member considers the effect of the proposed change on his or her area of responsibility. Each method has its advantages and disadvantages. If formal committee meetings take place at monthly intervals, the wait for change decisions can hold up progress, or result in the greater disruption to work that late changes cause. On the other hand, frequent committee meetings take up too much of the members' time. Informal committees, not meeting collectively but relying instead on the circulation of documents, suffer from a communication problem and can take longer to discuss and resolve misunderstandings or make decisions. Neither approach can be classified as right or wrong, but it will be assumed here that a formal procedure exists, with a change committee meeting at regular intervals.

Decision criteria

When each change request is considered for approval, the committee must weigh up all the possible consequences before making their decision. Points which have to be examined are listed below (not necessarily in order of importance):

- Is the change actually possible to make?
- Is it a customer-requested or a self-inflicted change?
- What is the estimated cost of the change?
- Will the customer pay? If so, what should be the price?
- If the change is not customer-requested, is it really necessary? Why?
- What will be the effect on progress?
- How will safety, reliability and performance be affected?
- If several identical sets of equipment are being produced, at what point in the production sequence should the change be introduced?
- Will scrap or redundant materials be created?
- Are any items to be changed retrospectively? Are these:
  - in progress?
  - in stock?
  - already delivered to the customer?
- What drawings, specifications and other documents will have to be modified?

The committee's response

When the committee has considered all these questions, it has the option to:

- authorize the change as requested;
- give limited approval only, authorizing the change with specified limitations;
- refer the request back to the originator (or elsewhere) asking for clarification, or for an alternative solution;
- reject the change, giving reasons.

Use of standard request forms

Individuals who wish to request a change should always be asked to put their request in writing to the committee. In order to save the committee's time and to ensure that all requests are properly controlled and progressed, it is essential to derive some sort of standard request form for this purpose. This form must be designed in such a way that the originator is induced to answer in advance all the questions that the change committee will want to ask. In some projects, even the customer can be persuaded to submit change requests using the contractor's standard forms.

Because there are several routes along which changes can arise within any organization, there are usually several different forms that can result in change requests. These forms are illustrated later in this chapter, in the section 'Forms and procedures'. However, the change coordination procedure described below is generally applicable to all of these different forms.

Coordination procedure

In any project organization where changes are expected (which really means all project organizations) it is necessary to nominate a change coordinating clerk. This is not usually a full-time role, and the person chosen will probably carry out other clerical or administrative duties for the project. The change coordinating clerk may reside in a contracts office, the project manager's administration group, the engineering department, or in some other department. His or her duties are likely to include:

- registering each change request and allocating serial numbers;
- distributing and filing copies of the change documents;
- following up to ensure that every request is considered by the change committee without avoidable delay;
- distributing and filing copies of the change documents after the committee's instructions have been given;
- Following up to ensure that authorized changes are carried out and that all drawings and specifications affected by the change are updated and reissued.

Numbering and registration

Upon receipt of any change request, the coordinator should enter brief details in a register from which subsequent progress can be controlled. Change registers are typically loose-leaf. Separate registers should be kept for project variations, engineering change requests, engineering queries, production permits and inspection reports. Usually a slightly different design of register sheet is used for each of these registers, but Figure 14.1 shows a layout that can be applied universally.

The change coordinator must allocate serial numbers from the appropriate register. The numbering systems should be kept simple, but must be designed so that no number is repeated on another project or in another register. The simple solution is to prefix each change with either the project number or a shorter code that is specific to the project, and to add one or two letters which denote the type of change. For example, if the project number is P123, engineering change request forms might be numbered in the series P123/EC001, P123/EC002, P123/EC003 and so on. Concessions or production permits for the same project would be numbered in the series P123/PP001, P123/PP002, P123/PP003 and so on.

Distribution

The change clerk's first duty after registering each change request is to arrange for its photocopying and distribution. This process will be speeded up if the forms are stocked in multi-part sets.

A typical distribution for any change request might be:

- engineering manager or chief engineer (who may wish to arrange further distribution within his or her department);
- change committee chairperson (the original 'top copy');
- other change committee members (one each).

The originator should retain a copy, and the coordinator will keep another on a 'changes pending file', with a different file for each type of form in use. All forms should be filed in sequential order of their serial numbers.

Register							

Project number: Sheet number:

For project variations, engineering change requests, engineering query notes and concessions or production permits

Serial number	Originated by	Description or title	Date of request	Approved? (Yes or no)	Date of final distribution	Price change ± (if any)

Figure 14.1 A general purpose change register sheet
A form such as this can be used for the serial numbering, registration and progressing of the various documents that can give rise to project changes and engineering modifications, such as project variations, engineering change requests, engineering queries and concessions or production permits. A separate register and numbering series must be set up for each of these document types.

Progressing

Change registers should be designed to highlight change requests that are with the change committee for consideration or which are otherwise still 'active', requiring monitoring to prevent delays. For example, a column can be provided on the register sheet headed 'final issue date' or something similar. The absence of a date in that column tells the coordinator that the change is still active and in need of monitoring and progressing.

Estimating the true cost of a design modification

Most changes will add to the cost of a project. It is not always appreciated, however, that the total costs of an engineering modification can far exceed the straightforward estimate of costs directly attributable to the modification itself. A simple example will help to demonstrate some of the extra incidental costs which can be introduced when a change is made to a project.

Suppose that a project is in hand to produce two competition cars within a small corner of a factory whose primary purpose is the quantity production of cars for general sale. The cars are being supplied to another company in the group for normal commercial profit and against that company's purchase order and standard contract conditions. The two racing cars are identical, one being intended as a back-up unit for the other in case of failure. Although these cars incorporate some standard components, practically everything about them is special. The engines are standard production units from the works stores, but they have to be stripped down, modified, rebuilt and bench-tested before they can be fitted.

During final assembly of the two cars the company is informed that the two engines will not comply with the current international competition rules, a mistake which has arisen because the purchaser did not realize that their copy of the rules was out of date. Suitable replacement engines are not available from within the company, but a different version of the engines, which will satisfy the competition rules, can be purchased from another company in the group (from their overseas factory).

These are almost interchangeable with the wrong engines and use the same fuel and ignition systems.

Asked to forecast the cost of this change, the company's cost estimating department might produce a set of figures something like the following:

		£
Cost of removing old engines		
5 man-hours at £8 per hour		40
Cost of preparing two new engines		
60 man-hours at £8 per hour		480
Cost of modifying engine mountings		
6 man-hours at £8 per hour		48
Sundry other changes		
10 man-hours at £8 per hour		80
Total direct labour		648
Overheads at 80 per cent		518
Materials:		
Two new engines	3 000	
Other materials	250	3 250
Estimated factory cost of modification		4 416
Mark-up at 50 per cent		2 208
Additional price		6 624

In reality, however, it might take six weeks to get the new engines delivered, during which time the project might have to be shelved temporarily. Even assuming that the fitters could be gainfully employed elsewhere in the works, it is unlikely that the total costs of the change would be limited to the £4 416 estimated. The cars, together with work benches, jigs, cradles and special tools, would probably occupy some 40 square metres of prime work space. Even when no work is taking place this space still attracts costs in terms of rent, business rates, heating, maintenance, cleaning, insurance and so on.

Here is an example of overhead under-recovery (the concepts of absorption costing, standard costing and the recovery of overheads were outlined in Chapter 4). The overall cost of factory floor space in this case might work out at about £250 per square metre per annum, so that the extra cost of leaving the car space idle for six weeks would amount to about £1 150. This sum would obviously not be recovered in the selling price calculated above.

Other projects for which the space and facilities are needed could suffer from a knock-on effect from the delay. Also, failure to meet the programme in the early part of a project can be reflected in increased activity later on, and this can cause problems and additional costs as a result of crash actions and overtime working.

Modifications often affect stocks of materials by making them redundant. If a spare engine had been ordered for the cars, this, too, might have to be replaced and prepared. It is by no means uncommon for items of quite high value to be overlooked completely, simply because they are out of sight in some remote storage area.

A direct result of the error in starting with the wrong engine might be that the cars were not ready in time to compete at the start of the racing season. This could lead to a loss of potential prize money and prestige for the competitor.

If the error in choosing the wrong engines had been the fault of the contractor, and not the purchaser, matters would have been far worse. The change would have to be classified as unfunded but essential, and the contractor would have to bear all the costs, both estimated and hidden. It is quite likely that the purchaser of the cars would seek compensation for his losses by way of liquidated damages or by invoking a contract penalty clause for late delivery. In the very worst case, the order might even be cancelled.

It is not reasonable to expect that all individuals will inevitably include all possible costs of modifications in their estimates, although this would be the ideal aim. In fact, the project manager must learn to expect that omissions of important cost factors are likely in many estimates. He or she will become experienced in asking significant and probing questions as a matter of routine, in order that the cost estimator's train of thought can be reset. Is there to be no inspection on this job? Are stocks affected? Does the prototype have to be modified too? What will the delay cost? Is this going to hold up other work and, if so, what will that cost? Such questions must always be asked in the quest for the whole truth about modification costs.

Recording the actual cost of a modification

Some of the difficulties to be expected in assessing the true costs of a modification have now been outlined, and it is apparent that there are many factors which can easily be overlooked. Nevertheless, an estimate can be made in most cases, and this can be used to work out and justify any possible increase in price which the contractor feels able to demand. Recording the actual costs of a modification can prove to be a far more difficult undertaking: it may even be impossible.

Difficulties underlying the measurement and recording of actual modification costs may not always be appreciated by some managers and others who, quite reasonably, would like to know just how much their budgets are being affected by changes.

Suppose that a modification is to be performed on a 'fuzzelbox', which is a complex piece of electronic equipment containing over 10 km of wire, with thousands of connections and many components. First take the case where the fuzzelbox has already been assembled, inspected and fully tested. Here there need be no problem in identifying the cost of the change, because a fresh works order or job ticket can be issued for the modification work and materials, complete with a new cost code. All the subsequent work of stripping, changing, inspecting and re-testing can be attributed directly to the change.

Now consider the different (but frequent) case in which drawings and specifications are modified during the course of production work. The fuzzelbox is in a semi-completed state, so that the modification will add new wires, delete others, re-route wires not yet installed and result in changed connections and components. How can anyone be expected to record accurately that part of the work which is directly attributable to the modification? It is also probable that many changes will occur on a job of this size before it is finished, so that the only apparent and measurable effect on costs will be an increase of expenditure compared with the initially-estimated production costs. This situation has to be accepted and, if the modification costs are needed for any purpose, they will have to be estimated.

Forms and procedures

A change can be introduced into a project through several different routes. This section describes some of these paths, with their origins and associated forms. The authorization and coordination procedures already described in this chapter will apply generally to all of these forms.

When is a formal procedure necessary?

When a designer, in a fit of rage or despair, tears up a drawing or clears the computer screen and starts again, there is obviously no need to invoke a formal change engineering procedure. Any new design might have to undergo many changes before it is committed to a fully checked and issued drawing. This is all part of the normal, creative development process. Provided that the design intentions remain within the requirements of the design specification, any internal changes made before drawings are formally issued are not generally considered to be modifications or engineering changes.

Some companies have a need to circulate early, pre-issue drawings for discussion, advance information or approval. These issues are often distinguished from the fully released versions by labelling them as revision A, revision B and so on, changing the revision numbers to the series 0, 1, 2 and so on, to denote official releases. A rule might, therefore, be suggested that formal engineering change procedures need only be applied to drawing revisions made after the first issue for manufacturing or construction. But such a rule can fall apart if preliminary issues are made for the manufacture of a prototype, in which changes must be properly controlled.

Another reason for invoking formal procedures is found whenever there is an intention to depart from the design specification, especially when the development work is being carried out for an external customer. This, again, is a case for using the formal change procedure before any drawing has been issued for manufacture or construction.

There is need, therefore, to seek some rule or criterion that can determine at which point in the design process the formal change procedure should be introduced. The question to be asked is 'Will the proposed change affect any instruction, specification, plan or budget that has already been agreed with other departments, the customer, or other external organization?' If the answer to this question is 'Yes', the probability is that formal change committee approval will be needed.

Design freeze

Sometimes project organizations recognize that there is a point in the design and construction of a project after which any change would be particularly irksome, inconvenient or potentially damaging. This leads to the announcement of a design freeze, after which the change committee will refuse to consider any change request unless there are compelling reasons, such as safety or a customer request. Ideally the customer should agree to be bound by the design freeze.

Project variations

Changes requested by the customer which affect price, delivery or any other aspect of the original purchase order or contract require formal documentation which, in effect:

* amends the purchase order or contract and describes the change;
* authorizes the contractor to make the change;
* promises payment;
* agrees to any associated timescale revision.

Where the original contract was in the form of a purchase order, the customer will usually request a change by issuing a purchase order amendment (see Chapters 12 and 13). In other cases, especially for projects involving construction, changes are recorded on project variation orders (sometimes called simply 'project variations' or 'contract variations'). An example is given in Figure 14.2. Similar changes arranged by a main contractor with site construction subcontractors are often known as site variation orders.

A procedure for simple, repetitive project variations
In projects where a considerable number of small changes are expected, it may be possible to streamline all the change procedures, perhaps with a prearranged scale of charges. Naturally such a procedure must be restricted to engineering changes of a routine nature, where safety and reliability cannot be affected. Provided that the scope of a change can be defined adequately, and that the work can easily be identified separately from other project work, the costs of small changes can be recovered on some agreed time and materials basis or, for construction projects, against an agreed schedule of rates per units of measured work.

Here is an example which shows how simplified change procedures can be used to avoid the need for hundreds of purchase order amendments or contract variations. For the project in question, the contractor was engaged on a defence contract for designing and building automatic test equipment for the electronic systems installed in military aircraft. Each complete tester was housed in a trailer which could be towed out to an aircraft, connected by cables, and left to carry out a whole range of measurements, 'go' or 'no-go' checks and diagnostic fault-finding routines. The testers were controlled by computers, programmed by means of special punched tapes.

Every time that the aircraft manufacturer wanted to change any of the test parameters (which occurred at least daily during prototype commissioning) a small amount of reprogramming was necessary in the test equipment. Some changes also required one, two or three wires to be re-routed inside the tester. Attempting to estimate the cost of each change and subjecting it to the formal change committee procedure was out

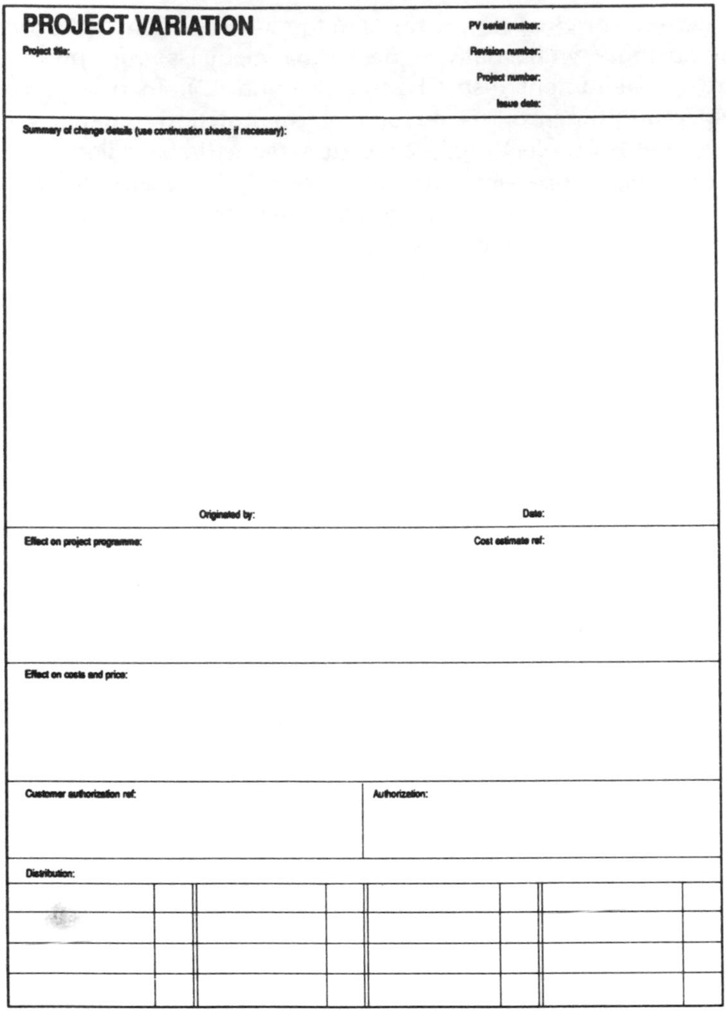

PROJECT VARIATION

Project title:

PV serial number:
Revision number:
Project number:
Issue date:

Summary of change details (use continuation sheets if necessary):

Originated by:
Date:

Effect on project programme:
Cost estimate ref:

Effect on costs and price:

Customer authorization ref:
Authorization:

Distribution:

Reproduced from *ProjectPlanner* by Dennis Lock, Gower, Aldershot, 1990.

Figure 14.2 A project variation
A form for recording and administering change requests from the customer.

of the question. Yet every change had to be recorded for later incorporation into drawings, and every change had to be paid for.

The matter was resolved by both companies agreeing to the

use of simple, serially numbered, all-one-price, program change request forms. These documented the details of each change, were authorized by the signature of the customer's senior engineer at the test site, and accepted for on-the-spot action by the contractor's senior commissioning engineer. A copy of each change was returned to the head office of the contractor, who kept the relevant drawings and programming records up to date. Invoices were sent to the customer periodically, each claiming payment for a batch of changes identified by their serial numbers.

The system was limited by mutual agreement to include only the simple changes needed to alter measurement data or test-point switching. Hundreds of changes were requested, actioned and charged for against these very simple pre-priced request forms, saving valuable time at the commissioning site, with the contractor collecting a satisfying level of revenue and the customer avoiding the expense of preparing, negotiating and issuing the more formal type of change orders.

Engineering change requests

The purpose of an engineering change request is to describe, document and seek formal permission for a permanent design change. The change may be unfunded, or it might be the result of a project variation order and, therefore, funded.

Engineering change requests of the type shown in Figure 14.3 are used widely in engineering projects, although they may be known by different titles, invariably abbreviated to sets of initials. The following are among those which may be encountered:

ECR – engineering change request
ECO – engineering change order
MR – modification request

Any person should be allowed to originate an engineering change request, since it can have no effect until it has been authorized by the change committee. The method for completing the form should be self-evident from Figure 14.3.

HONEYCOMB PRODUCTS LIMITED, LUTON, BEDFORDSHIRE Engineering change request						Mod number		
						Sheet　of　　　　sheets		

PROJECT _____

DRAWINGS AFFECTED

NUMBER	Issue	NUMBER	Issue	NUMBER	Issue	NUMBER	Issue

UNITS TO BE SUBJECTED TO EMERGENCY CHANGE ACTION (IF ANY)

Part number	Serial numbers

CHANGE DETAILS

REASON (IF CUSTOMER REQUESTS ENTER CUSTOMER REFERENCE_____)

ORIGINATOR _____　Date_____　Estimated cost £ _____

COMMITTEE DECISION: LIST POINT OF EMBODIMENT, ACTION ON STOCK, LIMITATIONS

Approved/rejected _____

Figure 14.3 Engineering change request form
A document which allows effective consideration and documentation of modifications.

Concessions or production permits

Manufacturing departments, faced with the need to keep to a budget or to accomplish work within a scheduled timescale, sometimes find that they need to depart from the specific instructions contained in the manufacturing drawings in order to achieve their objective. Naturally, the quality control department will keep a wary eye open to ensure that no unauthorized shortcuts or botching is allowed.

Suppose, however, that a drawing specifies the use of chromium-plated screws, but that these are simply not available when required because they have an unusual thread. The purchasing department may be able to obtain alternative screws with a different plate finish, or possibly some other thread size could be substituted. If the production team decided to make this substitution without reference to the design engineers, there would be a danger (remote in many companies) of an inspector noticing the difference and rejecting the work because it deviated from the drawing.

But would the use of these alternative screws really matter? It all depends, of course, on the actual circumstances and whether the screws are in a prominent position where they will be easily seen if they do not match adjacent chromium parts. Someone has to decide, and either authorize or reject the change.

Other requests for concessions might not be simply cosmetic. The use of alternative materials, different adhesives, acceptance of wider tolerances, are all reasons for originating requests for concessions. These might represent a risk to performance, reliability, safety or interchangeability. As a general rule, therefore, concessions require the formal approval of the design authority.

Concessions (or production permits) usually fall into the classification of temporary changes. It is unlikely that the drawings will be updated to suit the change, it being assumed that the manufacturing department will either be able to adhere to the drawings in any future production, or will apply for a further concession.

Procedures for requesting concessions vary greatly from one company to another. They can range from the very informal 'Is it all right if we do it this way instead, George?' to a rigid

REQUEST FOR CONCESSION | Serial number

PART NUMBER .... ISSUE .... BATCH/SERIAL NUMBERS ....

WORKS ORDER NUMBER ....

This requests a deviation from the above drawings for the parts defined by the above batch/serial numbers only in the following respects

Requested by .... Date ....

Reason for request

This concession does not affect
Reliability
Safety
Interchangeability

Approved/rejected *

....
CHIEF ENGINEER

....
CHIEF INSPECTOR

HONEYCOMB PRODUCTS LIMITED, LUTON, BEDFORDSHIRE

* Delete as appropriate

Figure 14.4 One type of concession form
A concession (also known as a production permit) provides a means for controlling, authorizing and documenting departures from drawings and other specific manufacturing instructions.

discipline supervised by the quality control department. Rigid procedures can be expected in the defence, aerospace and nuclear industries, and in any other case where safety and quality rank high as objectives. Figure 14.4 shows a suitable form.

The reasons for instituting a formal concession discipline are fairly obvious, because any departure from the instructions contained in issued drawings or specifications must either be disallowed or treated with a great deal of caution. Concession records may have less significance than other project records once a project has been finished and handed over. Nevertheless, they can prove useful in the quality and reliability control function. Concession records are part of project records which a contractor needs in order to trace the possible causes of poor performance, faults or failures in delivered equipment. If one of a number of identical units should fail in service, it may be vital to trace all other units which contain the same concession in order to prevent further failures.

The procedures associated with the granting of concessions can exist in a variety of permutations and combinations of the methods described in this chapter. Whichever method a company decides to adopt, the concession register will be complementary to the manufacturing drawings, modification records, inspection and test records and build schedules in defining the exact composition of the completed project.

Engineering query notes

A feature which is typical of project manufacturing is that the drawings are usually completely new and untried. It is not surprising, therefore, that a higher incidence of production problems is a characteristic of project work. The problems which can arise range from design errors to difficulties in interpreting the manufacturing instructions. Design errors must, of course, be corrected by the re-issue of amended drawings, for which the full-scale engineering change procedure will usually be invoked. Simple problems associated with the interpretation of drawings can be resolved by an explanation on the spot from the appropriate engineer. Between these two extremes lies a no man's land of production difficulties which are not a direct result of design errors, but which demand more than a simple explanation to get production on the move again.

In some firms any problems that cannot be resolved on the spot are channelled into a formalized 'engineering query' procedure, which relies on the use of forms similar to that shown in Figure 14.5. The general idea is that the production individual who comes up against a problem explains the difficulty on one of these forms and submits it to the engineering department for investigation and reply. Naturally, this system can only operate effectively and be accepted if each query is afforded reasonably urgent consideration. The advantages provided by adopting this routine are that all queries can be

ENGINEERING QUERY	Serial number

PART NUMBER _____ ISSUE _____ WORKS ORDER NUMBER _____

Is work held up? YES/NO

QUERY to engineering department

Department _____ Date _____ Raised by _____ (FOREMAN)

ANSWER

Signed _____ (SENIOR ENGINEER) Date _____

CONCESSION APPROVAL (if appropriate)
The above instructions to deviate from drawings
will not affect reliability/interchangeability/safety   (CHIEF ENGINEER) _____

(CHIEF INSPECTOR) ____

HONEYCOMB PRODUCTS LIMITED, LUTON, BEDFORDSHIRE

Figure 14.5 Engineering query note
This form provides a means of controlled communication between
design engineers and manufacturing departments whenever design-
related production difficulties are encountered.

registered and progressed by the coordinating clerk to ensure that none is forgotten. Regrettably, there are engineering managers who prefer the formal system because it tends to keep production personnel, oil and grease out of the engineering design offices.

The type of problem which could give rise to an engineering query note would be that concerned with, for example, the use of adhesives. Suppose that the specified adhesive, when used according to the appropriate process specification, failed to produce the specified bond strength, so that when the clamps were removed the work disintegrated into its constituent parts. The production team would need to ask the engineers what to do, and they could use an engineering query note for the purpose. If the problem were to prove too difficult to sort out on the spot, the engineers might be forced to return the query note with a temporary solution suggested. The instruction might read: 'Clean off adhesive, and use six equally-spaced pop rivets instead. This instruction applies only to batch 1. Drawings will be re-issued with alternative adhesive for batch 2.'

If, as in this case, an engineering query note is returned to a production department with instructions that conflict with those given in the manufacturing drawings, the query note becomes a document which carries authority to deviate from drawings. It has therefore become a concession or production permit. Because engineering query notes are often converted into concessions in this way, companies which use them should consider combining the concession and engineering query systems into one procedure, with a single common-purpose form designed to cope with both needs.

Inspection reports

Suppose that a block of extremely expensive raw material has been subjected to a protracted period of machining by highly skilled operators but, on final inspection, one of the measurements is found to be marginally below the limits of tolerance. Too much material has been cut away; the error has resulted in the work being undersized and no rectification is possible. Any inspector would have to reject the job. In many companies the inspector would fill in an inspection report ticket or form, detailing the 'non-conformance'.

The design engineers, if shown the inspection report, might decide that the error was too trivial to justify scrapping such an expensive workpiece. Perhaps it could still be used for the project or, alternatively, it might be possible to use it for a prototype assembly on the understanding that it must never be re-fitted into another assembly. A design engineer having the appropriate authority might feel able to annotate the inspection report accordingly, thus countermanding the inspector's rejection. This is another method by which a job can be passed through an inspection stage, even though it does not conform to the issued drawings. The inspection report has been translated by the design authority into a concession or production permit.

Figure 14.6 shows an inspection report form which has been designed so that it can be converted into a concession in appropriate cases.

Emergency modifications

We live in an impatient age, and project time can usually be regarded as a scarce commodity. If the need for an essential modification is discovered during the active production phase of a programme, there may simply be no time available in which to issue suitably changed drawings. There are right and wrong ways of dealing with this situation and the following case history is a good, all too common, example of the latter.

Case history – the Kosy-Kwik Company

Kosy-Kwik were a company which specialized in the design, supply and installation of heating and air-conditioning systems. In 1985 they were awarded a contract, as subcontractors to a large building group, to plan and install all the heating and ventilation arrangements in a new multi-storey office block commissioned by the Coverite Insurance Company Ltd. Two engineers, Clarke and Jackson, were assigned to the project. While Clarke was given overall design responsibility, Jackson was detailed off to plan the central control panel and its associated controls and instrumentation.

```
┌─────────────────────────────────────────────────────────────┐
│              INSPECTION  REPORT          │                    │
│                                          │ Serial number      │
├──────────────────────────────────────────┴────────────────────┤
│ PART NUMBER _____ ISSUE _____ BATCH/SERIAL NUMBERS _____ │
│ TEST SPEC _____ ISSUE _____ WORKS ORDER NUMBER _____   │
│ The above unit(s)/assembly/part(s) have failed to satisfy the  │
│ requirements of the relevant drawings and specifications in    │
│ the following respects                                         │
│                                                                │
│                                                                │
│                                                                │
│                                                                │
│                                                                │
│                                                                │
│                                                                │
│                                                                │
│                                                                │
│                    INSPECTOR _____ Date _____         │
├────────────────────────────────────────────────────────────────┤
│ REQUEST FOR CONCESSION (to be completed if appropriate)        │
│   The above discrepancies do not affect reliability/safety/    │
│   interchangeability                                           │
│   Other remarks                                                │
│                                                                │
│                          Signed _____            │
│                                   (CHIEF ENGINEER)             │
├──────────────────┬──────────────────┬──────────────────────────┤
│ DISPOSAL DECISION│ SERIAL NUMBERS   │ AUTHORIZATION            │
├──────────────────┼──────────────────┼──────────────────────────┤
│ SCRAP AND REMAKE │                  │                          │
├──────────────────┼──────────────────┼──────────────────────────┤
│ RECTIFY AND RE-INSPECT │            │ (CHIEF INSPECTOR) _____ │
├──────────────────┼──────────────────┼──────────────────────────┤
│ CONCESSION GRANTED │                │ _____ Date          │
├────────────────────┴────────────────┴──────────────────────────┤
│ HONEYCOMB  PRODUCTS  LIMITED, LUTON, BEDFORDSHIRE              │
└─────────────────────────────────────────────────────────────┘
```

Figure 14.6 Inspection report form
A method for reporting and recording defects and deficiencies discovered by the inspection or quality control department. The version shown here has provision for conversion into a concession, should the design authority decide that the degree of non-conformance is acceptable.

We join the project near the end of the preparation period in the Kosy-Kwik factory. By this time most deliveries of plant and equipment had been made to the Coverite premises, except for the control panel, which was still being fabricated, later than scheduled.

Jackson was a conscientious engineer who took a great interest in his jobs as they passed through the factory. He was in the habit of making periodical tours, in order to keep a check on progress and the results of his design. It was during one of these tours that Jackson was approached by the sheet metal shop foreman. It appeared that the Coverite control panel, now welded together, was weak and wobbly.

Jackson could only agree with the foreman. The front panel was indeed decidedly flimsy, as a result of a glaring design error in specifying a gauge of steel that was far too thin. Delivery of this panel to site was already late, and threatened to delay the whole project. There was simply no time available in which to start building a new control panel. In any case, the extra cost would have been unwelcome. A simpler solution had to be found – a rescue package in fact.

The engineer asked the foreman to weld some suitably chunky pieces of channel iron to the rear face of the panel in order to stiffen it up. The foreman agreed, but was worried about getting the job past the inspection department without a drawing. 'No problem!' said Jackson, who took a pen from his pocket, marked up the foreman's copy of the drawing, and signed it to authorize the alteration.

The modification was successful. Everyone concerned was very relieved, not least Jackson, whose reputation had been likely to suffer. Only a few hours were lost, and the panel was duly delivered. The remainder of the project went ahead without further mishap, and the Coverite Insurance Company Ltd joined the long list of Kosy-Kwik's satisfied customers.

In the summer of 1990 Kosy-Kwik were awarded a follow-up contract by the Coverite Insurance Company. Their offices were to be extended, with a new wing to house computer services and staff. Coverite were working to a well-planned but tight schedule, which demanded that the new wing should be opened on the first working day of 1991. Because of the rigid timescale restrictions, several contract conditions were imposed on Kosy-

Kwik. In particular, the only complete shut-down period allowed for the existing heating and ventilating plant (for connecting and testing the additional circuits and controls) was to be during the Christmas break. Otherwise the Coverite Company would suffer loss of work by their office staff. There was also to be a penalty payment of £400 for every week or part of a week by which Kosy-Kwik failed to meet the scheduled end-date.

During the five years which separated these two projects several changes had occurred in the Kosy-Kwik organization. Clarke received a well-deserved promotion to a remote branch office, where he became area manager. Jackson retired to enjoy his pension. The engineering department expanded and attracted several new recruits. Among these was Stevens, an experienced contract engineer. He had no means of contact with Clarke or Jackson, and was unlikely ever to meet either of them.

Stevens was appointed as engineer in charge of the new Coverite project. He decided that the best policy would be to prefabricate as many parts of the project as possible in the factory. This would reduce the amount of work to be done on site, and ensure that the final link-up and testing could be accomplished during the Christmas break. Stevens found a roll of drawings labelled 'Coverite Project' in a dead file drawer, dusted them off and set to work.

Most of the system was found to be straightforward, and the final tying-in with the existing installation was to be achieved by providing the installation engineers with a bolt-on package that could be fitted to the original control panel. This package was duly designed, manufactured and delivered to site along with all the other essential materials. By the time Christmas arrived, all equipment, pipes and ducts were in place in the new wing. All that remained was for the final installation team to arrive, shut down the plant, modify the control panel with the kit provided, and then test and set-up the whole system.

Early on Christmas Eve, two Kosy-Kwik fitters were sent to shut down the plant and start work on the control panel. Their first job was to cut a large rectangular hole in an unused part of the original panel in order to fit the new package. A template had been provided for this purpose, which they now placed in position. When they started cutting, the engineers met un-expected resistance in the shape of several large channel iron ribs welded to the rear face of the panel. The engineers had come prepared only to tackle the thin sheet shown on the old drawings. It took them over two hours and many saw blades before the hole was finished. Then they found that the connections to the new control package were fouled by what remained of the channel iron. Worse still, the panel was now weak and wobbly again.

The two engineers were experienced and trained as skilled installation fitters, but were equipped neither materially nor mentally to deal with problems of this magnitude without help. They suffered an acute sense of frustration and isolation, although they found different (shorter) words with which to express their feelings. A cry for help was indicated but, unfortunately, the response to their impassioned telephone call to Kosy-Kwik headquarters was less than satisfactory. Against the background accompaniment of a spirited office party they learned that all the senior engineering and management staff had already left to start their holiday. The operator wished the fitters a 'Merry Christmas' and suggested that they 'Have a nice day'. The two engineers interpreted these greetings as good advice, gave up and went home to start their unexpected holidays.

There is no real need to dwell at length on the consequences of this case, or to describe the scenes of anguish and recriminations back at headquarters in the New Year. A short summary of the additional cost items follows:

		£
1	Design and manufacture another control panel modification kit	3 500
2	Wasted time during first visit of the two fitters	250
3	Costs for repairing weakened panel, on site	180
4	Contract penalty clause, invoked by the Coverite Company, operative for four weeks at £400 per week	1 600
	Total additional costs, directly attributable	5 530

A retrospective glance at the circumstances which led to the disastrous consequences of the Coverite project will provide a useful basis for describing a more reliable method of dealing with very urgent modifications. In this example, all troubles can be traced back to the use of a marked-up print on the shop floor, the details of which were not passed on to the master drawings in the contract file. The use of marked-up prints is generally to be deplored, but we have to be realistic about this problem and accept that occasions will be encountered when they are unavoidable, when there is simply no time in which to update the master drawings and issue new prints. Under these circumstances, some sort of temporary documentation must suffice, but only where safeguards are in place to ensure that the original drawings do get changed to show the true 'as-built' condition of the project.

Safeguards

One way in which the updating of final drawings can be safe-guarded in the event of emergency changes relies on a stream-lined version of the formal modification procedure, without bypassing any of the essential control points. The originator of the emergency modification must write out an engineering change request and get it registered by the clerk. After seeking the immediate approval of the chief engineer (or the nominated deputy), the originator must pass one copy to the design office in order that the change will eventually be incorporated in the drawings. Another copy of the change request is kept by the coordinating clerk, who must make certain that it is seen at the next change committee meeting. The original change request form is passed to the production department for action, where it becomes part of the issued manufacturing instructions.

If a working print does have to be marked up, which may be inevitable if there is insufficient space on the change request form, an identical marked-up print must be deposited in the design office, together with their copy of the change request. A photocopy is preferred for this purpose, to ensure that the duplicate is indeed a true copy, eliminating any possibility of clerical errors or omissions.

The original change request must accompany the job right through all its production stages, particularly until it reaches final inspection and testing.

Document modification discipline

It is necessary to examine one or two pitfalls that can trap the unwary project engineering staff into issuing drawings or specifications that are not what their revision numbers would make them seem to be.

Central registry procedure

In the straightforward case of a drawings registry holding all original hand-drawn drawings, the modification procedure can be made foolproof. The rules are:

1 As soon as an original drawing has been checked and approved for issue, it is handed over to a secure registry.
2 The registrar will thenceforth issue only prints of the drawing, and the original will not be allowed out of the registry unless it is to be changed.
3 Any person taking an original drawing away from the registry for modification must sign for it in the register.
4 When the drawing is returned to the registry, the registrar will check that the revision number has been updated and record this in the register.
5 The only prints valid for manufacture or construction are those issued from the registry, certified by the registry stamp.

With the advent of modern reprographic techniques it is possible to produce copies of drawings that are almost indistinguishable from the originals. The existence of more than one apparent original of any drawing can lead to confusion and dangerous errors if any change is made, so that it is important to label or mark each copy in some way to show that it is not the master original.

Computer-plotted drawings

More risks are introduced when drawings are produced by a digital plotter connected to a computer, in which case each print not only resembles an original but *is* a true original. Further, unless rigid safeguards are introduced, the designer can alter the design information in the computer and then cause a new 'original' to be produced without making the necessary change to the drawing or revision number. Without the registrar, there is no independent check to prevent such mistakes.

The author once asked a design department to produce a small group of drawings for fitting out a new design office. The designs were first class. One master outline of the building had been created in the computer and used as the basis for partition layouts, electrical distribution and lighting, seating arrangements and other services. But every one of these drawings bore the same number, that of the original outline drawing. In this case it was the first project designed on a brand new CAD system, so perhaps there was some excuse.

Microfilm discipline

Some companies operate 35 mm microfilm systems, with each drawing filmed on to 35 mm aperture cards as soon as it has been approved for issue. There are some simple safeguards for such systems, especially where several copies of the microfilms are distributed around large engineering offices in satellite files. The rules are:

1 Colour code the aperture cards, using one colour for cards that are to be kept as the official masters, and different colours to distinguish cards that must not be used to produce officially issued prints.
2 Modify any microfilm reader/printers available to non-registry staff by inserting a mask bearing the message 'reference print only'. It should be possible to make a small transparency for this purpose, and attach it in the plane of the print paper along one edge, so that every print will bear the message.
3 Keep all original drawings in the registry after filming and only allow official prints to be issued by the registry (either from the drawings or from the master microfilm).
4 When an original drawing is removed from the registry for modification (it should not be allowed out for any other reason) the corresponding master microfilm aperture card is withdrawn from the pack and replaced by a plain marker

card (to indicate that it has been removed). The obsolete aperture card is then used as a loan card for the original drawing, signed by the engineer or draughtsman, and placed in a separate loan file. Thus, there is no risk that either the original drawing or the obsolete microfilm master can be used to produce an official print while the modification is in progress.

The interchangeability rule

The usual practice when a drawing is changed is to re-issue it with a new revision number. If, however, a change results in a manufactured component or assembly being made different from other items with which it was previously interchangeable, it is not sufficient merely to change the drawing revision number. The drawing number itself (and therefore the part number) must also be changed. This is a golden rule to which no exception should be allowed, whether the item is a small component or a major assembly.

Suppose, for example, that a project requires the use of 1 000 small spacers, and that after 500 had been produced in brass the design was cheapened to use mild steel. These spacers are truly interchangeable, and the part number need not be changed. But the drawing for the steel spacers would have to be given a new revision number.

Now suppose that the design had been changed instead to moulded nylon because on some later manufactured assemblies it became necessary for the spacers to be electrically insulating. Because the metal spacers can no longer be used on all assemblies, the nylon spacers must be given a new distinguishing drawing number.

Build schedules

In the case of the Kosy-Kwik company's Coverite project (described earlier in this chapter), only one set of equipment had to be provided, the details of which could all be recorded at the time using one set of drawings and specifications.

Many engineering projects involve the repetitive manufacture of parts or assemblies which have to be supplied or used in production over an extended period. When this happens there is a strong possibility that changes introduced during the course of the project will result in only the later parts or assemblies being affected. The change committee might, in fact decide to withdraw some or all of the units which have already been supplied in order that these can be modified to bring them up to the latest design standard. On the other hand, the committee could arrange for modifications to be introduced selectively, specifying the point at which a particular change is to be introduced. If a project has reached the state where a number of identical items are scattered about the production area, the stores, the customer's premises, and possibly even farther afield, it is obviously important that the contractor knows the exact standard to which every one of these items has been made.

The first requirement is that each unit should be identifiable by some mark or number which distinguishes it from its fellows. This objective is usually achieved by the allocation of batch or serial numbers. These, together with a type or part number, enable any unit to be identified positively, with no possible fear of misinterpretation. An a.c. generator type 10256, serial number 1023, leaves no room for doubt. If this unit is received back at the factory for servicing, repair or modification, there is no question regarding its origin, and its design status should be known. It should be possible to look at the general assembly drawing and parts list or bills of material for the generator and so discover the numbers of all the drawings and process specifications that went into its making. But would it be possible in this way to find out the relevant revision numbers and modification status of those drawings?

Suppose that generators of this type have been supplied for a major project over a number of months or even years. All are called a.c. generator type 10256, but they are not all identical. A number of modifications have been introduced over the period, so that different production batches contain small but significant design differences. How now can anyone tell exactly what went into the making of one of these generators, knowing only its type number and serial number?

The most common method of circumventing this problem is to compile a build schedule. This is tedious but possibly unavoidable. A build schedule comprises a list of all the drawings and specifications used in the manufacture of every unit, with the correct revision number of every drawing shown. If there is any drawing which has more than one sheet, the revision number of every sheet must be given. A separate build schedule must be compiled for every project item that is made and assembled as a single unit, but one build schedule can be used to cover a number of items where these are made as an identical batch.

Forms such as that shown in Figure 14.7 allow all the essential details to be recorded. They can be used singly for small assemblies or in multiple-sheet stacks for whole projects.

Note that there is little point in maintaining build schedules of units with differing build standards if all the drawing information cannot be retrieved. It follows that reference prints or microfilm records must be kept of all relevant revisions of each drawing in such cases. Also, the comfortable premise that the latest issue of a drawing must be the correct issue is destroyed. Indeed it can happen that different revisions of the same drawing are in use at the same time when a factory is dealing with assemblies or batches of different modification status.

The build schedule procedure should obviously be supported by labelling the actual products. Each label should show the part number and the batch or serial number. Some companies also make provision on the labels to allow for modification numbers to be added as each modification is carried out.

Recording the 'as-built' condition of capital projects

Whereas the build schedules just described relate particularly to manufacturing projects, it is no less important that the 'as-built' condition of mining, petrochemical, civil engineering and other capital projects is adequately recorded. This is vital if the contractor is to be able to fulfil his post-contract obligations to the client. The listing, although possibly bulky, is simpler than for multiple-batch manufacturing projects, because there is only one set of drawings and specifications to consider and, with few (if any) exceptions, the final revision of each drawing is always the correct issue.

The format of a drawing schedule is shown in Figure 14.8, although this version is for clerical use and it is likely that the listing will be produced from a computer system in practice.

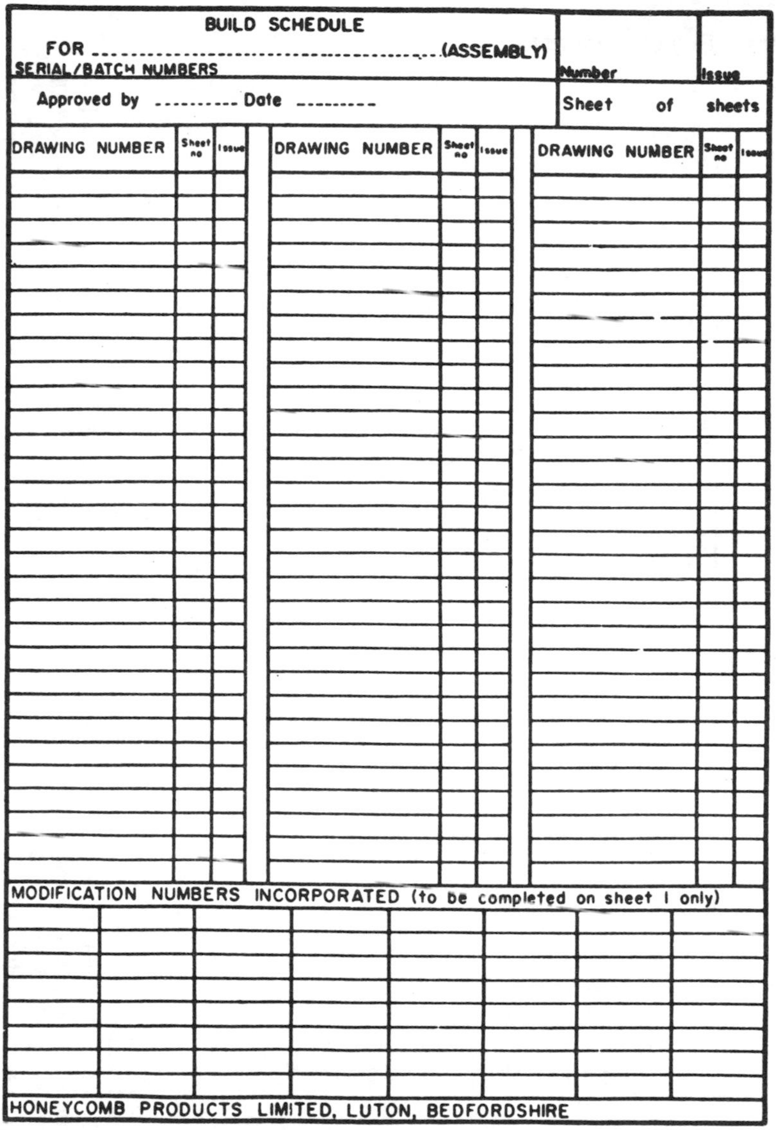

BUILD SCHEDULE
FOR ....(ASSEMBLY)
SERIAL/BATCH NUMBERS

BUILD SCHEDULE FOR ...(ASSEMBLY) SERIAL/BATCH NUMBERS / Approved by ... Date ...	Number	Issue
	Sheet of sheets	

DRAWING NUMBER	Sheet no	Issue	DRAWING NUMBER	Sheet no	Issue	DRAWING NUMBER	Sheet no	Issue

MODIFICATION NUMBERS INCORPORATED (to be completed on sheet 1 only)

HONEYCOMB PRODUCTS LIMITED, LUTON, BEDFORDSHIRE

Figure 14.7 A build schedule sheet
A build schedule is used to specify the modification status and content of a manufactured project. It is particularly useful in defining the content of project hardware items which exist in different versions. This is achieved by listing all drawings and associated documents together with the revision numbers that apply to the unit or batch being defined. The schedule may be prepared clerically (as here) or using a computer system.

Drawing schedule

Drawing schedule for:

Project number:

Sheet number: of: sheets

Issue date:

Drawing number	Size	Drawing title	Client's approval			Released for construction		Notes
			Needed?	Date requested	Date received	Date issued	Revision number	

Figure 14.8

Figure 14.8 Drawing schedule

Drawing schedules list all drawings needed for a one-off project. They can also be used to record aspects of progress (this version shows the status of the client's design approvals). This form demonstrates the basic content of a drawing schedule. In practice the schedule should be set up in a computer system so that it can be updated easily to show every drawing and its correct revision status. When the project is finished the drawing schedule (with the purchase control schedule) should show the final 'as-built' condition of the project.

The final, completely updated issue of the drawing schedule should carry the number of every drawing used on the project, with its correct revision number.

Equipment purchased for the project is defined by the final issue of the purchase control schedule, which should list all the purchase specifications, their associated requisition numbers and the resulting purchase order and purchase order amendment numbers. These schedules, together with the register and file of vendors' documents, provide the definitive detail. A purchase schedule form was shown in Chapter 13.

Drawing and purchase schedules are prepared in sets and subsets according to main plant sections, plant subsections and engineering design disciplines to agree with the work breakdown and hierarchical numbering system.

The continuous definition process

Chapter 3 describes the project definition process, and Figure 3.1 shows how this process is a continuous one. In any major project, whether it is for manufacturing or for construction, definition continues until the project has been finished, when the last document has been updated, registered and filed. Formal project variation, modification and concession procedures are all part of this process. The project engineers must ensure that any deviations from drawings are fed back for incorporation. This can be a particularly significant problem where there is construction work at a site remote from the contractor's home office.

15

Cost control and achievement analysis

Cost control is not really a separate function of project management. While it is true that some people specialize in the cost aspects of project management, possibly holding titles such as 'cost and planning engineer' or even the more specialized 'cost engineer', their roles are part of a far wider framework of project cost control, which must involve many people working throughout the project organization. A common misconception in this connection is to confuse *cost reporting* with *cost control*. Accurate and timely cost reporting is essential but, by itself, is not cost control. It is, therefore, necessary to start this chapter by examining some of the objectives and principles of project cost control.

The nature of project cost control

Objective

What is the objective of project cost control? There are several possible answers to this question, depending upon the datum from which the cost objective is measured.

Taking the narrowest view, the project contractor should be concerned (for many obvious reasons) that the project is completed successfully without exceeding his own planned costs (authorized budgets). In many cases, this is the cost objective set for the project manager. Most of the conventional cost reporting and control procedures, including those described in this chapter, are aimed at achieving that objective.

The contractor usually has some degree of responsibility for ensuring that the project purchaser's cost objectives are also satisfied. The most obvious manifestation of this is the firm *price* contract, in which the contractor's price is the customer's firm *cost* so that, unless the customer rocks the boat by asking for changes or the contractor goes bankrupt or is otherwise unable to finish the project successfully, the customer can plan his capital expenditure with confidence against a fixed budget.

Where large capital investments are involved, the managing contractor (and his project manager) assumes a specific cost-management duty to the client, which broadens the cost objective still further. The project cost control function extends to reporting costs to the client and helping him to schedule and control his funding and expenditure authorizations.

Factors in cost control

Many things can happen during the life of a project to alter the expected rate and magnitude of expenditure. The direction of change is usually upwards. Some of the reasons may be unavoidable or unforeseen but, in many cases, the fault will lie somewhere within the project organization. The purpose of cost control is to ensure that no preventable wastage of money or unauthorized increase in costs is allowed to happen. Here are some of the essential factors in a complicated mix of ingredients:

1 Cost awareness by those responsible for design and engineering, preferably involving a 'total cost' approach.
2 Cost awareness by all other project participants throughout the life of the project.
3 A project work breakdown which yields work packages of manageable size
4 A code of accounts system which can be aligned with the work breakdown structure.
5 Cost budgets, divided so that each work package is given its own share of the total budget.

6   A cost accounting system that can collect and analyse costs as they are incurred and allocate them with minimum delay to their relevant cost codes.

7   A practicable work schedule.

8   Effective management of well motivated staff, to ensure that progress is kept in line with the work schedule

9   A method for comparing expenditure on all parts of the work breakdown with the progress actually achieved.

10   Control of purchasing and subcontracts, to ensure that order values do not exceed budgets and that improper supplier's invoices are not paid.

11   Proper consideration and control of modifications and contract variations, including the passing of justifiable claims for price increases on to the customer.

12   Recovery from the customer of all incidental expenses allowed for in the contract charging structure (for example, telephone calls, printing, travel).

13   Effective and regular cost/progress reports to management, highlighting potential schedule or budget overruns in time for corrective action to be taken.

14   Proper invoicing, especially ensuring that claims for progress payments or cost reimbursement are made at the appropriate times and at the correct levels. Incorrect invoicing can cause disputes and delays in receiving payments.

15   Effective credit control, to expedite overdue payments from the customer.

Some of these factors were covered in earlier chapters. Others are considered in greater detail in the remainder of this chapter.

The total cost approach

The total cost approach is a way of regarding costs holistically. It demands that managers in the project organization work together, each considering how the work contribution of their department is likely to affect the costs incurred by other departments. An obvious example is where a suggested change in design approach might save considerable time and money in the resulting production or construction methods. Sometimes this may involve actually increasing the costs of one department in order to generate greater cost savings in another.

The author was once privileged to witness a convincing demonstration of the total cost approach in action. The scene was a meeting in an engineering director's office in the USA. The company was about to start three new projects, each for the design and manufacture of specialized heavy machinery for customers. The engineering director was in the chair. Also present at the meeting were the chief engineer and other senior engineers, and the production manager and senior production engineers. Various design proposals were passed back and forwards between the design engineers and the production people and, one by one, solutions were adopted that would lead to the lowest total company cost, while maintaining high quality standards. A high level of enthusiasm, motivation and co-operation was generated from the start. These projects, planned with multi-project resource allocation and given effective project management, were all subsequently completed on or before time and well below their originally budgeted costs (that is, below the cost levels previously experienced by the company for similar projects).

The true total cost approach should extend to include the costs of operating the completed project. This principle was well known to the same US company, who have since widened their total cost approach even further, to involve their customers in continuous design, quality and cost discussions. The design of the machines to be supplied, the design and development of the customer's machined parts, and the subsequent operation and maintenance of the machines all form part of continuing discussion and co-operation between the supplier and the purchaser in a process which is called 'integrated engineering', and which strives to achieve the customer's performance and quality requirements at lowest total cost.

Budgets

The initial project budgets must be derived from the cost estimates used when the tender was prepared. These become the authorized levels of expenditure for all departments engaged on the project.

Budget timing

It is not only the top budget limits that are important, but also the rate at which expenditure is scheduled to take place. When plotted as a graph against time, the typical cumulative project expenditure describes an *S* curve (see Figure 15.3, for example).

Labour budgets

It is often said, with good reason, that managers and supervisors should be given their work budgets in terms of manhours rather than as the resulting costs of wages and overheads. The argument is that a manager should never be held accountable for meeting targets where he or she has no authority to control the causal factors. Project managers are rarely responsible for wage and salary levels, increases in wages and salaries, and company overhead expenses. They are, however, responsible for progress and (through supervision) the time taken to complete each work package.

Budgets for purchases and subcontracts

Budgets for purchases and for subcontracts have to be expressed in the appropriate project currency. Relevant packaging, transport, insurance, duties and tax must be included.

The *S* curve for purchasing and subcontracts (see Fig. 12.3) can be drawn in different versions, displaced in time depending on whether the budgeted expenditure is timed at:

1   the dates when orders are placed (committed costs);
2   the dates when payments are scheduled to be made (actual costs).

There is a third, later time for recording the materials costs, especially for manufactured items, because job costing is carried out when the materials are withdrawn from stores (which may be long after they have been paid for).

The costs of purchases are determined during the preparation of purchase specifications and purchase orders, because once the orders have been issued the costs are committed. For that reason, purchasing cost control is dependent upon the procedures described in Chapters 12 and 13.

Currency units

The currency units used are obviously important. For projects conducted entirely within the borders of one country there should be no problem, and the national currency is the obvious choice for all budgeting and reporting purposes. If the project is to use imported services or materials, the logical method for expressing both the budget and the expenditure is to convert all sums into the 'home' currency, being careful to state the exchange rate used in each case.

When a project involves working for a foreign client, the contractor may be obliged by the terms of the contract or the agreed project procedures to prepare budgets and report all expenditure in the currency of the client's country, or in some other major currency (such as US dollars). The currency chosen may then have to become the control currency for the project. Again, it is obviously essential that the exchange rates used are shown.

Budget changes

Budgets on most projects are not static. They increase each time a contract variation order results in an agreed increase in the project price. At any time it should be possible for the budget for a work package to be stated in terms of the initial budget, additions approved by the client and, therefore, the total current budget.

Taking authorized budget changes into account, as time proceeds the typical project budget graph should resemble an *S* curve on to which a series of stepped rises have been grafted.

Adjustments for below-the-line allowances

If the project spreads over more than a few months, it is likely that cost escalation and (for international projects) foreign exchange fluctuations will have to be taken into account in budgets, cost reporting and control.

Any relevant allowances made in the original project estimate for cost escalation, exchange-rate fluctuations and contingencies, provided these have been built into the pricing or charging structure, can be regarded as 'reserve budgets'. Appropriate sums can be 'drawn down' from these reserves from time to time to augment the control budget.

Cost collection

It can be assumed that every established company will have procedures in place for collecting and recording project costs. It is vital that analysis and reporting of costs incurred and committed are carried out promptly. If the figures are a month or more old when they are made known to the project manager, what chance does he or she have of taking action in time to reverse any bad trend?

Most of the procedures for collecting costs and allocating them to the project cost codes are the responsibility of the company's cost accountant. Provided that the accounts department does its job properly, it is the reported figures rather than the day-to-day operation of the cost accounting procedures that usually concerns the project manager. There are, however, one or two areas where the project manager and others outside the accounts department have specific responsibilities for ensuring that cost collection is as accurate and timely as possible. The remainder of this section describes some of these areas.

Labour

A common method for recording and collecting the time spent on projects by professional and other office staff on projects is to ask each individual to complete a weekly timesheet. Timesheets usually require the person to declare the time spent against each cost code or job number, probably expressed to the nearest half-hour. An important part of this procedure is that the person's supervisor should check and verify the entries before adding an approval signature.

Whatever the method used, it is obviously necessary that the time records should be as accurate as possible. If the project is organized as a team, so that everyone works on the project all the time, the only errors to be expected would be in allocations to subcodes within the project. If, however, the organization is a matrix, people may be working on more than one project during a week, or even on the same day, and the apportionment of time between projects becomes more subjective and open to error or abuse.

People should be encouraged to fill in their timesheets on a daily basis. If this chore is left until the end of the week, mistakes will inevitably be made as individuals strive in vain to remember what they were doing earlier in the week.

Timesheet errors on firm price contracts can throw up false profit-and-loss assessments and reduce the value of historical cost records as the basis for future analysis and comparative cost estimating. In cost-plus contracts, timesheet mistakes will result in billing errors to the customer, which could be at best unethical and, at worst, fraudulent. Timesheets should, therefore, only be signed as approved by those nominated as being authorized to do so. It may be necessary introduce a higher-level check by arranging for a suitable independent person to carry out an occasional timesheet audit. In cost-plus contracts the customers will probably insist on some such safeguard.

Staff supplied by external agencies to work in the contractor's offices will be provided with their own agency timesheets, which the project contractor is expected to sign to show that the company agrees with the hours for which the temporary employee will be paid by the agency, and which will eventually appear on the agencies' invoices. These timesheets are rarely suitable as project cost records, and it will probably be necessary to ask the agency staff also to fill in the contractor's own timesheets (which can be colour coded to distinguish them from the timesheets used by permanent staff if required).

The time spent by agency staff working in agency offices will usually be charged for weekly, supported by detailed timesheets from the agency. The contractor may wish to specify and supply the timesheets that are to be used. Checking and correct authorization are obviously important, and the contractor may decide to arrange random, unannounced inspection visits to the external office as a precaution against fraud.

An example of a weekly timesheet is shown in Figure 15.1.

Casual work from subcontractors

A common method for dealing with miscellaneous work carried out by subcontractors depends on the use of dayworks sheets. Some such subcontractors submit their bills infrequently, or after long delays. It can prove very difficult trying to reconcile invoices received six months or even longer after the work has been done, especially since dayworks sheets tend to be scrappy tear-offs from duplicate pads. Even longer delays in invoicing have been known. One instance known to the author involved such incidentals as sundry plant rentals, the provision of skips, charges for a site hut, sundry materials and hundreds of dayworks sheets. The total costs amounted to many thousands of pounds, much of which was attributable to the dayworks sheets. The invoice, from the major construction company responsible, was received a year late and proved very difficult to reconcile. It is therefore important that the contractor checks, approves and carefully files his copies of all dayworks sheets until relevant invoices have been received and cleared for payment.

Purchases and subcontracts

It can be assumed that the organization's purchasing, account-ing and stores procedures will ensure that materials and bought-out equipment costs are collected and recorded. The routine cost accounting systems would normally cover costs associated with the payment of invoices, and the later job costs when materials are issued from stock for manufacturing jobs. However, the project manager should be concerned particularly to see that a system is in place for recording and tabulating the values of purchase orders at the times of issue, because these give the earliest possible indication of cost trends against the budget.

Gower

MANAGEMENT UPDATE

Gower is the leading publisher of business and management books in the UK and with over 400 titles in print it is one of the largest in the world in this area. The range embraces handbooks, practical management guides, reference works, personal skills books, audio manuals, and state-of-the-art studies in specialist areas of business activity. The subjects covered span from training, personnel and management development through manufacturing, sales and marketing to accountancy and finance.

We would be pleased to send you details of our publications in your chosen areas of interest. Just fill in the section below and we will send you the relevant information.

Please send me information on the books and other materials you publish in the following subject areas:

(please write clearly)

Name ....

Job Title..

Company ....

Address ....

....

.... Postcode..............

Please include the names of any other colleagues in your company who would benefit from this service:

....

....

....

If you do not wish to receive information from other organisations please tick here ☐

Gower Press
Gower House
Croft Road
Aldershot
Hampshire GU11 3BR

Timesheet

Department: Name: _____   Staff or clock number: _____

For week ending: _____

For accounts department use only

Job number	Saturday	Sunday	Monday		Tuesday		Wednesday		Thursday		Friday	
			Normal time	Overtime	Normal time	Overtime	Normal time	Overtime	Normal time	Overtime	Normal time	Overtime
Daily totals												

Notes: Fill in times to the nearest half hour. For holidays use account number 0099; sickness 0098; authorized special leave 0097; waiting or idle time 0096.

Signature: _____   Approved by: _____

Figure 15.1 A weekly timesheet

Incidental expenses

Some contracts, for example in the mining and petro-chemical industries, allow the contractor to claim reimbursement of sundry expenses such as telephone calls, plan printing, photocopying and some clerical tasks. Such costs can prove very difficult to collect; they are often difficult to isolate from the costs of other activities within the organization, which are not associated with the project. The effort should, however, be made. It is unlikely that the sums involved will be large compared with mainstream project activities, but they are usually worth having. A more important consideration is that every expense which can be charged directly against a project should be so charged. Otherwise these expenses will simply inflate the general overhead costs, which must always be kept as low as possible if the contractor is to remain competitive in the market place.

Suggested methods of collection include:

- The use of a simple requisition system for all bulk photocopying, plan printing and other reprographics services, with mandatory use of cost codes.
- Mandatory use of cost codes on petty cash vouchers.
- The installation and proper day-to-day management of an automatic call logging system covering all telephone, telex and facsimile lines. Unlike many modern innovations, these typically result in savings beyond those claimed for them by their manufacturers.

Achievement analysis

If a project has been running for three months, and the planned expenditure after three months should be £500 000, there are those who would be well satisfied on being told that the reported expenditure is at or below £500 000. Such people fail to ask some of the questions at the heart of cost control, namely; 'What have we achieved for this expenditure?', 'What should we have achieved?' and 'What can we read from the result about the likely total cost of the project?' The remainder of this chapter deals with these important questions and describes methods which can provide some of the answers.

The concept of achievement measurement

Achievement analysis is not part of the normal accounting or progress management procedures for many companies. It can be regarded as the missing link between cost reporting and cost control.

Imagine a bricklayer, engaged in building a wall which is to be 30 m long and 2 m high. This person might, in fact, be working on a tiny part of a project, so that the bricklaying activity could be represented on the project network diagram by one arrow labelled 'lay bricks – boundary wall', or something to that effect. If, at any time during the course of the bricklayer's labours, it was necessary to know what proportion of the work had been achieved, a simple count of the number of bricks laid might provide the answer. Alternatively, the area of wall built could be measured. Simple arithmetical processing of the result can yield an answer expressed as a percentage of the whole job. If, for example, the completed wall should contain 7 000 bricks, the work is obviously about 75 per cent finished when 5 250 bricks have been laid.

Now consider the very different case of a design engineer, also engaged on one project activity, and suppose that this particular task has a cost budget of 10 man-weeks. Assume that the work is continuous, so the duration is also scheduled to be 10 weeks. How can any sensible measurement of achievement be made during the progress of this intangible task? It might be suggested that the passage of time could be used as a rough guide, so that when three weeks (say) have elapsed the job is considered to be 30 per cent complete. Alternatively, the time booked to the job could be investigated, with achievement assessed on the basis of the proportion of budgeted man-hours spent. Any assumption based on these precepts would be most unwise, and dangerous for obvious reasons. The work may have been interrupted through lack of design information, or the engineer may simply be a slow worker. There may have been a bad false start in the design attempt, forcing the engineer to begin again. It is also more than possible that the original estimate was intrinsically wrong. In most such design jobs the only way to assess progress is to ask the engineer, or the engineer's superior, for a considered opinion. 'What percentage of this task do you consider has been achieved?' might be asked, or, perhaps more provocatively, how much longer is this job going to take?'

In the case of the bricklayer the answer obtained was objective, accurate and proof against fear of contradiction. Many other jobs on a project, especially the software activities, are far less straightforward and much more difficult to assess quantitatively in terms of progress achieved. The engineer may be guilty of unwarranted optimism or poor judgement when giving his or her progress report. This is the penalty which must be paid when changing from an objective measurement to subjective assessment of progress. Nevertheless, there is no need to abandon the quest. At least an answer of sorts can be extracted and, although by no means perfect, surely this is better than having no answer at all? In fact it will be shown later (in the section on design achievement) that good use can be made of such answers.

Now suppose that, instead of looking at only one activity, a progress assessment has to be made for a large project. Many hundreds of different activities might be involved, some of which are not started, while others are in progress and several could be completely finished. Design tasks, purchasing, production, inspection, testing and commissioning are all possible fields of activity which might have to be taken into account. Now where does the answer lie? There is no individual who can be approached for an achievement assessment on this scale. The chief engineer, production manager, or in fact any other manager, will not be able to comprehend the full scope of achievement single-handedly. No answer will be forthcoming at all unless special steps are taken to set up a measurement system.

The first stage in establishing an effective procedure for assessing achievement is to choose which work elements are to be subjected to measurement, analysis and reporting. In fact, this choice is usually very simple; the work packages from the project work breakdown, together with their cost estimates or budgets, must provide the framework. It is important to carry this breakdown through to the level of individual departments or work groups, so that each responsible manager or supervisor can be given quantifiable objectives for performance and subsequent progress assessment.

Design achievement

Most projects start their lives in a design department, and the first illustration of achievement analysis can conveniently be taken from that area.

The easiest approach is to determine how many drawings are to be produced, and then divide this number by the number of drawings actually issued, multiply the answer by one hundred and declare this as the percentage of design completed. Although some companies do use this method, it is really too crude because it fails to take into account all the conceptual design work needed, and assumes that the work involved in producing one drawing is equivalent to the amount of work needed to produce any other drawing. It can however be used in limited cases, such as for a department which is producing a large number of electrical running diagrams or piping and instrumentation diagrams.

Taking a more analytical approach, suppose that an engineering team has been charged with the responsibility for completing the design of a project containing 200 separate design activities. The total departmental budget, derived by adding all the estimates, is 1 000 man-weeks, but the estimated times for individual activities vary from as little as half a man-week to 20 man-weeks.

Now imagine that the project is spread over an extended time span, and that a point has been reached where 500 man-weeks of engineering (half the budget) have been spent. By simple prediction, if half the budget has been spent one should expect that half the work has been done or, in other words, that the achievement is 50 per cent. No right-minded person could assume this direct relationship to hold good, however, because there is no guarantee that the estimates were right in the first place or that work has proceeded according to plan.

No attempt to assess a complex situation of this kind can start without a detailed breakdown of jobs or activities, with their corresponding estimates or budgets. Each of these budgets can be regarded as the 'work value' for its associated task, expressed in man-hours, man-weeks or other convenient units. Assume that man-hours are to be used. As each job is finished, the appropriate number of man-hours can be considered as achieved, and added to a tally of completed work. Remember that this process uses the estimated or budgeted quantities, and has nothing to do with the man-hours actually spent at this stage. An allowance must also be made for work already achieved on activities that are still in progress. The running total of work values completed can be compared at any time with the total design budget for the project. This comparison allows an achievement figure to be calculated:

$$\text{Percentage achieved} = \frac{\text{man-hour values of work done}}{\text{total man-hours in the budget}} \times 100$$

This process is less complicated than it sounds. It is possible to combine the exercise with progress updating of the project network, because that task also requires progress monitoring and the reporting of achievement for all activities.

Now it is possible to demonstrate how this would operate in the design department. A good first-shot can be made by counting up the estimates for all the activities which have been completely finished. Suppose that 80 activities have been finished, and that the estimates for these particular activities add up to 450 man-weeks. This can be regarded as a true 'work value' of 450 man-weeks and, remembering that the total departmental estimate for this project is 1 000 man-weeks, this represents a measured achievement of 45 per cent.

Turn now to the question of the actual time spent in carrying out these same activities. This would be reported back to the project engineering manager at regular intervals by the accounts department, obtained from analysis of hours booked to the relevant job cost codes on daily or (more likely) weekly timesheets. Suppose that 17 500 man-hours had been booked. If this company operated a 35-hour week, this would be equivalent to 500 man-weeks.

At first sight an achievement of 450 work value units for the expenditure of 500 appears to indicate overspending, to the tune of 50 man-weeks. However, a significant amount of additional achievement could be tied up in work in progress. The original assessment of 45 per cent is, therefore, likely to be too low. It must be re-examined by taking the work in progress into account.

The remedy lies in obtaining a percentage progress report for all jobs that have not been reported as complete, but which were started before the day when the measurement data were collected. Corresponding portions of the estimates for all of these activities can then be added to the completed work tally to give a more accurate picture of the true total achievement.

The work-in-progress assessments will inevitably be less accurate than the data for completed activities, because they can only be opinions, and are subjective rather than objective. However, because work in progress should account for only a small proportion of the total work, assessment errors should be diluted by the larger, more reliable, estimates for jobs that are definitely finished. This will, of course, be less true for short-term projects, or at the start of any project, where the proportion of work in progress to completed work may be higher. If the individual activities are large, owing to insufficient work breakdown, then again the work in progress could rank high because it will take correspondingly longer to cross off the completed activities. It must be assumed, however, that the project work breakdown was undertaken correctly, so that it is really only in short-term projects that work in progress errors will prove significant. In any case, it is in the longer-term projects that achievement measurement becomes of most use because:

1   it allows any trend towards overspending to be predicted as early as possible, in time for action to be taken;
2   it provides a basis for assessing fair amounts for charging to the customer when progress payments are due.

If, in the example taken, 40 man-weeks was the assessed achievement value of work in progress, then this would bring the total departmental achievement up from 450 man-weeks to 490 man-weeks (that is, from 45 to 49 per cent). Thus the amount apparently overspent so far on this design work is not the 50 man-weeks first indicated, but only 10 man-weeks. Even if the assessed value of work in progress was in error by as much as ± 50 per cent, this would only affect the total result in the ratio of ± 20:490, or about ± 4 per cent.

In this example, therefore, it can be declared with a fair degree of confidence that, at the instant of measurement, 49 per cent of all engineering design has been achieved. Naturally, care must be taken to ensure that the actual costs of 500 man-weeks were recorded up to the same time as the achievement check. Given the information which has been recorded or derived so far, it is possible to embark upon a process of simple linear extrapolation in order to predict the final departmental expenditure at project completion.

Information received so far:

500 man-weeks have been spent
490 man-weeks' worth of work has been achieved
1 000 man-weeks is the total departmental estimate

Unless the general level of performance changes, the predicted total expenditure for the department at the end of the project is given by:

$$\frac{500}{490} \times 1\ 000 = 1\ 020 \text{ man-weeks}$$

In more general terms, the predicted end-of-project expenditure is given by:

$$\frac{\text{actual hours spent} \times \text{corresponding estimate}}{\text{related achievement (expressed in man-hours)}}$$

Man-weeks were used in the example rather than the more usual man-hours in order to emphasize the broader approach which engineering design control demands. The inaccuracies inherent in estimating for design tasks do not really justify the expression of any results in terms of man-hours. However, in practice, all figures would probably be calculated in man-hours, especially since timesheets and cost accounting are usually based on these units. It is nevertheless necessary to bear in mind that any result deriving from calculations in man-hours should be pruned back to remove all digits or decimal places which the measurement accuracy cannot support.

The actual mechanism of an achievement calculation for an engineering design department is demonstrated in Figure 15.2. In this example an engineering project is well under way. The total department estimate (the work-value of this project) is seen to be 85 man-weeks. An analysis of the work completed or in progress reveals that 39.7 man-weeks of this total have been achieved (which is 46.7 per cent). Against this, expenditure (the time booked) measured at the same date is unfortunately higher, at 49.5 man-weeks. Although 58.2 per cent of the budget has been spent, only 46.7 per cent of the work has been done.

These results can be extrapolated in order to predict that, if things are allowed to go on in the same way, the final expenditure for this department can be predicted as:

$$\frac{49.5 \times 85}{39.7} = 106 \text{ man-weeks}$$

This represents a departmental overspend of 21 man-weeks. If this rate of expenditure were allowed to continue unchecked, not only would profits be eroded away, but the timescale might also suffer. Much can often be done to improve performance, however. Escape may even be possible from an apparently hopeless situation, provided that suitable action is taken in time.

Stricter control of modifications should help to curb unnecessary expenditure and conserve budgets. While changes requested by the customer will be paid for, and so should augment the budget, all other requests for changes must be thoroughly scrutinized before authorization. Only essential unfunded changes should be permitted. Modification control, a very important aspect of project management, was described at greater length in the previous chapter.

In the face of vanishing budgets, the demands made on individuals will have to be more stringent, but this can only be achieved through good communications, by letting all the participants know what the position is, what is expected of them and why. It is important to gain their full cooperation. The project manager will find this easiest to achieve with a project

ACHIEVEMENT ANALYSIS

Department: __Engineering_____ Date: __March 1992__

Project: _SERVO CONTROL & SENSOR UNIT___ Sheet: _1 OF : 1____

	ACTIVITY	ESTIMATE MAN-WEEKS	% ACHIEVED	MAN-WEEKS ACHIEVED	MAN-WEEKS ACTUAL
0001	System Design	10	100	10	25
0002	Write Design Specification	1	100	1	1
0003	Design + 35v Power Supply	3	100	3	4
0004	Breadboard Stage	2	100	2	1
0005	Package	2	100	2	1
0006	Prove prototype	1			
0007	Write test spec	1			
0008	Design + 10v Power Supply	3	100	3	2
0009	Breadboard stage	2	100	2	1
0010	Package	2	50	1	0.5
0011	Prove prototype	1			
0012	Write test spec.	1			
0013	Design - 15v Power Supply	3			
0014	Breadboard stage	2			
0015	Package	2			
0016	Prove prototype	1			
0017	Write test spec	1			
0018	Design sensor circuit	10	100	10	8
0019	Breadboard stage	3	100	3	2
0020	Package	3	40	1·2	1·5
0021	Prove prototype	2			
0022	Write test spec	1			
0023	Design servo control	5	20	1	2
0024	Breadboard stage	4			
0025	Package	2			
0026	Prove prototype	3			
0027	Write test spec	1			
0028	Design main chassis	2	25	0·5	0·5
0029	Carry out system test	2			
0030	Environmental test	2			
0031	Write overall test spec	4			
0032	Write operating instructions	3			
0033					
0034					
0035					
0036					
0037					
0038					
0039					
0040					
	Departmental totals	85	46.7%	39.7	49.5

Figure 15.2 Departmental achievement analysis
Estimates, progress and costs are compared on this form in order to
predict the probable final expenditure.

team organization. If a matrix organization exists, the project manager must work through all the departmental managers involved to achieve good communications and the desired level of motivation.

The performance of individuals can often be improved considerably by setting short- and medium-term goals or objectives. These must always be quantifiable, so that the results can be measured objectively rather than subjectively, removing any question of favouritism or bias in performance assessment, and enabling the individual to monitor his or her own performance. In the project context, these personal objectives must be equated (by means of the work breakdown structure) with the overall project objectives of time, cost and perform- ance. The three go hand in hand and, if work is done on time, the cost objective should be met. Although all the objectives should have been set at the start of a project, they can be reviewed if things are going wrong and budgets appear to be at risk. However, care must be taken not to set objectives that cannot possibly be met.

If, in spite of all efforts, a serious overspend still threatens, there remains the possibility of replenishing the project coffers from their original source – the customer. This feat can sometimes be accomplished by re-opening the fixed-price negotiation whenever a suitable opportunity presents self. An excuse to renegotiate may be provided, for example, by a major customer modification, or as a result of economic factors that are beyond the contractor's control. Failing this step, smaller modifications or project spares can be priced generously in order to offset the areas of loss or low profitability. Care must also be taken to ensure that every item that the contract allows to be charged as an expense to the customer is so charged.

A significant point to bear in mind is that, without achieve- ment analysis, forewarning of possible overspending may not be received in time to allow any corrective action at all. The project manager must always be examining cost trends, rather than simple historical cost reports. When the predictions are bad, despair is the wrong philosophy. It is obviously far better to carry out a careful reappraisal of the remaining project activities and to explore all possible avenues which might lead to a restoration of the original project profit targets.

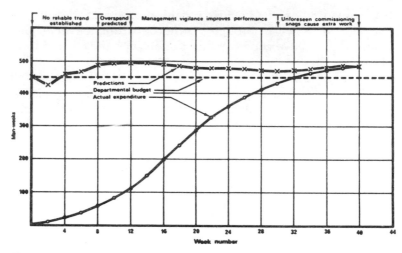

Figure 15.3 Graph of departmental achievement and cost predictions
Curves can be drawn to compare actual costs, achievement and the probable final project costs. This example shows the graphs as they might appear at the end of a project in which achievement analysis and predictions have been carried out at two-weekly intervals.

Regular achievement analysis

If achievement analysis is performed for every department at regular intervals, any trends indicated by the first few results are likely to be unreliable owing to the high degree of extrapolation needed. After an initial 'settling down' period, however, a consistent pattern of prediction should begin to emerge as the actual cost and achievement measurements build up. The intervals at which measurements are taken must depend partly on the nature and overall scale of the project and also on the preference of the individual project manager.

It is a very good plan to plot a graph of all the results, along with the relevant budgets, in order that any trends may be seen to better advantage. Figure 15.3 illustrates one possible pattern of results. This example, still concerned with engineering design, has been plotted from checks made at two-weekly intervals. Although the illustration is fairly typical, wide variations could of course be encountered in practice. Several features of this particular prediction curve are, however, worth noting. The first point plotted, taken at zero project time, is the initial prediction for design expenditure before it has been influenced by actual experience. In other words, this is the original estimate and budget taken straight from the total task list and work breakdown.

The next one or two points on the prediction graph display rather startling variations because they are based, in statistical parlance, on samples that are too small. These early results also contain a high proportion of assessed progress rather than activities that have definitely been completed. As time proceeds and the tally of completed work begins to mount up it is not very long before a more consistent trend shows so that, after a couple of months, the results carry sufficient weight to be taken seriously in determining any need for corrective action.

At about the sixth week in the example, a fairly consistent overspending condition has become apparent. Any manager faced with the prospect of overrunning budgets must take some action, and a degree of success in holding down the rate of expenditure was obviously gained in this case. In fact, a steady improvement is seen up to about week 30.

In most projects a danger exists that expenditure will not be cut off immediately when the last scheduled task has been finished. Clean-up operations, on-site activities, drawing corrections and commissioning problems are all possible causes of a last-minute addition to costs. Sometimes feverish activity takes place during the final phases of a project in order to get it finished on time, and this too can give rise to unexpected expenditure. Something of this nature has obviously happened over the last eight weeks of the project in Figure 15.3.

Now compare the graph showing predicted expenditure with that drawn to record actual costs, which is also included in Figure 15.3 (expressed in man-hours in this case). The curve of actual costs is cumulative, showing the total build-up of costs rather than just the costs incurred during each period of measurement. Notice how much more information can be gleaned from one glance at the prediction curve than can be derived from the cumulative cost curve, especially during the early and middle part of the project. The overspending danger is simply not shown up at all by the actual cost curve until very late in the project, at which time it is far too late to take any corrective action.

Measuring manufacturing achievement

So far, the main discussion of achievement measurement has been confined to one department only: engineering design. Production departments, at first sight, seem to be a very different proposition, being concerned with hardware rather than software and far removed from the abstract world of design and development. Fortunately, however, there is no practical reason preventing use of similar methods to cover all production activities. In fact, the process is made easier, since one is dealing not with theories and subjective assessments but with the tangible fruits of productive labour.

The basis for allocating work values to each production activity again derives from the project work breakdown, together with its associated estimates. For the purposes of project work measurement and achievement analysis it is not necessary or desirable for the project manager to consider production task breakdowns in any greater detail than this. The day-to-day level of operations planning needed within the production department can be ignored by the project manager, and the managers responsible for production should instead be asked to report progress against the list of specified project tasks or activities.

Steps must be taken to ensure that the collection of cost data from production aligns with the project work breakdown. This is achieved using a structured cost coding system, and by paying particular attention to the allocation of job numbers. The time booked to every production operation will then be recorded against a number which incorporates an identifier code, enabling the work and its costs to be related to the correct project task. This argument, and the cost coding methods, will become clearer by reference back to Chapter 4.

There are many ways in which production activities can be recognized as being complete. These might include acceptance into a finished goods store, dispatch to the customer, or the signature of an inspection docket. Alternatively, the information can be collected on progress sheets filled out by the various foremen and supervisors or by progress chasers. Work-in-progress achievement should also be assessed by production management, especially where the project contains activities of long duration.

Production activities often employ a wide range of different labour grades drawn from several departments. Which of these should be subjected to achievement analysis must depend to some extent on the degree of control considered necessary. It is probably unwise to attempt a detailed analysis for every conceivable cost centre. Overambition in this direction, leading to a multiplicity of facts, figures and prediction curves, could involve so much effort for so little return that disillusionment with the whole process of achievement measurement might set in. Probably the best course is to analyse the performance of departments, rather than individual labour grades. In this way, each departmental manager can be provided with a feedback of departmental performance against budgets. The vital factor is to ensure that each major cost centre is analysed regularly and given its separate place in the achievement measurements, in order that effective cost versus budget comparisons can be made.

Purchasing achievement

Measurement of purchasing achievement, in terms of the cost of materials, components and equipment against their estimates, differs from the measurement and consideration of labour costs. If a person is asked to work on a particular job, the hours and associated labour costs are incurred then and there. If ten hours are worked, ten hours should be booked against the appropriate job number and ten hours will appear in the records as the cost of the job. Purchase orders, on the other hand, are usually originated well in advance of the time when the goods will be received and invoiced, and there may be a further delay before they are actually used. The costs are committed irrevocably some time before the day of reckoning arrives.

Committed expenditure graph
A curve can be plotted to show the cumulative value of purchase orders as they are placed. This curve of committed expendi-

ture can be compared with the original budget (similar to the example of Figure 12.3).

If a curve of material commitments is to be drawn, care must be taken to allow for any materials that do not have to be ordered specifically for the project, but which will be issued from normal stocks. The quantities of these stock items must be estimated, and their costs have to be added to the cumulative totals in the curve so that the predicted cost shown reflects the total materials cost for the project.

Any curve showing materials commitments will be far more useful if a budget comparison curve is first plotted on the graph, like a track along which the committed expenditure is expected to run as the points are plotted. The points for plotting the timed budget curve must be calculated by adding together the materials cost estimates for each task, and timing them according to the dates when the orders are scheduled to be issued, not forgetting to include the value of common stock items. The inclusion of milestones on the graph (as described later in this chapter) will enhance its value.

Regular material cost estimate revisions

Another approach to monitoring purchasing cost performance is to compare actual costs with the corresponding estimates whenever a new purchase order is issued. If this is done at regular intervals a pattern should emerge which shows, for all the orders committed to date, whether any trend towards over- or underspending is emerging. The experience gained can be used in carrying out regular reviews of the cost estimates for all goods yet to be ordered. This will allow regular predictions to be made of the likely total materials expenditure, so that these can be compared with the authorized budgets to help in updating the forecast project profitability.

Where it is intended to use this method, four sets of data have to be gathered. These are:

1   the total value of all orders already placed;
2   the total estimated value of all purchase orders yet to be placed (using the task list or purchase control schedule as a check);
3   the cost of any materials already issued from general stock;

4 the estimated cost of any materials still to be used from general stock.

Surplus materials

When the final reckoning of project material costs is made, the total cannot be restricted only to those materials which have actually been used, scrapped or wasted. Any items which have become surplus to requirements must be included in the total. Such surpluses may have resulted from over-ordering, design modifications and other causes. The only surplus stocks that need not be taken into account are those which can be returned to the supplier for full credit, or which can be used *profitably* on a *known* alternative project for which a *firm* order exists.

There is often an understandable reluctance to write off materials left over at the end of a project. Individuals are sometimes tempted to take these items into general stock in the hope that one day, some time in the future, they may eventually become useful. It is surprising how quickly a storage area can become completely cluttered with such stock. Not only can large volumes of storage space be taken up, but the value to be written off eventually can accumulate to embarrassing proportions if it is allowed to mount up unchecked. The day of reckoning has to come, and it is better to recognize stock as redundant at the time when it first deserves that description.

Construction achievement measurement

Arrangements for measuring progress quantitatively on most construction tasks are well established compared with those for other project work, as a result of many contracts where various payment arrangements have been linked directly to the measurement of construction quantities. This is the domain of the professional quantity surveyor, who not only measures and reports achievement but is often called upon to certify the results.

Subcontract achievement

Achievement measurement may have to include subcontracted activities. If the subcontracts are for construction work, the remarks in the previous section will apply. If the subcontracted work is being obtained on a fixed-price basis, achievement analysis and cost control is the internal responsibility of the subcontractor.

Assurance that subcontractors will be able to meet their quality and delivery objectives is, of course, always a matter for concern. This was, however, discussed in Chapter 11.

The project manager will have to pay close attention to the achievement measurement techniques used by subcontractors whenever they submit claims for progress payments. Such claims for payment must be made against the achievement of recognizable events, or against properly assessed and certified achievement.

Effect of modifications on achievement

Every modification or other change introduced into a project can be expected to have some effect on the level of achievement attained by the departments involved. Before this effect can be measured, one significant question must always be answered. Can the customer be held liable for any additional costs, or must the additional work be paid for out of the existing budget (and, therefore, out of the potential profits)? Control of modifications is a subject worthy of separate discussion, and Chapter 14 has been devoted to that purpose. It can be assumed, however, that by the time that any modification reaches the stage of implementation, approval must have been granted by the designated authority. One duty of this person or committee will be to label each change as 'customer funded' or 'unfunded', as the case may be.

Unfunded modifications
Each unfunded modification must obviously affect the total workload remaining, usually with no corresponding change to the authorized budgets. In most cases the effect will be to increase the remaining workload, so that the proportion of work achieved is depressed in all the departments affected.

It would be possible to make an appropriate correction for modifications to the achievement measurement for each department. Each modification would have to be added to the task list, along with a cost estimate for the additional work needed. There can, of course, be no corresponding increase in the authorized budget. In practice, however, such adjustments are unnecessary, and unfunded modifications can be ignored provided that:

- they are not too numerous or horrendous;
- they do not cancel out work already reported as achieved.

Modification costs are often extremely difficult to estimate and record, because of the way in which the work is intermingled with the original task affected. If, for instance, a wiring diagram is changed for a complex piece of equipment, it can be impossible to work out the changed cost of carrying out the wiring task.

Unfunded modifications will therefore simply show up as apparent overspending, which is of course just what they really are. Achievement predictions will be self-correcting as these overspends are picked up, even if they are not immediately identifiable as being expressly due to unfunded modifications.

Unfunded modifications which nullify work already carried out must always be taken into account by erasure of the relevant achievement from the records. This should be done for every department affected, and either whole tasks or parts of them may have to be reinstated into the remaining workload. In this way, the achievement calculations can be kept on a true course. Taking an example, suppose that in the case illustrated by Figure 15.2 there arose a modification which demanded a complete restart of activity 0020, 'package design sensor circuit'. Achievement for this item would have to revert to zero, which would mean subtracting 1.2 man-weeks from the column total of man-weeks achieved. This would cut the measured achievement back to 38.5 man-weeks. The predicted final expenditure for this department would then be calculated at 109 man-weeks, compared with the budget of 85 man-weeks and the previous prediction of 106 man-weeks final expenditure.

Customer-funded modifications
Funded modifications can be considered as new tasks, for addition both to the task list and its authorized budgets.

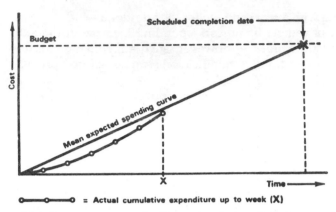

Figure 15.4 Costs compared with a simple predicted expenditure curve
This departmental cost curve shows costs compared with a planned rate of expenditure (expressed as a simple straight-line graph). The value of this display is limited because there is no indication of the corresponding achievement.

The customer should be asked to pay for any work which is scrapped as a result of the modification, in which case that work can be considered as having been sold and, therefore, achieved. It need not be subtracted from the achievement tally.

Monitoring by milestones

If achievement analysis is considered to be too complicated or too time consuming, it is possible to make better use of actual expenditure curves by annotating them or by adding more information. These alternatives, if less effective than full-scale achievement analysis, may appeal to the project manager who lacks the time or facilities for carrying out the procedures so far described. Two possible avenues of approach can be considered.

First, as seen in Figure 15.4, the rate of expenditure can be monitored and plotted cumulatively against time. At one extreme, if no money is being spent at all, then it is a fair assumption that no progress is being made either. No one could argue with this statement. It is also true that an inadequate rate

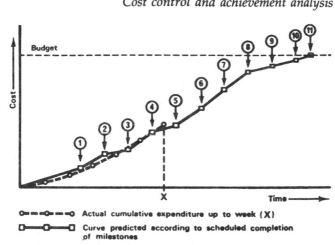

Figure 15.5 Costs compared with project milestones
Here the achievement of each milestone can be checked as the costs are accumulated. This affords some degree of cost versus performance monitoring.

of expenditure usually indicates an inadequate rate of progress and achievement. This statement also stands up well to logical argument. Unfortunately, the method then proceeds to the less acceptable assumption that if expenditure is being incurred at the planned rate, then progress and achievement must also be either on plan or 'about right'. This can only be regarded as a very rough and ready guide and it could lead to dangerously wrong conclusions. Mention of the scheme is made here, however, because it has been used by more than one company.

A variation of the method just described is illustrated in Figure 15.5, where the predicted rate of expenditure has been calculated and plotted with a good deal more care and attention. This has been done by picking out certain key project events which can be designated as significant steps along the road to project completion. Not surprisingly, these particular events are referred to as 'milestones'. It is important to choose as milestones only events that can be recognized easily and identified positively when they occur.

The curve of predicted expenditure is built up by adding the cost estimates for the work necessary to achieve each milestone, taking care to ensure that the grand total is equal to the project total and that no estimates are left out. The expected achievement date for each milestone is then found by reference to the project schedule. A planned expenditure curve can now be drawn for each department and for the project. Each curve is drawn by plotting the estimates cumulatively on a graph against time, with each progressive addition to expenditure placed at the scheduled date for the achievement of its associated milestone.

Monitoring the results then consists of plotting the actual expenditure cumulatively on the same axes and checking to see whether or not each milestone is in fact achieved on time. If any milestone is not passed on the expected date, the subsequent part of the programme must be rescheduled. When the revised dates for remaining milestones are known, the curve of predicted expenditure can be skewed over in the general direction of programme slippage by replotting these late milestones. This ensures that the predicted rate of expenditure is kept in line, broadly speaking, with known achievement. A low rate of actual expenditure, for example, might possibly be shown to correspond to a relatively low rate of progress, in which case the programme is suffering directly, and not the budget. On the other hand, expenditure could be shown as 'on plan', but with the milestones being achieved too late, indicating that overspending is taking place.

Disadvantages of the milestone method

Three disadvantages can be identified with the use of the milestone method. These are:

1   The information which can be extracted for management use in controlling the project is often obtained after the damage has been done, and certainly much later than the predictions possible with achievement analysis.
2   If programme slippages are going to occur very often, the curves may have to be redrawn frequently, unless a computer can be used or some flexible charting method devised.
3   Most important of all, the method only shows up qualitative results, indicating trends rather than the more accurate

quantitative measurements obtainable with achievement analysis.

However, the method involves comparatively little effort, and may therefore commend itself to the busy project manager.

The project ledger concept

A picture has now been built up of a collection of methods by which data can be displayed on graphs to show the predicted and measured performance of each department against plans and budgets. Successful budgetary control and cost prediction obviously require a certain amount of accurate book-keeping, not only within the boundaries of the accounts department, but also under the administration of the project manager.

The dossier of achievement returns, estimates and budgets, all collated with respect to the project task list, can be regarded as a project ledger. The ledger account is credited with the initial cost budgets plus any authorized additions, such as those arising from customer-requested modifications and contract variation orders. The value of work achieved, in cost terms, is debited from the ledger as it is reported, to leave a balance outstanding which represents the estimated cost of work remaining. At any time it should be possible to consult the ledger in order to determine the cost/budget/achievement status of every department engaged on the project.

Calculating aids for the project ledger

Computer systems
If a suitable computer program is available, it would seem sensible to set up the project ledger in a computer file. It may be possible to arrange this as part of an integrated database project management system, or as part of a company management information system.

If a computer system is used, the reports have to be treated with extreme caution until they have been checked. Such systems can generate reports whether or not all the budget information and progress data have been fed in. The results might be:

• correct;
• very obviously wrong (quite likely!);
• credible, but still wrong.

It can be very difficult to get project staff to feed budget and progress data into the computer without errors and at the appropriate, regular times.

A mechanical aid

There is a mechanical method which can work well for very simple projects. This is now somewhat outdated, but still worth mentioning because of its ingenuity and because it illustrates the principle of the project ledger quite well.

The method depends on the project having been planned and resource-scheduled using an adjustable bar chart. Figure 15.6 shows the bar chart from the garage project (Figure 7.6), but with an extra section marked out at the right-hand side containing vertical 'progress ladders'.

Each progress ladder has been constructed by counting up the total length of strip used on the chart for each department or cost centre. A scale is provided alongside each ladder, using the same time units as those for the main chart and enabling the height at any point to be read off with facility. These markings can be made using adhesive tape or paint. It is seen that the total height of the skilled section is 32 man-days, and that of the labourer section is 29 man-days.

It is assumed, in Figure 15.6, that the garage project has been in progress for some days. The actual date reached is indicated by the movable date-line cursor. It is apparent from the diagram that the project is on schedule. Completed activities, and parts of activities, to the left of the cursor have been removed from the chart. But, instead of being discarded, the strips have been plugged into their respective progress ladders.

Note that the skilled labour progress has reached 11 man-days out of the total 32 required. The achievement for this grade of labour is therefore:

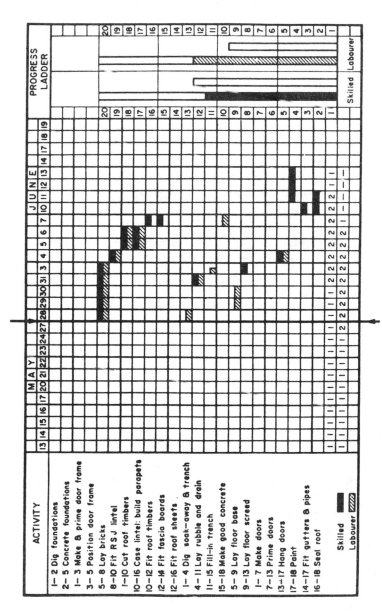

Figure 15.6 Bar chart with progress ladders

The usefulness of the garage project bar chart has been extended by the addition of 'progress ladders', a simple mechanical aid to progress measurement which allows achievement to be read off.

$(^{11}/_{32} \times 100) = 34$ per cent

Similarly, the achievement for the labourer's tasks is shown to be 41.4 per cent.

Predicting project profitability

Once a basis has been established for the collection of achievement analysis statistics from all parts of the project organization, it is a logical and progressive step to put all these results together into a composite prediction of total project costs. Of course, the first such prediction is that made before the start of the project, when the initial cost estimates and budgets are prepared and when progress can confidently be declared as zero. Subsequent achievement analysis and cost predictions can be regarded as a continuous process by which the original estimate is steadily refined. As more work is completed, the total estimate to completion contains an increasing proportion of actual cost data, so that the predictions should become more accurate. For the purposes of cost control, it is necessary that these data are presented in a way that shows up unwanted trends as early as possible, before it becomes too late for anything to be done.

Graphical method

As in the case of departmental performance, the total cost predictions can be plotted on a graph against project time for direct comparison with the budget, so that any upward or downward trends can be seen clearly.

Before the cost data for all the various departments or groups can be brought together and combined with the cost of purchased equipment and materials, they must all be expressed in terms of one common denominator, which must be the control currency for the project. The man-hour units that were appropriate for scheduling and supervisory control must now be converted into costs, using the appropriate rate for each labour grade. The man-hour records must, however, be kept because these will provide the stable and reliable yardsticks (unaffected by cost inflation) when comparative cost estimates for future projects are made.

Cost monitoring and prediction are aimed primarily at containing costs within budgets but, when a project has been sold commercially for profit, the profit becomes the end objective. Accordingly, the final prediction graphs should relate the cost and budget levels to the effective net selling price. Both the targeted and predicted gross margins will be displayed so that, as time passes, a wary eye can be kept on the likely outcome. Notice that the budget and price levels will have to be readjusted whenever a variation order, modification or other change is introduced that affects the contract price.

Figure 15.7 shows the type of curve that can result from the regular plotting of cost predictions for the whole project. In this example, the project has been finished. It is possible to recapture some of the sense of occasion which would have existed during the active stages of the project by placing a piece of card over the diagram and moving it from left to right to expose the graphs in two-weekly steps.

Spreadsheet presentation

Project cost summaries and predictions are commonly presented in tabular or spreadsheet form, with or without accompanying graphs. Figure 15.8 shows a widely used arrangement, suitable for preparation from purely clerical methods or from computer systems. Tables such as this are typically bound into regular cost and progress reports, often produced at monthly intervals. A description of this format on a column-by-column basis will serve to round off this chapter with a recapitulation of the principles embodied in the interpretation of cost and progress data. The columns have been labelled A, B, C and so on for ease of reference.

The form is headed with the obvious and necessary project title and project number information. The report date is important, being the effective common reference date for all measurements and progress assessments. The report issue date would be later, because of the time needed for data collection and report preparation.

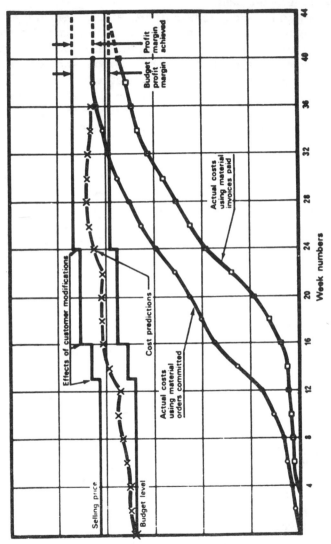

Figure 15.7 A cost/profit prediction graph for a project

A curve of this type is the reward gained by carrying out detailed achievement analysis. It enables management to be given an early warning of any possible overspending. Try placing a piece of card over the diagram, and then move it slowly to uncover the graphs from left to right. Notice how, as each week is uncovered, the predicted cost curve yields information which is far more significant than that provided by the simple cost accumulation graphs below it.

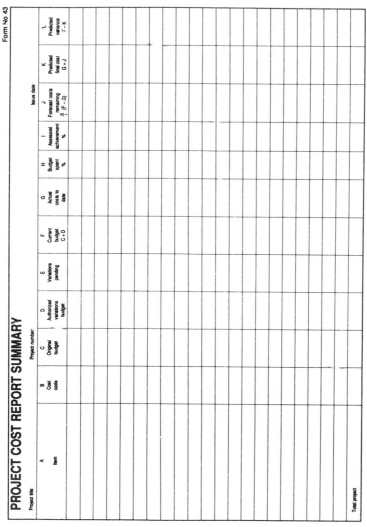

Figure 15.8 Project cost report in tabular form
A tabular presentation of project cost data, including forecast costs to completion and final variances.

The time lag between the effective report date and the report issue date depends on the size and complexity of the project to a great extent: it obviously takes more time to collect results from a remote overseas site than it would where the whole project is conducted within one factory. Nevertheless, all possible steps must be taken to produce these reports before they become outdated and too late for provoking constructive management response. Some companies, for example, take over two weeks to analyse man-hour bookings on their internal timesheets. An effective computer system, coupled with good timesheet discipline, should allow such analyses to be finished in two or three working days.

Column A lists the main project sections from the project work breakdown. The example in Figure 15.8 is taken from an engineering company which referred to these main sections as plant sections. The listing in column A must include all cost items, including software tasks and summarized miscellaneous items. If more detail is required, this can be provided on back-up sheets.

Column B lists the cost code of every main project section. This makes it easier to refer back to the original estimates and budgets and to audit the data presented.

In column C the original budgets for the project sections are shown, and these add up to the total original project budget at the foot of the column. This is the cost budget originally authorized and approved, which should be equal to the original cost estimates. Consideration must be given to the inclusion or otherwise of escalation and other below-the-line estimates, and it may be necessary to add explanatory notes in the accompanying report text.

As the project proceeds, it can be expected that a number of variations or modifications will arise that are agreed with the client, and for which the client will pay. These must obviously increase both the project revenue and the budget. Budget increments from this cause are listed in column D. These, when added to the original budget for each project section give the current revised authorized budgets, in column F (the current budget).

In any project of significant size there are usually variations under consideration or awaiting approval that could ultimately affect the budget (and progress assessment). Until such variations have been agreed with the client it is obviously not possible to take the additional revenue for granted. It may, nevertheless, be of considerable interest to know the value of any such proposals which happen to be 'in the pipeline' at the report date. Column E can be included in the report layout, if desired, to give this advance information.

Column G lists the costs actually recorded as at the report date. These comprise:

1 All labour hours booked to the project (on timesheets or job tickets) converted at standard cost or other appropriate rates into the project control currency.
2 Overheads and administrative costs.
3 Payments for directly relevant insurance premiums, licences, legal fees and consultants' fees.
4 Payments made to, or legitimately claimed by, subcontractors.
5 The cost of all materials committed, which includes the cost of all materials and equipment already used or delivered, plus the value of all other materials and equipment for which orders have been placed at the report date. In all cases freight, packing, insurance, agents' fees and duties paid or committed must be included.
6 Any other costs incurred or committed up to the report date than can be directly attributed to the project.

In column H a straightforward calculation is made to express the actual expenditure to date (column G) as a percentage of the current budget (column F).

The percentage achievement in column I is the best assessment of progress that can be made, using achievement analysis methods such as those described earlier in this chapter and taking care to include allowances for work in progress.

In column J, the forecast remaining costs are listed. If the achievement to date has been exactly in line with expenditure (that is, the percentages in columns H and J are equal), then the forecast costs remaining to completion should be equal to the unspent portion of the current budget. In practice there will usually be a difference between the percentage of work achieved and the percentage of budget spent. The forecast costs remaining to completion will then not be equal to the remainder of the budget, and these must therefore be calculated using the formula printed at the head of column J.

Adding the forecast remaining costs to the actual expenditure to date yields the best possible estimate of what the project final total cost will be (column K). As time passes, the forecast element of this figure will become less, the proportion of actual costs will become greater, and the final prediction will grow more accurate. Eventually this will provide the definitive estimate, as classified in Chapter 4.

The final column, L, shows the expected difference between the final project costs and the approved budget. In this example, a negative variance indicates an overspend, and a positive result forecasts a cost saving (these meanings are reversed in some companies).

Post mortem

When the project is finished and the final costs become known an investigation can be conducted to compare the actual expenditure with the original estimates. Such post-mortem examinations are obviously far too late to be of benefit to the completed project, but they can be helpful in pointing out mistakes to be avoided when estimating or conducting future projects.

16

Closing the project down

Project management activities do not necessarily end with the physical completion of an industrial project. A number of loose but important ends usually need to be tied up.

Formal closure notice

Just as it was necessary to issue a formal document of authority to open a project and allow expenditure to begin, so the end of a project should be marked by a formal announcement forbidding further expenditure against the main project cost codes. This is essential if hard-won profits are not to be eroded by an insidious continuation of time-sheet bookings to the project simply because the account still happens to be open. It is well known that the recording of man-hours on timesheets is open to abuse; there is always a tendency for the less scrupulous staff to try and 'lose' unaccountable time by booking it to large projects where, it is hoped, it will go unnoticed. Obviously, good supervision will minimize this risk, but an instruction to the computer to reject all further timesheet entries against the project number is more effective.

Company accountants may wish to hold a project account open for their own use beyond the official project closure date to collect a few 'tail-end' costs. Although further man-hour time bookings are banned after the closure date, there are usually items such as late invoices from suppliers and subcontractors. On a large project these can be delayed for several months and represent considerable sums, but they should not affect the calculated profit significantly because (unless there has been loose control of subcontracts and dayworks) these costs should have been known and accrued in the accounts at the time when they were committed (when the orders were issued).

Although a guillotine must be imposed on time bookings at project closure, it must be recognized that large projects often leave a backwash of documentation work in their wake. These activities are summarized in the remainder of this chapter. They may require considerable effort, although much of this can be assigned to clerical and fairly junior engineering staff. Just how well such tasks are performed depends upon how much money the contractor is prepared to spend on them. In some firms, final documentation will be treated as an overhead expense, while others may be more fortunate in having budgets contractually agreed with their clients for this purpose, with funds provided. Whether treated as an overhead cost or as a directly recoverable expense, post-project work should be allocated its own, separate, strictly budgeted account number. Thus the closure activities become a small work package, separately identifiable from the main project and relatively easy to monitor and control.

The formal closure notice need only be a very simple form, but it should list the following information:

- project title;
- project number;
- the effective closure date;
- reason for closure (usually, but not always, because the project has been finished);
- any special instructions;
- closure authorization signature;
- distribution, which should at least include all those who received the authorization notice when the project was opened.

The formal notice of project closure can be designed to include a checklist of all the closedown activities. Figure 16.1 illustrates a form that also acts as an authorization document for the related expenditure, stating the budgets allowed and the account number to be used for timesheet bookings. By no means typical, this form would obviously need modification in practice to suit each contractor's own project circumstances and management systems. It does, however, demonstrate a method that can help to ensure the orderly closedown of a project.

Documentation

Purchased equipment

For the purposes of illustration, suppose that a client has formally accepted the handover of a complex manufacturing plant, the result of a major turnkey project. Everything has been managed for the client, including the construction of the buildings, purchasing and installation of all the plant, cranes and other equipment, and final commissioning. Quite obviously, the contractor retains a follow-up responsibility to the client for arranging service under guarantee, assisting with operating problems, and in being able (if required) to carry out future modifications or extensions to the plant.

In order to provide such a service, the contractor needs adequate technical records of the equipment purchased from external suppliers. These records have to be obtained from the vendors during the course of the project in the form of layout drawings, technical specifications, operating and maintenance instructions, lists of recommended spares, lubrication charts, test certificates and so on.

In most cases a copy of all such documents would be sent to the client. It would, however, be a foolish contractor who did not keep his own set of such documents. While it should theoretically always be possible to go back to the relevant vendor for information in the event of a subsequent problem, companies have a distressing habit of going out of business, or of losing their former identities in mergers and takeovers. There may also be a considerable benefit to the contractor in keeping

PROJECTS UNLIMITED LTD
NOTICE OF PROJECT CLOSURE

The following project will be closed to time bookings and all expenses with effect from the date given below

Client   Lox Chemicals Limited   **Closure date** 7 August 1987   **Project No.** 42 - 050

Project title Loxylene Plant

The following budgets are hereby authorised for the closedown activities described in the checklist

Cost allocation code number:

DEPARTMENT	MAN-HOURS BY STAFF GRADE								£
	1	2	3	4	5	6	7	8	
Project Engineering	10			20			50		720
Planning					10				50
Purchasing			15			50			610
Installation									
Commissioning									
Construction Management	5		10				—		230
Computing				1		2			28
Central Archives			10				200		1,340
Microfilming (bureau)									750
TOTALS	15		35	21	10	52	250		3,728

Special Instructions: Take special care with filing - a follow up plant expansion might be required later
All files not marked for destruction to be retained for five years unless otherwise
stated below.

CHECKLIST OF PROJECT CLOSURE ACTIVITIES

ITEM	ACTION REQUIRED	DOCUMENT FILES	
		Microfilm?	Destroy?
Project case history	Keep it brief but ensure performance data correct	Yes	No
Project specification	Should be up to date, but check carefully	No	No
Project variations	List and check file complete	Yes	No
Drawing schedules		Yes	Yes
Our own drawings	Check all are 'as built' and none missing	Yes	No
Design calculations	Ensure all handed in by project engineers	Yes	No
Client's drawings		Yes	Yes
Purchase control schedules		Yes	Yes
Vendors' drawings		Yes	Yes
Purchase orders		Yes	Yes
Expediting/inspection reports		No	Yes
Test certificates		Yes	No
Operating/maintenance instructions	Keep all sets	No	No
Spares lists		Yes	No
Maintenance contracts	Discuss with client and agree terms	-	-
Subcontract documents	Keep six years	Yes	No
Correspondence files	Keep two years	Yes	No
Final cost records	.	Yes	Yes
Progress reports		No	No
Photographs	Send to publicity department for picture library	-	-
Critical path details	Erase computer files and destroy all printouts	No	
Management information system	Delete records from MIS at this year end		

Prepared by: Peter Wilkins   **Project Manager:**   **Authorised by:**

Figure 16.1 Project closure notice, with checklist

detailed records of equipment purchases, because these can often be of use to engineers when specifying equipment for future, non-related projects.

The key to all these data must be the final edition of the purchase control schedules (Figures 13.3 and 13.4) which should give the relevant purchase specification numbers with their correct revision status.

Engineering design

For engineering design records the first obvious need is to keep a set of project drawings. Sometimes a client will, having paid for the engineering design of a project, consider all project drawings to be his own property. The client's own drawing sheets may even have been used. The contractor will still want to keep a set of drawings. These may be in the form of reproducible (translucent) master prints, on microfilm, or in some digital form suitable for the company's computer-aided design systems.

Drawings are usually indexed for filing and retrieval according to the contractor's drawing numbering system, but the specific project 'as-built' record is provided by the final set of drawing schedules (Figure 14.8). For multiple-batch manufacturing projects the control tool is the more complicated form of drawing schedule, namely the build schedule (Figure 14.7).

Design calculations are a vital part of project records. It is essential that these are numbered, indexed and stored with at least as much care as that given to the main drawing files. They may be called for in the unfortunate event of subsequent malfunction or structural failure, especially if personal injury results.

All contract variations, modifications, concessions, final inspection reports and similar documents helping to define the final design status and quality of the project should be filed and indexed.

Cost records

Final cost accounting information provides an important data-bank from which comparative cost estimates can be made for future projects. This is especially true of the man-hour records. Costs for materials and purchased equipment, and the expression of man-hours in terms of wages plus overheads, are less useful records because these become invalidated by cost inflation as time passes. Those needing to retrieve information from any of these records will find their task made immeasurably easier if all the data have been filed under a logical cost-coding system which has been rigidly applied.

Correspondence and internal memoranda

Letters to and from vendors can be filed with the relevant purchase order files, where they form part of the technical and contractual record. Other correspondence, not least that with the client, can be filed by date order.

When large projects come to their end, an embarrassing problem sometimes arises because files have been built up in at least two places, in the central filing registry and in the project engineering department. One way of turning this difficulty into an advantage is to have all the project correspondence filed by subject according to the project work breakdown structure. Provided that the project files are properly managed, they can be added to the central files when the project ends. This then ensures that any document should be retrievable if either its date or its subject is known.

Internal correspondence between departments is usually of less importance, but can be kept along with the relevant subject files if required.

Case history or project diary

If sufficient time and money can be spared for the purpose, it is sometimes useful for the project manager to write a brief case history or diary of the project. This document does not have to be a literary masterpiece, but it should record every significant event, and list all serious problems together with their solutions. When filed with the project specification, minutes of meetings and other key documents, a case history becomes a valuable asset in the future if legal or other questions arise about the project. Reference to past case histories may also help when formulating the strategy for new projects, and reading about past mistakes can help new managers to avoid repeating them in the future.

File management

The amount of work needed at the end of a project to close down all the files and store the information safely will be indirectly proportional to the care and attention given to files during the active life of the project.

It is very easy to build up substantial files in a very short space of time. These can occupy large areas of expensive office floor. In fact, it can be said that no company can hope to have an infinite life, because as time tends to infinity so will the space needed for its records become infinite, and the company will choke to death on its own files.

There are several ways of overcoming the filing space problem. These are:

1 Hire off-site space for the storage of non-active files, possibly in a secure repository managed by one of the specialist archive companies. This method has the drawback that the files can easily be forgotten, the only reminder of their existence being the regular invoices for space rental.
2 Label each file prominently with a review date, at which time the file must be considered for microfilming and/or destruction.
3 Invest in space-saving filing equipment. Lateral filing cabinets use less space than drawer-type filing cabinets. Motorized rotary files can be purchased which extend upwards into ceiling voids.
4 File bulk can easily be reduced very dramatically by microfilming. Drawings are stored on 35 mm roll film or aperture cards. Other documents can be filmed using 16 mm film mounted in cassettes or (for semi-active files) on jacket-fiche. While microfilm is usually adequate for longevity, subsequent retrieval and printing, drawings should be kept as originals if they are likely to be needed again in accurate scale dimensions.

5 Provided that adequate safeguards are taken to ensure compatibility with existing and future equipment, some form of electronic digital storage can be used, resulting in even smaller storage space requirements, fast retrieval and the possibility of high-quality printouts.

Finding any document in a large file store, whether this is on microfilm, electronic storage, or as original 'hard copy', demands that all records are carefully indexed. It should be possible, for instance, to be able to search for an individual letter from a client either by reference to its subject, or by its date, or by both of these.

Records are usually at risk from fire, flood or loss and it is always good sense to consider maintaining a security copy (on the basis that tragedy is unlikely to strike in two places simultaneously). If, however, there should be a fire which consumes the original files, the back-up copy will be of little practical use without an index of its contents. An up-to-date copy of the index for the main files must therefore form part of the security files.

Information held in computer files has to be remembered at project closure time. Unwanted files should be erased. While a few unwanted items left on the floppy disks of personal computers may not present a problem, a forgotten set of project management files held on-line on a hard disk (possibly including a large network analysis exercise, drawing schedules and purchase control schedules) is a needless waste. Any such files that are not required as part of an on-line database should be erased or transferred to some more suitable off-line storage.

Disposal of surplus material stocks

Surplus stocks will almost certainly remain upon completion of a manufacturing project. Whether these are contained in a bonded project store or are merely pre-allocated on stock records, they will represent a useless investment of funds unless positive instructions are given for their release and sensible disposal.

Some specialized components may be saleable to the customer as part of a recommended holding of spare parts. Other items must be returned to common stock, sold, or scrapped as appropriate. Redundant stockholdings use floor space unprofitably. Their presence adds to the work of counting at each annual stocktaking, while their value can be expected to dwindle steadily towards zero as they deteriorate or become obsolete.

Index